HELLSTORM

HELLSTORM

The Death of Nazi Germany

1944–1947

by

THOMAS GOODRICH

ABERDEEN BOOKS
Sheridan, Colorado
2010

Hellstorm: The Death of Nazi Germany, 1944–1947
By Thomas Goodrich

First printing, 2010
ABERDEEN BOOKS
3890 South Federal Boulevard
Sheridan, Colorado 80110
303-795-1890
aberdeentp@earthlink.net · www.aberdeenbookstore.com

ISBN   1494775069

Design by Ariane C. Smith
Capital A Publications, LLC
Spokane, Washington

To the voiceless victims of
the world's worst war

TABLE OF CONTENTS

ILLUSTRATIONS

MAP BY JOAN PENNINGTON

PROLOGUE

ON THE NIGHT OF October 20, 1944, the village of Nemmersdorf lay mantled in sleep. Dark and still, only the twinkling of street lamps suggested life in the tiny town. It was now the sixth autumn of the war. The once-mighty German nation teetered at the brink. Her cities lay in ruins, her industry had been shattered, her economy was on the verge of collapse and worse, the Allied armies of the world were locking a death-grip on the very borders of the Reich itself. No one with eyes to see or mind to think could doubt that utter defeat was not only certain, but imminent. And yet, the village of Nemmersdorf slept.

For six years now the Third Reich had been mortally engaged in the most violent and cataclysmic war the world had ever known. Millions of Germans were already dead, millions more were crippled or maimed and many others who had survived in tact were staggering toward starvation. And yet, Nemmersdorf slept. The children of the village lay snug, warm and seemingly secure beside their mothers, as they always had and as they imagined they always would; in the bedrooms below, grandfathers, now the only men remaining, coughed quietly in the night, then rose from time to time as they always had for a cup of water, a glass of shnapps or perhaps a quiet moment's draw on the pipe. Just beyond, in the barns that adjoined most homes, milk cows rustled softly among the hay and fodder. In the dark village square, the old town clock patiently tolled the passing hours as it had night after night, year after year, century after century. Outwardly, at least, and despite a world engulfed in smoke and flame, nights in Nemmersdorf passed peacefully, predictably, as they always had. But

EASTERN GERMANY 1945

COURLAND   °Riga

SWEDEN

Baltic Sea

SOVIET UNION

Memel °

Pilau °

°Königsberg

Gotenhafen°

Nemmersdorf

Danzig

° Allenstein

EAST PRUSSIA

°Stettin

POMERANIA

GERMANY

Vistula River

★ BERLIN

Oder River

★ WARSAW

Neisse River

POLAND

SILESIA

Breslau

0   100 miles

MAP BY JOAN PENNINGTON

that was about to change; all was about to be violently swept away forever. The war, like a wall of angry red lava, was rushing down on the sleeping hamlet and was only moments from arrival.

For six hundred years East Prussia had served as the frontier outpost of Germany. Jutting eastward into often hostile Slavic lands, the old Teutonic province, unlike the rest of Germany, had faced a host of real or potential enemies for the entirety of its long existence. As a consequence, a strong military tradition had developed. It was here, in the "Breadbasket of Germany"—a fertile plain of large estates and proud, noble families—that much of the leadership for the German Army, past and present, had come. Thus, it was with no small amount of irony that despite its martial reputation, East Prussia was one of the few spots in Germany that had not been devastated by the current war. While the rest of the Reich's urban centers had long since been reduced to smoking rubble, the cities and towns of East Prussia, beyond the range of Allied bombers, remained, for the most part, untouched.

Although the unscathed condition of the province was envied elsewhere in Germany, Prussians, especially those nearest the eastern frontier, knew better than most that the war was reaching its climax. Each day the rumble to the east grew more distinct; each night the red glow on the horizon throbbed more angrily. By mid-October 1944, the Soviet Army had finally reached the Reich's border. And yet, as was the case at Nemmersdorf, there was no panic.

As a dedicated National Socialist, as a fanatical follower of Adolf Hitler, it was Erich Koch's duty as district chief of East Prussia to hold the line, no matter the cost. With the battered and bleeding remnant of the German Wehrmacht now fighting desperately on the nation's eastern approaches, Koch was determined to stamp out all forms of panic and defeatism among the populace. Except for a five-mile buffer directly behind the front, the district leader forbid any and all attempts at flight or evacuation. Civilians disregarding the order faced summary execution. Moreover, any manifestation of panic—withdrawal of bank funds, slaughtering of farm animals, packed luggage—could bring down the death penalty.[1]

---

1. Juergen Thorwald, *Flight in the Winter* (New York: Pantheon, 1956), 13; Martin K. Sorge, *The Other Price of Hitler's War* (Westport, Conn.: Greenwood, 1986), 126.

"[N]o true German would allow himself even the thought that East Prussia might fall into Russian hands," the Nazi die-hard announced menacingly.[2]

While Koch's threats and iron rule were no doubt needed to bolster some nervous Prussians, for most it was not necessary. Hopeless debacle that the war had become, faith in the Fatherland and trust that the beleaguered Wehrmacht would yet hold the "East Wall" against the red tide predominated. As was the case during the First World War, there was a general feeling that in this war too, the front would stabilize on the frontier and the Russians would be ground down through attrition. Concerning the rumors of "Bolshevik bestiality" and the horrible hints of what might be expected should the "Asiatic hordes" overrun Germany, most Prussians only laughed. Such notions, many felt, were merely the government's attempt to harden their will to resist.[3]

Thus it was, that on the night of October 20, as Nemmersdorf and other communities nearest the front slept in imagined security, the unthinkable occurred. After punching a hole through the German line, the Red Army suddenly burst into the Reich. Within hours, the Soviets widened the gap and swarmed over the countryside. After several days of desperate fighting the Wehrmacht regrouped, launched a furious counterattack, then eventually drove the Russians back across the border.[4] What German troops found upon reclaiming the lost ground, however, was staggering.

"[T]hey tortured civilians in many villages . . . ," reported one German officer, "nailed some on barn doors and shot many others."[5] Along the roads, "treks" of fleeing refugees had been overtaken by the communists, the people pulled from their carts, then raped and murdered on the spot. It was at Nemmersdorf, though, where stunned soldiers first viewed hell on earth. Recorded a physician with the army, Lt. Heinrich Amberger:

> On the road through Nemmersdorf, near the bridge . . . I saw where a whole trek of refugees had been rolled over by Russian tanks; not only the wagons and teams,

2. Thorwald, 13.
3. Marlis G. Steinert, *Hitler's War and the Germans* (Athens: Ohio University Press, 1977), 292.
4. Alfred M. deZayas, *Nemesis at Potsdam* (London: Routledge & Kegan Paul, 1977), 61.
5. Ibid.

but also a goodly number of civilians, mostly women and children. . . . [They] had been squashed flat by the tanks. At the edge of the road and in the farm yards lay quantities of corpses of civilians who evidently . . . had been murdered systematically.[6]

Added another horrified witness:

In the farmyard further down the road stood a cart, to which four naked women were nailed through their hands in a cruciform position. . . . Beyond . . . stood a barn and to each of its two doors a naked woman was nailed through the hands, in a crucified posture. In the dwellings we found a total of seventy-two women, including children, and one old man, 74, all dead . . . all murdered in a bestial manner, except only a few who had bullet holes in their necks. Some babies had their heads bashed in. In one room we found a woman, 84 years old, sitting on a sofa . . . half of whose head had been sheared off with an ax or a spade.[7]

"Every female, including girls as young as eight, had been raped," noted another viewer.[8]

Old men who had feebly tried to protect their wives, daughters and granddaughters, were themselves knocked down, then sawed in half or chopped to bits. A group of over fifty French POWs and Polish workers who had instinctively stepped in to protect the people were likewise castrated and killed.[9] Lt. Amberger continues:

On the edge of a street an old woman sat hunched up, killed by a bullet in the back of the neck. Not far away lay a baby of only a few months, killed by a shot at close range through the forehead. . . . A number of men, with no other marks or fatal wounds, had been killed by blows with shovels or gun butts; their faces completely smashed. . . . [I]n the near-by villages . . . similar cases were noted after these villages were cleared of Russian troops. Neither in Nemmersdorf nor in the other places did I find a single living German civilian.[10]

Staggered by the enormity of the crime, German authorities requested that neutral investigators and medical personnel from Spain, Sweden and Switzerland view the sickening carnage close up. When the visitors filed their reports, however, and when word finally reached the out-

---

6.   Ibid., 62–63.
7.   Ibid., 63.
8.   Sorge, *Other Price*, 119.
9.   Ibid., 117.
10. DeZayas, *Nemesis,* 63.

side world, there was only silence. By the winter of 1944, the vicious propaganda war waged against Germany had been won. By that late stage
of the conflict, the war of words had reached such hideous extremes that
few individuals beyond the Reich's borders were concerned about
brained German babies or crucified German women. By the final months
of the war, the enemy to be destroyed was not merely Adolf Hitler, the
Nazi Party or even the soldiers in the field. By the end of the war the aim
of the approaching Allies was nothing less than the utter extinction of
the German nation, including every man, woman and child.

In his 1925 political testament, *Mein Kampf*, Adolf Hitler laid out in
unmistakable terms his plan to rid Germany of all Jewish influence—
economic, political and cultural—should he ever some day rise to
power. When that seeming fiction became fact eight years later and
Hitler was elected chancellor to one of the mightiest industrial giants
on earth, alarmed Jews world-wide declared war on Germany. Fearful lest Nazism spread and jeopardize their hard-won position around
the globe, influential Jews met in July 1933 at Amsterdam to invoke
global economic sanctions against Hitler's Germany. The campaign,
said boycott organizer, Samuel Untermeyer of the United States, was
a "holy war . . . a war that must be waged unremittingly . . . [against]
a veritable hell of cruel and savage beasts."[11] As a consequence, Germans responded in kind with a boycott of their own. While citizens
were encouraged to shun Jewish businesses, a series of laws were
enacted designed to not only drive Jews from German arts, media
and the professions, but force them from the nation as well.

As the economic struggle continued, Jewish journalists, writers, play-
wrights, and filmmakers around the world joined the fray. With the
outbreak of war in 1939 and the entry of the United States into the conflict two years later, the war of words reached pathological proportions. Increasingly, as rumors of savage persecution against Jews under
Nazi control spread, the propaganda campaign directed at Hitler and

11. *New York Times*, August 7, 1933; Ralph Grandinetti, "Germany's Plan to Resettle Jews in Mada-
gascar," *The Barnes Review* 4, no. 3 (May/June 1998): 26.

Fascism devolved swiftly into a fanatical cry of extermination. No where was hatred more intense than among American Jews. Wrote Hollywood script writer and director, Ben Hecht:

> [A] cancer flourishes in the body of the world and in its mind and soul, and ... this cancerous thing is Germany, Germanism, and Germans. . . . I read in their watery eyes, their faded skins, their legs without feet, and their thick jaws, the fulfillment of a crime and the promise of another. The German hates democracy because he does not like himself. He has only one political ideal. It is based on his fat neck, his watery eyes, and his faded skin. . . . He is a pure murderer. The thought of killing defenseless people brings a glow into his fat German neck. . . . The Germans outraged me because they are murderers, foul and wanton, and because they are fools such as gibber at a roadside, with spittle running from their mouths. They outraged me because they raised their little pig eyes to their betters and sought to grunt and claw their way to the mastery of men. . . . That this most clumsy of all human tribes—this leadenhearted German—should dare to pronounce judgment on his superiors, dare to outlaw from the world the name of Jew—a name that dwarfs him as the tree does the weed at its foot—is an outrageous thing. . . . It is an evil thing.[12]

"GERMANY MUST PERISH," echoed Theodore N. Kaufman in a widely-read book of the same name.

> This time Germany has forced a TOTAL WAR upon the world. As a result, she must be prepared to pay a TOTAL PENALTY. And there is one, *and only one,* such Total Penalty: Germany must perish forever! In fact—not in fancy! . . . The goal of world-dominion must be removed from the reach of the German and the only way to accomplish that is to remove the German from the world. . . . There remains then but one mode of ridding the world forever of Germanism— and that is to stem the source from which issue those war-lusted souls, by preventing the people of Germany from ever again reproducing their kind.[13]

To implement his plan, Kaufman recommended that when the war was successfully concluded all German men and women should be sterilized. The result, wrote the author, would be "the elimination of Germanism and its carriers."[14] Far from being shocked by such a genocidal scheme, leading American journals were thrilled by the concept.

---

12. Ben Hecht, *A Guide for the Bedeviled* (New York: Charles Scribner's Sons, 1944), 120, 125, 130, 144, 155, 156.

13. Theodore N. Kaufman, *Germany Must Perish!* (Newark, N. J.: Argyle Press, 1941), 6, 7, 28, 86.

14. Ibid., 88–89; Michael F. Connors, *Dealing in Hate* (Torrance, Calif.: Institute for Historical Review, 1970), 28.

HELLSTORM

"A Sensational Idea!" cheered *Time* magazine.

"A provocative theory," echoed the *Washington Post*.

While many in America and Great Britain could understand and even commiserate with Jewish emotions, many more were initially aghast by the flaming rhetoric and the murderous cries for extermination of innocent and guilty alike. Nevertheless, the sheer weight and persistence of the propaganda, both subtle and overt, in film, radio, books, magazines, and newspapers, gradually worked its way into the thoughts and attitudes of the public mainstream. Eventually, in the minds of a sizable percentage of Americans and Britons, little distinction was drawn between killing a Nazi soldier and killing a German child.

On September 15, 1944, President Franklin Roosevelt made the demand for extermination official when he endorsed the so-called "Morgenthau Plan." Named for Roosevelt's Secretary of the Treasury, Henry Morgenthau, but actually conceived by the secretary's top aide, Harry Dexter White—both of whom were Jewish—the program called for the complete destruction of Germany after victory had been won. In addition to the dismantling or destruction of German industry and the permanent closure of mines, the Morgenthau Plan called for a reduction of the Reich's land area by one half. As many calculated, and as Roosevelt, Gen. George C. Marshall and other proponents of the plan well knew, this act guaranteed that roughly two-thirds of the German population, or fifty million people, would soon die of starvation. With the remnant of the population reduced to subsistence farming, and with the shrunken nation totally at the mercy of hostile European neighbors, it was estimated that within two generations Germany would cease to exist.[15]

"They have asked for it . . . ," snapped Morgenthau when someone expressed shock at the plan. "Why the hell should I worry about what happens to their people?"[16]

"You don't want the Germans to starve?" Roosevelt's incredulous son-in-law asked the president in private.

---

15. Russell D. Buhite, *Decisions at Yalta* (Wilmington, Del.: Scholarly Resources, Inc., 1986), 25; Eugene Davidson, *The Death and Life of Germany* (New York: Alfred Knopf, 1959), 6; Gregory Douglas, *Gestapo Chief 3* (San Jose, Cal.: R. James Bender, Pub., 1998), 187.
16. Buhite, *Yalta*, 23.

"Why not?" replied Roosevelt without batting an eye.[17]

Another advocate of the plan was Winston Churchill. Despite his earlier protest of the scheme as "cruel [and] unChristian," the British prime minister's attitude was soon softened when millions of dollars in much-needed "lend-lease" supplies and equipment were dangled before him by the Americans.[18] Unlike Roosevelt, Churchill's endorsement of the Morgenthau Plan was little known in the prime minister's home country. Even had the plot been common knowledge, however, it likely would have caused hardly a ripple in a nation that had been locked in war with "evil" for five years and where much anti-German propaganda from the First World War was still warmly embraced.

"One can't think of anything bad enough for the diseased Germans," hissed an English housewife. "They are like a loathsome disease spreading and spreading over Europe."[19] Added a British naval officer:

> Twice running they had been the criminals who had turned Europe into a slaughterhouse, their present leader was a "bloodthirsty guttersnipe," they themselves must "bleed and burn," and there were "no lengths in violence" to which the British would not go to destroy their wicked power. . . . Germans [were] first cousins to the devil. . . . The population of the British Isles had been worked up by propaganda to a state of passionate hatred of Hitler, the Nazi party, the German Armed Forces, and the German people. They had been told repeatedly that "the only good German was a dead one."[20]

Curiously, the genocidal agreement so recently made official by the western democracies had long since been state policy in communist Russia. There, because of the massive deaths and destruction caused by the German invasion in 1941, as well as the great number of Jews who perished as a consequence, it was guaranteed Germany would receive no mercy should the Red Army ever gain the upper hand. Perhaps the most influential Jewish writer anywhere in the world was the Soviet, Ilya Ehrenburg. Unlike Morgenthau, White, Hecht, Kaufman, and others who aimed to influence men in high places, Ehrenburg lowered his sights on the common Red soldier himself,

17. Diary of Henry Morgenthau, entry for March 20, 1945.
18. Buhite, 25; *The Memoirs of Cordell Hull*, (New York: Macmillan and Co., 1948), 207–208.
19. Paul Fussell, *Wartime* (New York: Oxford University Press, 1989), 122.
20. Russell Grenfell, *Unconditional Hatred* (New York: Devin-Adair, 1953), 117.

or those most likely to encounter German civilians. Whether in the
columns of Moscow dailies such as *Pravda* and *Isvestja*, or whether
in the front-line soldier's newspaper, *Red Star*; whether in mass dis-
tribution leaflets dropped from planes on the front, or whether in
his book, *The War,* Ehrenburg urged the Red Army forward with a
cry of total, complete and utter extermination:

> The Germans are not human beings. . . . If you have not killed at least one
> German a day, you have wasted that day. . . . If you cannot kill your German with
> a bullet, kill him with your bayonet. . . . [T]here is nothing more amusing for
> us than a heap of German corpses. Do not count days. . . . Count only the
> number of Germans killed by you. Kill the German—that is your grandmother's
> request. Kill the German—that is your child's prayer. Kill the German—that is
> your motherland's loud request. Do not miss. Do not let through. Kill. . . . Kill,
> Red Army men, kill! No fascist is innocent, be he alive, be he as yet unborn.[21]

In public, Russian premiere Josef Stalin sought to distance himself
from such sentiments. "Some time we hear silly talk about the Red
Army intending to exterminate the German people and to destroy
the German state," smiled the Soviet dictator with an eye to the world.
"This is, of course, a stupid lie."[22] But if Josef Stalin dismissed Ehrenburg's blood-thirsty words as "silly talk," his soldiers did not. Already
bursting with hatred and revenge, such admonitions from sanctioned
individuals writing in official Soviet organs lent an air of legality to
those already eager to act out their own savage fantasies.

"There will be no mercy—for no one . . . ," grimly warned one
Russian commander. "It is pointless to ask our troops to exercise mercy.
. . . The land of the fascists must be made a desert."[23]

Most Germans actually knew little of thoughts such as those above.
Most Germans were yet living under the illusion that the war still
had rules. Few could bring themselves to believe that the horror at
Nemmersdorf was anything other than an aberration; that the butchery was only a bloody mistake destined never to be repeated. Unbeknownst to those in Prussia and other German regions facing east, the

---

21. DeZayas, *Nemesis*, 65–66; Thorwald, *Flight*, 33.
22. DeZayas, 66.
23. Sorge, *Other Price*, 127.

nightmare at Nemmersdorf would soon prove only the faintest foretaste of what was ahead.

Meanwhile, as Russian pressure in the east grew ever more menacing, further west, Soviet allies were already engaged in their own brand of extermination. Here, in its western and central provinces, Germany was within easy striking distance of enemy bomber fleets. Here, the United States, and especially Great Britain, seemed determined to make atrocities attributed to the Nazis seem like child's play by comparison. Unlike the war further east, here in western Germany hell came not from the ice and mud below, but from the clouds and heavens above.

1

HELL FROM ABOVE

O N THE NIGHT OF July 24, 1943, air raid sirens sounded in Hamburg for the hundredth time.[1] No city the size of this great German port could hope to escape for long in a major European war and Hamburg had not. To date, however, the Royal Air Force raids and the sirens they elicited had been more a trial than terror. With a population of over one million, Hamburg was a huge northern city of harbors, canals, lakes, and rivers, and citizens in one part of town often were oblivious to enemy air raids in another part. While the bombing attacks proved destructive and caused significant loss of life, they were no greater, and in many cases far less, than raids on other communities across Germany. Because of pre-war economic and cultural ties to Great Britain, many felt that Hamburg, the "most English city in Germany," was being spared as a result of this relationship.

And thus, as the population responded dutifully to the wailing sirens and sought shelter on this mid-summer night in 1943, the first waves of British bombers appeared overhead. Few below doubted that this raid would be any different from those of the past. Soon, hundreds of planes began raining down tons of high explosives on the heart of Hamburg, blowing to bits schools, churches, hospitals, and homes. The onslaught increased in fury with each succeeding wave of bombers, building minute by minute to a fiery, devastating crescendo. Then, the planes suddenly disappeared, the skies were clear and all was silent again. When the stunned survivors reemerged from their cellars later that night, they saw that their once beautiful city was now a smoldering ruin.

---

1. Sorge, *Other Price*, 101.

The following day, as rescue crews and firefighters from through-out northern Germany battled the blaze, bombers of the US Army Air Force appeared over Hamburg.[2] As planned, the Americans sur-prised not only the emergency workers, but columns of fleeing refugees as well. During the ensuing massacre, thousands perished.

The next night, RAF bombers returned. In addition to the normal payload of high explosives, the British sent down tons of phosphorous bombs to accelerate the fires. The resulting conflagration ignited a "fire storm." Hurricane-force winds created by the intense heat and sub-sequent updraft uprooted trees, ripped roofs from buildings and sucked screaming victims back into the inferno. Some who escaped the 150 mph winds in the streets became mired in melting asphalt and quickly burst into flames. Those who threw themselves into the city's canals died of thermal radiation to the lungs, then, as they floated on the water's surface, they too ignited. In the center of the holocaust, tem-peratures reached 1,500 degrees and when the great mass of flames joined they rose to a height of three miles.[3] The hellish drama below was not lost on those above.

"As I looked down, it was as if I was looking into what I imagined to be an active volcano," said one horrified British crewman. "Our actual bombing was like putting another shovelful of coal into the furnace."[4]

"Those poor bastards!" another airman muttered as he gazed down in disbelief.[5]

The attacks against Hamburg continued unabated for another week. Finally, there was nothing left to destroy. Aptly dubbed by the Allies "Operation Gomorrah," the raids had been a cold and calculated attempt to scorch Hamburg and its people from the face of the earth. The plan succeeded. With thirteen square miles of total destruction, with 750,000 homeless, with an estimated 60,000 to 100,000 dead, mostly women and children, Hamburg, for all intents and purposes, had ceased to exist. For those who had harbored hopes that the British and American war against Germany would be waged in a humane

---

2.   Ibid., 102.
3.   Ibid.
4.   Martin Middlebrook, *The Battle of Hamburg* (New York: Charles Scribner's Sons, 1981), 244.
5.   Ibid.

manner and directed solely at the fighting forces, the events at Hamburg was final and powerful proof that indeed it would not. It was now clear to all that the Allied air war had become a war of massacre and unmasked terror.

The obliteration of Hamburg was only the most graphic and egregious example of a pattern that had been building since 1940. During the summer of that year, when the struggle for the skies over England was in progress, an embattled Winston Churchill gave the go-ahead to a plan that would take the air war to Germany. The architect of the idea was Arthur Harris, chief of British Bomber Command. Unlike the "Battle of Britain," which was a military contest from first to last, it was Harris's belief that intense, sustained air strikes against German population centers could prove decisive. The devastation of ancient cities and the destruction of priceless art works, coupled with the massive slaughter and "de-housing" of civilians would, Harris felt, soon lower German morale on both the home and battle fronts to the point that utter collapse was inevitable. While countenancing the plan, Churchill initially vacillated between striking at purely military targets and aiming at "the man in the street."

"My dear sir," protested the prime minister to an advocate of indiscriminate bombing during the height of the Battle of Britain, "this is a military and not a civilian war. You and others may desire to kill women and children. We desire . . . to destroy German military objectives."[6]

As with the Morgenthau Plan, however, the mercurial Churchill soon reversed himself and gave Harris and his scheme the go-ahead. Four months following the onset of the British bombing campaign, the German Luftwaffe finally retaliated with raids of its own, notably the ancient English city of Coventry, where nearly four hundred civilians were killed.[7] With the invasion of the Soviet Union the following year, however, much of Germany's air arm was diverted for the desperate contest in the

---

6. Stephen A. Garrett, *Ethics and Airpower in World War II* (New York: St. Martin's Press, 1993), 44.
7. Sorge, 90.

east. As a consequence, swarms of British bombers began the system-
atic destruction of Germany. "German cities . . . will be subjected to an
ordeal the like of which has never been experienced by a country in con-
tinuity, severity and magnitude . . . ," vowed Churchill. "[T]o achieve this
end there are no lengths of violence to which we will not go."[8]

Upon entry of the United States into the war, hundreds of additional
planes were eventually available for the assault on Germany. Publicly, Ira Eaker, commander of the US Eighth Air Force, expressed horror and contempt at the indiscriminate British bombing raids, usually
carried out under cover of darkness. Although the risk to his own crews
were infinitely greater, the American general opted for daylight "pre-
cision bombing" where the targets would be military and industrial
installations alone.[9] This course, most agreed, was the more "manly
and civilized" approach.

"[W]e should never allow the history of this war to convict us of
throwing the strategic bomber at the man in the street," Eaker
announced.[10]

Unfortunately, and despite such promising pronouncements, the
Americans did not hesitate when occasions arose to "pitch in" and join
their British comrades for raids on residential areas, as the survivors
of Hamburg could sadly attest.

Although Churchill, Arthur Harris and RAF communiqués continuously referred to their air campaign against Germany as area-, car-
pet-, saturation-, or unrestricted-bombing, the old, the young and the
weak who were forced to endure the nightmare and who made up
the overwhelming majority of its victims called it by a simpler, more
accurate name—"Terror-Bombing."

Beep—beepbeep—beep. . . . Beep—beepbeep. . . . beep. Silence, then the cool,
detached voice of the announcer: "Incoming flight in zero-five north, course
south-southeast. . . ." My heart beats, and the uncontrollable shaking takes

8. Garrett, *Ethics and Airpower*, 31.
9. Max Hastings, *Bomber Command* (New York: Dial Press/James Wade, 1979), 181.
10. Garrett, xiii.

over. . . . There is a voice again. "The bomber formations have now passed Hamburg, still flying east-southeast. An attack on the capital is to be expected." We are in our coats, out on the street with the bike in no time at all. The bike will be faster. The bags are easier to carry this way, and on the even stretches of road Mutti can sit on the baggage rack. . . . I pedal hard, furiously, with the strength of fear.

House doors slam, garden gates squeak, dark figures hurry through the night. They come from everywhere, out of every street. A constantly swelling stream that turns into a solid black mass. Like a flood-swollen river at springtime, it moves with irresistible force toward the bunker. Individual faces become visible for a second when a red flare illuminates the sky. No, they are not faces, they are spooky masks, frightening. The sirens howl "Alert". . . . Still three hundred yards to go over an open field. Hundreds race toward the one door.

Luckily, the door is at the side, right next to the fence, where I leave my bike, even lock it. And then we are catapulted, sluiced, past the soldier guards with their rifles at the ready, pushed by those behind us, through the steel door. Inside, we are forced against those already there. There's no room, and still we get packed tighter. A little more and we won't be able to breathe. Flattened, squeezed to death in the fight to stay alive. Screams . . . and shouting outside. The guards have closed and locked the door and it's suddenly quiet.[11]

So wrote a young Berliner, describing what was for her and millions of other Germans the central event of their lives—the air raid alert. By 1944, the bombing of the Third Reich had become so pervasive that almost every person in every city and town was affected. For the frightened fraulein above and her fellow urban-dwellers, the radio was more than a temporary escape from the horrors of war—it was the front line in their struggle to survive. In the words of Ilse McKee:

> A steady "ping, ping, ping" would . . . come over whenever there were enemy aircraft over German territory either attacking or on their way to attack. At regular intervals an announcer would give the exact position, number and type of the aircraft and warn the district or town for which the formations were heading. Any alteration in direction was of course reported immediately and a warning given to the town or district concerned. As soon as the enemy aircraft formation had left Germany the "ping" was replaced by a monotonous "tick-tock" like that of a clock.
>
> In this way we were able to get our warning when the bombers were still hundreds of miles away, and we knew that we could expect sirens later. Special

---

11. Ilse Koehn, *Mischling, Second Degree* (New York: Greenwillow, 1977), 194–195.

maps were issued to each household on which we followed the course and
progress of the aircraft formations right to their final point of attack. . . . With
so many people in the house and the constant air alarms we had soon worked
out a plan for a proper . . . shift duty. Every adult in turn had to sit up at night
and listen to the air reports. The first shift was from 10 P.M. until 2 A.M. and
the second from 2 A.M. until 6 A.M. This system gave everybody else in the house
a chance to get a little sleep between the five trips to the cellar which on average we now made every night.[12]

Such watching and waiting, and the seemingly endless trips to the
shelters, taxed the endurance of everyone, especially the young and the
old. Although the great majority of alerts were naturally false alarms,
those weary individuals who treated any with indifference did so at
their peril.

"Most of the time I didn't even wake my children when there was an
alarm," admitted one mother. "But on this particular evening, when
I turned on the radio—I always turned on the radio when the sirens
began wailing—I was horrified to hear that large bomber formations
were on their way and that we were to take shelter immediately. I woke
and dressed my three small daughters and helped them into their
little rucksacks containing extra underwear. I took along a briefcase,
which held a fireproof box with family documents, all of my jewelry,
and a large sum of money."[13]

"Shuffling feet. Suitcases knocking against walls . . . ," another woman
recounted. "The way leads across a courtyard with stairs above. . . .
Some more steps down, thresholds, corridors. Finally, behind a heavy,
rubber-rimmed iron door which can be locked by two levers, our
cellar. Officially called Shelter, we call it by turns cave, underworld, cat-
acomb of fear, mass grave."[14]

"It was terrible sitting and waiting in those stone cellars from which
there would have been no escape," said Gisela-Alexandra Moeltgen.
"Our nerves were at breaking point, the fear of death was constantly
with us."[15]

---

12. Ilse McKee, *Tomorrow the World* (London: J.M. Dents & Sons, 1960), 130–131.
13. Peter Pechel, Dennis Showalter and Johannes Steinhoff, *Voices from the Third Reich* (Wash-
    ington, D.C.: Regnery Gateway, 1989), 224.
14. Anonymous, *A Woman in Berlin* (New York: Harcourt, Brace, 1954), 19.
15. Alexander McKee, *Dresden 1945* (New York: E.P. Dutton, 1982), 261.

As was often the case, however, after enduring hours, even days underground, the anticipated attacks usually failed to materialize. Bomber formations, reportedly on a collision course with a city, often veered right or left for other targets or sometimes passed harmlessly overhead. Consequently, among many apathy unavoidably set in. Some, like young Jan Montyn, were claustrophobic and dreaded the thought of sitting passively in "sealed tombs."

> Having seen inside an air raid shelter a couple of times, I had decided that even a minute in there was more than I could stand. The very thought of being shut away in an underground hole with hundreds—sometimes even thousands— of others, waiting for the inevitable, made me break out in a cold sweat. . . . I preferred lying behind a wall in the open air to crouching behind a hermetically sealed steel door underground—completely at the mercy of blind fate.[16]

And others, like sixteen-year-old Olga Held, soon became bored with the monotonous routine:

> In the beginning, when the air raid siren sounded, we would run the one kilometer to the shelter that was always crowded. We had to squeeze through the door and stand on the jam-packed stairway. In a way it was fun because I had ample opportunities to flirt with the soldiers who were home on leave. But we quit running after several months. Too many times the air raid siren sounded and the bombers flew on. . . . Thereafter, we went to a shelter only if we happened to be near one, if it was convenient.[17]

Nevertheless, the great majority of prudent adults heeded each warning as if it were their first . . . or their last. Terrifying as the spate of alarms had been, Germans suddenly realized the true meaning of the word once the real thing began.

"Sirens! A drill? An alert? Probably one or two reconnaissance planes . . . ," thought Ilse Koehn when she found herself one day in an unfamiliar part of Berlin. "I look for a shelter just in case."

> I keep on walking, hoping to reach the shelter before there's a full alarm. The sirens blare, howl. Full alarm! Oh my God, where is everyone . . . ? We

---

16. Jan Montyn and Dirk Ayelt Kooiman, *A Lamb to Slaughter* (New York: Viking, 1985), 68–69.
17. Olga Held Bruner, unpublished manuscript, 97.

race onto the bridge, stop for breath in the middle of the hundred-yard span. What's that noise? A swarm of hornets? Where? And then we see them, and for one long moment we stand frozen.

"Oh my God!" What a sight! Hundreds, thousands of airplanes are coming toward us! The whole sky is aglitter with planes. Planes flying undisturbed in perfect V formation, their metal bodies sparkling in the sun. . . . Only the terrifying, quickly intensifying hum of engines, thousands of engines. The air vibrates, seems to shiver; the water, the ground and the bridge under us begin to tremble. . . . We run. The first formation is already overhead.[18]

"There was a brilliant flash in the sky as the lead elements of several formations opened their bomb-bay doors, catching the sun like many mirrors," recalled another awe-struck witness.[19]

For those tardy or doubting individuals who viewed the onset of a night raid, the sight was even more spectacular. To aid the waves of bombers that followed, advance aircraft staked out the area to be destroyed by dropping clusters of colored markers. Because they cascaded in a brilliant shower of red, green and white lights, the flares were called "Christmas trees" by those on the ground. "When my husband and I came out of the house, we could already see the Christmas trees nearly overhead . . . ," one woman near Hamburg wrote. "They lit up the street so brightly that we could have read a book. We knew what these meant and we were frightened."[20]

Generally, to witness the flash of bomb-bay doors by day, or flares by night, almost always meant that it was too late for the viewer to find shelter since the rain of death was only moments away.

"Then came a roar, similar to a thousand trains moving through the air," remarked one listener. "Those were the bombs beginning to cascade to earth. . . . [T]he roar became louder and louder. . . . Women ran in with their hair pinned up, mop buckets and brooms in hand . . . some were screaming in terror."[21]

As she sat trembling in her shelter, Rosa Todt of Neustadt also recalled

---

18. Koehn, *Mischling*, 188–189.
19. Sorge, *Other Price*, 109.
20. Middlebrook, *Battle of Hamburg*, 147.
21. Sorge, 109.

the horror when doubters outside the steel doors first heard the hellish roar. "All at once, crowds of people who had been standing on the street and in front of the entrance to the air-raid shelter wanted to come into it . . . ," Rosa remembered. "People drummed with their fists against the entrance to the air-raid shelter but it was closed because it was full. People were running around outside, frantically trying to save their lives."[22]

"Mother of God, pray for us . . . ," a woman in Ilse McKee's bunker cried. "Holy Virgin, please protect us."

> The next moment there was an unpleasant whistle, followed by an explosion. In an instant everybody was flat on the floor. The cellar shook, mortar came trickling down, and all was quiet again. We raised our heads, hoping that it was over. There were a few more explosions in the distance and then the aircraft returned. This time the whole earth seemed to tremble. There were a number of crashes outside. It sounded as if the house were breaking into pieces. We listened and then the planes came back. We put our heads down. Nobody was praying now. The mothers were lying on top of their children, protecting them with their bodies. Some of the suitcases came tumbling down the stairs where we had put them.[23]

"It felt as if the whole house had come down on us with one gigantic crash," said a terrified ten-year-old from her shelter. "The dogs were frantic, rushing around in the darkness; their owners kept calling them. . . . 'Everything is going to be all right,' mother told us. 'Just keep calm and don't worry.' "[24]

"It was like an earthquake," added Eva Beyer. "We all crouched together, and cried, and prayed, and trembled, absolutely terrified. One of the women was so fearful that she had diarrhea, two other women passed out, the children screamed, the baker's wife started to have a bilious attack. It was like a lunatic asylum."[25]

Wrote Liselotte Klemich:

---

22. Middlebrook, 147.
23. McKee, *Tomorrow the World,* 133.
24. Kamilla C. Chadwick, *The War According to Anna* (Woodside, Calif.: Seven Stones Press, 1986), 53.
25. McKee, *Dresden,* 208.

The people in the shelter reacted in very different ways. Some screamed every time there was a hit. Some prayed. Some sobbed. I was choked up with emotion. I kept thinking, "My poor, innocent children. They will be taken now." I kept trying to protect them. What's more, I was pregnant.

Finally it stopped and we were all still alive. I couldn't believe it, because no one had thought we could come out of that shelter alive.[26]

Unfamiliar with air raids as most were, some like Liselotte naturally assumed that the first wave of attacks was the last. All too often, however, it was not. The haggard mother continues:

I thought it was over, but my poor Annemarie kept crying out, "They're coming back, they're coming back." She was right. . . . We ran into the shelter again. The children were at the end of their ropes; they cried and clung to me. We stood in the hallway—we couldn't get back into the shelter because the windows had been blown in. We stood crowded together. Some were sitting on the floor. My little Karin, who was five years old, began to pray very loudly, "Dear God protect us, dear God protect us." Her little voice kept getting louder and more penetrating.[27]

"The children immediately started screaming again," noted Eva Beyer.

[T]hen three women began to scream and rage like mad, while one old woman stood in a corner and prayed from the bottom of her heart to God. It was horrifying. I got down under an arch and waited for what was to come. I crouched on my knees with my face buried in my arms, and my heart doing overtime out of fear. I experienced an incredible dread of being buried alive, for it is absolutely terrible to lie there and wait for the end when you don't know what the end is going to be like.[28]

No amount of crying or praying could protect the people from direct hits. A variety of bombs were used by the Allies to reach the huddled crowds, including incendiaries, aerial mines and the 11-ton Blockbuster, which, like its name, was designed to level an entire city block and kill every living thing in it. Special delayed-action devices were also developed to penetrate buildings and explode in basements and shelters. While relatively few bunkers actually suffered direct hits, death came in many ways.

26. Pechel et al, *Voices From the Third Reich*, 225.
27. Ibid.
28. McKee, *Dresden*, 137–138.

"An elderly lady had a heart attack and died right in front of us," revealed a little girl from one terror-filled shelter. "There was nothing anybody could do for her, Mother said. The strange thing was that nobody seemed to care very much that she had died."[29]

Added a witness from another shelter:

> She had been sitting on the floor with her back against a mirror. The mirror had been fixed low down on the wall. . . . And after the house had been hit the whole mirror had smashed in a thousand splinters which had penetrated the woman's back and head. Very quickly, without anyone noticing it in the dark and excitement, the old woman bled to death.[30]

"A cloud of dust from the cellar ceiling settled over us as a gigantic explosion boomed and the lights went out," Olga Held wrote from Nuremberg. "The force of the blast pushed me down the foundation wall and a sharp pain stabbed my right ear. I screamed. Mother held me tightly and it seemed to relieve the pain for a minute or two, but the damage was done. . . . I had lost half of the hearing in my right ear."[31]

For those forced to endure the seemingly endless assault, the strain soon took its toll. "The earth shook, the walls cracked and the plaster came down like flour until the whole basement was one cloud of dust . . . ," recorded Elli Nawroski of Hamburg. "No one spoke a word. Then, the nerves of one of my colleagues snapped. There was complete silence in the shelter when this girl suddenly started to laugh. . . . Someone said, 'This is nothing to laugh about,' to which the girl replied, 'This is all I have ever wanted.' She really had no idea what she was saying. Her mother and grandmother were both killed that night."[32]

"It was not death that was terrible that night," explained Jacob Schutz of Darmstadt, "but the *fear* of death—the whimpering, the shrieks, the screams."[33]

With fingers "still trembling round the fountain pen," one woman who had experienced other air raids tried to block from her mind the death above and the "fear of death" all around by jotting in her journal:

---

29. Chadwick, *Anna*, 53.
30. Anonymous, *Woman in Berlin*, 273–274.
31. Bruner manuscript, 113.
32. Middlebrook, *Hamburg*, 258.
33. Hastings, *Bomber Command*, 315.

I'm drenched, as though after heavy work. . . . Ever since I myself was bombed out and during that night had to help rescue the buried, I've been attacked by the fear of death. The symptoms are always the same. The palms of my hands begin to sweat. Then a circle of sweat round the scalp, a boring sensation in the spinal cord, a twitching pain in the neck, the roof of the mouth dries up, the heart beats in syncope, the eyes stare at the chair leg opposite, memorizing its carved knobs and curves. To be able to pray now. The brain gropes for fragments of sentences: 'Let the world go by, it's nothing. . . . And no one falls out of this world. . . . *Noli timere.*[34]

And then, continued the woman, to the relief of all "the wave subsides" and there was only silence overhead. "As though by command a feverish babbling broke out. Everyone began to laugh, to outshout the others, to crack jokes."[35]

Too often, however, such laughter and levity was cut short by yet more waves of bombers. As nightmarish and surreal as conditions were in the shelters, the situation was vastly more terrible for those trapped outside. Caught in the open with an old woman and her grandchildren, Ilse Koehn lay helpless as "all hell breaks loose."

[B]ombs fall like rain. Millions of long, rounded shapes come tumbling down around us. The sky turns gray, black, the earth erupts. The detonations begin to sound like continuous thunder. . . . "Grandma! Grandma!" wails the little girl, pulling at her skirt. "Grandma, let's go to the bunker; please, please, Grandma!"

I'm flat on the ground. Bombs, bombs, bombs fall all around me. It can't be. It's a dream. There aren't that many bombs in the whole world. Maybe I'm dead? I get up, drag pail, old woman and girl with me toward a porch, a concrete porch with space underneath. Above the detonations, flak fire, [and] shattering glass, rises the old woman's high-pitched voice: *God in Heaven! God in Heaven!*" And now the baby's wailing, too.

Hang on to the earth. It heaves as if we are on a trampoline, but I cling to it, dig my nails into it. Why is it so dark? The old woman crouches over the baby. She shakes a fist at the little girl, then screams: "God in Heaven forgive her. Forgive her her ugliness, her sin. . . . O Lord, I know she didn't say her prayers!" Her fist comes down on the little girl's head.

A sizzling piece of shrapnel embeds itself in the concrete of the porch. The little girl grabs me, her nails dig into my neck. Her voice, as if in excruciating pain, pierces my eardrums: *Mama! Mama! Where are you, Mama?*" A clod of soil

34. Anonymous, *Woman*, 24.
35. Ibid.

hits me in the face. I'm still alive. Alive with fear and ready to promise any powers that be that I'll become a better person if only my life is spared.

Warrrooom. Warrrooomwarroomwaroom. My whole body is lifted off the ground, dropped again, up and down again. . . . "You wicked girl . . . O Lord! . . . Why didn't you say your prayers?" Over and over again. . . . "Mama! Mama! Mama!"

Rrrahrrahrrahhhh!

Grandma, little girl and baby wailing over the bombs, the flak. Will this ever end?[36]

And then, like a miracle, there was nothing. Ilse continues:

Suddenly, it's quiet. Dead quiet. A spine-chilling, eerie quiet. I'm breathing. We're all breathing. Strange to hear our breaths. What's that? Oh, only a fire engine. Sirens. Sirens again? All Clear. That means I can leave.

"I'm sorry, but I have to go. I have to collect some pig fodder," I say.

"Of course, my dear," the old lady replies. "I'm sorry you have to leave so soon. You must come again. Come visit us. We'll have tea. It's very nice to have met you." We shake hands very formally.[37]

As the above experience illustrated, one of the few advantages survivors caught outside possessed was that they could generally stagger away to safety once the "All Clear" had sounded. Those underground often could not. Moments after a raid, frantic rescue squads set to work. One searcher, naval recruit Jan Montyn, left a vivid account of devastated Mannheim:

Smoke. The crackling of fire. The smell of sulfur and TNT. A rumbling of houses collapsing. The occasional delayed explosion. And people. People giving orders, calling out, shouting, screaming, crying. Footsteps. Running. Shuffling. People scrambling about in a daze amid the debris—not knowing what they are looking for, much less where.

The first rescue teams were already feverishly clearing access routes to allow fire engines and ambulances to reach those streets that could still be made to some extent passable. Others roamed about the ruins, clambering over heaps of rubble, in search of gas leaks and burst water mains. There was a risk of further explosions. The cellars might fill up with water. Anyone who had not

36. Koehn, *Mischling*, 189–190.
37. Ibid., 190.

been buried, who had not been asphyxiated, had not been roasted in the heat, could still drown. With the aid of maps, efforts were made to locate the air raid shelters. Then the rubble had to be cleared: with spades, with our bare hands, a wet cloth in front of our faces, our eyebrows and lashes scorched. Stone by stone, fragment by fragment. The debris is removed by a living chain of hands. And look out. Be careful. A floor can cave in without warning under the weight of the rubble—be careful. Meanwhile the fire is still burning everywhere and, from time to time, far away or close at hand, comes the sound of an explosion. Unexploded time bombs. You might trip over one at any moment.[38]

Their havens buried beneath tons of debris, survivors could only huddle together, choke back the terror and await what they prayed would be their deliverance. Wrote one little girl:

People were weeping and saying, "Oh my God, oh my God, where is the water coming from?" I could feel my feet getting wet. Some candles were lit so we could see where the water came from, but one man went around blowing out all the candles again, shouting, "You blockheads. Do you want us all to blow up? Can't you smell the gas? . . ." Nobody could find where the water was coming from; it just kept on rising slowly. We pulled up our feet onto the benches and waited for something to happen.

"Don't worry," Mother told us again. "They'll find us in a minute or two."

A woman started singing a hymn about God being a strong fortress and a mighty defense who would help us through whatever happened. I knew that hymn and sang along as other people joined in. . . . Singing helped a lot. While I was singing, I didn't have time to be scared.

And then the cellar door opened with a loud crash and I saw a man poking his head in. He held a large flashlight and said, "The party is over. Let's go." Then everybody shouted "Hurray" and "Thank God" and "What took you so long?" It was as if nobody had been frightened and shouted and cried just a little while earlier.[39]

While the search for those buried in the ruins continued, others emerged from hiding to discover a landscape turned surreal. "As we slowly made a cautious move out of the cellar we were shocked by the darkness," said a survivor of one Berlin raid. "Two hours earlier it was a beautiful summer day. Now we couldn't see the sun. All there was to see was a putrid looking greenish blue sky, with scraps of burned

38. Montyn, *Lamb to Slaughter*, 71.
39. Chadwick, *Anna*, 53–54.

cloth and paper floating through the air. It was dark in the middle of the day."[40] Recalled little Traute Koch:

With great apprehension we stepped out on to the street. There was only one way, in front of us, but what a way! There was a great heat and leaden gloom over us. Where there had been houses only a few hours before, only some single walls with empty windows towered upwards. In between were large heaps of rubble, still glowing. Torn overhead wires were hanging everywhere. . . . Suddenly, I saw tailors' dummies lying around. I said, "Mummy, no tailors lived here and, yet, so many dummies lying around." My mother grabbed me by my arm and said, "Go on. Don't look too closely. On. On. We have to get out of here."[41]

From Hamburg, Otto Mahncke recorded a new horror at every step:

On the corner . . . a woman who had come back from a birthday party was screaming, "My child! My child! Up there!" None of the men or women dared to go into the house to save the baby. . . . [W]e saw sailors rescuing people out of a burning house, passing them from balcony to balcony. Some people were saved. Then, suddenly, the house collapsed like a pack of cards. Everybody standing on the balconies fell into the ruins. . . . An old woman of seventy was calling for help from the third-floor window of a half-timbered house. The room was ablaze. I ran with some other men to fetch a ladder. We found a long one and a number of men climbed up to save the woman. But they all came back after the second floor; it was too hot. I tried, too, but had to retreat only a few steps under the window. The heat was too great. When I got to the ground, I saw the woman looking down with wild eyes and then fall back to her death among the flames.[42]

From the same city, seventeen-year-old Helmut Wilkens witnessed similar scenes in his burning neighborhood:

Someone stood at a second-floor window, calling for help. It was Mr. Schwarz, who never went down to the shelter; only his wife did that. People called up to him to jump. We stretched out some blankets for him to jump into but he was afraid. The blankets would not have saved him. Suddenly, there were two sailors. . . . They said, "Shoot him. He won't suffer in agony any more. He's burning already." They started to fire at him with their pistols. He fell forward, then, and smashed on to the pavement.[43]

---

40. Sorge, *Other Price*, 109.
41. Middlebrook, *Hamburg*, 274.
42. Ibid., 169–170.
43. Ibid., 295.

"People with an arm or leg caught under heavy burning timbers cried for help . . . ," remembered Olga Held as she ran through the streets of Nuremberg. "Screams came from under tons of burning debris. In every direction I looked trapped people begged to be freed."[44]

To the shattered survivors following a raid, the dead seemed to outnumber the living. One victim, noted a horror-struck man in Darmstadt, was "lying like a statue, her cold heels in their shoes stuck up in the air, her arms raised . . . , her mouth and teeth gaping open so that you did not know whether she had been laughing or crying."[45]

"One fat air-raid warden lay, his little lantern beside him, his hands peacefully folded on his enormous chest," another witness reported from the same city. "He looked like a sleeper replete after a banquet."[46]

Not everyone discovered was a nameless stranger. "My two children were pulled out dead," agonized one mother in Cologne. "You could hardly see any injuries on them. They only had a small drop of blood on their noses and large bloody scrapes on the backs of their heads. I was in a state of total shock. I wanted to scream . . . I wanted to scream."[47]

Even as stunned survivors escaped their shelters and wandered through the streets, workers frantically searched for those still trapped underground. For many victims, it was far too late. When would-be rescuers finally broke through to buried bunkers they often found scenes of unimaginable horror. In cellars suffering direct hits, walls were awash in blood, with bone, brains and body parts splattered everywhere. In some shelters, broken water mains had slowly drowned the occupants. Ruptured steam pipes had boiled alive other screaming victims. Nevertheless, the grisly search for life went on. Jan Montyn:

> We were busy for hours, stone after stone. The rubble was piled up metres high. Chalk, cement, straw, broken furniture, beams. From time to time we stuffed some food into our mouths, at a hastily erected aid post. And on we went again. Grimly, unthinking, uncomprehending. Our eyes ran with tears, but we were oblivious, our hands were raw and covered in blood, but we felt nothing. We heard tapping signals. We heard voices coming from the depths of the

44. Bruner, 120–121.
45. Hastings, 315.
46. Ibid.
47. Pechel, *Voices*, 463.

earth. And we worked faster. Stone after stone. But the time passed. Hour after hour. The night passed. The tapping signals grew fainter. We quickened our speed. The sun came up. We no longer heard any voices. Nor any tapping sounds.

Towards noon we managed to open up the entrance to the shelter. But we found nothing but death. We sat down, scorched and sooty, defeated, exhausted. And then suddenly a miracle happened. It was Bo'sun Heyne. He tore like a madman at a mansize hunk of masonry, his face contorted like an idiot's. His eyes bulged. He became redder and redder. The veins in his temples seemed about to burst. But the wall of stone yielded and he had to jump aside to avoid being crushed. A cavity was revealed. And in that cavity there was a large rush basket.

"I knew it, goddammit, I knew it, goddammit, goddammit," stammered Bo'-sun Heyne. And he took something in his arms. Something that was very small, that moved. Something that cried.[48]

And then, after hours, even days, of death, screams, tears, irony, and occasionally, miracles, something often occurred that many thought impossible—the sirens sounded again. For many incredulous victims of the first raids, the sound seemed—and often was—the end of the world. As was the case with the attacks against Hamburg, Berlin, Nuremberg, Darmstadt, Cologne, and other German cities, after first blasting a targeted town to splinters, the British and American bombers soon returned in hopes of catching survivors and rescuers in the open and igniting with fire bombs all that remained.

Stumbling once again to the shelters, few could have imagined that they were returning to death traps. When the roaring bombers released their lethal cargo, a veritable rain of fire descended on a doomed town.

"[A] huge burning cloud . . . slowly settled on the city . . . ," said a witness from Wurzburg. "This fiery cloud knew no pity. It sank on churches and houses, palaces and citadels, broad avenues and narrow streets. At the outset burning drops spurted from the cloud causing isolated fires, then the burning veil enveloped Wurzburg. In a few moments a gigantic path of flame lit up the dark night and turned the clouds to scarlet."[49]

48. Montyn, *Lamb*, 71–72.
49. Garrett, *Ethics and Airpower*, x.

"It was as if fire was poured from the sky," added one horror-struck viewer from another town.[50]

"Everything, everything is burning!" shouted a man who rushed into the shelter occupied by Martha Gros.

> There was a dreadful crash, the walls shook, we heard masonry cracking and collapsing, and the crackle of flames. Plaster began to fall and we all thought the ceiling would collapse. . . . About thirty seconds later there was a second terrible explosion, the cellar-door flew open, and I saw, bathed in a brilliant light, the staircase to the cellar collapsing and a river of fire pouring down. I shouted "Let's get out!" but the [captain] gripped me: "Stay here, they are still overhead." At that moment, the house opposite was hit. The armored plate in front of our cellar flew up in the air, and a tongue of fire about fifteen feet long shot through at us. Cupboards and other furniture burst and fell on to us. The terrible pressure hurled us against the wall.[51]

Many victims initially tried to toss hissing fire bombs out windows. To discourage such attempts, some incendiary sticks carried deadly delayed charges.[52]

Soon, the thousands of small fires joined to form one huge blaze, creating a vortex of wind and flame. "The noise," one terrified listener remembered, "was like that of an old organ in a church when someone is playing all the notes at once."[53] Now, for the first time, many in the cellars and bunkers realized that their havens would soon become ovens. Wrote Rolf Witt of Hamburg:

> Word of what was happening in the street must have spread to the people at the back of our shelter because they broke down the wall to the next-door basement. That was a great mistake because, when they did this, they found that they were looking into a furnace. The street door was half open and, with the air being drawn out of our basement, the smoke and fire came pouring through the break in the wall. Everyone became severely affected by smoke. I heard people screaming but this became less and less. . . . We were within seconds of death. I could not speak to my parents because of the gas mask I was wearing. I tapped father on the shoulder as a sign that I was going. I thought they would follow me. A few seconds before I would have suffocated, I must have had a

---

50. McKee, *Dresden*, 169.
51. Hastings, *Bomber Command*, 311–312.
52. McKee, *Dresden*, 140.
53. Middlebrook, *Hamburg*, 269.

tremendous burst of strength. At a moment when the door was open and when no burning debris was falling down, I sprang out into the street.[54]

Like young Witt, other trapped victims were frantic to escape the blistering heat. Martha Gros:

> [S]omebody shouted: "Get out and hold hands!" With all his strength he pulled me out from under the wreckage. I dropped my cash box and pulled the others with me. We climbed through the hole leading to the back. . . . More bombs were already falling into the garden. We crouched low, each of us beating out the small flames flickering on the clothes of the one in front. Phosphorous clung to the trees and dripped down on us.[55]

"People who got phosphorous on them presented a fearful sight," recalled Rosa Todt. "Their skin was bright red, water dripping out of the pores of their skin; their ears and nose, their whole face, was a nauseating mask."[56]

Despite almost certain death in the streets, most instinctively knew that their only hope was to escape the shelters. "Mother wrapped me in wet sheets, kissed me, and said, 'Run!'" recounted Traute Koch. "I hesitated at the door. In front of me I could see only fire—everything red, like the door to a furnace. An intense heat struck me. A burning beam fell in front of my feet. I shied back but, then, when I was ready to jump over it, it was whirled away by a ghostly hand. I ran out to the street. The sheets around me acted as sails and I had the feeling that I was being carried away by the storm."[57]

Hellish as the earlier raids had seemed, many now, for the first time, discovered the true meaning of the word. "The heat from the surrounding houses . . . was unbearable," said a teenage boy as he staggered through the furnace. "We whimpered and cried from the pain of it."[58]

"Burning people raced past like live torches," Martha Gros remembered, "and I listened to their unforgettable final screams."[59]

---

54. Ibid., 265.
55. Hastings, 312.
56. Middlebrook, 147.
57. Ibid., 264.
58. Ibid., 268.
59. Hastings, 312.

"All we could hear were the terrible screams for help from the cellars of the streets around us," added a girl from Darmstadt.[60]

With every fiery step, a new nightmare appeared. "I struggled to run against the wind in the middle of the street . . . ," wrote nineteen-year-old Kate Hoffmeister. "We . . . couldn't go on across . . . because the asphalt had melted. There were people on the roadway, some already dead, some still lying alive but stuck in the asphalt. . . . They were on their hands and knees screaming."[61]

In a desperate bid to escape the inferno at Hamburg, fifteen-year-old Herbert Brecht and several other rescue workers fled in a car and small trailer.

> Burning people ran and staggered after us. Others were lying on the road, dead or unconscious. . . . [O]ur trailer got stuck in a bomb crater. We unhitched it and jumped into the car which was still running; there were six of us crammed inside. After another 200 metres we were forced to a halt between the trams standing in front of the tram depot. Our car caught fire immediately. We all managed to get out and we stood there in those fires of hell. The storm pulled me, unwillingly, into an enormous bomb crater in the middle of the road. Those of us who did not get into this crater had no chance of survival. . . .
>
> There was a smashed water main in the bomb crater. Although there was no pressure left in the pipe, the water still ran into the crater and we had to fight against the flood. Some people drowned or were buried when the sides of the crater caved in. . . . Because I always wore my goggles on duty, I could see everything very clearly. The burning people who were being driven past our bomb crater by the storm could never have survived. Eventually, there were about forty people lying in the crater. There was a soldier in uniform near me with a lot of medals. He tried to take his life with a knife. . . .
>
> About this time, I noticed that a car had driven into our crater and had buried some people beneath it. . . . I hadn't seen this happen. It was only through the crying of a small boy that I noticed it. He was lying with the front bumper of the car on top of him. . . .
>
> The screams of the burning and dying people are unforgettable. When a human being dies [like that], he screams and whimpers and, then, there is the death rattle in his throat.[62]

60. Ibid., 313.
61. Middlebrook, 266–267.
62. Ibid., 268–269.

Like the badly burned Brecht, some miraculously survived the holocaust, reaching safety in rivers, canals and parks. Thousands more, however, did not. When the raids finally ended and the firestorms began to recede, the fortunate few began to reemerge. Again, young Herbert Brecht:

> At midday—it never got light—a man came and pulled some of us survivors out of the crater. He was an elderly man who also had a burnt face. When he pulled me out by the hands, my skin stuck to him in shreds. He looked at me— I cannot describe his look—and he could only say, "Child! Child! . . ." The air was hardly breathable and my injuries hurt hellishly. Dead lay everywhere. Most were naked because their clothes had been burnt away. All had become shrunken, really small, because of the heat. . . . I saw a burnt-out tramcar in which naked bodies were lying on top of each other. The glass of the windows had melted.[63]

"There was a deathly silence in the town, ghostly and chilling," remembered Martha Gros as she stumbled through the ruins of Darmstadt. "It was even more unreal than the previous night. Not a bird, not a green tree, no people, nothing but corpses."[64]

"Four-story-high blocks of flats were like glowing mounds of stone right down to the basement," Anne-Lies Schmidt noted as she searched for her parents in a section of Hamburg.

> Everything seemed to have melted. . . . Women and children were so charred as to be unrecognizable. . . . Their brains tumbled from their burst temples and their insides [spilled] from the soft parts under the ribs. . . . The smallest children lay like fried eels on the pavement. Even in death, they showed signs of how they must have suffered—their hands and arms stretched out as if to protect themselves from that pitiless heat.[65]

Many survivors, including Martha Gros, now returned to the deathtraps they had fled in hopes of recovering valuables.

> We climbed over the wreckage into the garden and proceeded to the burntout cellar. The ashes were almost two feet deep. I found the place where I had dropped our cash box, picked it up and opened it. The 1,000 Reichmark note

---

63. Ibid., 274, 275.
64. Hastings, 321.
65. Middlebrook, 276.

which I had saved for emergencies was a heap of ashes. The little boxes of jew-elry had been burned. The best piece, a large emerald, had cracked. Around our safe lay large lumps of melted silver, and in the wine-racks, there were melted bottles hanging in bizarre long ribbons. For this to have happened the tem-perature must have been something like 1,700 degrees.[66]

Sad and disappointing as discoveries such as these were, others who returned to cellars found scenes straight from the blackest of nightmares. Due to the tremendous heat, some bunkers contained only dozens of log-like shapes, charred and shriveled to only a quarter their original size. Dogs and cats had been reduced to the size of rats. In still other cellars, only a powdery gray ash remained. When rescuers entered some shelters they found floors covered in up to a foot of greasy fat—the victims having been rendered into a dark, evil liquid.[67]

Because of sickening sights and smells such as the above, many dazed rescuers quickly slipped into a state of "nervous hysteria." When offered liquor by understanding officials, not a few workers drank to drunk-enness in an effort to bear up.[68] One of those ordered to bring in burn victims prior to their transfer to a waiting hospital ship was Otto Muller. Relates the Hamburg policeman:

> The burnt people were marked with a label round their neck giving their per-sonal details and their degree of burns. I talked to a doctor and he told me that the larger the area of burn, the less pain the people felt but that, when the burns had reached a certain percentage of the body area, death was inevitable. The doctor went through the rows of injured and those with too much area of burn he left behind because there was only room for those with a chance of survival. He was looking for those who were still in pain and these were cho-sen to be put on the ship. The people being left behind knew that they had no chance. One man dragged himself up my leg to get at my pistol holster—it was simply dreadful.[69]

In many cases, nurses and doctors could do little more than soak sheets in salad oil and spread it over the wretched victims. Officer Muller continues:

66. Hastings, *Bomber Command,* 321.
67. Middlebrook, *Hamburg,* 266, 272; Hastings, 319.
68. Hastings, 321, 322.
69. Middlebrook, 374.

I was going through burning streets . . . when I suddenly saw a young girl. I thought it might even be my own daughter. . . . I stopped my motor cycle and the girl came running towards me. Her face was black with soot except for two streams of tears which were running down her face. She was dragging her little dead brother behind her; the right side of his face was already scraped smooth. She had been wandering around aimlessly for three days and two nights. . . . This little girl put her hand round my neck and said . . . "Please take us along with you."[70]

Not surprisingly, because of the severe and continuous emotional shock such as Muller and others experienced—shock, not only from the devastating air raids and firestorms, but also from the hellish aftermaths—hundreds of survivors soon lost their reason and ran through the smoldering streets shouting and screaming at everything, or nothing. "One man has gone mad," noted Anne-Kaete Seifarth. "He's standing in front of a mound of bricks from a collapsed wall, on top of which he had erected the swastika flag. He is screaming at the fugitives with a steel helmet on his head—his face mad—and he is bombarding the fugitives with bricks."[71]

More often the case, however, unhinged survivors simply staggered aimlessly amid the rubble, babbling and gesturing incoherently. Others were so utterly stunned as to be all but dead to further emotion. Liselotte Klemich recalled seeing refugees resting on a toppled tree trunk after one shattering air raid. "And from under [the] fallen tree," observed the woman, "a hand in a white glove was slowly opening and closing. No one even tried to lift up the huge tree trunk."[72]

Frantic to escape the stricken cities, terrified that the bombers would return, survivors fled pell-mell toward the countryside. "We were carried along by the stream of people who had been bombed out, their faces gray and their backs bent, heavily laden with their belongings," recorded Ursula von Kardorff in her diary. "When evening fell over the burning city one hardly noticed it, because it had been so dark all day."[73]

"It was the most pathetic sight I had ever seen . . . ," Margot Schulz added as one flight of victims passed through her village.

---

70. Ibid.
71. Ibid., 279.
72. Pechel, *Voices*, 226.
73. Ursula von Kardorff, *Diary of a Nightmare* (New York: John Day, 1966), 191.

They were in their night dresses—half burned sometimes—and pajamas, sometimes a coat thrown over their shoulders. They pushed their belongings in a
pram, still with the baby in. . . . You have to imagine the hysteria, with some of
the people burnt and crying. It went on for days. It was just endless. . . . I remember a woman suddenly collapsing on the pavement across the road from where
I lived and giving birth to a baby. The baby came after about a quarter of an hour
or twenty minutes of moaning and groaning. . . . There was another woman,
sat on the pavement near by, breast-feeding her baby. She was only dressed in
a nightdress and all her hair was burnt away. And, all the time, the exodus
went on. It was a constant stream of misery.[74]

Carolin Schaefer, herself desperate to flee burned-out Darmstadt,
tried to shield her sons' eyes from the hideous sights in the corpse-
strewn streets, "I felt that if the boys were to see this, they could never
grow up to lead happy lives," explained the mother. Carolin soon abandoned her efforts, however, since a new horror arose at seemingly every
step. Spotting an old friend pushing a bicycle with melted tires, the
woman quickly noticed a box fastened to the back.

"Silently she embraced me," said Carolin. "Then she began to cry,
pointing to the box. 'In there is my husband,' she said."[75]

When word first filtered to the outside world of the butchery being
visited upon the women and children of Germany by the RAF, the
British government initially tried to deflect criticism by simple denial.
Well aware that many voices at home and abroad would denounce
such slaughter in the strongest terms, military and civil spokesmen
of the United Kingdom were trotted out on a regular basis to solemnly
assuage the world.

"The targets of Bomber Command are always military," Air Minister Sir Archibald Sinclair assured the House of Commons in early
1943.[76]

"There is no indiscriminate bombing," chorused Deputy Prime Minister Clement Attlee a short time later. "As has been repeatedly stated

74. Middlebrook, 279–280.
75. Hastings, 322,
76. Ibid., 171.

in the House, the bombing is of those targets which are most effective from the military point of view."[77]

Added political leader Harold Balfour: "I can give the assurance that
we are not bombing the women and children of Germany wantonly."[78]

Despite the power and persistence of government denial, grim truth
could not be skirted long. Some voices of conscience were outraged,
calling the massacre of innocent civilians "savage," "inhuman and
un-English."[79] Many critics, however, were more concerned by the
apparent "moral collapse" of any nation that could commit such crimes
than for the nation who was a victim of it.

"To bomb cities as cities, deliberately to attack civilians, quite irrespective of whether or not they are actively contributing to the war
effort, is a wrong deed, whether done by the Nazis or by ourselves,"
announced George Bell, the Bishop of Chichester.[80]

"It will be ironical," added the preeminent British historian, Basil
Liddell Hart, "if the defenders of civilization depend for victory upon
the most barbaric, and unskilled, way of winning a war that the modern world has seen. . . . We are now counting for victory on success
in the way of degrading it to a new level—as represented by indiscriminate (night) bombing."[81]

"The ruthless mass bombing of congested cities is as great a threat
to the integrity of the human spirit as anything which has yet occurred
on this planet . . . ," author Vera Brittain later protested. "There is no
military or political advantage which can justify this blasphemy."[82]

Evidence that the much dreaded moral demise of Great Britain
had already arrived was provided by many RAF bomber crews themselves. To many airmen, the almost total lack of Luftwaffe opposition in the skies over Germany made the bombing of cities less and
less like war and more and more like murder. While open criticism
of government policy could have earned a reprimand, court-martial,
imprisonment, or worse, the turmoil raging within many a young flyer

---

77. Ibid.
78. Ibid., 173.
79. Sorge, *Other Price,* 107.
80. Middlebrook, 346.
81. Hastings, 176.
82. Sorge, 108.

occasionally surfaced. During one pre-flight briefing for yet another carpet bombing raid, an anonymous voice from the back of the room cried out, "women and children first again."[83]

"There were people down there," another crewman confessed, "being fried to death in melted asphalt in the roads, they were being burnt up and we were shuffling incendiary bombs into this holocaust. I felt terribly sorry for the people in that fire I was helping to stoke up."[84]

While public criticism by bomber crews themselves was considered tantamount to treason, many a troubled young soul revealed itself in private ways.

"[M]y navigator and I cycled to Huntingdon and took a boat out on the river," remembered one RAF pilot following a raid. "We drifted quietly downstream and Nick said, 'What about those poor sods under those fires?'"

The young pilot reflected on the words for a moment or two, but remained silent.

"I couldn't think of anything to say. We drifted quietly on."[85]

Surprisingly, though duty-bound to obey orders, members of the military hierarchy occasionally gave vent to personal anger and outrage at their government's actions. Incensed by the British media's bloodthirsty gloating over the massacres—"ALL GERMANS ARE GUILTY!" ran one headline; "NO PITY! NO MERCY!" screamed another[86]—Brigadier Cecil Aspinall-Oglander at last lashed out in a letter to the *London Times*:

> Britain and her Allies and well-wishers must all be devoutly thankful that the RAF is at last able to repay Germany in her own coin and to inflict upon her cities the same devastation that she has inflicted on ours. But it must offend the sensibilities of a large mass of the British population that our official broadcasts, when reporting these acts of just retribution, should exult at and gloat over the suffering which our raids necessitate. . . . Let us at least preserve the decencies of English taste. An Englishman does not exult when a criminal is condemned to the scaffold, nor gloat over his sufferings at the time of his execution.[87]

83. Garrett, *Ethics and Airpower*, 82.
84. Ibid.
85. Middlebrook, *Hamburg*, 368.
86. Garrett, 103.
87. Hastings, 174.

While Arthur Harris was the man planning and implementing the bombing campaign, and did so with undisguised glee, Winston Churchill was the individual responsible for its onset and, ultimately, its outcome. Far from bending to the cries of mercy and humanity, the prime minister pursued the bomber offensive with a dogged determination that brooked no deviation. Even so, the enigmatic British leader was not without his moments of doubt and on occasion, pangs of conscience surfaced in an otherwise stubborn demeanor. "In the course of the film showing the bombing of German towns from the air, very well and dramatically done," a guest of the prime minister jotted in his diary, "W. C. suddenly sat bolt upright and said to me: 'Are we beasts? Are we taking this too far?' "[88]

Such rare sparks of compassion, however, were quickly doused by Churchill's abiding antipathy toward "the Boche." Despite the persistent, though largely weak and easily ignored pleas for restraint, the sentiments of the British prime minister, as well as a majority of his countrymen, could be summed up succinctly by the popular phrase: "The only good German is a dead one!"

As a consequence, the fiery massacres continued. Statistics on those killed, maimed or left homeless are horrific enough. But figures failed to reveal, another category of casualties that touched the lives of many millions more. Of all segments of German society affected by the bombing terror, children suffered most.

"Mommy! Mommy!! Airplanes! MOMMY, AIRPLANES!" screamed two-year-old Freddy Schrott when he heard the sirens wail at his home in Wolfsburg. Although it had only been bombed once, and that but lightly, the town unfortunately found itself situated on the Allied flight path to Berlin. Hence, nightly the sirens sounded and nightly the terrible travail began. "He would stand in his little crib, shaking his arms and crying, 'Mommy, Airplanes! Mommy, AIRPLANES!!' " remembered an older sister. "He was a nervous wreck."[89]

"[T]he tears come. The tears and the terrible shaking," said another child who experienced the air raids. "The tears stop, but the shaking doesn't. I shiver, shake, tremble as if I had fever chills."[90]

---

88. F. J. P. Veale, *Advance to Barbarism* (New York: Devin-Adair Co., 1968), 194.
89. Interview with Emma Schrott Krubel, Topeka, Kansas, 1/9/97.
90. Koehn, *Mischling*, 192.

Horribly, and in a tragedy fully as great, where frightened, confused children should have found most solace from the terror above,
they often found instead only more terror below. Because of the rad-
ical disruption in their lives, parents faced incredible stress. Whether
it was the loss of jobs caused by bombed-out factories and shops, or
whether it was an actual increase of jobs as when those on the home
front were compelled to perform air raid work at night in addition
to their normal duties during the day; whether it was disruption in
water, gas and electric services or whether it was simply the day-in,
day-out uncertainty of their children's safety and their own—all
worked to grind down parents as surely as if their homes had received
direct hits. Recalled one troubled eight-year-old:

> During this time I noticed that Father wasn't very nice to Mother. He'd get
> angry over nothing at all, and when he was very angry, he would hit her. I did-
> n't like that. He was bigger than she was, and we had been taught never to hit
> anybody smaller than ourselves. It was awful to hear Mother cry in her bedroom
> and to listen to the arguments coming from there. Afterward, Father would go
> to work and Mother would come out from her room again and say, "Don't
> you worry, we just had a little disagreement." Then she'd give me a big smile
> and tell me that everything was fine. . . .
>
> Around that time, both Dieter and Erich started wetting their beds every night,
> and Mother and Father had arguments about that, too.[91]

In an effort to save their children, both emotionally and physically,
many urban parents sent offspring to the country for safekeeping. The
evacuations—sometimes of entire schools, complete with teachers and
books—were shattering, heart-wrenching moments for adults. Ultimately, some two and a half million children were relocated to camps
and homes throughout the German hinterland.

With most of their crushing burden removed, adults who remained
could now turn much-needed energies elsewhere. Despite the almost
utter obliteration most cities and towns suffered, Germans who steadfastly held to their homes soon discovered that total destruction was
no guarantee of sudden immunity. Operating under the premise that
"bombing something in Germany is better than bombing nothing,"
Allied war planes returned to old targets again and again, blasting

---

91. Chadwick, *Anna*, 34.

buildings to bricks and bricks to dust. Nevertheless, thousands of determined Germans with nowhere to go merely dug deeper and deeper into the rubble.[92]

"If they destroy our living room, we'll move into the kitchen," one tenacious woman exclaimed. "If the kitchen goes, we'll move into the hallway. And if the hallways fall into ruins, we'll move into the basement. As long as we can stay . . . a little corner of home is better than a strange place."[93]

"Like 'little moles in their holes,' " thought Paula Kuhl as she viewed the phenomenon first-hand. The resiliency of her neighbors was as amazing and remarkable as it was sad and pathetic.

> In the ruins, where basement cellars had defied all the bombs, people were quick off the mark to take possession of any four walls still standing, even if they were half underground. The cellars would soon be cleared of any debris, a ceiling fixed up and windows put in; enough building material was lying around anyway, free for the taking. Having managed to make some sort of living quarters habitable, one would find they were surprisingly comfortable, considering the unusual circumstance; even little rags of curtains adorned the windows. . . . Gradually, the enterprising "do-it-yourselfers" gathered more bricks and sticks together and built a little more "on and up" and, like mushrooms, little houses were sprouting out of the ground again.[94]

Beyond the natural human inclination to abide amid familiar surroundings, another explanation for the seemingly suicidal tendency to remain was simply that many Germans were learning to cope. Explained a chronicler from the heavily bombed city of Kassel:

> Three hundred times the people of Kassel ran terrified to their air-raid shelters as giant British and American planes dropped their bombs. Nearly 10,000 were killed in the first terrible bombing. . . . That was largely an incendiary attack, which set the whole center of the city afire. . . . From that night on they never knew when; they just knew they were doomed. Sometimes they got only a few bombs; often raiding parties which couldn't reach objectives farther east around Berlin picked Kassel on the way home. Occasionally swarms of planes went directly overhead and nothing happened; other times they went overhead, and when the people of Kassel thought they were going on eastward, they wheeled around and came back to drop their powerful tons of TNT.

92. Ralph Barker, *The RAF at War* (Alexandria, Va.: Time-Life, 1981), 161.
93. Sorge, 94.
94. Middlebrook, *Hamburg*, 359–360.

They got so they knew all the tricks, those that remained in Kassel. Steadily their town was beaten down upon their heads. . . . They learned how to dig in, to escape the coal fumes, the fire. Somehow, I thought it was with just a touch of pride that the Mayor said, "And then our latest raid. . . . It was by far the biggest. Perhaps a thousand big bombers, one of the biggest raids in all Germany; and we lost very few killed—less than 100.[95]

That thousands of people, at Kassel and elsewhere, could survive amid the debris was nothing short of miraculous. Another miracle, and one which consistently baffled, bewildered and ultimately frustrated Allied leaders, was the failure of terror-bombing to deal a death blow to German morale. "Our walls are breaking, but not our hearts," ran a typical sign poking up from the bricks of Berlin.[96] Despite enduring five years of the worst war known to modern man, trust in Germany and faith in the Fuhrer remained surprisingly strong. Although morale occasionally cracked, particularly after a heavy air raid or yet another land defeat, it never quite crumbled. By January 1945, Adolf Hitler and the Third Reich had become so inextricably intertwined with one another, that for Germans to lose faith in the one would have been to lose faith in the other. And this, the bombed, burned and battered people never did.

With the armies of the world closing in for the kill by land, sea and air, Germans still looked to their leader for a miracle.

"Faith in the Fuhrer is so great," revealed one observer, "that just a small victory would quickly change the mood of many for the better."[97]

Though few believed any longer that Germany could win the war, most felt that this incredible man who had triumphed so long and often against impossible odds would nevertheless pull off a miracle in the last hour. And this, as he paced his bunker deep beneath the ruins of Berlin, poring over maps with his generals, this was the very thing Adolf Hitler, with every ounce of energy he possessed, was striving to do— to save the German nation in this, the eleventh hour of the war.

---

95. Ralph Franklin Keeling, *Gruesome Harvest* (rpt., 1947; Torrance, Calif.: Institute for Historical Review, 1992), 3–4.

96. Terry Charman, *The German Home Front, 1939–1945* (New York: Philosophical Library, 1989), 147.

97. Steinert, *Hitler's War and the Germans,* 296.

2

THE DEAD AND
THE DEAD TO BE

B Y THE BEGINNING of the new year, 1945, the greatness and glory
that had been Berlin was little more than a fast-fading memory.
Gone were the notes of blaring brass bands and victory parades,
the stirring speeches, the cheering crowds. Replacing these sounds were
the wailing of air raid sirens, the pulsating roar of Allied war planes
as they darkened the skies overhead, the earth-shaking thunder of
death-dealing bombs. And when the bombers banked for home to take
on yet another load of destruction, only silence settled over the smoking hulk of what had once been one of the world's grandest and most
glittering capitals. As a symbol of the Third Reich, as the most obvious example of Germany's will to fight on, more bombs had been
devoted to Berlin than any other German city and in total tonnage,
more explosives were dropped on the capital alone than the Luftwaffe had dumped on all of England throughout all the war. Hence,
of an original population of nearly four and a half million, roughly
half had now vanished; some as refugees, some as casualties. An estimated 50,000 Berliners had been killed by the incessant raids.[1]

Despite being the most heavily defended city in the world, Berlin
had nevertheless become little better than "a vast heap of rubble."[2]
To those survivors who rode out the storm in the hundreds of shelters scattered about the capital, each raid was seemingly heavier and

---

1.   Tony LeTissier, *The Battle of Berlin, 1945* (New York: St. Martin's Press, 1988), 16.
2.   Charman, *The German Home Front*, 144.

more devastating than the last. The destruction was so complete that one Berliner was heard to quip, "If they want to hit more targets, they'll have to bring them with them."[3]

For those refugees reentering the capital after a lengthy absence, the transformation was staggering. Lali Horstman returned via train:

> On coming up the steps of the underground to the daylight, I was shocked by the grimaces of abandoned buildings, by the ruins of the last disastrous bombings, and the streets now empty of traffic. A few shivering people walked by quickly, muffled up against the intense cold, as drab and sad as their surroundings. Although all life seemed extinct, every one individually was full of spirit. The city was like a snake of which the parts continued to live after it had been cut into small pieces. A vivifying spiritual current made it resist being killed outright.[4]

As Lali suggested, though their once-magnificent city was in ruins, the morale of those who remained had not been broken. Like survivors in other German towns, Berliners who had endured countless air raids had become inured to fear and were learning to deal with even death itself.

"I feel a growing sense of wild vitality within myself . . . ," Ursula von Kardorff confided to her diary after surviving yet another Berlin air raid. "If the British think that they are going to undermine our morale they are barking up the wrong tree. . . . [T]hey are not softening us up."[5]

"I was amazed at their excellent spirit," waxed Minister of Propaganda, Dr. Joseph Goebbels, who visited victims on a regular basis. "Nobody is crying, nobody complaining . . . the morale shown here by the population of Berlin is simply magnificent."[6]

With wit, humor and irrepressible optimism, the little doctor was himself a source of comfort to the stricken, as an employee of the Propaganda Ministry, Rudolf Semmler, makes clear:

> Goebbels drives round the whole city. Everywhere desolation. At several points he takes charge of the firefighting. . . . Wherever he is recognized he gets a friendly

3. Christabel Bielenberg, *The Past is Myself* (Dublin: Ward River, 1982), 194.
4. Lali Horstmann, *We Chose to Stay* (Boston: Houghton Mifflin, 1954), 39.
5. Charman, *Home Front,* 145.
6. Ibid., 144.

greeting in spite of everything. Even bombed-out people come and shake him by the hand. He is always ready for a jest. A woman who is engaged to be married complains that her whole home has been wrecked the very night before her wedding. She is no longer young: she tells Goebbels she is 55. "Well then," he says to comfort her, "be thankful that it's your furniture that's gone and that your future husband is still alive. You can get new furniture all right but do you think you would find a new husband easily?" Many people gather round and laugh.[7]

To Goebbels' chagrin, and despite his repeated promptings, Adolf Hitler could not be induced to go among the victims and offer words of encouragement. When Hitler traveled by train through the blasted cities of Germany, he did so with the curtains drawn tight and when photos of ruins crossed his desk, he refused to view them. No doubt, the German Fuhrer feared that even a glimpse of a war gone wrong might weaken his resolve to fight on—that to have walked amid the smoking embers and witness for himself the dismembered bodies of women and children or see first-hand the destruction of Germany's centuries-old culture might have caused him to waver, to despair, to doubt. To meet the coming crisis, the German chancellor simply could not afford even a slight crack in his will to persevere.

Few in devastated Berlin were aware of the fact, but their leader had now returned to his command post in the bunker beneath the Reich Chancellery. Since the onset of war in 1939, Hitler had seldom worked from the capital. Moving his headquarters with the army, from west to east, then back again, the supreme commander chose to direct operations close to the fronts. When he was not actively engaged in the war, Hitler was at Berchtesgaden, his mountain retreat in the Bavarian Alps. Now, without fanfare, the German leader had returned to Berlin, his greatest gamble of the war a failure.

Had the operation taken place earlier in the war, the brilliant surprise would almost certainly have pushed the Allies back to the Channel coast and perhaps ended the war in the west then and there. But the story of the Ardennes offensive was the story of Germany over the past several years—Allied air superiority. When the winter skies finally cleared over the Belgium battlefield after Christmas 1944, British

---

7.   Rudolf Semmler, *Goebbels—The Man Next to Hitler* (London: Westhouse, 1947), 110.

and American aircraft reappeared with a vengeance, halting the attack and forcing the Wehrmacht back to its starting point.

Much through the incompetence, even indifference, of Hermann Goring, head of the Luftwaffe, the once invincible German Air Force had fallen into a condition whereby it could no longer offer serious opposition to the enemy. Prior to hostilities, Goring had pompously assured his countrymen that no German need fear British bombs striking the Fatherland. If so, the field marshal winked, "you may call me Maier." It had long since become the stalest of jokes that among bombing victims the rotund Luftwaffe chief was commonly known as "Hermann Maier." Despite persistent, frantic efforts by his advisors, Hitler refused to sack his old friend and fellow fighter from the days of Nazi Party struggle.

Although nothing could stop the rain of death pouring down on Germany, Adolf Hitler was determined to trade terror for terror. While damage was trifling compared to that of the Reich, it was a boost to German morale when the first "wonder weapons," or V-rockets, began slamming into England during the summer of 1944. Outraged by this "inhuman, criminal" new device, Churchill made plans to saturate Germany with poison gas and deadly anthrax germs, despite an international ban on such warfare.[8]

"We could drench the cities of . . . Germany in such a way that most of the population would be requiring constant medical treatment," the prime minister argued to his advisors.[9]

Fearful, no doubt, that Hitler would respond in kind from his own stockpile of such weapons, Churchill wisely hesitated.

In addition to V-rockets, many, including volunteers, urged the chancellor to deploy suicide planes, as Germany's ally, Japan, was doing with such striking success. Hitler, however, quickly vetoed the idea. "Every person who risks his life in the battle for his Fatherland must

---

8. Hastings, *Bomber Command*, 287; Richard Landwehr, *Charlemagne's Legionnaires* (Silver Spring, Maryland: Bibliophile Legion Books, Inc., 1989), 14–15; Mark Weber, "Churchill Wanted to 'Drench' Germany with Poison Gas," *The Journal of Historical Review* 6, no. 4 (Winter 1985–86): 501–502.

9. Garrett, *Ethics and Airpower*, 194.

have a chance for survival, even if it's small," explained the Fuhrer. "We Germans are not Japanese kamikaze."[10]

Like many of his beleaguered countrymen, Adolf Hitler still believed in miracles. He had to. To toss away this final hope would have been to admit defeat. With the weight of the world against him, with "unconditional surrender" the adamant Allied demand, Hitler was determined to continue the fight unto death . . . or a miracle. No one need remind him of the worsening odds—a simple glance at the map was proof enough. The Soviet Union, the United States, Great Britain and its Commonwealth, France and her colonies—with well over half a billion people to draw from, the Reich's enemies dwarfed Germany's tiny population of 70 million. Great as the demographic disparity was, it seemed trivial compared to the industrial imbalance. With almost unlimited natural resources—coal, oil, ore, rubber—a seemingly inexhaustible supply of tanks, planes, ships, and guns were ready to replace enemy losses with ease. On the other hand, Germany's shattered and rapidly shrinking industries were merely struggling to survive, with many operations forced underground into caves and tunnels.

Against such impossible odds, with such an overpowering enemy closing on all sides, a normal man might have gone mad. Indeed, suspecting such was the case, Allied propagandists reported that Hitler frequently frothed at the mouth following each new disaster, rolling in a rage on the floor as he chewed rabidly on the carpet.

"I was with him every day and almost every night to the very end," revealed one confidant. "Long fits of sullen silence, yes. Volcanic explosions, yes—although the lava was usually controlled. Hitler was a consummate actor, not a rug-chewer."[11]

Hopeless as the odds were, impossible as the situation became with each passing day, for Adolf Hitler surrender was simply not an option. As a common soldier during World War I, well did Hitler remember the last German surrender. Although the troops were more than willing to fight on in 1918, the politicians in Berlin had caved in and

---

10. Leni Riefenstahl, *A Memoir* (New York: St. Martin's Press, 1993), 320–321.
11. James P. O'Donnell, *The Bunker* (Boston: Houghton Mifflin Co., 1978), 318.

capitulated. As a consequence of this "stab in the back," Germany had been humbled and humiliated, dismembered, then all but enslaved by the victors. It was the lesson of 1918—a time when hatred of Germany was not a tithe as great as now—that steeled Hitler's resolve by reminding him that surrender was tantamount to national suicide. Even after the death-knell in the Ardennes, the Fuhrer was firm.

"You should not infer that I am thinking even in the slightest of losing the war," Hitler confided to a group of generals. "I have never in my life learned the meaning of the word capitulation, and I am one of those men who have worked their way up from nothing. For me, therefore, the circumstances in which we find ourselves are nothing new."[12]

Additionally, Hitler had the towering figure of Frederick the Great to serve as his model. During another dark time in Germany's past, a time when enemy armies also stood poised to devour the Reich, Frederick had stood firm. Because of "Old Fritz's" determination to fight to the last ditch, the impossible had occurred when the Czarina of Russia, Elizabeth, had died, throwing the alliance against Germany into disarray and enabling the improbable victory. It was this amazing eleventh hour miracle of the eighteenth century, more than anything else, that buttressed Hitler's will to hold out in hope of a similar occurrence in the twentieth century. That he might never forget this lesson and weaken, a portrait of Frederick hung wherever the Fuhrer established headquarters, including now, in his tomb-like bunker beneath Berlin.

"When bad news threatens to crush my spirit," mused Hitler, "I derive fresh courage from the contemplation of this picture. . . . We have reached the final quarter of an hour. The situation is serious, very serious. It seems even to be desperate. While we keep fighting, there is always hope. . . . All we must do is refuse to go down!"[13]

Abysmal as conditions were in the west, where American, British and

12. Earl F. Ziemke, *The Soviet Juggernaut* (Alexandria, Va.: Time-Life Books, 1980), 179.
13. Christopher Duffy, *Red Storm on the Reich* (New York: Atheneum, 1991), 39; John Toland, *The Last 100 Days* (New York: Random House, 1965), 72–73.

French forces were now free to advance on the Rhine, and as devastating and deadly as the bombing massacres had been, these were mere sideshows to the main event. While the embattled chancellor's gaze might be distracted momentarily in these directions, his eyes always reverted east. It was here, Hitler knew, that the war would be won or lost. It was here that diametrically opposed ideologies were locked in a fang and claw fight to the finish. And thus, it was here, more than anywhere else, that the German Army had to hold. If the approaching red storm could be weathered, then turned back, all else would manage itself. Weak, bleeding and decimated as it was, the Wehrmacht was still more than a match for threats from the west. But above all, it was the communist peril looming to the east that had to be faced and overcome. If not, if there was no modern miracle for Germany, then not only would the Reich cease to exist, but much of Europe would pass into darkness as well.

Since the German invasion of the Soviet Union in September 1941, the fight on the Eastern Front had been little better than a savage war of annihilation. A contest between "European Nationalism" on the one hand, and "International Bolshevism" on the other, would have been a most desperate struggle under any conditions. But then, fighting for his life, Josef Stalin deliberately exacerbated the situation.

Dubious over the loyalty of his armed forces, aware of the massive Russian surrenders during the First World War, the Red premier steadfastly refused to sign the Geneva Convention on prisoners of war or the Hague Treaty regarding land warfare. It was Stalin's belief that if a soldier had no guarantee of survival in captivity, then he must of necessity fight to the death in battle. Despite such ruthless measures, Soviet troops surrendered by the hundreds of thousands in the first weeks and months of the war. Swamped by the flood of prisoners, strained to adequately clothe, feed and house such numbers, and understandably hesitant to even do so unless the Russians reciprocated, the Germans time and again tried to reach an accord with Stalin. The efforts were flung back with contempt.[14]

Soviet soldiers do not surrender, communist officials airily announced. "[A] prisoner captured alive by the enemy [is] *ipso facto* a traitor. . . . If they had fulfilled their duty as soldiers to fight to the last they would not have been taken prisoner."[15]

"Everyone who was taken prisoner, even if they'd been wounded . . . was considered to have 'surrendered voluntarily to the enemy,'" wrote Stalin's daughter, Svetlana, whose own brother was captured and promptly disowned by her father. "The government thereby washed its hands of millions of its own officers and men . . . and refused to have anything to do with them."[16]

Hence, growled a disgruntled captain of Russian artillery, Alexander Solzhenitsyn, "[Moscow] did not recognize its own soldiers of the day before."[17]

Not surprisingly, many Red Army men, including General Andrei Vlasov, swiftly turned on their government after capture and became "traitors" not only in name, but in fact, by joining the Germans in their anti-communist crusade.

That the Soviets would treat their own troops in such a deplorable manner bode ill for that German soldier, or Landser, unlucky enough to fall into enemy hands. Although responses varied greatly among Soviet units and some captured Germans were treated as POWs, most were not. During the first glorious days of German victory in 1941, the Red Army's headlong retreat precluded the likelihood that large numbers of Landsers would be captured. Nevertheless, thousands of unwitting Germans did fall into communist hands and were dispatched on the spot.

On July 1, 1941, near Broniki in the Ukraine, the Soviets captured over 160 Germans, many of them wounded. In the words of Corporal Karl Jager:

14. Mark Elliott, *Pawns of Yalta* (Urbana: University of Illinois Press, 1982), 9, 168; Nikolai Tolstoy, *The Secret Betrayal, 1944–1947* (New York: Charles Scribner's Sons, 1977), 323.
15. Elliott, *Pawns*, 168.
16. Ibid., 169–170.
17. Ibid., 9.

After being taken prisoner . . . other comrades and I were forced to undress. . . . We had to surrender all valuable objects including everything we had in our pockets. I saw other comrades stabbed with a bayonet because they were not fast enough. Corporal Kurz had a wounded hand and . . . could not remove his belt as quickly as desired. He was stabbed from behind at the neck so that the bayonet came out through the throat. A soldier who was severely wounded gave slight signs of life with his hands; he was kicked about and his head was battered with rifle butts. . . . Together with a group of 12 to 15 men I was taken to a spot north of the road. Several of them completely naked. We were about the third group coming from the road. Behind us the Russians commenced the executions . . . panic broke out after the first shots, and I was able to flee.[18]

"My hands were tied up at my back . . . and we were forced to lie down . . . ," said another victim in the same group. "[A] Russian soldier stabbed me in the chest with his bayonet. Thereupon I turned over. I was then stabbed seven times in the back and I did not move any more. . . . I heard my comrades cry out in pain. Then I passed out."[19]

In all, 153 bodies were recovered by advancing Germans the following morning. Despite the summary slaughter of their own men at Broniki and elsewhere, Wehrmacht field marshals strictly forbid large-scale reprisals. One group which could expect no mercy from the Germans was the communist commissars who traveled with Red Army units. Composed "almost exclusively" of Jews, it was these fanatical political officers, many Germans felt, who were responsible for the massacres and mutilations of captured comrades.[20] Explained one witness, Lieutenant Hans Woltersdorf of the elite SS:

One of our antitank gun crews had defended itself down to the last cartridge, really down to the last cartridge. Over thirty dead Russians lay before their positions. They then had to surrender. While still alive they had their genitals cut off, their eyes poked out, and their bellies slit open. Russian prisoners to whom we showed this declared that such mutilations took place by order of the commissars. This was the first I had heard of such commissars.[21]

With the threat of torture and execution facing them, many idealistic German soldiers had an added impetus to fight to the death. In

18. Alfred deZayas, *The Wehrmacht War Crimes Bureau, 1939–1945* (Lincoln: University of Nebraska Press, 1989), 163.
19. Ibid., 164.
20. Ibid., 167; Douglas, *Gestapo Chief, II,* 223; Sorge, *Other Price,* 7.
21. Hans Werner Woltersdorf, *Gods of War* (Novato, Calif.: Presidio Press, 1990), 214.

the minds of most Landsers, the war in the east was not a contest against the Russian or Slavic race in particular, but a crusade against communism. In the years following World War I, Marxist revolutionaries had nearly toppled the German government. Because most of the leaders were Jews, and because Lenin, Trotsky, and many other Russian revolutionaries were Jewish, the threat to Nazi Germany and Europe seemed clear. Hence, from Adolf Hitler down to the lowliest Landser, the fight in the east became a holy war against "Jewish Bolshevism."

"The poor, unhappy Russian people," said one shocked German soldier as he moved further into the Soviet Union. "Its distress is unspeakable and its misery heart-rending."[22]

"When you see what the Jew has brought about here in Russia, only then can you begin to understand why the Fuhrer began this struggle against Judaism," another stunned Landser wrote, expressing a sentiment shared by many comrades. "What sort of misfortunes would have been visited upon our Fatherland, if this bestial people had gotten the upper hand?"[23]

Following the devastating German defeat at Stalingrad in 1943, the "upper hand" did indeed pass to the enemy. Supplied by the US with a seemingly inexhaustible amount of goods, from tanks and planes to boots and butter, the resurgent Red Army assumed the offensive.[24] As the heretofore invincible Wehrmacht began its long, slow withdrawal west, a drama as vast and savage as the steppe itself unfolded, the likes of which the modern world had never witnessed. In dozens of major battles, in thousands of forgotten skirmishes, a primeval contest was waged wherein victory meant life and defeat meant death.

Overwhelmingly outnumbered in men and materiel, especially the dreaded tank, for young German recruits sent to fill depleted ranks there was no subtle transition from peace to war on the Eastern Front—

22. Stephen G. Fritz, *Frontsoldaten* (Lexington: University Press of Kentucky, 1995), 52.
23. Ibid., 195.
24. LeTissier, *Battle of Berlin*, 7.

they simply stepped straight from the train or truck into the inferno. Likewise, the step from boy to man could, and often did, come within a matter of moments once the recruit reached the lines. Guy Sajer's youth ended abruptly one day when his convoy was ambushed.

> "Anybody hit?" one of the noncoms called out. "Let's get going then. . . ." Nervously, I pulled open the door [of the truck]. Inside, I saw a man I shall never forget, a man sitting normally on the seat, whose lower face had been reduced to a bloody pulp.
>
> "Ernst?" I asked in a choking voice. "Ernst!" I threw myself at him. . . . I looked frantically for some features on that horrible face. His coat was covered with blood. . . . His teeth were mixed with fragments of bone, and through the gore I could see the muscles of his face contracting. In a state of near shock, I tried to put the dressing somewhere on that cavernous wound. . . . Crying like a small boy, I pushed my friend to the other end of the seat, holding him in my arms. . . . Two eyes opened, brilliant with anguish, and looked at me from his ruined face.
>
> In the cab of a . . . truck, somewhere in the vastness of the Russian hinter-land, a man and an adolescent were caught in a desperate struggle. The man struggled with death, and the adolescent struggled with despair. . . . I felt that something had hardened in my spirit forever.[25]

"The first group of T34's crashed through the undergrowth," another terrified replacement recalled when Russian tanks suddenly shattered his once peaceful world.

> I heard my officer shout to me to take the right hand machine. . . . All that I had learned in the training school suddenly came flooding back and gave me confidence. . . . It had been planned that we should allow the first group of T-34's to roll over us. . . . The grenade had a safety cap which had to be unscrewed to reach the rip-cord. My fingers were trembling as I unscrewed the cap . . . [and] climbed out of the trench. . . . Crouching low I started towards the monster, pulled the detonating cord, and prepared to fix the charge. I had now nine seconds before the grenade exploded and then I noticed, to my horror, that the outside of the tank was covered in concrete. . . . My bomb could not stick on such a surface. . . . The tank suddenly spun on its right track, turned so that it pointed straight at me and moved forward as if to run over me.
>
> I flung myself backwards and fell straight into a partly dug slit trench and so shallow that I was only just below the surface of the ground. Luckily I had

---

25. Fritz, *Frontsoldaten*, 176.

fallen face upwards and was still holding tight in my hand the sizzling hand grenade. As the tank rolled over me there was a sudden and total blackness. . . . The shallow earth walls of the trench began to collapse. As the belly of the monster passed over me I reached up instinctively as if to push it away and . . . stuck the charge on the smooth, unpasted metal. . . . Barely had the tank passed over me than there was a loud explosion. . . . I was alive and the Russians were dead. I was trembling in every limb.[26]

Another Landser who found truth facing Russian tanks was eighteen-year-old Guy Sajer. Armed with single-shot "Panzerfausts," a shoulder-held anti-armor weapon, Sajer and five comrades cowered in a shallow hole. "Our fear reached grandiose proportions, and urine poured down our legs," admitted the young soldier. "Our fear was so great that we lost all thought of controlling ourselves."

Three tanks were moving toward us. If they rolled over the mound which protected us, the war would end for us in less than a minute. I. . . . [raised] my first Panzerfaust, and my hand, stiff with fear, [was] on the firing button.

As they rolled toward us, the earth against which my body was pressed transmitted their vibrations, while my nerves, tightened to the breaking point, seemed to shrill with an ear-splitting whistle. . . . I could see the reflected yellow lights on the front of the tank, and then everything disappeared in the flash of light which I had released, and which burned my face. . . . To the side, other flashes of light battered at my eyes, which jerked open convulsively wide, although there was nothing to see. Everything was simultaneously luminous and blurred. Then a second tank in the middle distance was outlined by a glow of flame. . . .

We could hear the noise of a third tank. . . . It had accelerated, and was no more than thirty yards from us, when I grabbed my last Panzerfaust. One of my comrades had already fired, and I was temporarily blinded. I stiffened my powers of vision and regained my sight to see a multitude of rollers caked with mud churning past . . . five or six yards from us. An inhuman cry of terror rose from our helpless throats.

The tank withdrew into the noise of battle, and finally disappeared in a volcanic eruption which lifted it from the ground in a thick cloud of smoke. Our wildly staring eyes tried to fix on something solid, but could find nothing except smoke and flame. As there were no more tanks, our madness thrust us from our refuge, toward the fire whose brilliance tortured our eyes. The noise of the tanks was growing fainter. The Russians were backing away.[27]

26. Ibid., 41–42.
27. Guy Sajer, *The Forgotten Soldier* (New York: Harper & Row, 1967), 446–447.

After pulling wounded from the burning tanks, Sajer collapsed in a heap. As the young Landser and his exhausted comrades well knew, however, the respite would be brief: "They would undoubtedly reappear in greater numbers, with the support of planes or artillery, and our despairing frenzy would count for nothing."[28]

Sajer was correct. In yet another contest between man and machine, the soldier and his companions could only watch in helpless horror as the steel monsters overran a gun emplacement.

> Our cries of distress were mingled with the screams of the two machine gunners and then the shouts of revenge from the Russian tank crew as it drove over the hole, grinding the remains of the two gunners into that hateful soil. . . . The treads worked over the hole for a long time, and . . . the Russian crew kept shouting, "Kaputt, Soldat Germanski! Kaputt!"[29]

Many scenes from the East Front, like the above, seemed scripted in hell. After a hastily organized force of mechanics, bakers and cooks had beat back one enemy assault, a group of Landsers, including Hans Woltersdorf, crept up to a damaged Russian tank. "The men looked into the tank," the lieutenant remembered, "and they were near vomiting, so they didn't look further but instead went away, embarrassed. A headless torso, bloody flesh, and intestines were sticking to the walls."[30] Several soldiers did succeed in pulling an injured driver from the wreck. "He lay there, wearing a distinguished award for bravery . . . ," noted Woltersdorf. "The back of his head was gaping open and bloody brains were pouring out. He was foaming at the mouth and his breath was still rattling, the typical rattle after an injury to the back of the head. You're dead but your lungs are still puffing. . . . I took his military papers and the award. Later, when it was all over, I would send them to his family and write to them that he had fought bravely to the last for his country . . . he had given his best . . . they could be proud of him . . . what does one write at such times?"[31]

Terrible in their own right, sights and sounds such as the above were

---

28. Ibid., 447.
29. Fritz, 42.
30. Woltersdorf, *Gods of War*, 73.
31. Ibid.

made doubly horrifying by the haunting suspicion that the viewer was gazing down on his own fate. "One always sees oneself sticking to the walls in thousands of pieces like that," confessed Woltersdorf, "without a head, or being dragged from the tank with a death rattle in one's throat."[32]

Facing cold, robot-like tanks was terrifying enough. When humans became such, the results were devastating. Perhaps the most frightening moment in any Landser's life came when he first faced the human wave. In a nation so vast that it compassed two continents, men were a resource the Soviets could afford to waste . . . and did. Following a Russian artillery barrage upon his position, Max Simon redeployed surviving soldiers along a ridge.

"Then," the SS general wrote, "quite a long distance from our positions there were lines of brown uniformed men tramping forward. The first of these crossed a small river and was followed at about 200 metres distance by a second line. Then there rose out of the grass—literally from out of the ground—a third wave, then a fourth and a fifth."[33]

"To see them, the Ivans, rise up from the ground and just stand there, thousands of them, was really frightening," said another who faced the human wave. "They would stand there, within range . . . silent, withdrawn and not heeding those who fell around them. Then they would move off, the first three lines marching towards us."[34]

Returning to General Simon:

> The lines of men stretched to the right and left of our regimental front overlapping it completely and the whole mass of Russian troops came tramping solidly and relentlessly forward. It was an unbelievable sight, a machine gunner's dream. . . . At 600 metres we opened fire and whole sections of the first wave just vanished leaving here and there an odd survivor still walking stolidly forward. It was uncanny, unbelievable, inhuman. No soldier of ours would have continued to advance alone. The second wave had also taken losses but closed up towards

---

32. Ibid.

33. James Lucas, *War on the Eastern Front, 1941–1945* (London: Jane's Pub. Co., 1979), 32.

34. James Lucas, *Last Days of the Third Reich* (New York: William Morrow and Co., Inc., 1986), 19.

the center, round and across the bodies of their comrades who had fallen with the first wave. Then, as if on a signal, the lines of men began running forward. As they advanced there was a low rumbling "Hoooooraaay. . . ."[35]

"The sound of that bellowing challenge was enough to freeze the blood," admitted one trembling Landser. "Just the sound alone terrified the new recruits."[36]

Again, Max Simon:

> The first three waves had been destroyed by our fire, but not all of the men in them had been killed. Some who dropped were snipers who worked their way forward through the grass to open fire upon our officers and machine gun posts. The rush of the fourth wave came on more slowly for the men had to pick their way through a great carpet of bodies and as the Soviets moved towards us some of our men, forgetful of the danger, stood on the parapets of their slit trenches to fire at the oncoming Russians. The machine guns became hot from continual firing and there were frequent stoppages to change barrels. . . .
>
> The great mass of the Soviet troops was now storming up the slope towards us but our fire was too great and they broke. About an hour later a further five lines of men came on in a second assault. The numbers of the enemy seemed endless and the new waves of men advanced across their own dead without hesitation. . . . The Ivans kept up their attacks for three days and sometimes even during the night. Suddenly they stopped and withdrew.[37]

While the slaughter of thousands in such suicidal assaults seemed senseless, the results were not altogether one-sided. The psychological wounds inflicted on the Germans were, as Gen. Simon acknowledged, perhaps an even greater blow than the physical havoc wrought on the Russians. "The number, duration and fury of those attacks had exhausted us . . . ," confessed Simon. "If the Soviets could waste men on our small move, and there was no doubt that these men had been sacrificed, how often, we asked ourselves, would they attack and in what numbers if the objective was really a supremely important one?"[38]

The carnage following battles such as the above was truly horrific. Although most recruits soon became hardened after two or three similar encounters, no soldier ever became complacent about war. The

---

35. Lucas, *Eastern Front*, 32.
36. Lucas, *Last Days*, 19.
37. Lucas, *Eastern Front*, 32–33.
38. Ibid., 33.

battlefield had many grim faces and no two were alike. Surprisingly, some of the most shattering moments in a Landser's life concerned the dreadful impact war had on horses, thousands of which served both armies. Harald Henry remembered vividly one animal in particular, laying by the wayside:

> It reared, someone gave it a mercy shot, it sprang up again, another fired. . . . [T]he horse still fought for its life, many shots. But the rifle shots did not quickly finish off the dying eyes of the horse. . . . Everywhere horses. Ripped apart by shells, their eyes bulging out from empty red sockets. . . . That is just almost worse than the torn-away faces of the men, of the burnt, half-charred corpses.[39]

After just experiencing what he imagined was all the horror one battle had to give, Lieutenant Friedrich Haag noticed a "beautiful white horse grazing by a ditch."

> An artillery shell . . . had torn away his right foreleg. He grazed peacefully but at the same time slowly and in unspeakable grief swayed his bloody stump of a leg to and fro. . . . I don't know if I can accurately describe the horror of this sight. . . . I said then . . . to one of my men: "Finish that horse off!" Then the soldier, who just ten minutes before had been in a hard fight, replied: "I haven't got the heart for it, Herr Lieutenant." Such experiences are more distressing than all the "turmoil of battle" and the personal danger.[40]

Although massed human assaults and tank battles were dramatic, earth-shaking events, surviving German soldiers could normally expect a welcome, if brief, respite between contests. Not so with the ever-lurking, ever-active partisan war. For that Landser behind the front who dropped his guard, the result could mean instant death . . . or worse.

"When German soldiers were captured by guerrillas, they were often abominably treated," one Wehrmacht general recounted. "[I]t was not unusual for the Soviets to torture their prisoners and then hang them up, sometimes with their genitals stuffed in their mouths."[41] Other Landsers were released, then sent staggering down roads toward their comrades, naked, bloody, eyes gouged from sockets, castrated.

39. Fritz, *Frontsoldaten*, 153.
40. Ibid.
41. John H. Nugent and George Fowler, "The Geneva & Hague Conventions—And the 'Holocaust,'" *The Barnes Review* 2, no. 2 (Nov. 1996): 16.

Unable to deal decisively with the civilian-clad irregulars, German reprisals against the surrounding communities were swift, grim and arbitrary.

"A partisan group blew up our vehicles," recorded one private, "[and] ... shot the agricultural administrator and a corporal assigned to him in their quarters. . . . Early yesterday morning 40 men were shot on the edge of the city. . . . Naturally there were a number of innocent people who had to give up their lives. . . . One didn't waste a lot of time on this and just shot the ones who happened to be around."[42]

As with commissars, "no quarter" was the standard fate of guerrillas who fell into German hands. Wrote a witness:

> Businesslike, the men of the field police emerge and tie with oft-practiced skill seven nooses on the balcony railing and then disappear behind the door of the dark room. . . . The first human package, tied up, is carried outside. The limbs are tightly bound . . . a cloth covers his face. The hemp neckband is placed around his neck, hands are tied tight, he is put on the balustrade and the blindfold is removed from his eyes. For an instant you see glaring eyeballs, like those of an escaped horse, then wearily he closes his eyelids, almost relaxed, never to open them again. He now slides slowly downward, his weight pulls the noose tight, his muscles begin their hopeless battle. The body works mightily, twitches, and within the fetters a bit of life struggles to its end. It's quick; one after the other are brought out, put on the railing. . . . Each one bears a placard on his chest proclaiming his crime. . . . Sometimes one of them sticks out his tongue as if in unconscious mockery and immoderate amounts of spittle drip down on the street.[43]

As the Wehrmacht was pressed inexorably west, the daily attrition was staggering. Repeated Russian attacks opened gaps in German ranks simply too great to be filled. Outnumbered sometimes ten to one, each Landser was thus expected to fight as ten if they were to survive. Many did. After beating back waves of Soviets with only a handful of men, Leopold von Thadden-Trieglaff refused to abandon his tiny section of

42. Fritz, 50–51.
43. Ibid., 51.

line. Holding on throughout the night, the surrounded squad again fought furiously the following dawn.

"[A] hail of fire rained on us, from right, from left," recorded the young soldier in his journal. "In a few minutes our bunker was full of wounded and I struggled to quiet the poor fellows. . . . Screams and groans, and singing. I had to strain every nerve in order to remain as calm as before."[44]

Finally, a German counterattack broke through and rescued the survivors, ending "the most terrible night and the hardest battle of my life . . . ," wrote Thadden-Trieglaff. "As I returned to my command post in the village I gaped at the dead comrades. I was so shaken that I almost cried. . . . When might this hideous defensive struggle come to an end?"[45]

For the heroic twenty-year-old, that end came the following day when he was killed.

As the crushing attrition ground the German Army into the Russian mud, the turnover rate from death and wounds was tremendous. Green recruits often found themselves within months, even weeks, the oldest veterans in their unit. "I noticed that it was particularly in the first few days that newcomers were most likely to get killed," observed Jan Montyn.

> Gert was one of those newcomers. He was sixteen. . . . I saw in his eyes, behind his round spectacles, the same bewilderment that I had felt myself when I was finding my way around that first day—almost a month ago now. His legs were trembling, he kept blinking. He had never held a real gun in his hands before. And I felt that he would not be with us for long.
>
> "You have to think carefully about everything you do," I told him. "You must not allow anything to become a habit. On the other side there are snipers on the look-out day and night. If you as much as strike a match, you are finished. They notice every regularity in your behavior. When you have to scoop out a trench, don't throw the earth over the side in the same place twice. . . .
>
> Gert nodded. He would remember. But less than two hours later I heard a cry. He had climbed out of the trench. He had been hit with his trousers down. In ten paces I was with him, and pulled him back into the trench by his legs. *Oh,*

---

44. Ibid., 40.
45. Ibid., 41.

you idiot! Did *I have* to say that . . . ? There was a big hole in his groin. I pulled
a roll of substitute bandage out of my breast pocket. But the poor quality paper
was drenched within a few seconds. I tried to close the wound by pressing on
it with my thumbs, begging and praying that someone might come along. I dared
not call; that might provoke mortar fire. Gert lay panting, his mouth half open.
He did not seem to feel any pain. For God's sake let someone come. No one came.
The blood that gushed through my fingers mingled with the mud. And Gert
no longer moved.[46]

Added to the trauma of watching comrades die one by one, was concern for the safety of loved ones at home. Unlike Allied soldiers, whose
words from home brought comfort and cheer, for the German Landser
a letter from a loved one was merely one more burden to bear. Penned
Martin Poppel in his diary:

My wife wrote to me: "Today we are worn out after this terrible hail of bombs.
To be hearing the howling of these things all the time, waiting for death at any
moment, in a dark cellar, unable to see. . . . Everything gone. . . ." No, here at
the front we musn't think about it. . . . We understood the feelings of the people at home, suffered with them and feared for our loved ones who had to bear
terror bombing.[47]

"A few days ago," scribbled a tormented sergeant, "I found out that
just at the same time as we dreamed of home, the rubble was smoking in my home city of Mannheim. What a bitter irony."[48]

"These pigs . . . think they can soften us up in that way. But that is
a mistake, a mistake," growled another sergeant. "Ah, if only the Fuhrer
would send a pair of . . . divisions to England. They would deal a death
dance that would give the devil himself the creeps. Oh, I have a rage,
a wild hatred."[49]

Despite official orders against killing prisoners, the unofficial reality was often quite different. Living without hope, dealing with death
on a daily basis, aware of the fate their loved ones at home were facing, as well as their own should they be captured, many crazed, bru-
talized individuals could not be restrained.

---

46. Montyn, *Lamb to Slaughter,* 97.
47. Fritz, *Frontsoldaten,* 84.
48. Ibid., 85.
49. Ibid., 86.

"A prolonged and penetrating cry rose from the hole on my left . . . ,"
Guy Sajer noted after one desperate fight. "Then there was a cry for help."

> We arrived at the edge of a foxhole, where a Russian, who had just thrown
> down his revolver, was holding his hands in the air. At the bottom of the hole,
> two men were fighting. One of them, a Russian, was waving a large cutlass, hold-
> ing a man from our group pinned beneath him. Two of us covered the Rus-
> sian who had raised his hands, while a young [corporal] jumped into the hole
> and struck the other Russian a blow on the back of his neck with a trenching
> tool. . . . The German who had been under him . . . ran up to ground level. He
> was covered with blood, brandishing the Russian knife with one hand . . . while
> with the other he tried to stop the flow of blood pouring from his wound.
>
> "Where is he?" he shouted in a fury. "Where's the other one?" In a few bound-
> ing steps he reached the . . . prisoner. Before anyone could do anything, he had
> run his knife into the belly of the petrified Russian.[50]

Following three days of frenzied fighting, Sajer and his sleepless comrades finally snapped.

> Sometimes one or two prisoners might emerge from their hideout with their
> hands in the air, and each time the same tragedy repeated itself. Kraus killed four
> of them on the lieutenant's orders; the Sudeten two; Group 17, nine. Young Lind-
> berg, who had been in a state of panic ever since the beginning of the offen-
> sive, and who had been either weeping in terror or laughing in hope, took Kraus's
> machine gun and shoved two Bolsheviks into a shell hole. The two wretched vic-
> tims . . . kept imploring his mercy. . . . But Lindberg, in a paroxysm of uncon-
> trollable rage, kept firing until they were quiet.
>
> We were mad with harassment and exhaustion. . . . We were forbidden to
> take prisoners. . . . We knew that the Russians didn't take any, . . . [that] it was
> either them or us, which is why my friend Hals and I threw grenades . . . at
> some Russians who were trying to wave a white flag.[51]

Nevertheless, amid the insane upheaval of combat, the same soldier who might one moment murder helpless prisoners could the next
risk his own life to pull men from burning enemy tanks. Hans Woltersdorf stood for one eternal instant, his machine-gun trained on several Russians he had surprised, the last flicker of humanity struggling mightily against all the dark forces of his past. "Do I shoot or

---

50. Ibid., 52–53.
51. Ibid., 53–54.

not? . . . ," the lieutenant asked himself, as the terrified prisoners begged for mercy. "They got up . . . , stumbled backwards a few steps more to the fir thicket, turned round, put their hands down and ran like the devil. . . . Did I try to shoot? Did my machine gun really fail to function, as I claimed later?"[52]

Very often, death was the highest act of kindness one could show an enemy. "On Tuesday I knocked out two T-34's . . . ," one Landser wrote. "Afterward I drove past the smoking remains. From the hatch there hung a body, head down, his feet caught, and his legs burning up to his knees. The body was alive, the mouth moaning. He must have suffered terrible pain. And there was no possibility of freeing him. . . . I shot him, and as I did it, the tears ran down my cheeks. Now I have been crying for three nights about a dead Russian tank driver."[53]

"From time to time one of us would emerge from torpor and scream," admitted Guy Sajer. "These screams were entirely involuntary: we couldn't stop them. They were produced by our exhaustion. . . . Some laughed as they howled; others prayed. Men who could pray could hope."[54] Sajer continues:

> We felt like lost souls who had forgotten that men are made for something else, . . . that love can sometimes occur, that the earth can be productive and used for something other than burying the dead. We were madmen, gesturing and moving without thought or hope. . . . Lindberg . . . had collapsed into a kind of stupor. . . . The Sudeten . . . had begun to tremble . . . and to vomit uncontrollably. Madness had invaded our group, and was gaining ground rapidly. . . . I saw . . . Hals leap to his machine gun and fire at the sky. . . . I also saw the [sergeant] . . . beat the ground with his clenched fist. . . . [I] shout[ed] curses and obscenities at the sky. . . . After hours and then days of danger . . . one collapses into unbearable madness, and a crisis of nerves is only the beginning. Finally, one vomits and collapses, entirely brutalized and inert, as if death had already won.[55]

"[We were] the dead or the dead to be," stated one Landser simply.[56] As the East Front moved steadily west, the struggle became even more

52. Woltersdorf, *Gods of War,* 34.
53. Fritz, 88–89.
54. Ibid., 88.
55. Ibid., 89.
56. Ibid., 84.

desperate. By the winter of 1944, the Red Army had finally driven the invaders from Russian soil and was pressing them through Poland. Although enormous losses had melted away much German manpower, and although the odds remained overwhelmingly in the Soviets' favor, the Red Army suffered grievously as well. For every German casualty on the field of battle, there were four Russians. Many Soviet units had been reduced to a mere 50% of their original strength.[57] Consequently, Red ranks were increasingly filled by troops from far eastern provinces.

"This is not the Red Army," spit one Russian officer. "The Red Army perished on the battlefields in 1941 and 1942. These are the hordes of Asia."[58]

In addition to Asians, Soviet officials called up a motley reserve—boys as young as thirteen, women, cripples, even convicts.[59] "We opened up our penitentiaries and stuck everybody into the army," Stalin admitted.[60] If possible, these raw levies were thrown away with more criminal disregard than ever. Wrote a German soldier:

> It does not matter that these conscripts are untrained, that many are without boots of any kind and that most of them have no arms. Prisoners whom we took told us that those without weapons are expected to take up those from the fallen. . . . I saw . . . attacks which were preceded by solid blocks of people marching shoulder to shoulder across the minefields which we had laid. Civilians and Army punishment battalions alike advanced like automata, their ranks broken only when a mine exploded killing and wounding those around it. The people seemed never to flinch nor to quail and we noticed that some who fell were then shot by a smaller wave of commissars or officers who followed very closely behind.[61]

"This was not war anymore," a Landser who witnessed the massacres confided. "It was murder."

Of all the horrors the East Front had to give—human waves, Red crewmen bolted inside burning tanks, murder of prisoners, partisan atrocities—the single facet most frightening to the average Landser was undoubtedly "Ivan" himself.

---

57. Duffy, *Red Storm*, 25, 54.
58. Aidan Crawley, *The Spoils of War* (Indianapolis: Bobbs-Merrill, 1964), 20.
59. McKee, *Dresden 1945*, 30.
60. deZayas, *Wehrmacht*, 179.
61. Lucas, *Eastern Front*, 35–36.

"The Russian infantryman . . . always defended himself to the last gasp . . . ," remembered Gen. Max Simon. "[E]ven crews in burning tanks kept up fire for as long as there was breath in their bodies. Wounded or unconscious men reached for their weapons as soon as they regained consciousness."[62] Added another German soldier, Erich Dwinger:

> Among the prisoners waiting to be ferried back across the river were wounded, many of whom had been badly burnt by flame-throwers. . . . Their faces had no longer any recognizable human features but were simply swollen lumps of meat. One of them also had had his lower jaw torn away by a bullet and this wound he had bandaged roughly. Through the rags his windpipe, laid bare, was visible and the effort it made as his breath snorted through it. Another soldier had been hit by five bullets and his right shoulder and his whole arm was a ragged mass of flesh. He had no bandages and the blood oozed from his wounds as if from a row of tubes. . . .
>
> Not one of them was moaning as they sat there in the grass. . . . Why did they not moan? But this was not the most tragic picture of that day . . . [S]ome of our soldiers brought out barrels of margarine and loaves of Russian bread. They began their distribution more than thirty metres distant from the place where the badly wounded were lying and these rose up, yes, even the dying rose up quickly and in an inexpressible stream of suffering hurried toward the distribution point. The man without a jaw swayed as he stood up, the man with the five bullet wounds raised himself by his good arm . . . and those with burned faces ran . . . but this was not all; a half dozen men who had been lying on the ground also went forward pressing back into their bodies with their left hands the intestines which had burst through the gaping wounds in their stomach wall. Their right hands were extended in gestures of supplication . . . [A]s they moved down each left behind a broad smear of blood upon the grass . . . and not one of them cried . . . none moaned.[63]

As Dwinger makes implicit, such scenes left a profound impression on thousands of Landsers. The almost unearthly stoicism of the Russian, his fatalism, his willingness to suffer and die in silence, was bewildering to German soldiers. To some, it was as if the harsh climate and crushing conditions of communism had molded a man in which normal human emotions were no longer important.[64]

---

62. Ibid., 52.
63. Ibid., 51–52.
64. Rauss, Erhard, et al, *Fighting in Hell,* (Mechanicsburg, Penn.: Stackpole Books, 1995), 22.

"It's not people we're fighting against here," one Landser burst out, "but simply animals."

Perhaps. And yet, as deep as their differences undoubtedly were, there were also similarities, some as elemental and ancient as the earth itself. On December 24, a strange, seemingly impossible understanding was reached by the deadly foes in which each side promised to stop hating the other "from four o'clock in the afternoon until six o'clock the following morning."

"An unreal silence fell," recalled Jan Montyn.

> Hesitantly, we crawled out into the open. We on our side. They on theirs. Step by step we approached one another, almost timidly. And the enemy, of whom we had seen nothing until then but the vague movement of a helmet or the barrel of a gun, suddenly turned out to be boys like ourselves. They too were dressed in rags, they too were starving, ill, filthy.
>
> We met in the middle of no-man's land. We shook hands, exchanged names and cigarettes. They tried out their few words of German, we our Russian. We laughed at one another's accents. Merry Christmas. We made big bonfires, shared out our Christmas rations. . . .
>
> When we withdrew, after midnight, each to his own side, the fires in no-man's land were still glowing. For several hours the silence lasted. Then firing broke out. Was it heavier than the day before? Not at all. But there were more casualties than ever. The break, however brief, had broken the resistance of many of us.[65]

Obviously, by the winter of 1944, German soldiers on the East Front were well aware that all their sacrifices during three years of war had been for naught; defeat was inevitable. Close as victory had once been, by invading the Soviet Union tiny Germany had unleashed a force of almost unlimited resources; a colossus spanning much of the globe. To continue the struggle against such a giant was hopeless. And yet, many German soldiers, especially those of the elite SS, were determined to fight to the death, or, as one private wrote, "to sell our skins as dearly as possible." Explained an observer:

> Even the last soldier was aware that the war was lost. He was aiming to survive, and the only sense he could see was to protect the front in the East to

---

65. Montyn, *Lamb*, 106.

save as many refugees as possible. . . . [H]e was hoping for a political solution for ending the war. . . . but . . . the demand for unconditional surrender left in the light of self-respect no alternative but to continue the hopeless fighting.[66]

As was the case during the Christmas truce, when "Fritz" looked into the face of "Ivan" the White Russian, or "Popov" the Ukrainian, he generally saw himself reflected. Not so the inscrutable Mongolians and other Asiatic "slit eyes" that usually followed just behind the front. In their faces the German saw something ferocious and frightening and something not seen in Europe since the days of Ghengis Khan. Lurking in the back of every Landser's mind, especially after the horror at Nemmersdorf, was the nightmare should this new "yellow peril" reach the Reich to run loose among the cities, towns and farms of Germany, among wives, sweethearts, sisters, and mothers.

------

66. Duffy, *Red Storm*, 56.

3

BETWEEN FIRE AND ICE

*About seven in the morning I was awakened by a monotonous roaring
and rumbling. The windowpanes were rattling. It sounded as if many
heavy trucks were standing around the building with their motors running uninterruptedly. In the dim light I could not distinguish anything.
I stood at the window and collected my thoughts. . . .*

*Toward noon the roaring became as loud as a falling avalanche. Vio-
lent gusts of wind made you gasp for breath. People looked meaning-
fully at one another, trying to take some comfort in the belief that all
this was only the effect of our new Wonder Weapon.*

Later on there was a sudden complete silence.[1]

S O RECORDED IN his diary army surgeon Hans Graf von Lehndorff of a day in mid-January 1945. Although miles behind the
front, the distant roll left little doubt in von Lehndorff's mind
as to what had occurred. "This could only mean the end," the doctor
noted solemnly.[2]

On the morning of January 12, Soviet forces unleashed the greatest
massed artillery barrage in history—a five hour inferno directed at the
German line along the Vistula River. Already bled white by years of
attrition, further weakened by the withdrawal of troops for the failed
Ardennes offensive, the paper-thin German front was blown to bits.

Fearing just such a disaster unless the lines were somehow strength-
ened, Field Marshal Heinz Guderian sought desperately to reason with

---

1.   Hans Graf von Lehndorff, *Token of a Covenant* (Chicago: Henry Regnery Co., 1964), 5.
2.   Ibid.

his leader three days earlier. Painfully aware of the gross imbalance—
twenty to one in artillery alone—Adolf Hitler nevertheless insisted
that the Wehrmacht not only could, but would hold.

"The Eastern front is like a house of cards," Guderian angrily warned.
"If the front is broken through at one point all the rest will collapse."[3]

His prophesy correct, when the Russian barrage finally lifted Guderian's lines had ceased to exist. "A dead, bloodstained silence settled
over the western bank of the Vistula," said a Soviet commander. "[J]ust
freshly ploughed land, fallen trees, dead horses, and mutilated bodies remained where the German lines had been."[4]

"As a rule—" added another Russian general, "and this rule was
repeatedly confirmed all through the war—German soldiers stayed
where they were ordered to stay and never retreated without permission, but on that day . . . the fire was so merciless that those who
remained alive lost all self-possession."[5]

With the remnants of the German army in headlong flight, hordes
of Red soldiers swarmed through the breach and poured into Greater
Germany. As word of the Russian breakthrough spread, millions of
Germans in their path hastily packed and fled into the freezing weather.
Those with the means escaped by car, train or boarded ships on the
Baltic coast. Most merely packed farm carts, hitched horses or cows,
and with a whip crack set off as fast as their animals would take them.
Except for the very old or the very young, the only males in the treks
were generally French, Polish and even Russian POWs and laborers
who, after years of working for German farmers had developed a loyalty for "their" families, particularly the children.[6]

As the refugees streamed west, thousands more joined the columns.
Wrote a witness, a German officer struggling against the tide to reach
his unit:

> [T]he treks . . . stood literally wheel to wheel. Their columns barely inched
> along. One could hardly see their faces. Many of them had potato sacks pulled

---

3.   John Strawson, *The Battle for Berlin* (New York: Charles Scribner's Sons, 1974), 75.
4.   Duffy, *Red Storm*, 88.
5.   Ivan Konev, *Year of Victory* (Moscow: Progress Publishers, 1969), 19.
6.   Duffy, 278.

over their heads, with holes for their eyes. . . . [M]ost of the wagons were open, and loaded in great haste. Old people, sick people, and children lay deep in snow-wet straw or under wet, soiled feather beds, occasionally with a cover or a tent thrown over them and tied down.

The treks were strangely silent, and that made them seem unspeakably sad. The hooves of the horses thumped on the snow, and here and there a wheel creaked. From time to time a tractor came chugging along with several wagons hitched to it. Any of those on foot held on to the wagons for support, and had their little sport sleighs tied to them. Cattle and sheep drifted along with the crowd.

The villagers of the Vistula valley stood in front of their homes, stiff with fright, watching the endless stream of people. Most of them, clearly, did not yet understand that the same fate was in store for them. In one village I saw a farmer getting excited because one of the wagons, in making way for a heavy truck, had damaged his fence. The East Prussian leading the wagon looked at him silently and kept going. Most of the houses were closed up tight, perhaps for fear they would have to take in refugees. From time to time, when my car got caught between piled-up wagons, I saw the curtains moving. During the past few years I have seen enough hard hearts, among all nationalities. Why should we Germans be an exception? It was all the more precious to see . . . some man or woman standing by the road with a pitcher of warm milk and calling for children.

The ice of the Vistula and Nogat Rivers was covered with wagon trains. Many horses had slipped and broken a leg. We shot one of them ourselves, because the Polish coachman, driving "his" family, asked us to. . . . [T]he roads were so congested that for a time we tried to make headway across country and along field paths. But even there, refugee treks were blocking the way. People of all kinds on foot leading fantastic vehicles, stragglers—an indescribable, ghostly procession, bundled up so that you could see only their eyes, but eyes full of misery and wretchedness.[7]

Already bitterly cold, several days after the exodus began the temperature plunged below zero. As a result, little children and infants dropped by the thousands. "It was so terribly cold, and the wind was like ice," said one young mother, "the snow was falling and nothing warm to eat, no milk and nothing. I tried to give Gabi the breast, behind a house, but she didn't take it because everything was so cold. Many women tried that, and some froze their breasts." When Gabi died, the distraught woman continued to cradle the tiny corpse until her own arm eventually froze. "I couldn't carry her any more after she was dead. I could-

7.   Thorwald, *Flight in the Winter*, 142–144.

't stand it any more," the mother sobbed. "I wrapped her up well and put her deep in the snow beside the road.... [T]housands of women . . . put their dead in the ditches by the roadside where they wouldn't be hurt by automobiles or farm wagons."[8]

Hideous as conditions were, the treks pressed steadily west, away from the terror looming somewhere behind. Although millions were on the roads in full flight, millions more remained at their farms, villages and towns. Despite the rumors of Bolshevik savagery and the reality of Nemmersdorf the previous autumn, many Germans were determined to ride out the storm, refusing to believe the situation was as bad as Nazi propaganda would have them believe.

"About one thousand inhabitants defied danger and remained in Schoenwald . . . ," ran a typical account. "[T]hey did not really believe that the Russians were as cruel and inhuman as they were reputed to be, but hoped to win over the latter by welcoming them and being hospitable."[9]

"Things never turn out either as well or as badly as one expects," explained an old German adage, an adage that those who remained now desperately embraced. Nevertheless, as a precaution, many in Schoenwald and elsewhere took time to bury valuables, hang out white flags and hide their liquor in cellars. When these last safety measures were taken, there was little the people could do but watch, wait and pray to God their decision had been correct. For many, an answer came soon enough. Wrote a priest from the city of Lauban:

> In the evening I climbed up onto the roof of the church and gazed at the countryside around me. Without being a prophet I realized that disaster was about to overtake us,—a terrible disaster, for the heathens were rapidly approaching. I could see the reflection of a fire on the horizon. It seemed to be moving. . . . It was as though a wind of destruction and desolation swept the countryside. . . . It was as though there were a sinister warning in the very air. The whole sky was ablaze and the air seemed to vibrate with the rumble of the Soviet tanks, as they came nearer and nearer.[10]

8. Ibid., 48–49.
9. Johannes Kaps, The Tragedy of Silesia, 1945–1946 (Munich: Christ Unterwegs, 1952/53), 155.
10. Ibid., 445.

The following day, in an effort to bring the aged and sick to the safety of a church cellar, the priest and several nuns raced through the streets with wheel chairs and hand carts.

Unsuspectingly, we proceeded down the Promenade. When we had gone about half-way and were just passing the old town-walls we suddenly heard a deafening crash. Bombs and shells exploded all around us and splinters whizzed past our heads. We threw ourselves flat on the ground and then crawled on all fours towards the low wall which runs along the old Lauban Brook. It was as though all the forces of hell had been let loose in order to destroy the town. The air vibrated with the deadly thunder, rumble and hiss of bombs and shells. We were paralyzed with fear. . . . Shell upon shell hit the buildings, gardens, and streets close by. "We can't get back to the cellar. We'll have to try to get to Goerlitz Street, away from the shelling," I shouted to the nuns. "I'm not coming with you. I'm going back," replied Sister Johanna-Franziska. Just as she said this, we all jumped up from the ground in order to seek shelter elsewhere. . . .

The shelling grew fiercer. Pieces of glass and bricks whizzed through the air and fell onto the streets. Some of the houses caught fire, and flames shot up amidst dense clouds of black smoke. We managed to get as far as the Protestant cemetery, which had likewise been hit by several shells. To my horror, I discovered that we were no better off here than we had been before, for a fresh volley of shells descended. We crawled along between the tombstones. Bombs and shells exploded with a deafening crash. The ground trembled under the violent impact of shells. We crouched down behind the tombstones whilst this inferno raged all around us. All of a sudden, enemy planes appeared over the town and began to launch an attack. To protect ourselves . . . we covered ourselves with the wreaths which lay on some of the graves. The ground was frozen hard and our hands and feet gradually became numb with cold as we lay there. We prayed to the Heavenly Father to protect us. . . .

When I reached the Promenade I saw a huddled form lying in the middle of the road, some distance away. It was Sister Johanna-Franziska. She was dead. A shell splinter had lacerated her head. There was a look of terror and rigidity on her face. . . . I managed to lift her onto the wheelchair and began pushing it up the slope of the Promenade.[11]

For the next several days, the fight for Lauban went on. "Shells and artillery fire rent the air and the concentrated fire of the tanks grew fiercer and fiercer," the priest continues. "The thunder of the cannon

---

11. Ibid., 446–447.

which continued without pause was deafening. There was a stifling smell of sulfur."[12]

> [A]bout noon some German soldiers came to the convent and told us that the Russians were likely to arrive in about an hour's time. . . . The tumult and commotion overhead grew louder and louder. We could hear soldiers tramping about overhead, but we could not tell whether they were Germans or Russians. . . . [B]efore we had a chance to get out of the cellar the first lot of Russians appeared. They stood at the entrance to the cellar and were obviously very surprised to find human creatures down here. They soon disappeared again, however. They did not look as bad as we had expected and most of us were rather relieved.[13]

In numerous other towns and villages, frightened German civilians were also "rather relieved" upon their initial encounter with the Red Army.

"[T]he first Russian troops entered the village from the east," remembered one witness from Schoenwald. "This went off quite peacefully, no shots were fired, the Germans served food and drink to the Russians, and the latter were very amiable. Any misgivings, which some of the inhabitants of the village might have had, vanished."[14]

"One moment the streets were deserted, and the next moment they were full of Russians," added a little girl from another village. "I was in our bedroom upstairs at the time, watching from a corner window partly facing the street. I thought I'd carefully lift a corner of the blanket covering that window to take a peek. . . . I was spotted by an old Russian soldier sitting in the front of a covered wagon pulled by two enormous horses. He smiled at me and waved."[15]

"Most of them were of strong and sturdy build," a resident of Kunzendorf observed. "And all of them, as they confronted us, were armed to the teeth—with revolvers and pistols of every type. . . . They were attired in dirty, brownish, padded trousers and jackets, and on their heads they wore fur-caps."[16]

12. Ibid., 448.
13. Ibid., 448–449.
14. Ibid., 155.
15. Chadwick, *Anna*, 113.
16. Kaps, *Silesia*, 283.

Composed largely of White Russians and Ukrainians, many Germans were shocked that the enemy often looked, sounded, and acted, much like themselves. Recalled Lali Horstmann:

> There was a loud hammering on the door, which echoed through the house. When my husband opened the door, a tall, fair-haired officer . . . stood on the doorstep. . . . When he entered the room, the Russian Army itself was in our home, taking possession. As always, reality differed from anticipation, for it was not he who was violent, but Bibi who flew at his legs before we could stop her, while the soldier made a friendly gesture towards the outraged little dog. . . . He talked in the serious tones of a kindly grown-up soothing frightened children, and helpless though we were, we had a mutual respect for each other's unalterable position. He stalked through the rooms in a formal search for German deserters. Then, his duty done, he gravely saluted with great dignity and departed, leaving us speechless and trembling.[17]

Unfortunately, the fact that one Russian like the above might display proper conduct did not guarantee that the next would. The lack of consistency or a predictable policy among Soviet front line troops was one of the most confusing and paralyzing aspects of the Russian occupation. From a rural estate, Renate Hoffman wrote:

> [W]e saw a Russian ride through the main gate on a horse. He must have been drunk because he fell off. A second Russian came, then a third. They staggered and reeled their way to the door and entered the house. It was worse than we had ever imagined. One of them went straight to the telephone, ripped it off the wall, and threw it on the floor. . . . Another Russian went to the radio and threw that on the floor, making sure we no longer heard any more news broadcasts. More men came in. They raged through the house, going from room to room. They stormed into the kitchen and demanded the cook make them something to eat. There must have been about forty soldiers.
>
> I took the children outside and hid them behind some bushes. Inside, we ran from one corner to the other, not knowing what to do. A man from the nearby village passed by and reported that the Russians were acting like animals everywhere. . . . After hours of this, a Russian officer showed up with an interpreter. . . . He was wearing a perfectly tailored uniform, an impressive looking man, and also wearing white gloves! This officer told us, through his translator, that he was confiscating the house and was giving us five minutes to leave the estate.[18]

---

17. Horstmann, *We Chose to Stay*, 82–83.
18. Pechel, *Voices From the Third Reich*, 443–444.

Continues a witness from Kaltwasser:

When the shelling ceased we ventured out of the cellar once more, but we had only got as far as the stairs when we saw . . . a Pole, coming towards us with a Russian officer and another man. We hoped for the best, but the interpreter promptly demanded our watches and rings. In fact, he actually tore my watch off its chain, and made the women remove all their rings, bracelets, and necklaces. We were horrified when the Russian officer and the interpreter seized hold of Mrs. M. and my aunt and dragged them off. When they eventually came back we went to the vicarage. The house was full of Russians and they had already wrought havoc in all the rooms. Some of them had ransacked the pantry and were gorging the food they had found there. Others had opened all the drawers and cupboards and thrown the contents onto the floor. . . . Russians continued to raid the house all day long. They played the mouth-organ and the harmonium and set the gramophone going. There was a bottle of pure alcohol in the house and they drained it undiluted. They swarmed into the pantry and ate all the preserves. . . . When it grew dark they set fire to the school. We did not dare go to bed as one lot of soldiers after another kept raiding the house. . . . At about three o'clock in the morning a savage-looking Russian appeared and searched us. We had already been searched innumerable times by other Russians. . . . In the course of their searches one of them opened the wardrobe and slashed all the garments to pieces with his dagger.[19]

Traumatic as first encounters were, when the shock troops moved off many Germans would concur that the experience had not been as bad as feared. While rapes had occurred and while many German men of military age had been marched east or shot on the spot, the front line soldier was more concerned with fighting and survival than with loot, rape and revenge. Not so with those who followed. In numerous instances, before Red combat officers and men pushed on they turned to the helpless civilians with stone-like faces: "The Mongols are coming. . . . Very bad men. You go quick. Go quick."[20]

Composed largely of Mongols, Kulaks, Kazakhs, Kalmuks, and other Asians, as well as convicts and commissars, these men who formed the second wave of troops were regarded, even by their own comrades,

19. Kaps, *Silesia*, 435.
20. Lucas, *Third Reich*, 69.

as utterly merciless. Terrified by the news, many Germans did attempt to flee and move in the wake of the first Soviet wave. Most, however, found themselves trapped and could do little more than hide young girls and once again pray that their worst fears were unfounded. After a wait of sometimes days, but normally only hours, the dreaded second wave arrived. There were no preliminaries. Unlike storm troops, who cautiously entered towns and villages and slipped nervously from door to door, the rear echelons burst noisily into communities atop trucks, tanks or peasant carts crammed high with loot. Often wildly drunk, many wore a bizarre array of stolen clothes and gaudy jewelry. Adding to the chaos were herds of bellowing cattle and sheep.

"It was almost like a scene from the Middle Ages—a migration, no less," said one stunned observer.[21]

Soon after the "carnival columns" halted in a German town, hell on earth was unleashed. "It seemed as though the devil himself had come . . . ," a witness from Silesia wrote. "The 'Mongol barbarism of the Asiatic plains' had come not in a propaganda phrase but in the flesh."[22]

While flames shot up from different corners of the towns and gunfire erupted as citizens were murdered in the streets, the invaders soon began kicking in doors to homes, shops and churches. "[A] whole horde of Asiatic-looking fellows appeared and started searching the cellar . . . ," recalled one priest. "The place was a dreadful sight by the time they had finished. The room was already full of smoke and I begged one of the Russians to let us out. . . . Were they going to let us be burnt to death? After a while, however, a more civilized-looking Russian appeared and I repeated my request. He led us out to . . . the courtyard of the convent. The noise was deafening—the raucous shouts of the Russians, the crackling of the flames, the crashing of beams and brickwork."[23]

Many horrified Germans tried to greet with a smile their strange visitors. Revealed one woman from a boarding house in Berbitz:

> As a precaution, the landlord, Mr. Grebmann, had lined the vestibule with liquor bottles in the naive hope that his house might thereby be spared from

21. Ibid., 41.
22. Thorwald, *Flight*, 53.
23. Kaps, 449.

ransacking. To the succeeding troop of slant-eyed Mongolians, the tenants brought their jewelry and watches. Hysterical, Mrs. Friedel embraced one of the greasy Kirgis and drank with him from the same bottle, and the elderly Mr. Grebmann patted them familiarly on the back. . . .One of the Mongolians held up my Tom's tall leather boots triumphantly, the other one put my rings into his pants pocket. . . .

Scarcely had this second detachment left the house and we were beginning to breathe freely, when fists once more thundered at the door: thus it kept up the whole day. The house doors were not permitted to be locked any more. Each took what he wanted either in a more or less harmless or in a malicious way. Soon we and the Russians were wading knee-deep in thrown-around clothing, laundry and bits of smashed dishes. . . .

As soon as a new detachment of Russians entered the house noisily, we squatted trembling about the round table in Grebmann's living room. One of the soldiers sat at the table with us with pistol disengaged and demanded schnapps or vodka, while the others rummaged around the house. . . . [N]o one dared to speak. We women sat with downcast eyes and lowered head. Someone had told us never to look a Russian in the eye, otherwise we would be lost. . . .

Before long the inside of the house looked as if a band of robbers had lived there. . . . The fellows had cut the beds up into little pieces, slit open the upholstered chairs, thrown furniture around; had slashed pictures, despoiled books, cracked eggs against the wall; had poured liqueur over the rugs, torn curtains down, and scattered the entire contents of all the closets and drawers all over. One of the most painful shocks for me was to see how two of the ruffians with their heavy boots kicked the chest in which I had my beautiful porcelain wrapped in tissue paper and cotton wadding. They were all treasured pieces. . . . My most beautiful piece . . . was used by one of them as a toilet.[24]

As a rule, the Soviets generally sought out gold and jewelry first, with an especial eye for "uri," or wristwatches. It was not unusual to see Red troops laden with necklaces and gold chains or sporting as many as a dozen watches on each arm. When the people had been plucked clean of valuables, interest usually turned to liquor. In their mad quest for "wodka," soldiers greedily imbibed everything from fine wines and champagne to rubbing alcohol and perfume. Red troops, observed one woman, were "crazy for anything even smelling of alcohol."[25]

And then. . . .

---

24. Elizabeth Lutz, "Rape of Christian Europe—The Red Army's Rampage in 1945," *The Barnes Review* 3, no. 4 (Apr. 1997): 11.

25. Anonymous, *A Woman in Berlin*, 218.

"Rape was a word that [had] occurred again and again in [our] conversation," admitted Lali Horstmann. "It was an expression which caused no pang of fear in our times for its meaning was purely figurative—'to be ravished' belonged to the realm of lyrical poetry. Now its original sense was terrifyingly restored and brought us face to face with a new peril."[26]

"Suddenly the door of the room we were in was opened and some soldiers entered," a frightened boy recalled as he sat with a group of women huddled in a dark room. "One or two matches were struck and I saw that there were about eight Russians in the room who were obviously looking for women."[27] The child continues:

> As I crouched there in my corner I saw one of the Russians coming towards me. The match he held in his hand went out. I felt, rather than saw, a hand reach out towards me. I had a fur cap on my head, and suddenly I felt fingers tracing curl-like movements on my temple. For a brief moment I did not know what to make of this, but the next instant, when a loud "No" resounded through the room, I thanked God with all my heart that I was not a woman or a girl.
>
> Meanwhile the beasts had spotted their victims and shared them out. Then they suddenly started shooting at random. But it was dark in the room and no one could see where the shots were being fired or who was hit. I heard wails and groans and voices calling out to me to help, but there was nothing I could do. Right next to me poor defenseless women were being ravished in the presence of their children.[28]

Merely because a female had been raped once was no guarantee she would not be assaulted again and again. "Many of the girls were raped as often as ten times a night, and even more," said a witness from Neustadt.[29]

"There was never a moment's peace either by day or at night," added another victim:

> The Russians were coming and going the whole time and they kept eyeing us greedily. The nights were dreadful because we were never safe for a moment. The women were raped, not once or twice but ten, twenty, thirty and a hundred times, and it was all the same to the Russians whether they raped mere chil-

---

26. Horstmann, 40.
27. Kaps, *Silesia*, 147.
28. Ibid.
29. Kaps, 192.

dren or old women. The youngest victim in the row houses where we lived
was ten years of age and the oldest one was over seventy. . . . I am sure that
wild and hungry animals would not have behaved any differently.[30]

Wrote a girl from Posen who desperately clung to a cousin for safety:

When we were lying in bed at night we kept hearing steps coming up the stairs.
. . . They beat on the door with their rifle-butts, until it was opened. Without
any consideration for my mother and aunt, who had to get out of bed, we were
raped by the Russians, who always held a machine pistol in one hand. They
lay in bed with their dirty boots on, until the next lot came. As there was no light,
everything was done by pocket torches, and we did not even know what the
beasts looked like.[31]

Like hunted prey leading predators from their young, some mothers instinctively sacrificed themselves. Recorded one little girl, ten-
year-old Mignon Fries:

[S]he told us in a stern voice to go outside to play and under no circumstances
to come back in. No matter what we heard, until she herself would come for
us, no matter how long it took. Fearfully we looked at her even though we did-
n't know exactly what we were afraid of. . . . We went outside and stood around
for awhile not knowing what to do, just listening to the noise in the apartment. My mother had just closed all the windows but we could still hear the soldiers talking, laughing and shouting. Then the music started and before long
the soldiers were singing. . . .

The day gave way to evening, it got rather chilly and still we were outside and
the "party" got noisier. Every once in a while a soldier would open a window and
throw an empty vodka bottle outside. Sometimes the music would stop for a while,
but the singing and shouting continued. As it got later and later we became very
hungry and cold, but having been raised in an atmosphere of strict obedience we
didn't dare go back in the house against our mother's orders and just huddled
against the wall of the shed in the garden trying to keep each other warm. . . .

The music and the singing broke off as suddenly as it had started. . . . Within
minutes it was all over and all the soldiers left the house. . . . But it was a long
time before our mother finally came out to get us. She was very pale and hugged
both of us very tightly for a long time and we could feel her body shaking.[32]

---

30. Ibid., 136.

31. Theodor Schieder, ed. *The Expulsion of the German Population from the Territories East of the
Oder-Neisse Line* (Bonn, Germany: Federal Ministry for Expellees, Refugess and War Victims,
1951–), 256.

32. Letter of Mignon Fries Baker, 1992 (copy in author's possession).

If front-line troops had displayed unpredictability regarding rape, the second wave did not. "All of us, without exception, suffered the same," revealed one victim.[33]

"And to make matters worse," added a witness from Neisse, "these atrocities were not committed secretly or in hidden corners but in public, in churches, on the streets, and on the squares. . . . Mothers were raped in the presence of their children, girls were raped in front of their brothers."[34]

"They . . . raped women and girls . . . in ditches and by the wayside, and as a rule not once but several times," echoed another viewer. "Sometimes a whole bunch of soldiers would seize hold of one woman and all rape her."[35]

For those Germans who had naively imagined that they might "win over" the Soviets with kindness and courtesy, they now understood, too late, that Nazi propaganda had in this instance grossly understated the threat, rather than exaggerated it. "[T]he atrocity reports in the newspapers were harmless, compared to reality," one incredulous victim revealed.[36] While many upright Russian officers courageously stepped in and risked their own lives to stop the murders and rapes, their efforts were little more than a drop of water to a forest fire.[37]

"[A]ll of us knew very well that if the girls were German they could be raped and then shot," admitted Alexander Solzhenitsyn. "This was almost a combat distinction."[38]

"There will be no mercy—for no one . . . ," ran one Russian general's order to his men. "It is pointless to ask our troops to exercise mercy."[39]

"Kill them all, men, old men, children and the women, after you have amused yourself with them! . . . ," urged Ilya Ehrenberg in his flaming broadsides. "Kill. Nothing in Germany is guiltless, neither the living nor the yet unborn. . . . Break the racial pride of the German

---

33. Thorwald, *Flight*, 180.
34. Kaps, *Silesia*, 228.
35. Ibid., 324.
36. Ibid., 192.
37. Heinrich von Einsiedel, *I Joined the Russians* (New Haven, Conn.: Yale University Press, 1953), 193.
38. DeZayas, *Nemesis at Potsdam*, 68.
39. Sorge, *Other Price*, 127.

women. Take her as your legitimate booty. Kill, you brave soldiers of the victorious Soviet Army."[40]

Springing from house to house and victim to victim "like wild beasts," the drunken horde was determined to embrace such words as the above at their literal worst.

"When the Russians eventually tired of looting, robbing, murdering, and ill-treating the women and girls, they set fire to a considerable part of the village and razed it to the ground," said a survivor of Schoenwald, the small community that had dismissed rumors of Russian ruthlessness and opted to welcome them instead.[41]

Much like Schoenwald, one town after another was swiftly enveloped by the howling red storm . . . with the same results.

"And as we were then hauled out of the cellar," recalled a woman who, along with her mother and grandmother had been raped repeatedly, "and as they stood there with their machine guns, my mother said, 'Well, now we'll probably be shot.' And I said, 'It's all the same to me.' It *really* was all the same to me."[42]

> You can imagine Asian cruelty. . . . "Frau, come," that was the slogan. "Frau, come." And I was *so* furious, because I'd had it up to here. . . . [H]e had me in such a clinch I couldn't free myself, with my elbow I hit him in the pit of his stomach. That definitely hurt him, and he yelled, "You, I shoot." And he was brandishing this kind of machine gun around my nose and then I said, *"Then shoot."* Yelled it, yelled it just like he did. *"Then shoot."*[43]

Though this woman miraculously lived, many who offered even token resistance did not. Wrote a witness from Bauschdorf:

> Emilie Ertelt . . . wanted to protect her fifteen-year old daughter, who had been raped sixteen times on one and the same day. Holding a lighted candle in her hand, Mrs. Ertelt, and all those present in the room began to pray for her daughter. . . . [F]our shots were suddenly fired at us. After a few moments some more Russians appeared and started shooting at Mrs. Ertelt, wounding her in the head.

---

40. Lutz, "Rape of Christian Europe," 13; *The Barnes Review* 4, no. 1 (Jan./Feb. 1998): 19. (title?)(author?)

41. Kaps, 155.

42. Alison Owings, *Frauen—German Women Recall the Third Reich* (New Brunswick, New Jersey: Rutgers University Press, 1994), 405.

43. Ibid., 406.

The blood streamed down her face, and the nuns who were present went to her assistance and bandaged her head. Soon afterwards another Russian appeared, a brutal-looking fellow . . . and fired a shot at close range. Mrs. Ertelt was killed instantaneously.[44]

Surrounded by Soviets, flight was simply not a sane option for females—and yet, some tried. One young teacher from Kriescht ran terror-stricken into the nearby woods. The woman was soon found, however, and, according to a chronicler, "They drove her out on the road stark naked, and many soldiers used her one after the other. She reached her village crawling on hands and knees along the ditch, through mud and snow."[45]

Another group of females found temporary haven in a woodland barn near Schoeneiche. But again, the refuge was swiftly discovered. Remembered one who was there:

They burst in, drunk with vodka and with victory, looking for women. When they saw only older women and children hiding behind a pile of carpets, they must have suspected that somewhere younger bodies were being concealed, and they started to ram their bayonets into the carpets. Here and there first and then systematically. . . . Nobody knows how many young girls were killed instantly that night. Eventually, the muffled cries of anguish and pain gave the hiding places away, and the victors started unrolling their prey. They chased those girls that had remained unhurt through the barn. . . . By then the barn looked like a battle field with wounded women on the floor right next to screaming and fighting victims forced to endure repeated and violent acts of rape.[46]

Faced by relentless assaults, with flight out of the question, females tried a variety of stratagems to save themselves. "Some of us tried to make ourselves as unattractive as possible by rouging the tips of our noses, putting gray powder on our upper lips to look like mustaches, and combing out our hair wildly," revealed Lali Horstmann.[47] Others placed pillows under their dresses and hobbled with sticks to appear like hunchbacks.[48] One crazed woman, clad in an alluring night-

44. Kaps, *Silesia*, 252.
45. Thorwald, *Flight in the Winter, 180.*
46. Erika M. Hansen, "A Woman's Odyssey" (unpublished manuscript, Glendale, Calif.): 158.
47. Horstmann, *We Chose to Stay*, 89.
48. Lutz, "Rape of Christian Europe," 11.

gown, left her door open purposely to attract soldiers to where she was lying in bed, in the hope of finding a protector. "Two Russians, who had entered for a moment stood speechless. Then both spat in disgust, using a coarse word, shocked to the core by a woman who could offer herself to them. They went on to the room next door, from where soon came cries for help from the girl's grandmother, aged sixty-nine. Her valiant defense of her honor had made her more attractive than the pretty, too willing girl."[49] Regarding "willing" women such as the above as "unclean," Red troops were as likely as not to kill on the spot such individuals.

Many frantic females mistakenly assumed a house of God would provide protection. In fact, churches were usually the rapists' first stop. Agonized a priest from Neisse:

> The girls, women and nuns were raped incessantly for hours on end, the soldiers standing in queues, the officers at the head of the queues, in front of their victims. During the first night many of the nuns and women were raped as many as fifty times. Some of the nuns who resisted with all their strength were shot, others were ill-treated in a dreadful manner until they were too exhausted to offer any resistance. The Russians knocked them down, kicked them, beat them on the head and in the face with the butt-end of their revolvers and rifles, until they finally collapsed and in this unconscious condition became the helpless victims of brutish passion, which was so inhuman as to be inconceivable. The same dreadful scenes were enacted in the hospitals, homes for the aged, and other such institutions. Even nuns who were seventy and eighty years old and were ill and bedridden were raped and ill-treated by these barbarians.[50]

Those women pregnant, on their menstrual cycle, or enduring diarrhea, suffered like all the rest. Nothing, it seemed—not age, ailment or ugliness—could repel the Red rapist. Even death was no defense.

"I . . . saw some twenty Red Army men standing in line before the corpse of a woman certainly beyond sixty years of age who had been raped to death," one sickened witness recorded. "They were shouting and laughing and waiting for their satisfaction over her dead body." As this viewer went on to add, and as numerous examples attest, such ghoulish depravities were not isolated events.[51]

49. Horstmann, 104–105.
50. Kaps, *Silesia*, 228.
51. Ibid.; Thorwald, *Flight*, 55.

✠   ✠   ✠

While those who remained endured unspeakable fates, Germans who fled with treks also suffered. "What surprised us most was the way they traveled," recalled a British POW, who, along with thousands of other Allied prisoners, was being marched west away from the advancing Soviets.

> There was not a car, lorry or even a bicycle to be seen—only a seemingly endless line of covered wagons and carts drawn by horses or mules. . . . They were a pitiful sight, frozen, hungry, shoes and clothes falling apart, dragging themselves along to an unknown destination, hoping only that it might be beyond the reach of the Russian army. It was so cold that even in the day-time any drink mixed with cold water froze solid before it was possible to carry it to one's mouth. At night men and women could keep alive only by huddling together in a wagon. . . . Those who fell asleep in the snow were dead within a few minutes. . . .
>
> Within an hour of taking the road prisoners and refugees had become indistinguishable. We were bound together by one common thought—to keep together so as to keep alive. . . . The refugees gladly let us climb on to their wagons and, as they had nothing with which to barter, we gave them what food we could spare.[52]

Given the chaotic conditions, and with freezing refugees clogging the way, many treks were quickly overhauled by the Russians. Some Soviet tanks refused to leave the roads and crashed straight through the columns, squashing all in their path. After heavy traffic, the victims—men, women, children, and animals—were eventually as flat as cardboard.

Young Josefine Schleiter records the horror when her group was overtaken:

> The [tanks] rushed through the rows of carts. Carts were hurled into the ditches where there were entrails of horses, and men, women and children were fighting with death. Wounded people were screaming for help.
>
> Next to me was a woman bandaging her husband who was losing blood from a big wound. Behind me a young girl said to her father: "Father shoot me." "Yes father," said her brother who was about sixteen years old. "I have no

---

52. Crawley, *Spoils of War*, 10–11.

more chance." The father looked at his children, the tears streaming down his cheeks and he said in a quiet tone: "Wait still a little while children."

Then came an officer on horseback. Some German soldiers were brought to him. He took his revolver; I shut my eyes, shots fell, and the poor fellows lay in front of us shot in the head, an expression of horror on their faces.[53]

Those terrified survivors who scattered to the icy countryside fell easy prey. "The Russians found us and pulled us out of the barn," said fourteen-year-old Horst Wegner. "They were Mongolians. They had huge scars and pockmarks on their faces. And they were draped in jewelry—they wore watches up to the elbows. They came in and pulled out everyone wearing anything military—a military coat, for example. They were taken behind the barn, shoved against a wall, and shot. They weren't even all Germans; some of them were foreigners. They even shot the private who had bandaged my father's leg."[54]

As always, for females the living death soon began. Renate Hoffmann:

Suddenly three Russian soldiers came around the corner. They pointed their guns at us and forced us into the house. . . . [W]e knew what they had in store for us. We were separated. They put their guns to our heads. Any attempt to defend ourselves meant certain death. The only thing you could do was to pretend you were a rock or dead. . . .

When the three men left the house, I opened the door of the room I was in. Another door opened down the hall and the nurse came out. We just looked at one another. . . . We were nauseated and felt miserable. Thank God there was still running water in the house.[55]

As he struggled by car over the crowded roads, Major Rudolf Janecke of the Medical Corp gained a glimpse of what seemed to him an "endless agony."

Near a small village . . . I saw for the first time a trek that had been destroyed from the air. Many wagons had caught fire in spite of the wet—perhaps phosphor bombs—and were entirely burned out. The dead lay around in strange positions, among them children pressed against their mothers' breasts. . . . Soon afterward we were stopped by a man waving desperately. . . . He had seen the red cross on our car. His excitement nearly choked him. He was pale as death,

53. Schieder, *Expulsion of the German Population*, 129–130.
54. Pechel, *Voices From the Third Reich*, 418.
55. Ibid., 445.

and raised his right hand in an imploring gesture. He kept pointing to a wagon that stood out in the open field. His left arm, probably broken, hung limply from his shoulder.

His wife would bleed to death, he managed to groan, if I did not help immediately. A Russian tank crew had caught them, two days ago, while they were resting in a village. Later they had got away. But now she was dripping blood. She hardly breathed any more—no one could help her.

I have performed some difficult operations in the field, under impossible conditions. But this was the first time I tried a tamponade of the uterus, on a snow-covered field over which an icy wind was blowing, with the patient lying on a filthy wagon in her blood-drenched clothes. . . . Some other women stood around. By the patient's head cowered a befuddled boy of about fourteen, all the while close to tears. "He had to watch it," the man said while I was giving the woman two injections I happened to have with me. "When the fifteenth man was on her they knocked me down because I dropped the light. He had to hold the light till they all were through." The other women nodded, with not a word of their own misery.[56]

As a rule, those who fled by train fared best. Speed did not always guarantee escape, however. Russian aircraft routinely strafed and bombed the cars from above and tanks cut the rails from below. When the Soviets suddenly captured the town of Allenstein, they forced the station master to signal the "all clear" to refugee trains still arriving from the east. As one unsuspecting train after another steamed into Allenstein, the Russians first slaughtered any men found on board, then passed their time raping carload after carload of females.[57]

For millions of Germans cut off on the Baltic coast by the rapid Russian advance, only one avenue of escape remained open—the sea. Even here, however, Soviet aircraft controlled the skies above and submarines prowled unseen below. In the various ports along the coast, thousands upon thousands of ragged, frozen refugees pressed to the water's edge in hopes of landing a spot on one of the few vessels available. The

56. Thorwald, 144–145.
57. Alexander Solzhenitsyn, *Prussian Nights—A Poem* (New York: Farrar, Straus and Giroux, 1977), 51, 63, 65.

numbers were so great and the fear so consuming that efforts to board when ships did dock often resembled riots.

"The crush to get on board was just terrible," a witness wrote from Pillau. "I saw a pram being squeezed out of all recognition by the pushing masses. One old man fell into the water and there was nothing one could do in the crush—also it was so cold he would have died on hitting the water."[58]

Because armed guards had orders to evacuate as many women and children as possible, babies were used like tickets, with half-crazed mothers tossing infants down to relatives on the pier. Some children landed safely; some did not.[59]

If anything, the situation at Gotenhafen was even more horrific. As the *Wilhelm Gustloff* made ready to take on passengers in late January 1945, the ship's crew were stunned by what they saw. "There must have been 60,000 people on the docks . . . ," remembered second engineer, Walter Knust. "[A]s soon as we let down the gangways people raced forward and pushed their way in. In the confusion a lot of children got separated from their parents. Either the kids got on board leaving their parents on the harbor or the children were left behind as their parents got pushed forward by the throng."[60]

A former cruise liner designed to accommodate two thousand passengers and crew, by the time the *Gustloff* cast ropes on January 30, the beautiful white ship had taken on as many as six thousand refugees. Even so, as she backed away from port, her path was blocked by smaller craft jammed with people.

"Take us with you," the refugees cried. "Save the children!"

"We put down nets and everybody on the small ships scrambled up as best they could," said the *Gustloff's* radio operator, Rudi Lange. "As we got under way I think I remember being told by one of the ship's officers to send a signal that another 2,000 people had come aboard."[61]

---

58. Christopher Dobson, John Miller and Ronald Payne, *The Cruelest Night* (Boston: Little, Brown, 1979), 25.

59. Ibid.; Toland, *Last 100 Days*, 31.

60. Dobson, *Cruelest Night*, 58.

61. Ibid., 84.

That black, stormy night, as she struggled through high winds and heavy, ice-filled waves, the *Gustloff's* ventilation and plumbing systems failed utterly. Strained far beyond its limits, the tightly-sealed ship filled with a hot, nauseating stench of urine, excrement, and vomit.[62] The groans and screams of severely wounded soldiers and the wails of separated families added to the ghastly horror. But the worst was yet to come. At approximately 9 P.M., three heavy jolts rocked the passengers on the *Gustloff.*

"Vroom—Vroom—Vroom! That's what it sounded like," recalled a young boy upon hearing the torpedoes.[63]

"I heard [the] explosions," wrote engineer Knust, "and I knew what had happened at once, because the engines stopped and then I saw a rush of water through the engine room. First the ship lurched to starboard under the force of the blast. Then she rose and began listing to port. I put on my shoes and jacket and hurried out into the corridor."[64]

Panic-stricken, thousands below deck stampeded through the narrow passageways crushing and clawing others in an attempt to reach the life boats.[65] "People were rushing about and screaming. Alarm bells shrilled," remembered one terrorized passenger.[66]

"We struggled through the crowd to one of the boats," said Paula Knust, wife of the ship's officer. "It was so cold as the wind hit us. I was wearing only slacks and a blouse and blazer. Already the ship had a heavy list. The waves seemed very high, and you cannot imagine how terrible it looked."[67]

Most lifeboats were frozen solid and even those that could be freed were mishandled in the panic and spilled their screaming occupants into the black sea. Walter and Paula Knust grappled with one boat that did manage to get away. "As we hit the water," the husband recalled,

---

62. Ibid., 90.
63. Ibid., 105.
64. Ibid., 102.
65. Thorwald, *Flight,* 122.
66. Dobson, *Cruelest Night,* 104.
67. Ibid., 112–113.

"I could see people leaping from the side of the ship into the sea. I thought those who escaped drowning would freeze to death. It was so cold."[68] Indeed, the water was so frigid that those who leaped overboard might just as well have jumped into boiling oil or acid for their chances of survival were almost as slim. In seconds, minutes at most, the struggling swimmers were dead.

While loud speakers blared words of comfort—"The ship will not sink. Rescue ships are on the way"—thousands of freezing people pressed along the decks.[69] Convinced that the sealed bulkheads had held and that indeed, the ship would not sink, many passengers fled indoors once more to escape the razor sharp winds and –20 degree temperature. The respite proved brief, however.

At ten o'clock a heavy tremor ripped the *Gustloff* as the bulkheads broke and the sea rushed in. Within seconds, the big ship began to roll on its side.[70] Sixteen-year-old Eva Luck was in the ballroom with her mother and little sister:

> [S]uddenly the whole music room tilted and a great cry went up from all the people there. They literally slid in a heap along the angled deck. A grand piano at one end went berserk and rolled across the crowded room crushing women and children in its path and scattering others before it. Finally it smashed into the port bulkhead with a discordant roar as though a giant fist had hit all the keys at once.[71]

Elsewhere, other victims went flying through glass enclosed decks into the sea.[72] Amid the screams, sirens and roar of rushing water, gunshots sounded throughout the doomed ship as those trapped below committed suicide.

Miraculously escaping the ball room with the help of a sailor, Eva Luck's family frantically tried to escape:

> My mother had forgotten to put her shoes on, and I moved clumsily on high heels towards the iron rungs of the ladder going up the ship's inside. People around us were falling about as the ship moved but I was able to grasp the rungs

68. Ibid., 114.
69. Ibid.
70. Thorwald, *Flight*, 123.
71. Dobson, *Cruelest Night*, 117.
72. Thorwald, 123.

and haul up my little sister. . . . My mother followed us to the upper deck. When we got there it was terrible. I saw with horror that the funnel was lying almost parallel with the sea. People were jumping in. I could hear the ship's siren and felt the ice-cold water round my legs. I reached out to try and grab my sister. I felt nothing but the water as it swept me out and over the side.[73]

Fortunately for Eva and a few others, the force of the flooding water freed a number of life rafts. As survivors scrambled aboard, the *Gustloff* began her swift descent. "Suddenly," remembered a woman in a lifeboat, "it seemed that every light in the ship had come on. The whole ship was blazing with lights, and her sirens sounded out over the sea."[74] Paula Knust also watched the drama:

> I cannot forget the loud clear sound of the siren as the *Gustloff* with all her lights on made the final plunge. I could clearly see the people still on board the *Gustloff* clinging to the rails. Even as she went under they were still hanging on and screaming. All around us were people swimming, or just floating in the sea. I can still see their hands grasping at the sides of our boat. It was too full to take on any more.[75]

When rescue ships later reached the scene, they pulled from the icy waters a mere nine hundred survivors. All else—roughly 7,000 men, women and children—were lost. Even then, however, the nightmare did not end. When rescue vessels touched land, scores of victims were disembarked at Gotenhafen. Thus, in less than twenty-four hours, after a harrowing night of incredible terror, some refugees found themselves on the very docks they had hoped to leave, once again searching desperately for a way to escape.[76]

Meanwhile, the red tide moved closer. In countless German cities and towns the pattern repeated itself, as the diary of a Catholic priest from Klosterbrueck reveals:

73. Dobson, 117.
74. Ibid., 120.
75. Ibid.
76. Ibid., 135.

January 21st, 1945. . . . Strange to say, the population intends to remain here, and is not afraid of the Russians. The reports that in one village they raped all the women and abducted all the men and took them away to work somewhere must surely have been exaggerated. How dreadful it would be if Goebbels was telling the truth after all! . . .

January 22nd. . . . the machine-guns sound very near and some shells must have hit some of the buildings close by, because the house keeps trembling. The occupants of the cellar keep asking me what the Russians will be like. I keep asking myself the same thing. . . .

[Later]—We have had our first encounter with them, and are somewhat relieved. They are not as bad as we had expected. When we heard the Russians moving about in the church up above, we went up to them. Two Russian soldiers looked in at the cellar-door and asked if there were any German soldiers there. There was a strange look of tenseness and fear on their faces. A Russian kept watch at the entrance to the cellar the whole night.

January 23rd. . . . After the fighting troops had moved on, a fresh lot of Russians arrived. Two of them entered the cellar, fired several shots into the ceiling, and asked us to give them our watches. They went off with fourteen wristwatches. Then three more Russians arrived. . . . [They] swallowed the food like wild animals, and they drank the wine as if it were water. "The war is good here," they kept saying. . . .

January 25th. All night long Russians entered the chapel and searched and questioned us. They ordered the woman to go outside with her small child. . . . [They] raped the woman and sent her back to us. She came back to the chapel, her small child in her arms, the tears streaming down her face. . . . During the morning three women from the village came to the chapel. The vicar hardly recognized them, for their faces were distorted with fear and terror. They told us that whole families had been shot by the Russians. . . . Girls who had refused to allow themselves to be raped, and parents who had sought to protect their children, had been shot on the spot. . . .

January 26th. Last night was very troubled again. Fresh lots of soldiers kept on arriving and searching the house. . . . Every time the door is opened we start with fear. . . .

January 27th. We priests were allowed out of the chapel for half an hour today in order to bury Margarethe in the yard. Poor girl, it is a good thing you were dead and so did not know what the Russians did to your body!

January 28th. The night was very troubled again. . . . Many of the nuns are getting very distressed and nervous. They sleep even less than we do. I often hear them say, "If only we had fled before the Russians arrived!"[77]

---

77. Kaps, *Silesia*, 179–181.

By the end of January, the routed German army was finally able to wheel and face its pursuer. Because the Red advance had been so swift, Soviet supply lines were unable to keep pace. Additionally, a sudden thaw melted icy rivers and turned roads into quagmires, making rapid pursuit impossible. While isolated enclaves continued to hold back the Russians, particularly along the Baltic coast, the bulk of the German Army took up defensive positions behind the Oder River, the last natural barrier before Berlin. Although the miraculous respite was spent regrouping and placing arms in the hands of the People's Army, or Volkssturm, the morale of the Wehrmacht had received a severe blow. The incredible force and fury of the Russian onslaught now convinced most military men that defeat was unavoidable. And for the huddled and stunned civilian masses, the sickening depth of Soviet savagery also clearly foretold that the end would be vastly more nightmarish than even the most lurid imagination had dreamed.

At first, only breathless rumors relayed by panic-stricken refugees revealed the nature of the approaching horror. Later, however, the extent of Russian atrocities was confirmed when stranded army units broke through to German lines or when the Wehrmacht launched small counterattacks and reclaimed bits of lost ground.

"In every village and town they entered," wrote one who spoke with soldiers, "the German troops came upon scenes of horror: slain boys, People's Army men drenched with gasoline and burned—and sometimes survivors to tell the tale of the outrages. In some villages, they surprised Russians warm in the beds of women they had taken, and found the bodies of the many French war prisoners who had died defending German women and children."[78]

Staggered by what he had seen and heard, a German officer tried desperately to make sense of the disaster; to understand the minds of men "who find . . . pleasure in raping the same woman over and over, dozens of times, even while other women are standing near."

There is a perverse hatred behind this which cannot be explained with phrases about Bolshevism, or the so-called Asiatic mentality, or by the assertion that

78. Thorwald, *Flight*, 79.

the Russian soldiers have always considered the women of the conquered as their booty. . . . I was in Poland in 1939 when the Russians moved in, and I did not see a single woman being molested.[79]

"This," concluded the young officer grimly, "shows the frightful power of propaganda."[80]

Hundreds of thousands massacred, hundreds of thousands raped, millions already enslaved—but this was nothing. Worse was to come.

"The Germans have been punished, but not enough," gloated Ilya Ehrenburg. "The Fritzes are still running, but not lying dead. Who can stop us now? . . . The Oder? The Volksturm? No, it's too late Germany, you can whirl around in circles, and burn, and howl in your deathly agony; the hour of revenge has struck!"[81]

---

79. Ibid., 145.
80. Ibid.
81. Toland, *Last 100 Days,* 72.

4

CRESCENDO OF DESTRUCTION

IN EARLY FEBRUARY 1945, leaders of the three most powerful nations on earth assembled for a final time at Yalta in the Soviet Crimea. Unlike previous meetings in Teheran, Casablanca and Quebec, this gathering on the Black Sea was not really a council of war or a summit to discuss strategy so much as it was a celebration of victory. No longer was it a case of "if" victory would be achieved, but merely a question of "when." Hence, the atmosphere at the gala banquet on the night preceding the formal talks was relaxed, friendly, festive. When the sumptuous feast was finished—consommé, sturgeon, beef, fried chicken, dessert—and when the champagne and vodka began to flow, the leaders engaged in small talk and banter.[1]

With perhaps one or two exceptions, the three men at Yalta were the most recognizable faces on earth. Winston Churchill—round, cherubic, a heavy drinker, though half-American he seemed to all the quintessential English bulldog with his ever-present cigar, dark bowler, and "stiff-upper-lip" attitude. Franklin Roosevelt—stately, urbane, though confined to a wheelchair and visibly ill—"slack-jawed," thought some—he still seemed every inch the polished world statesman. Josef Stalin—twinkling eyes, wry smile, hair like a thick carpet, although but 5' 2", the dictator's solid, massive frame seemed to personify the great red behemoth he headed.[2] Despite the obvious dissimilarities of the men, intellectual as well as physical, each shared a

---

1. Diane Shaver Clemens, *Yalta* (New York: Oxford University Press, 1970), 128; Ziemke, *Soviet Juggernaut*, 183.
2. Eugene Davidson, *The Death and Life of Germany* (New York: Alfred Knopf, 1959), 32.

characteristic with the other that shrank into insignificance all outer contradictions—all three harbored a inveterate hatred of not only Adolf Hitler and Nazism, but Germans and Germany.

In spite of campaign promises to keep the US out of World War II— "I have said it once, and I will say it again and again, your boys will not fight in any foreign war"—Franklin Roosevelt had worked assiduously behind the scenes to bring his country into that war once his reelection was secured. Still unable to convince Americans that a war with Germany was in their best interest, Roosevelt slapped a crippling embargo on the Reich's ally, Japan, in hopes of provoking an attack and slipping into the war via the "back door." When the Japanese, facing slow strangulation, dutifully responded at Pearl Harbor in December 1941, it was Roosevelt's dream come true. Later, when his Secretary of the Treasury, Henry Morgenthau, proposed a plan to pastorialize Germany upon victory, thereby assuring the death of millions, Roosevelt was its strongest supporter.

"I would like to see the Germans on the breadline for 50 years," the president admitted in private.

At a meeting with Churchill at Casablanca in 1943, Roosevelt declared that nothing short of "unconditional surrender" would be accepted from Germany. Thus, by removing any possible latitude Hitler might have had for negotiation, the American president's pronouncement insured that not only would Germany fight to the death, but it also guaranteed that hundreds of thousands of Allied airmen and soldiers would perish as well. Additionally, that such a protracted war would enable the Red Army to reach and no doubt enslave much of Europe seemed a foregone conclusion.

Though he could be warm and sympathetic, and few doubted that beneath an often gruff exterior beat a sensitive heart, Winston Churchill's loathing of the "Bosche" dated back to at least the First World War. Nothing illustrated the prime minister's antipathy more than the RAF terror campaign. Churchill's eagerness to unleash the horrors of germ warfare, as well as his willingness to invade neutral countries to reach the Reich, was further evidence of his deep enmity.[3]

3.   Landwehr, *Charlemagne's Legionnaires*, 14–15; Fussell, *Wartime*, 284.

Unlike Roosevelt and Churchill, Josef Stalin's hatred was not directed so much at the Germans as a race as it was aimed at the Germans as political opposition. Stalin's fits of paranoia were legendary and his murderous suspicion found vent as readily on countrymen as outlanders. During the 1930s, millions of independent-minded Russian and Ukrainian farmers were deliberately starved to death during a famine engineered by the dictator. An estimated ten to twenty million more who resisted collectivization or were considered politically unreliable were give a sentence tantamount to death when they were marched off to Siberia as slave laborers.[4] Thousands of army officers who lacked sufficient Marxist zeal were likewise liquidated.

"Neither dismissal, nor ostracism, nor the insane asylum, nor life imprisonment, nor exile seemed to him sufficient punishment for a person he recognized as dangerous," wrote one who later came to know Stalin's methods well, Alexander Solzhenitsyn. "*Death* was the only reliable means of settling accounts in full. And when his lower lids squinted, the sentence which shone in his eyes was always *death*."[5]

When Soviet forces invaded Poland in 1939, one of Stalin's first moves was to round up and execute upwards of 15,000 army officers and intellectuals, thereby removing in one stroke much potential opposition.

Well aware of his past, nervous about the impact his future acts in Europe would have upon a squeamish British public, desperate to hold an unnatural alliance together, Churchill's government tried mightily to cover for the bloody behavior of their communist ally. Ran a secret memo of the British Department of Intelligence to high-ranking civil servants and opinion-molders in the press:

> We cannot reform the Bolsheviks but we can do our best to save them—and ourselves—from the consequences of their acts. The disclosures of the past quarter of a century will render mere denials unconvincing. The only alternative to denial is to distract public attention from the whole subject. Experience has shown that the best distraction is atrocity propaganda directed against the enemy. Unfortunately the public is no longer so susceptible as in the days of the "Corpse Factory," the "Mutilated Belgian Babies" and the "Crucified Canadians" [of World War One]. Your cooperation is therefore earnestly sought to distract public atten-

---

4. Keeling, *Gruesome Harvest*, 20.
5. Strawson, *Battle for Berlin*, 54.

tion from the doings of the Red Army by your wholehearted support of various charges against the Germans . . . which have been and will be put into circulation by the Ministry.[6]

Lest anyone doubt Stalin's intentions once his legions gained control in Germany, the reality was made crystal clear at the Teheran Conference in 1943. Lifting his glass of vodka for the "umpteenth toast," the communist leader suddenly announced, "I propose a salute to the swiftest possible justice for all of Germany's war criminals—justice before a firing squad. I drink to our unity in dispatching them as fast as we capture them, all of them, and there must be at least 50,000 of them."[7] When Churchill, well into his cups, angrily protested—"The British people will never stand for such mass murder. . . . without a proper trial!"—Stalin smiled, his eyes twinkled and overall he seemed "hugely tickled."[8]

"Perhaps," the American president interrupted, "we could say that instead of summarily executing 50,000 we should settle on a smaller number. Shall we say 49,500?"[9]

Asked his opinion on the matter, Roosevelt's son, Elliott, a brigadier-general in the US Army, stepped in diplomatically:

> Isn't the whole thing pretty academic? Russian, American and British soldiers will settle the issue for most of those 50,000 in battle, and I hope that not only those 50,000 war criminals will be taken care of, but many hundreds of thousands more Nazis as well.
>
> Stalin was beaming with pleasure. Around the table he came, flung an arm around my shoulders. An excellent answer! A toast to my health! I flushed with pleasure.[10]

Despite Stalin's well-earned reputation as the greatest mass murderer in history, Franklin Roosevelt was a staunch supporter and admirer of the dictator and defended him at every turn. In an effort to put a friendly, folksy face on the Russian premier and convince Americans that he was a "magnificent" and "gallant" ally, Roosevelt began referring to Stalin as "Uncle Joe."

---

6. Udo Walendy, *The Methods of Reeducation* (Vlotho/Weser, Germany: Verlag fur Volkstum und Zeitgeschichtsforschung, 1979), 5.
7. Veale, *Advance to Barbarism*, 216.
8. Ibid.
9. Ibid., 217.
10. Ibid.

"He is a man who combines a tremendous, relentless determination with a stalwart good humor," explained the president to the American public. "I believe he is representative of the heart and soul of Russia; and I believe that we are going to get along very well with him and the Russian people—very well indeed."[11]

In private, Roosevelt's strange need to be liked and accepted by the dictator was at times embarrassing and comical. "Stalin hates the guts of all your top people," the president wrote Churchill, sounding much like a schoolboy bragging of a favorite teacher. "He thinks he likes me better, and I hope he will continue to do so."[12]

For his part, Stalin remained aloof, regarding his American admirer as little more than a tool to be used. Despite the fact that neither he or his nation would have survived long against the German war machine without massive aid from America, Stalin was testy with the US president in the best of times and openly contemptuous in the worst. Once, during the Teheran summit, Roosevelt attempted to interrupt the Russian leader while he was examining a document. "For God's sake let me finish my work!" Stalin snarled, much to the embarrassment of those around.[13]

Nothing better illustrated the one-way relationship between the two men than Stalin's insistence on staging the 1945 summit in his own backyard at Yalta, thereby forcing a frail and terminally ill American president to travel half way around the globe to attend.[14] Nevertheless, despite the insults, slights and shocking lack of gratitude on Stalin's part, Roosevelt persisted in his efforts to woo the dictator.

"There is one thing I want to tell you," Roosevelt confided to Stalin at the Yalta dinner banquet. "The Prime Minister and I have been cabling back and forth for two years now, and we have a term of endearment by which we call you and that is 'Uncle Joe.'"[15]

---

11.   Harry Elmer Barnes, "Sunrise at Campobello: Sundown at Yalta," *The Barnes Review* (Sept. 1997): 6.

12.   Ibid., 5.

13.   Remi Nadeau, *Stalin, Churchill, and Roosevelt Divide Europe* (New York: Praeger, 1990), 211–212; Ziemke, *Soviet Juggernaut*, 71.

14.   Stewart Richardson, ed., *The Secret History of World War II* (New York: Richardson & Steirman, 1986), 209, 213.

15.   Clemens, *Yalta*, 128–129.

Unaware that such familiarity showed disrespect in Russia, Roosevelt was surprised when a visibly angered Stalin made motions to leave. The situation was salvaged somewhat when Churchill broke the tension with a toast. The eyes of the world were now upon Yalta, said the prime minister, and what the "Big Three" accomplished during talks over the next few days would affect mankind for a hundred years.[16]

Actually, despite Churchill's toast and the ensuing press releases, Yalta was little more than a stage for Stalin and Stalin alone. By February 1945, the relationship between the three men could more accurately be described as the "Big One and little two." Roosevelt would not refuse Stalin's requests for reasons philosophical and psychological and Churchill could not for want of might. With his massive armies poised to end the war, Josef Stalin was now clearly in the driver's seat. Additionally, of the three victor nations it was an indisputable fact that Russia had by far suffered most from the war. As a consequence, when the spoils were divided Russia should logically receive the lion's share.

Although the communist leader paid lip-service to "free and unfettered elections" in the nations his army would soon overrun, neither the American president or the British prime minister could seriously doubt the fate of eastern Europe. Nothing more graphically demonstrated Stalin's plans for the countries he conquered than recent events in Warsaw. There, emboldened by the approach of the Red Army and swayed by Allied promises of aid, Polish freedom fighters had risen against the Germans. Rather than move in and assist the uprising, however, as he was certainly capable of doing, Stalin halted his army a few miles away and merely watched, thereby allowing the Germans to eventually crush this potential threat to communism.[17] Nevertheless, little or nothing the Soviet strongman did damaged him in the eyes of his allies, especially Roosevelt.

Such incidents as that at Warsaw, as well as their government's craven acquiescence to seemingly every Soviet demand, did not go unnoticed by a number of Americans, including James V. Forrestal. Jotted the Secretary of the Navy in his journal:

---

16. Ibid., 129.
17. Nadeau, *Stalin*, 106–107.

I find that whenever any American suggests that we act in accordance with the needs of our own security he is apt to be called a god-damned fascist or imperialist, while if Uncle Joe suggests that he needs the Baltic Provinces, half of Poland, all of Bessarabia and access to the Mediterranean, all hands agree that he is a fine, frank, candid, and generally delightful fellow who is very easy to deal with because he is so explicit in what he wants.[18]

As Forrestal found from experience, all protests against Soviet policy were swiftly silenced.

Another subject Stalin was explicit about at Yalta concerned the return of over two million Soviet citizens who had either fled to Germany to avoid persecution at home or who had joined the enemy to fight against communism. Again, to this demand Roosevelt promised his complete cooperation.[19]

But of course, the main topic of discussion at Yalta was the fate of their mutual enemy, or, as Churchill grimly phrased it, "The future of Germany, if she had any."[20] In the west, the Allies were just recovering from their near catastrophe in the Ardennes. In the east the fate of Germany was being written in blood red letters as the Soviet Army continued its rampage across Prussia, Pomerania and Silesia. Once victory was complete, the three leaders agreed that the former Third Reich would be carved up like the evening's meal and her people marched off as slaves to the Soviet Union. Although Roosevelt had solemnly announced earlier that "the united Nations do not traffic in human slavery," when Stalin proposed the plan, the president called it "a healthy idea."[21]

Another subject broached at Yalta, albeit a seemingly minor one, was Stalin's request for the massive bombing of eastern Germany to smooth the way for the Red Army's final sweep across the Reich. Eager to demonstrate to his ally that Britain, and especially the RAF, was yet a force to be reckoned with, Churchill quickly agreed. And as he did, one target in particular came to mind; it was a target Air Marshal Harris had urged destroyed for months now. This city and its destruction, the prime minister was convinced, would provide the grand

---

18. Davidson, *Death and Life*, 28.
19. Elliott, *Pawns of Yalta*, 2.
20. Clemens, *Yalta*, 140.
21. Keeling, *Gruesome Harvest*, 19.

opportunity to show Stalin and the world that the sun had not quite set on the once-mighty British Empire.[22]

When the Yalta talks were finally concluded on February 11, the three Allied leaders signed a joint statement for press release, then bid each other a fond adieu.

"It is not our purpose," explained the declaration, "to destroy the people of Germany."[23]

Some newsmen who reported on Yalta may have actually believed this statement and many who read the words world-wide no doubt did. Those most directly affected, however, the surviving Germans themselves, suffered no such illusion. From past experience, most already knew what lay ahead far better than words could ever tell.

Fashing is an annual German event similar to the Latin celebration of Mardi Gras. On this particular evening of "Shrove Tuesday," normally staid, reserved Teutons don outlandish costumes, join friends or complete strangers, swarm into bars, restaurants and theaters, then partake for several hours in pointless, yet harmless, merry-making. Because of the exigencies of war, however, the celebration, like most else in the devastated Reich, had been all but abandoned. In only one city did the Fashing tradition continue much in the manner it always had and on the night of February 13, women and children, along with the few remaining men, flooded its streets to celebrate.

Dresden was truly one of the world's great cultural treasures. Known as the "Florence on the Elbe," the ancient show-case in the heart of Saxony was a virtual time-capsule of Gothic architecture and medieval culture. At every turn on every narrow, cobbled street of the old town was an ornate palace, a museum, an art gallery, or a towering, centuries-old cathedral. Like Paris, Rome and Venice, Dresden was both beautiful, romantic and enduring. For decades, the city had been one of the "must stops" for continental travelers, especially those from Britain and America.[24]

22. Hastings, *Bomber Command*, 341–342.
23. Keeling, xi.
24. Pechel, *Voices From the Third Reich*, 224; Veale, *Advance*, 189.

Welcome as it was, the fact that a city the size of Dresden had survived when all else was destroyed, mystified some residents and troubled others. Since only two tiny daylight raids had occurred during
five years of war, many assumed Dresden's salvation was due to its reputation as an "art city"; that as a priceless, irreplaceable gem of Western culture even "terror-bombers" lacked hatred sufficient to efface
such beauty.[25] Others surmised that since Dresden had almost no heavy
industry—and what little it did have had no bearing on the war—
the enemy simply did not deem the city a viable target. When skep-
tics pointed out that many other beautiful German towns with little
or no industry had been systematically obliterated, rumors invented
new reasons for Dresden's miraculous survival.

One belief embraced by many stated that an aunt of Churchill's lived
in Dresden. Another hinted that the town was spared because of huge
American investments. The fact that Dresden had become a "hospital city" with numerous medical facilities seemed a rational explanation to others. To some, the twenty-six thousand Allied POWs interred
in the town appeared a more logical answer.[26] Among many Dresdeners, however, perhaps the greatest explanation as to why their
city lived when all else died was that undoubtedly a spark of mercy
yet burned in the hearts of British and American flyers. Of all the many
names it was known by, nothing better described Dresden in February 1945, than "refugee city."

Since the Soviet invasion in January, millions of terrified trekkers, desperate to put as much space between themselves and the Red Army as
possible, had fled through Dresden in trains, cars, wagons, or afoot. Hundreds of thousands more, though—injured, wounded, starving, or simply separated from their families—washed up in Dresden like castaways
on an island. At the main train station, a city within a city had sprang
up wherein thousands of people, many of them lost or orphaned children, lived a semi-permanent existence. A seventeen-year-old Red Cross
worker, Eva Beyer, offers a glimpse at the heart-rending agony:

> Children were searching for their parents, parents were searching for their
> children, there was constant calling and asking. A boy of about nine years of age,

---

25. David Irving, *The Destruction of Dresden* (1963), 173; Owings, *Frauen*, 191; McKee, *Dresden 1945*, 137; Pechel, *Voices*, 137, 224.
26. Owings, 191; Pechel, 228, 463–464; Sorge, *Other Price*, 105.

holding his little four-year-old sister by the hand, asked me for food. When I asked him where his parents were, the boy said to me: "Grandma and grandpa are lying dead in the carriage and Mummy is lost." The children had no tears any more. . . . In one compartment we found a woman. She had twenty-three children with her, and not one of them was her own. She had buried her own child three weeks ago. Her child had died of cold and tonsillitis. I asked her where all those other children came from, and she told me that all these were children whose parents were lost or dead. "After all, somebody has got to take care of them," she said. . . . [T]hose children's faces were not the faces of children any more. They were the faces of people who have gone through hell. Starving, wounded, lice-ridden, in rags. And the most treasured thing they had, security and the love of their parents, they had lost.[27]

As truly appalling as the situation at the railroad station was, conditions were little better in the surrounding city. From a normal population of 600,000, Dresden had swollen by the night of February 13 to perhaps double that figure.[28] Every which way residents turned they found frightened, ragged refugees.

"[E]ach restaurant, cafe, pub, and bar . . . was crammed full of people with suitcases, rucksacks and bundles," a woman wrote. "You literally fell over these people and their possessions. It was so bad that you did not like to watch it, and it spoiled all the usual happy atmosphere of the Fashing."[29]

Nevertheless, in spite of the crowds and the fact that the Russians were a mere seventy miles away, thousands of Dresdeners were determined to take to the streets and celebrate what was certain to be the last Fashing of the war.

Just before ten P.M. the Dresden sirens sounded. There was no panic. Most residents simply ignored the sounds. Even had there been any public air raid shelters few would have fled to them for there seemed little doubt on this cold, yet cheery night, that like the 171 false alarms that preceded it, this warning too would end in nothing.[30] Instead of

27. McKee, *Dresden 1945*, 44–45.
28. Ibid., 45.
29. Ibid., 144.
30. Ibid., 145; Owings, *Frauen*, 191; Irving, *Dresden*, 173.

the "All Clear" siren, however, seconds later Dresden heard another sound.

"Suddenly," said one startled woman, "a thundering and roaring which made the whole earth tremble. An earthquake?"[31]

Almost before this lady and others could guess the answer, the black sky above Dresden turned brilliant. Many spectators were dazzled by the colored lights and stared in awe. "It's getting light, it's getting light, it's bright as day outside!" shouted an incredulous friend to young Gotz Bergander who was indoors listening to his radio.[32]

Weary Red Cross worker, Eva Beyer, had just awakened moments earlier and paid a visit to the restroom:

> I saw a green light shine through the window. What was this? When I opened the door, I could see what it was. The "Christmas Trees" were in the sky. . . . I went to warn the other people in the building. . . . I ran through the whole house, calling out: "Alarm! Alarm!" and waking everyone up. . . . Another five families lived in this building and together we totaled eleven women, six children, and one man—Kurt, the wounded ex-soldier. Then I went back to the flat and fetched the children from their beds. . . . [T]hey started to scream because they didn't know what was happening and there was no time to explain anything to them.
>
> We all went down into the cellar and I put just a blanket round each child, because there was no time for anything else. I myself was only in my nightgown, but I didn't even feel the cold.[33]

At the railroad station, Gisela-Alexandra Moeltgen was standing at the window of an idle train talking to her husband on the platform when the chilling lights showered down.

> Many optimists stayed in order to secure a good seat, but I broke the window—it was only made of cardboard—grabbed the handbag in which I carried my jewelry, grabbed my fur, too, and got through the window. The others followed suit. We ran along the completely blacked-out platform in the dark and found that all the barriers were closed. Over the barriers, then! The police wanted us to go into the already overcrowded air raid shelter at the station, but we had only one urge—out, and away from the station! . . .
>
> We ran across the road to the Technical High School where, it was claimed, there was a good cellar. And above us—very low—the planes. Masses of people were already in the cellar when we arrived, and I collapsed then. It was my heart.

31. McKee, *Dresden 1945*, 125.
32. Pechel, *Voices*, 228.
33. McKee, 45, 137.

I was still very weak and all the running had exhausted me completely. Somebody asked us to move on, further into the crush in the cellar, and we did so.[34]

"Air raid warning!" grumbled an indignant SS officer, Claus von Fehrentheil, as he lay in a military hospital with half his hip shot away. "After all, we understood we were in an open city, world-famous for its art, undefended, declared a 'hospital town.'"

Only after very intensive efforts urging us to shelter, did we concede to go into the cellar. . . . For one thing, we regarded the whole affair as probably a mistake at this time. Then also, a soldier who had been on the Front felt too restricted in a cellar, a place where he could not dodge any threatening dangers. . . . So we stood in the passages and on the staircases outside the air raid shelter.[35]

"Get dressed, get dressed! Quickly, get down to the cellar," cried nuns in the hospital where twenty-year-old Annemarie Waehmann was a patient. "Bedridden patients were put into push-chairs, and there was nothing but hurrying and rushing about. We had hardly been in the cellar for five minutes when [the bombs fell]. . . . This is the end, we thought. . . . Many screamed in fear, and prayed, and we crept trembling under the beds."[36]

"All hell broke loose over us so suddenly that no one really had a chance to perceive what was actually going to happen," recalled Erika Simon, whose parents had only seconds before whisked the little girl and her brother and sister to the cellar. "I remember I had my head in my mother's lap under a blanket and was putting both hands over my ears in an attempt to blot out the horrific noise."[37]

As wave after wave of RAF bombers appeared overhead, ton upon ton of bombs tumbled down. "It was as if a huge noisy conveyor belt was rolling over us," Gotz Bergander thought when he heard the strange, terrifying noise, "a noise punctuated with detonations and tremors."[38]

Added to the normal payload of high explosives, hundreds of two- and four-ton "Block-busters" slammed into Dresden, effacing entire neighborhoods.[39] Centuries-old cathedrals, palaces, museums, and

---

34. Ibid., 131–132.
35. Ibid., 147.
36. Ibid., 126.
37. Ibid., 151–152.
38. Pechel, *Voices*, 228.
39. Irving, *Dresden*, 146.

homes were reduced to rubble in seconds. At the railroad station, those hundreds of individuals on the trains who had refused to leave their coveted seats were blown to bits. At the huge indoor circus, spectators, performers and animals were slaughtered by blast and hissing shrapnel. In the streets, on the sidewalks, atop the bridges over the Elbe, costumed revelers with nowhere to run were slain by the thousands. Without let-up, the massacre continued.

Because Dresden lacked any sort of anti-aircraft weapons, enemy planes were able to fly so low that victims could be seen running through the streets. Despite this, and the fact that night was "as bright as day," the numerous hospitals were not spared.

"We patients," Claus von Fehrentheil recalled, "had been reassured that even the smallest hospital had the distinctive red cross on a white background painted on its roof. It seemed to us as the night went on that these served as excellent markers for the bombs of the English."[40]

Said Annemarie Waehmann from her own hospital: "There was crashing and thundering, whistling and howling. The walls trembled, swayed by the impact of the bombs. This is the end, we thought. . . . Then some of the doctors screamed: 'Everyone out of the cellar, the whole building is going to collapse!' . . . I too ran for my life into the next building. . . . Everyone was in such a panic that all we wanted was to save our naked lives."[41]

Elsewhere, as the bombing rose in fury, horror-struck Dresdeners huddled against the onslaught. "Time and again I gazed at the ceiling, expecting everything to collapse on us," confessed Margret Freyer from a cellar containing forty-three women. "Somehow I had switched off and was expecting the final catastrophe; it must have been for this reason that I did not join in the weeping and praying of the totally terrified women, but tried to calm them down as best I could."[42]

"The attack continued and the mood among us reached panic pitch," remembered Gisela-Alexandra Moeltgen from the crowded high school basement. "Then a shout—'At once, everyone leave, there is danger of collapse!' Out through the narrow cellar windows we went, flames

40. McKee, *Dresden 1945*, 147.
41. Ibid., 150–151.
42. Ibid., 145–146.

whipping down the staircase, the whole building alight. . . . Flames, flames wherever one looked."[43]

"I can see my father leaning against this wall," reminisced Erika Simon, "and I felt that the walls were coming towards us and that my father was trying to stop them from falling down on us."[44]

"And then," said the surprised little girl, "suddenly, the noise ceased."[45]

"There was absolute quiet," another listener added.[46]

Several minutes later, the welcome silence was broken by the even more welcome sound of the "All Clear" signal. Those who had clocks or watches and thought to look were stunned—what had seemed an all night trial by fire had actually occurred in just under half an hour. In those thirty minutes, however, one of the world's most beautiful treasures had all but vanished. As the people stumbled from their holes they were stunned at the strange sight that greeted them.

"[C]oming out of the cellar was unforgettable," wrote teenager Gotz Bergander. "[T]he night sky was illuminated with pink and red. The houses were black silhouettes, and a red cloud of smoke hovered over everything. . . . People ran toward us totally distraught, smeared with ash, and with wet blankets wrapped around their heads. . . . All we heard was, 'Everything's gone, everything's on fire.'"[47]

"I saw only burning houses and screaming people . . . ," added Margret Freyer when she entered the street. "It was frightening—I found myself completely alone, and all I could hear was the roaring of the fires. I could hardly see, due to the flying sparks, the flames and the smoke."[48]

Those who managed to reach the streets found their way almost entirely blocked by fallen trees, poles, wires, and collapsed buildings.[49] As the dazed survivors scrambled for safety, fire brigades arrived from outlying communities to battle the blaze. Red Cross workers also appeared and began pulling victims from the rubble.[50]

43. Ibid., 153.
44. Ibid., 152.
45. Ibid.
46. Pechel, 228.
47. Ibid., 229.
48. McKee, 146.
49. Ibid., 153.
50. Sorge, *Other Price*, 105.

Meanwhile, at the great city park in the center of town, another type of rescue was in progress. Like everything else in Dresden, the magnificent zoo had been heavily damaged. Remembered Otto Sailer-Jackson, the sixty-year-old zoo inspector:

> The elephants gave spine-chilling screams. Their house was still standing but an explosive bomb of terrific force had landed behind it, lifted the dome of the house, turned it around, and put it back again. The heavy iron doors had been completely bent and the huge iron sliding doors which shut off the house from the terraces had been lifted off their hinges. When I and some of the other men . . . managed to break in to the elephant house, we found the stable empty. For a moment we stood helpless, but then the elephants told us where they were by their heart-breaking trumpeting. We rushed out on to the terrace again. The baby cow elephant was lying in the narrow barrier-moat on her back, her legs up to the sky. She had suffered severe stomach injuries and could not move. A . . . cow elephant had been flung clear across the barrier moat and the fence by some terrific blast wave, and just stood there trembling. We had no choice but to leave those animals to their fate for the moment.[51]

In other areas of the zoo, cages had been blown open and frantic animals had escaped to the park. When Sailer-Jackson approached a monkey, the terrified little animal reached to him for help. To the old man's horror, he saw that the monkey had only bloody stumps for arms. Drawing his pistol, Sailor-Jackson sadly put the poor creature out of its misery.[52]

As rescue work continued into the early morning of February 14, those in Dresden whose homes had escaped the flames began to mechanically sweep the glass and plaster from their beds and floors or fasten cardboard over windows to keep out the returning cold. "My God, the work was pointless!" admitted one woman, "but it calmed their nerves and their conscience."[53]

As shattering as the destruction of their beautiful city had been,

51. McKee, *Dresden 1945*, 193–194.
52. Ibid., 194–195.
53. Ibid., 153–154.

no one in the stricken town was emotionally prepared for what came next. At 1:30 A.M., the earth began to shake again.[54]

"[S]omeone yelled, 'They're coming back, they're coming back,'" young Gotz Bergander recalled:

> Sure enough, through the general confusion we heard the alarm sirens go off again. The alarm system in the city had ceased to function, but we could hear the sirens from the neighboring villages warning of a second attack. That's when I was overcome with panic, and I'm also speaking for the rest of my family and those who lived in our house. It was sheer panic! We thought this couldn't be possible, that they wouldn't do such a thing. They wouldn't drop more bombs on a city that was already an inferno. . . . We rushed into the cellar.[55]

Margret Freyer was equally stunned: "[M]y friend and I looked at each other, terrified—surely it wasn't possible? Are they coming a second time? I just caught the radio announcer's message: 'Several bomber units are approaching Dresden.' The voice of the announcer was anything but steady. I felt sick—so they *were* coming a second time. Knees shaking, we went down into the cellar."[56]

Once more, the pathetic patients at Claus von Fehrentheil's military hospital hobbled, crawled or were carried to shelter below. "From the sound of the engines," noted the SS officer, "we could hear that this time a very large number of aircraft were taking part, definitely more than in the first wave."[57]

Yet again, as more than a thousand bombers roared overhead, a veritable rain of death showered down on Dresden. In addition to the usual payload of explosives, the second wave brought thousands of incendiary bombs. "[A] non-stop hail of bombs . . . ," thought a terrified Margret Freyer. "The walls shook, the ground shook, the light went out and our heavy iron door was forced open by [a] blast. In the cellar now, there were the same scenes as had occurred before . . . a crowd of crying, screaming, or praying women, throwing themselves on top of each other."[58]

---

54. Pechel, *Voices*, 225.
55. Ibid., 229
56. McKee, 170.
57. Ibid., 177.
58. Ibid., 170.

"This was hell, hell itself . . . ," said Gisela-Alexandra Moeltgen. "I thought: 'Surely this will have to stop some time.'"

> I had the feeling that each individual plane tried to hit our house, because it was not on fire yet but brilliantly lit up by the burning house next to it. The planes flew just across the roofs, or at least, that is what it sounded like. I kept shouting: "Open your mouths!" The sound of the bombs—"bschi-bum, bschi-bum"—came wave after wave. There was no end to it. . . . The house seemed to come crashing down and shook continuously. When the direct hit came, no one noticed it, for the whistling noise of the bombs drowned all other noises. In any case, it was the others who confirmed that the house was on fire. From that moment on I felt a little calmer. My feeling was: "Thank God they have hit it at last and yet we are still alive."[59]

Unbeknownst to Gisela-Alexandra and thousands more, many of the bombs they heard hitting their homes were phosphorous. While Eva Beyer and the other women and children in her cellar huddled in terror, the wounded ex-soldier, Kurt, disappeared briefly.

> Suddenly Kurt was beside me as I crouched. He whispered very quietly into my ear: "We have fire bombs in the coal cellar, come quick and help me throw the things out!" I gathered all my courage and went with him. Three incendiaries lay there, and we managed to throw out two. The third one we could only throw sand over because it had already started to smoke, and then there was supposed to be only thirty seconds before the thing would explode like a firework.[60]

In a matter of minutes, the thousands of fire bombs ignited the debris in Dresden and a racing furnace of flame erupted. Unfamiliar with bombing raids and fire storms, most Dresdeners reacted slowly. Erika Simon and the nuns at a military hospital stood frozen in terror.

> So there we were, paralyzed by horror and fear, clinging to the Sister in a corridor amongst the dead, the wounded, and soldiers who had just had their legs amputated and were now lying on stretchers, helpless amongst the chaos. Gruesome . . . [were] the Catholic Sisters constantly saying their prayers, murmuring over their rosaries. I am sure nobody bothered to save the screaming soldiers.[61]

One patient who had no intention of being broiled alive was the severely wounded officer, Claus von Fehrentheil.

---

59. Ibid., 191–192.
60. Ibid., 138.
61. Ibid., 190.

Now I was in the open, no longer surrounded by walls, but by flames instead. . . . No path was recognizable between the buildings, no obvious path of escape, because walls were collapsing and adding to the heaps of rubble. The suction of the flames was . . . strong. . . . Even the pieces of clothing which I had hurriedly picked up and thrown over myself began to smolder. Because of the flying sparks my eyes became useless. I was blind. Small holes must have been burnt into the cornea, which were incredibly painful. They made it impossible for me to open my eyes even briefly, just to see where I was.[62]

Another person determined to escape was Margret Freyer:

Out of here—nothing but out! Three women went up the stairs in front of us, only to come rushing down again, wringing their hands. "We can't get out of here! Everything outside is burning!" they cried. . . . Then we tried the "Breakthrough" which had been installed in each cellar, so people could exit from one cellar to the other. But here we met only thick smoke which made it impossible to breathe. So we went upstairs. The back door, which opened on to the back yard and was made partly of glass, was completely on fire. It would have been madness to touch it. And at the front entrance, flames a metre and a half high came licking at short intervals into the hall.

In spite of this, it was clear that we could not stay in the building unless we wanted to suffocate. So we went downstairs again and picked up our suitcases. I put two handfuls of handkerchiefs into a water tub and stuffed them soaking wet into my coat pocket. . . . I made a last attempt to convince everyone in the cellar to leave, because they would suffocate if they did not; but they didn't want to. And so I left alone. . . .

I stood by the entrance and waited until no flames came licking in, then I quickly slipped through and out into the street.[63]

"[S]omebody screamed: 'Everyone out of here, the place is on fire!'" Maria Rosenberger recalled. "When we arrived upstairs we saw that the street was on fire. . . . Burning curtain material was flying towards us and glowing pieces of wood came flying down on us from above. . . . Now everyone started to make a run for the outskirts in order to reach some open space."[64]

As with Maria and her companions, once in the streets victims did everything they could to escape the ancient inner city where the fire storm seemed centered. Here, in the heart of old Dresden, tempera-

---

62. Ibid., 180.
63. Ibid., 171.
64. Ibid., 169.

tures reached upwards of 3,000 degrees.[65] Metal roofs, copper cupolas, glass, even sandstone, liquefied in the furious heat and poured down like lava. A hurricane of smoke, flame and dust roared toward the vortex from all directions as the cold air beyond Dresden was drawn in by the fire ball. Many disoriented victims, especially the thousands of refugees, took wrong turns on strange streets and were swept like feathers into the furnace.

"The whole of Dresden was an inferno," said one teenage boy. "In the street below people were wandering about helplessly. I saw my aunt there. She had wrapped herself in a damp blanket and, seeing me, called out. . . . The sound of the rising fire-storm strangled her last words. A house wall collapsed with a roar, burying several people in the debris. A thick cloud of dust arose and mingling with the smoke made it impossible for me to see."[66]

"[I]t was like 'The Last Days of Pompeii,'" remembered Eva Beyer. "People came crawling on their hands and knees, so as to be near the ground and be able to breathe better, but not knowing, as they crawled, whether they were really getting away from the fire-storm or merely heading into other burning areas of the city."[67]

As he groped blindly through the holocaust, Claus von Fehrentheil well knew he was only seconds from death:

> One could forecast what must happen next: the oxygen in the air becomes completely burnt away, so one becomes unconscious and hardly notices that one is burning to death. Blind, I accepted that this must happen. Suddenly, someone touched my shoulder and asked me to come along. He had found a way through the rubble to the outside. And so, holding on to the arm of a comrade, I was led through burning Dresden.[68]

Like von Fehrentheil and his timely guide, others were desperately trying to reach the huge city park or the open spaces along the Elbe River. The trials of twenty-four-year-old Margret Freyer were the trials of many:

> Because of flying sparks and the fire-storm I couldn't see anything at first. . . . no street, only rubble nearly a metre high, glass, girders, stones, craters. I tried to

---

65. Ibid., 176.
66. Ibid., 141.
67. Ibid., 209.
68. Ibid., 180.

get rid of the sparks by constantly patting them off my coat. It was useless. . . . I took off the coat and dropped it. Next to me a woman was screaming continually: "My den's burning down, my den's burning down," and dancing in the street. As I go on I can still hear her screaming but I don't see her again. I run, I stumble, anywhere. I don't even know where I am any more. I've lost all sense of direction because all I can see is three steps ahead.

Suddenly I fall into a big hole—a bomb crater, about six metres wide and two metres deep, and I end up down there lying on top of three women. I shake them by their clothes and start to scream at them, telling them that they must get out of here—but they don't move any more. . . . Quickly, I climbed across the women, pulled my suitcase after me, and crawled on all fours out of the crater. To my left I suddenly see a woman. . . . She carries a bundle in her arms. It is a baby. She runs, she falls, and the child flies in an arc into the fire. It's only my eyes which take this in; I myself feel nothing. The woman remains lying on the ground, completely still. . . .

[T]here are calls for help and screams from somewhere but all around is one single inferno. I hold another wet handkerchief in front of my mouth, my hands and my face are burning; it feels as if the skin is hanging down in strips. On my right I see a big, burnt-out shop where lots of people are standing. I join them, but think: "No, I can't stay here either, this place is completely surrounded by fire." I leave all these people behind, and stumble on. . . . In front of me is something that might be a street, filled with a hellish rain of sparks which look like enormous rings of fire when they hit the ground. I have no choice. I must go through. I press another wet handkerchief to my mouth and almost get through, but I fall and am convinced that I cannot go on. It's hot. Hot! My hands are burning like fire. . . . I am past caring, and too weak. . . .

Suddenly, I saw people again, right in front of me. They scream and gesticulate with their hands, and then—to my utter horror and amazement—I see how one after the other they simply seem to let themselves drop to the ground. . . . I fall then, stumbling over a fallen woman and as I lie right next to her I see how her clothes are burning away. Insane fear grips me and from then on I repeat one simple sentence to myself continuously: "I don't want to burn to death—no, no burning—I don't want to burn!" Once more I fall down and feel that I am not going to be able to get up again, but the fear of being burnt pulls me to my feet. Crawling, stumbling, my last handkerchief pressed to my mouth . . . I do not know how many people I fell over. I knew only one feeling: that I must not burn. . . .

I try once more to get up on my feet, but I can only manage to crawl forward on all fours. I can still feel my body, I know I'm still alive. Suddenly, I'm standing up, but there's something wrong, everything seems so far away and I can't hear or see properly any more. . . . I was suffering from lack of oxygen. I must have stumbled forwards roughly ten paces when I all at once inhaled fresh air. There's a breeze! I take another breath, inhale deeply, and my senses clear.[69]

Through sheer will, some, like Margret, did succeed in reaching safety—but most did not. Standing alone on the far hills outside Dresden, one viewer stared in silent awe at the fiery massacre.

> I did not understand what my eyes were seeing. I stood in the darkness, paralyzed, numbed, with my eardrums aching from the hellish uproar. . . . It was simply beyond comprehension, beyond the wildest imagination. It seemed actually unreal. . . . I saw the rising of a flaming sea which . . . inundated the entire city in one huge glowing wave. . . .[T]he entire area was in flames. Huge red and yellow tongues of fire were roaring toward the sky. Streaming, trembling, madly onrushing clouds . . . intermingled with brilliant white, red, and yellow explosions out of which the big bombers seemed to rise like flocks of giant birds. . . . Without ever having been through a big air raid before, I knew at once that here something quite different was happening.[70]

The view from above was even more compelling. "Dresden was a city with every street etched in fire," said one RAF navigator.[71]

"At 20,000 feet," a comrade added, "we could see details in the unearthly blaze that had never been visible before."[72]

For those planes which ventured down, the view quickly became more personal. "I saw people in the streets," admitted one crewman. "I saw a dog run across a road—and felt sorry for it."[73]

"Oh God," one airman muttered over and over again, "those poor people."[74]

After half an hour or so, the bombers broke off the attack and banked for home. Equipped with a movie camera, a single aircraft remained to record the drama:

> There was a sea of fire covering in my estimation some 40 square miles. The heat striking up from the furnace below could be felt in my cockpit. The sky was vivid in hues of scarlet and white, and the light inside the aircraft was that of an eerie autumn sunset. We were so aghast at the awesome blaze that although

---

69. Ibid., 171–174.
70. Tony March, *Darkness Over Europe* (New York: Rand McNally, 1969), 188–189.
71. Irving, *Dresden*, 143.
72. Ibid.
73. McKee, *Dresden 1945*, 165.
74. Ibid., 199.

alone over the city we flew around in a stand-off position for many minutes before turning for home, quite subdued by our imagination of the horror that must be below. We could still see the glare of the holocaust thirty minutes after leaving.[75]

It was on that dark return flight home, when crewmen had a chance to ponder, that some first came to realize that the war had gone "a step too far."

"[F]or the first time in many operations," a Jewish pilot confessed, "I felt sorry for the population below."[76]

"I was sickened," echoed a comrade simply.[77]

With the merciful departure of the planes, rescue teams soon began inching toward the center of town. "Because of the fire-storm, at first it was possible to give help only at the periphery of the fires," explained one worker. "I had to look on, helpless, as people who were clinging to iron railings were seized mercilessly by the suction and plucked off into the flames. And not human beings only, but all sorts of things, even prams, were seized by this force and sucked into the sea of fire."[78]

When the inferno finally abated later that morning, rescuers and relatives entered the still flaming city to search for survivors.

> What we saw . . . was indescribable, horrible. Thick smoke everywhere. As we climbed with great effort over large pieces of walls and roofs which had collapsed and fallen into the street, we could hear behind us, beside us, and in front of us, burnt ruins collapsing with dull crashes. The nearer we came to the town center, the worse it became. It looked like a crater landscape, and then we saw the dead.[79]

"Dead, dead, dead everywhere," gasped Margret Freyer as she stumbled through the ruins.

> Some completely black like charcoal. Others completely untouched. . . . Women in aprons, women with children sitting in the trams as if they had just nodded

75. Irving, 146.
76. Ibid., 143.
77. McKee, 144.
78. Ibid., 182.
79. Ibid., 218.

off. Many women, many young girls, many small children, soldiers who were only identifiable as such by the metal buckles on their belts, almost all of them naked. Some clinging to each other in groups as if they were clawing at each other. From some of the debris poked arms, heads, legs, shattered skulls. . . . Most people looked as if they had been inflated, with large yellow and brown stains on their bodies. . . . [T]here were also so many little babies, terribly mutilated.[80]

"Never would I have thought that death could come to so many people in so many different ways . . . ," noted a stunned rescue worker.

[S]ome times the victims looked like ordinary people apparently peacefully sleeping; the faces of others were racked with pain, the bodies stripped almost naked by the tornado; there were wretched refugees from the East clad only in rags, and people from the Opera in all their finery; here the victim was a shapeless slab, there a layer of ashes. . . . Across the city, along the streets wafted the unmistakable stench of decaying flesh.[81]

Indeed, of all the hideous scents wafting through Dresden—sulfur, gas, sewage—the heavy, sweet stench of cooked flesh blanketed all. "There is nothing like it; nothing smells so," one nauseous woman wrote.[82] What were at first mistaken to be thousands of burnt, blackened logs scattered about the streets were soon found to be charred corpses, each reduced to roughly three feet. "All the way across the city," said a horrified rescuer, "we could see [these] victims lying face down, literally glued to the tarmac, which had softened and melted in the enormous heat."[83]

"The thin and elderly victims took longer to catch fire than the fat or young ones," observed another witness.[84]

Horribly, many frantic relatives were compelled to examine countless such bodies in hopes of identifying loved ones. "I can still see my mother," remembered eleven-year-old Erika Simon, "bending down and turning over dead children, or bits of dead children, for she was still desperately searching for my little brother."[85]

"One shape I will never forget," a rescue worker recalled, "was the

80. Ibid., 175.
81. Irving, 189.
82. McKee, 223.
83. Irving, *Dresden*, 189.
84. Ibid., 205.
85. McKee, *Dresden 1945*, 190.

remains of what had apparently been a mother and child. They had
shriveled and charred into one piece, and had been stuck rigidly to the
asphalt. They had just been prised up. The child must have been underneath the mother, because you could still clearly see its shape, with
its mother's arms clasped around it."[86]

At every turn, a new nightmare awaited. When she kicked from
her path what seemed a burnt piece of wood and discovered it was not,
young Eva Beyer ran screaming round a corner. Once there, she froze
in horror: Hanging with claw-like hands from a metal fence, like so
many blackened rats, were those—men, women and children—who
had vainly tried to scale the barrier to safety. The sight was too much;
Eva vomited on the spot.[87]

Wrote another witness:

> In the middle of the square lay an old man, with two dead horses. Hundreds
> of corpses, completely naked, were scattered round him. . . . Next to the tram-
> shelter was a public lavatory of corrugated iron. At the entrance to this was a
> woman, about thirty years old, completely nude, lying face-down on a fur-
> coat. . . . A few yards further on lay two young boys aged about eight and ten
> clinging tightly to each other; their faces were buried in the ground. They too
> were stark naked. Their legs were stiff and twisted into the air.[88]

Curiously, while most victims had been burned to cinders in the
streets, others, according to one viewer, "sat stiff in the streetcars,
bags in hand, open eyes, dead, with but a slight trickle of blood having run down their noses or coming from their closed lips."[89]

"One woman was still sitting in a destroyed tramcar as if she had
merely forgotten to get out," recorded Maria Rosenberger. Another victim, she continued, was a completely shriveled corpse of a man, naked,
his skin like brown leather, but with his beard and hair in tact.[90]

Adding even more horror to the scene, terribly burned and mutilated zoo animals screamed in pain amid the rubble.

86. Irving, 188.
87. McKee, 240.
88. Irving, 191.
89. Letter of Thomas Andreas Weyersberg (Rigaud, Quebec, Canada), Jan. 31, 1990, to Mathias F.
    Kuester (copy in possession of the author).
90. McKee, 259.

At the main railroad station, where thousands upon thousands were sheltered prior to the attack, few escaped. In the vast basement under the station, no one survived. Unlike those above, victims below died from smoke and carbon monoxide poisoning. "What I saw," said one who entered the tomb, "was a nightmare, lit as it was only by the dim light of the railwayman's lantern. The whole of the basement was covered with several layers of people, all very dead."[91] Added another who witnessed the scene: "What we noticed . . . were not so much dead bodies as people who had apparently fallen asleep, slumped against the station walls."[92]

Aware that those in the old city would flee the flames to the open spaces, the RAF had hurled tons of high explosive bombs into the huge central park. Here, the slaughter was ghastly. "I could see torn-off arms and legs, mutilated torsos, and heads which had been wrenched off their bodies and rolled away," commented a Swiss visitor who attempted to cross the park. "In places the corpses were still lying so densely that I had to clear a path through them in order not to tread on arms and legs."[93]

At the numerous hospitals in Dresden, the survival rate was naturally much lower and many wretched victims could only lay helpless as they slowly burned to death. When Eva Beyer passed a women's clinic she made the mistake of glancing over as clean-up crews brought out victims.

"I went down on my knees, trembled and cried . . . ," the young Red Cross worker recounted. "Several women lay there with their bellies burst open . . . and one could see the babies for they were hanging half outside. Many of the babies were mutilated. . . . Scenes like that one saw everywhere and very slowly one became numbed. One acted like a zombie."[94]

Later that morning, recalled Erika Simon,

the news spread in a most mysterious way, that all those people who were walking about lost and helpless should assemble in the [city park]. Thus a gray

---

91. Irving, 176.
92. Ibid.
93. Ibid., 193.
94. McKee, 252–253.

mass of people began to move along in a line. One had ceased to be an individual and was only part of a suffering mass. The gray line of people climbed over debris and over the dead. One's feet stepped on burnt corpses and one didn't even think about it.[95]

As the stunned survivors assembled at the park and along the grassy banks of the Elbe, some found missing loved ones. Most, however, did not. Absorbed as they were with the hell all about, few were aware of their own condition. When Margret Freyer asked for a mirror, she was staggered by what she saw: "I . . . did not recognize myself any more. My face was a mass of blisters and so were my hands. My eyes were narrow slits and puffed up, my whole body was covered in little black, pitted marks."[96] Others suddenly realized that they themselves were seriously injured, or that their hair and much of their clothing had been burned away.

By noon, February 14, a strange silence settled over what once was Dresden. "The city was absolutely quiet," Gotz Bergander remembered. "The sound of the fires had died out. The rising smoke created a dirty, gray pall which hung over the entire city. The wind had calmed, but a slight breeze was blowing westward, away from us."[97]

And then, shattering the calm, came the sounds. "I suddenly thought I could hear sirens again," continues Bergander. "And sure enough, there they were. I shouted, and by then we could already hear the distant whine of engines. . . . The roar of the engines grew louder and louder."[98]

As US bombers began blasting the rubble to dust, American fighter planes zeroed in on the thousands of refugees at the park, along the river and in other open spaces. Recalled Annemarie Waehmann:

We looked up and saw how they flew lower and lower. "They're coming here . . . ," we screamed. A few men took over and gave commands: "Split up! Scatter!

95. Ibid., 190.
96. Ibid., 175.
97. Pechel, *Voices From the Third Reich*, 230
98. Ibid.

Run into the fields! Down on your faces!" While we were lying in the dirt, our hands clawing at the earth as if we wanted to crawl inside it, they came after us, wave after wave, circling, flying low, shooting with their machine-guns into the defenseless people. Popping noises right and left, clods of earth flying up, screams. Like everyone else, I expect, I prayed: Dear God, please protect me. A few seconds' pause, as the planes circled in order to come back at us again. The men screamed: "Up, up! Run on! Run towards the trees!" . . . But again that popping noise as they fired without mercy into the people, and screams and clods of earth flying around. . . . I took Hilde by the hand and without turning round once, without even looking to see how many people did not get up again, we ran.[99]

"[P]anic broke out," said fifteen-year-old Gerhard Kuhnemund. "Women and children were massacred with cannon and bombs. It was mass murder. . . . While we literally clawed ourselves into the grass, I personally saw at least five American fighter-bombers, which from an altitude of approximately 120–150 metres opened fire with their cannon on the masses of civilians. My companion . . . was killed beside me in this attack. There was a hole in his back the size of a palm."[100]

Near the park, zoo-keeper Otto Sailer-Jackson watched in stunned disbelief as one American pilot mowed down people running in the street. "He attacked several times, flying very low, firing from cannon and machine-guns into the refugees. Then he flew low over the Zoo and made several firing runs at anything he could see that was still alive. In this way our last giraffe met her death. Many stags and other animals which we had managed to save, became the victims of this hero."[101]

Although the raid lasted only ten minutes, the Americans returned the next day, and the next, and the next, seemingly determined that not a single living thing should survive in Dresden. "There seemed to be no end to the horror," said Eva Beyer.[102]

Desperate to prevent epidemics, the survivors of Dresden scurried between raids to dispose of the corpses. With thousands of bodies

99. McKee, *Dresden 1945*, 219–220.
100. Ibid., 221.
101. Ibid., 222.
102. Ibid., 253.

littering the streets and parks, the task initially seemed simple. "They had to pitchfork shriveled bodies onto trucks and wagons and cart them to shallow graves on the outskirts of the city," a British POW engaged in the cleanup observed.[103] As the ghastly work continued, however, it soon became clear that in no way could such a slow process handle the enormous amount of bodies. Hence, huge grills were fashioned from girders in various parts of town and corpses were stacked on them like logs. When the piles reached roughly ten feet high and thirty feet wide, flame throwers were used to ignite the mass.[104] Elsewhere, workers simply built great mounds. Eva Beyer watched in horror as men poured gasoline over a large pile composed entirely of heads, legs and other body parts. While that mound was ablaze trucks arrived and dumped more such loads.[105]

As the recovery continued and workers entered the ruins, even greater horrors were in store. Acting like vast ovens, super-heated cellars had rendered their victims into liquid fat.

"[R]escuers were walking about up to their ankles in sludge," recounted Margret Freyer.[106]

With his father, ten-year-old Thomas Weyersberg entered the basement of his family's business to salvage from the ruins. In spite of the horror already experienced, neither father or son was prepared for what they found. "We literally waded into the pit of hell," the boy said, "carrying out fat-soaked documents, company books, stationery[,] even some typewriters. . . . The walls . . . were still warm when we progressed . . . wading ankle-deep in the fried human drippings."[107]

Despite Dresden's frenzied efforts to recover the dead, ten days after the raids, "mountains of bodies" still awaited disposal and for weeks workers with carts and trucks hauled thousands of corpses through the streets.[108] Clearly, the dead in Dresden outnumbered the living.

One month after the massacre, the Dresden Chief of Police reported that over 200,000 bodies had been recovered from the ruins. The

---

103. Sorge, *Other Price*, 108.
104. Toland, *Last 100 Days*, 157.
105. McKee, 246.
106. Ibid., 144.
107. Weyersberg letter.
108. March, *Darkness Over Europe*, 190; McKee, 246.

official added that the toll might possibly reach 250,000. Later, the International Red Cross estimated that 275,000 had died in the raids. Because of the incredible density of Dresden's population on the night of February 13–14, because thousands of victims were refugees with no records, because many bodies either lay buried forever in the ruins or had simply melted like wax, other estimates that place the death toll at 300,000 to 400,000 may well be closer to the mark.[109]

As news from Dresden spread slowly throughout the rest of the Reich, there was shock and horror, but mostly their was anguish. "Dresden was a glorious city . . . ," wrote Ruth Andreas-Friedrich in her diary. "It's a little hard getting used to the idea that Dresden, too, no longer exists. I almost feel like crying." And Rudolf Semmler, aide to the propaganda minister, also took note that public facades of strength and courage could easily crumble in private: "For the first time I saw Goebbels lose control of himself when two days ago, he was given the stark reports of the disaster in Dresden. The tears came into his eyes with grief and rage and shock. Twenty minutes later I saw him again. He was still crying and looked a broken man."[110]

When word of the Dresden bombing first reached Great Britain there was initial joy. That the seventh largest city in Germany should be scorched from the map was "wondrous news," trumpeted the British press; that hundreds of thousands of women and children should be burnt to cinders in the process was also "an unexpected and fortunate bonus." Cabinet minister, Sir Archibald Sinclair, heartily agreed with this attitude and lyrically termed the firestorm a "crescendo of destruction."[111]

As more facts and information from neutral Swiss and Swedish sources began to arrive, however, many throughout the world were

109. Daily order, no. 47 (Mar, 22, 1945), Office of the Chief of Police, Dresden; Report of International Red Cross, Joint Relief (1941–1946); Douglas, *Gestapo Chief*, 1, 41; McKee, *Dresden 1945*, 182.

110. Semmler, *Goebbels*, 181.

111. Grenfell, *Unconditional Hatred*, 193; Toland, *100 Days*, 158.

horrified. For the first time in the war, those in England, America and elsewhere learned what Germans had known for three years—the Allies were engaged in "deliberate terror-bombing."[112] Angered and shamed by such a course when the war was clearly on its last leg, Richard Stokes lashed out in the House of Commons: "What happened on the evening of 13th February? There were a million people in Dresden, including 600,000 bombed-out evacuees and refugees from the East.... When I heard the Minister speak of the 'crescendo of destruction,' I thought: What a magnificent expression for a Cabinet Minister of Great Britain at this stage of the war."[113]

Most outrage, high and low, was directed at Arthur Harris, Chief of Bomber Command.

"[W]e were told at the briefing that there were many thousands of Panzer troops in the streets [of Dresden], either going to or coming back from the Russian Front," one angry RAF crewman later explained. "My personal feeling is, that if we'd been told the truth at the briefing, some of us wouldn't have gone."[114]

"To just fly over it without opposition felt like murder," added a comrade. "I felt it was a cowardly war."[115]

Once known affectionately by many of his men as "Bomber" Harris, after Dresden the air marshal earned a new nickname—"Butcher."

"Butcher Harris didn't give a damn how many men he lost as long as he was pounding the shit out of German civilians," growled one British airman.[116]

Meanwhile, the man directly responsible for the Dresden massacre began to publicly distance himself from both Harris and terror bombing. Winston Churchill:

> It seems to me that the moment has come when the question of bombing of German cities simply for the sake of increasing the terror, though under other pretexts, should be reviewed. The destruction of Dresden remains a serious query against the conduct of Allied bombing. . . . I feel the need for more precise

112. Hastings, *Bomber Command*, 343.
113. Toland, 158.
114. McKee, *Dresden 1945*, 66.
115. Ibid., 199.
116. Ibid., 116.

concentration upon military objectives . . . rather than on mere acts of terror
and wanton destruction.[117]

Public pronouncements to the contrary, the air terror continued
unabated. Lost almost entirely in the furor over Dresden was the
February 23 leveling of Pforzheim in western Germany. Although much
smaller than Dresden, in nineteen minutes the city was utterly
destroyed with nearly 20,000 dead.[118] A short time later, the "hospital city" of Wurzburg was likewise incinerated.[119] Additionally, in what
appeared an attempt to broaden the war, American planes struck neutral Switzerland, raiding Schaffhausen in late February and striking
Basel and Zurich on March 4.[120]

Working in tandem with the bombing of German cities was the "targets of opportunity" policy on the countryside. Under this order,
anything moving in the Reich was fair game for Allied fighter planes.
Ships, trucks, cars, ambulances, bicyclists, farmers in fields, animals in
pastures, even children in school yards, provided potential targets.
Steaming locomotives were especially vulnerable, as thousands, including Olga Held, soon discovered.

> [S]uddenly four American P-51 Mustangs swooped down on us at tremen-
> dous speed. One second they appeared right outside the train window, and in
> a blink disappeared with a roar. Minutes later the Mustangs attacked from ahead
> of us, firing at the engine.
>
> "Olga! Under the car!" Heiner cried out when the train came to a halt.
>
> We jumped to the ground, but before I could crawl under the car, the airplanes
> attacked again. This time they strafed the passenger cars. I heard the ratta-tat-
> tat of bullets as they hit above me. Some of the passengers ran from the train
> across a field, trying to reach a wooded area. One of the planes pursued them.
> None of the passengers made it. . . .

117. Veale, *Advance to Barbarism*, 194.
118. Dagmar Barnouw, *Germany 1945* (Bloomington: Indiana University Press, 1996), 66.
119. Garrett, *Ethics and Airpower*, x.
120. McKee, *Dresden 1945*, 253–254.

[A]fter the last plane roared away I was drenched with sweat and so weak I could hardly stand.[121]

Merciless attacks such as the above were a double blow to many victims. Unlike the British, American airmen had always been considered by most Germans, rightly or wrongly, as honorable, even "chivalrous," warriors. As one German explained: "The Americans were regarded by us as *soldiers*. Their attacks were during the daytime and were nearly always directed on military targets, even if the civilian population sometimes suffered heavy casualties because of them. They flew in good visibility and risked the aimed fire of our Flak. Hence a certain respect for the 'Amis' as we called them."[122]

After Dresden, however, and the targets of opportunity "turkey shoot," most German civilians sadly saw little distinction between British and American "terror flyers."

In response to the air war against Germany, Joseph Goebbels urged Hitler to abrogate the Geneva Convention. Recorded Rudolf Semmler:

> He said this Convention had lost all meaning when enemy pilots could kill 100,000 non-combatants in two hours. The Convention made us helpless, because it prohibited any reprisals on the enemy air crews, while giving them the best possible cover for their terror tactics. By cutting loose from the Convention we would be able to condemn to death by summary trial all the British and American airmen in our hands, on a charge of murdering civilians. That, said Goebbels, would stop the heavy air raids.[123]

Many Germans agreed with Goebbels and at the local level some leaders already considered the Geneva Convention a dead-letter. Read a decree from one outraged county official:

> The general public is to be informed that what enemy fliers are doing in our country has nothing whatsoever to do with the war. One must consider it plain murder when a woman with a white scarf around her head is working in the field or a child is in the field and a flier shoots and kills such persons. There-

121. Bruner manuscript, 131–132.
122. Middlebrook, *Battle of Hamburg*, 340.
123. Semmler, *Goebbels*, 183.

fore I demand that when enemy fliers are shot down and the pilots are able to rescue themselves, they are not to be captured alive.[124]

Though isolated instances of reprisal against downed Allied airmen did occur, such acts never became state policy. Indeed, despite the angry protests, Hitler and his military staff continued to abide by the Geneva Convention throughout the war. As a result, roughly ninety-nine percent of Allied POWs survived to reach home.[125] Even as the news of Dresden was reaching the rest of the Reich, a nurse in Vienna recorded in her diary on what was the typical fate of captured Allied airmen:

> Just as we were finishing, two American pilots, who had been shot down yesterday morning, were brought in. They arrived supported on either side by a German soldier. They seemed badly injured and could barely drag their feet. One had a burnt face that was quite black, with yellow hair standing up stiffly. By now we have about thirty American pilots in our hospital. They are treated well, but are taken down into our basement shelter only during exceptionally heavy raids. . . . One nurse . . . brought one of them some flowers.[126]

Despite attempts such as the above to maintain a modicum of civility in a hopelessly uncivil war, after Yalta there was no doubt whatsoever in the minds of the Nazi leadership of Germany's fate should she fall.

"So much for the drivel talked by our coffeehouse diplomats and foreign ministry politicos!" snapped Hitler. "Here they have it in black and white—if we lose the war, Germany will cease to exist. What matters now is to keep our nerve and not give in."[127]

In the west, a massive Allied army under the American, Gen. Dwight Eisenhower, was pressing to the Rhine, poised for a crossover into the heart of Germany. To the south, another Allied force was aiming for the Alps. And to the east. . . . It was here, in the east, more than anywhere else, that Hitler's words to fight on were directed for it was

---

124. Joseph Halow, *Innocent at Dachau* (Newport Beach, Calif: Institute for Historical Review, 1992), 69.
125. Sorge, *Other Price,* 107.
126. Marie Vassiltchikov, *Berlin Diaries, 1940–1945* (New York: Alfred A. Knopf, 1987), 250.
127. Duffy, *Red Storm on the Reich,* 124.

here that the looming end seemed most nightmarish. A glimpse at the tremendous pressure grinding down on even the strongest of all German nerves is offered by a secretary from the Berlin bunker:

> The battle fronts were drawing threateningly closer. . . . The atmosphere in the bunker was characterized by desperate efforts to maintain a tiny spark of hope in life. No one wanted to be alone—everyone sought the companionship of others. We looked for human company, and yet none of us expressed his or her true innermost feelings. We talked of trivial matters, distracted ourselves, consoled ourselves with memories, thought of our families at home, and deadened our fear and doubt with alcohol, cigarettes and silly chatter—and yet each of us was in themselves quite alone. . . .
>
> Appalling news came from the occupied towns and villages: children massacred, women raped. When we gathered for tea in the evenings Hitler's eyes were wild as he showed us photos from the eastern Front—nothing but death and despair. He swore vengeance and let his fury against the Russians explode. "These aren't men," he'd shout, "they're wild animals from the steppes of Asia. The war I'm waging against them is the battle for the dignity of the peoples of Europe. They're going to pay for this—no price is too high for our final victory. We must remain inflexible, and fight these savages with all the means at our disposal.[128]

---

128. Pierre Galante and Eugene Silianoff, *Voices From the Bunker* (New York: G.P. Putnam's Sons, 1989), 139–140.

5

THE DEVIL'S LAUGHTER

ALTHOUGH SOVIET FORCES had reached the Oder River by the end of January 1945, thereby threatening Berlin and much of Germany, several enclaves behind the front remained firmly in Wehrmacht hands. Within these encircled islands of the Reich, soldiers and militiamen dug in and refused to surrender.

"[O]ur conduct of war must become fanatical . . . ," declared Adolf Hitler. "Every bunker, every block in a German city, and every German village must be turned into a fortress against which the enemy will either bleed to death or its garrison be buried in man-to-man combat."[1]

No individual was more determined to faithfully follow every word of his Fuhrer's directive than the district leader of Silesia, Karl Hanke. Even before his capital, Breslau, was surrounded by the Soviets, Hanke readied for siege. Stirred by the fact that the city had heroically resisted another Mongol invasion almost exactly seven hundred years before, the grim Nazi leader was determined to "do or die."

"Breslau has become a fortress and will be defended to the last house," Hanke vowed.[2]

Unfortunately for the one million residents and refugees crammed into the city, Hanke ordered all but able-bodied men to leave. Not only would thousands of women and children place an unbearable strain on medical facilities, but food stocks could never last a protracted siege. Hence, wrote one Wehrmacht officer who witnessed the expulsion,

---

1. Steinert, *Hitler's War*, 279.
2. McKee, *Dresden 1945*, 32.

> On all roads leading to the railway stations masses of people were in flight, panting and sweating under the loads of their emergency packs. Train after overcrowded train moved off.... But there were still hundreds of thousands of people in the town when the ground began to tremble with the distant drumfire of the enemy guns. Then ... to the horror of the entire population, the street loudspeakers blared out: "All women and children are to leave the city *on foot.* ..."
>
> The Oder was completely frozen, the temperature was now down to 20 degrees below zero, and yet thousands of young and old women with prams, sledges and little carts were moving along the snow-covered streets into a freezing winter's night. The human cost of this unprepared exodus has never been counted. For town dwellers the ordeal was especially severe, and in particular it was women and children who died. The ditches on both sides of the roads were choked with corpses, mainly of children who had frozen to death and been abandoned there by their mothers.[3]

Though the draconian act enabled the garrison at Breslau to face the foe unencumbered, the measure was a virtual death sentence to thousands of women and children. North of Silesia, the plight of trekkers in East Prussia was even worse. As isolated Wehrmacht units desperately defended their shrinking Baltic beach-heads, millions of refugees poured into the coastal pockets. Unlike the situation at Breslau, military authorities to the north could not simply order superfluous civilians from their lines; with their backs literally to the sea, only the slow and treacherous evacuation by boat was an option. Consequently, at Memel, Konigsberg, Kolberg, Danzig, and other besieged "cauldrons," the situation was appalling.

Juergen Thorwald describes the chaotic conditions at Pillau, where thousands of refugees sought shelter.

> Every alley, every street was packed with their vehicles. People were waiting in every harbor shed, in every wind-sheltered corner. Among them stood their beasts, bleating, snorting, lowing.... The pregnant women giving birth somewhere in a corner, on the ground, in a barracks. Some of them had been raped on their flight ... [and] now they were trembling for fear they would give birth to a monster. The strangely pale faces of girls going up and down the streets asking for a doctor. The wounded and the sick, in constant fear they would be left behind, concealing weapons under their blankets to force someone to take them along, or to end their own lives if the Russians came. The orphans who

---

3.   Ibid.

had been saved from their asylum somewhere at the last moment and tossed onto carts with nothing around them but a blanket, and who were now lying on the floors with frozen limbs. The Russian prisoners of war, brought west under orders from above, walking on wooden soles, their tattered overcoats held together with paper strings. The old people who had lain down in some door-way at night, and had not awakened. The hungry for life who found each other to mate among the ruins in broad daylight. And the wild-eyed insane ones who rushed from house to house, from wagon to wagon, crying for their moth-ers or their children. . . . Over it all the gray sky, snow, frost, and thaw, and thaw and frost and snow, and the chill, killing wet.[4]

Impossible to adequately feed such a host from existing stocks, starvation swiftly made its appearance. "The food ration was so mea-ger," said soldier Guy Sajer,

> that the occasional distributions which were supposed to feed five people for a day would not . . . be considered enough for a school child's lunch. . . . A crowd stretched as far as the eye could see, in front of a large building crammed with people. From the building a faint smell of the gruel cooking in large caldrons washed over the tightly compressed mass of people, who stood stamping their feet to keep from freezing. The thudding of their feet against the pavement sounded like a dull roll of muffled drums. . . . People with the faces of mad-men were wolfing down the flour which was the only food distributed to them. . . . Soldiers also had to stand in interminable lines, to receive, finally, two handfuls of flour apiece, and a cup of hot water.[5]

Because of chronic overcrowding and freezing temperatures, roofs were at a premium. Wrote young Hans Gliewe when his family reached a coastal village:

> We opened the door of one of the wooden barracks. A cloud of stench came to meet us. Hundreds of people sat in there, crowded together on filthy straw piles. The wash hung from strings across the room. Women were changing their children. Others were rubbing their bare legs with some smelly frost ointment. Brother pulled Mother's coat and said: "Please, Mummy, let's go away from here." But we were grateful to find room on a pile of straw next to an old, one-armed East Prussian. . . .
>
> Near me lay a very young woman whose head was shorn almost to the skin and whose face was all covered with ugly sores. She looked terrible. Once when she got up I saw that she walked with a cane. The East Prussian told us that

4.   Thorwald, *Flight in the Winter*, 127–128.
5.   Sajer, *Forgotten Soldier*, 416,438, 441.

she had been a woman auxiliary; the Russians had caught her in Rumania in the autumn of 1944 and had taken her to a labor camp. She had escaped somehow and made it up here. He said she was only eighteen or nineteen. I tried not to, but I couldn't help looking at her.

A few hours later we couldn't stand the barracks any more and ran away. We preferred the cold.[6]

Like this family, many others joined the teeming thousands who were encamped near the docks in hopes of securing passage on anything that would float. Sub-zero weather was not the only deadly foe faced by the campers. In the skies above, Soviet planes returned again and again to strafe and bomb huge holes in the waiting crowds below. After the aircraft briefly disappeared, thousands dashed forward over the mangled corpses in hopes of boarding the next ship.[7]

When a long-sought vessel finally tied up and lowered the walkways, pandemonium erupted on the docks. Because of an order granting priority to men or women with little children, the latter became more valuable than gold. According to an army chaplain:

[W]omen who had got aboard with their babies threw them to relatives still on the pier to get them, too, aboard. Often the children dropped into the water between the ship and the pier, or they fell into the frantic crowd and were trampled underfoot. Or they were caught by strangers who used them to swindle their way aboard. Children were stolen from their sleeping mothers. . . . Among the marauding stragglers . . . were soldiers—and some of them stole children. With these, or even with empty bundles in their arms, they pushed aboard, claiming that they had to save their families. Soldiers appeared in women's clothing that they had stolen or been given by their mistresses.[8]

Among the mob, wounded soldiers awaited their turn to board. "The groaning crowd of men, clinging to a last hope of evacuation, was divided into two categories," remembered Guy Sajer. "The most severely wounded—those whose chances of survival were doubtful, who would at best be hideously mutilated—were not embarked. For them, everything was over. The rest, who might still have some hope of a decent life, were eligible for the boats."[9]

---

6. Thorwald, *Flight*, 174.
7. Sajer, *Forgotten Soldier*, 416, 448.
8. Thorwald, 126.
9. Sajer, 438.

One soldier lucky enough to be carried aboard was Jan Montyn. "An endless stream of refugees poured into the holds. Women, children, old men. Bundles on their backs, leaning on sticks, pushing ramshackle prams. . . . Farewells were said to those who stayed behind; there were shouts to be quick. Anyone who did not hurry would be too late."[10]

Even without children, wounds or passes, some still managed to get aboard. Admits sixteen-year-old Hans Gliewe:

> We walked along with them as if we belonged. Then we hid in the cold, drafty hold of the ship. We huddled close together, but still we were terribly cold. But we did not dare to move, let alone go up, for fear they would recognize us as stowaways. The night went by. The rumble of artillery . . . grew very loud. A man who had been up on deck said the sky was all red with the fires. We were so happy and grateful that we could lie in the drafty hold of the ship. But we were shaking with fear that we would be found out and put ashore.
>
> Then the ship pulled out, and we breathed again.[11]

For the fortunate few who sailed from the besieged ports, their prayers appeared answered; for those left standing on the docks, their doom seemed sealed. Many men, "in a surge of madness," shot themselves. Crazed mothers, with starvation gnawing and the red horror looming, found cyanide and poisoned their children, then themselves. Old people merely crawled into snow banks, fell asleep, and never awoke.

Among the great majority of those who scrambled onto ships, boats, tugs, barges, and naval craft sailing west, their flight was safe and successful. Not only was the warmth and food aboard ship a God-send, but the realization that they were at last escaping the dreaded Bolsheviks proved the first peace of mind many had know in weeks. As the wretched survivors of the *Wilhelm Gustloff* could aver, however, there often was no escaping the nightmare . . . even at sea.

While most of the passengers and crew slept, the old luxury liner *General Stueben* plowed through the icy, black Baltic in the early morning minutes of February 10. Heavily weighed down with refugees and

10. Montyn, *Lamb to Slaughter*, 113.
11. Thorwald, *Flight*, 175.

wounded soldiers, the ship was in the middle of its second such evacuation in less than a fortnight. Just before one A.M., two torpedoes
slammed into the *Stueben's* side.

"The whole ship shivered and vibrated. People were screaming and
shouting," said soldier, Franz Huber. "The ship rocked violently and
those wounded men still capable of getting up were thrown against
the sides. The rest just slid about while we somersaulted, fell on each
other, and made our wounds even worse. But somehow I managed
to put on my lifejacket."[12]

Unlike Huber, who made his way above, few wounded soldiers,
including those strapped to stretchers, were capable of moving as
the ship rapidly sank. "I sat there in the dark alone and heard screams
from all over," Huber continues. "I heard them praying the Lord's
Prayer in such a voice as I will never hear again. Somewhere the ship
was burning and people everywhere were jumping into the water."[13]

As the *Stueben's* stern rose high out of the water, hundreds leaped
overboard, including some who were torn to pieces by the still-turn-
ing propellers. Within seven minutes, the ship plunged beneath the
waves, swiftly silencing a final mass scream that seemed to arise from
a single voice. Of the 3,500 passengers aboard, only Franz Huber and
a few hundred more survived.[14]

"Once you have heard an underwater explosion you never forget it
. . . ," revealed another wounded soldier, Jan Montyn, whose hospital
ship was torpedoed on the Baltic.

> Everything hits the ceiling and bounces back again. For a moment the port-
> holes are darkened as the water crashes down. Stretchers are upturned, every-
> one screams and shouts at once. The engine dies. . . . And then arose a sound
> which none of the survivors would ever forget. A sound so dreadful and terri-
> fying that no words can describe it: the cries of thousands of people, their screams
> reverberating round the ship's hold. Already we were listing badly. Everything—
> people, stretchers—slid to one side. I tried to raise myself, but sank back in pain.
> Then, through a red haze, I saw a shadow coming towards me. Two arms picked
> me up like a child. I catch a glimpse of a face, a familiar face, grimacing with

---

12. Dobson, *Cruelest Night*, 155.
13. Ibid.
14. Ibid., 154; Thorwald, 131.

the exertion—then I lose consciousness. Thereafter everything seems to be happening very far away. Sometimes I am there, then I am not. Light comes and goes, noise alternates with utter silence.

A heavy panting close to my ear. A tottering. We are falling. But we don't fall. A steel door slams shut. Sunlight. My head knocks against the side of a gangway. And at once everything goes dark.

We are floating on a life raft, rising and falling with the waves. White foam, spray sparkling in the sunlight. . . .

I catch a glimpse of the ship behind me. It is listing heavily and, like a lumbering, bloated carcass, it is slowly sinking beneath a churning crest of foam. The wild screeching of seagulls. And darkness. Then light again, as if a veil has been rent apart. We bump against the gray-painted side of a ship. *The Navy*, that's what gray means. Again I am being lifted, by many people this time, and passed from hand to hand.

I am lying on the packed forward deck of a small coastguard vessel, shivering inside a blanket that freezes solid in seconds. The man bending over me is called Schneider. But he looks away to gaze back, like everyone else on deck, at a certain point in the water. It must be a place where the surface of the sea is still whirling madly and the water surges up metres high from the pressure far below. I am lying on my back. I cannot see that place. And yet I *can* see it. I see it reflected in the horror in everyone's eyes.[15]

Tragically, for thousands who successfully traversed the treacherous Baltic, American and British bombers were often the first to greet them when their ships docked. At the port of Swinemunde in northern Germany, the arrival of a navy destroyer loaded with evacuees coincided almost exactly with an Allied air raid. As the horrified captain recalled:

There was a deathly hush on the bridge of the craft, and we could already hear the dull drone of a large number of heavy bombers reverberating from above the low-hanging clouds. Vessels of all kinds were fleeing in panic from the harbor. They rushed past us at full speed in an attempt to reach the safety of the sea before the raid began. . . .

We steamed out again at fifteen knots. We had just passed the lighthouse when we heard the roar of a carpet of bombs landing on the town and harbor of Swinemunde. A high white wall signified where a line of bombs descended on the exact

15. Montyn, *Lamb*, 113–114.

place where we had turned. The paralyzing tension gradually relaxed, and while we were repassing the moles on the way out two refugee children appeared on deck. They were holding hands and laughing with joy. That made us happier than anything for a long time.[16]

Few such raids ended so innocently. At the same port, the freighter *Andross* tied up just as another attack occurred.

"I had gone on deck to find a restroom and a bomb hit very close to me . . . ," related ten-year-old Manfred Neumann, who, like everyone else on board, had but moments before felt himself finally safe. "I managed to get my mother and brothers up on deck. The *Andross* was sinking very quickly. We were led across planks from our ship to [another] ship. People were trying to jump to the other ship, and got squashed between them. I shall never forget the screaming of all those people trapped in the hold of the freighter as it sank. . . . The *Andross* took at least 2,000 people—refugees—to the bottom of the sea."[17]

While the slow, dangerous evacuation of women, children and wounded comrades continued, the German Landser remained in the ever-shrinking pockets, ferociously fighting on so that others might live. That most in the enclaves were already doomed, all fighting men understood. "For every thousand persons embarked, some three thousand more arrived from the east," calculated Guy Sajer. The soldier continues:

> This population, to which we could give only the most rudimentary help, paralyzed our movements and our already precarious system of defense. Within the half circle we were defending, ringing with the thunder of explosions which covered every sort of shriek and scream, former elite troops, units of the Volkssturm, amputees . . . women, children, infants, and invalids were crucified on the frozen earth. . . .
>
> At Memel, no one could stay out of the fighting; children and young girls dried their tears and helped the wounded, distributing food, resisting their desire to devour it, and suppressing horror and fear which were so fully justified. They

---

16. Duffy, *Red Storm on the Reich*, 234, 235.
17. Letter of Manfred Neumann (Appin, Ont., Canada) to the author, Jan. 14, 1998.

performed tasks which their overburdened elders gave them, without argument or complaint. One either died or lived. . . . In the disorder of our advanced positions, civilians sometimes became directly involved in the fighting beside the soldiers; these civilians were often women."[18]

Failed Soviet assaults on the enclaves by armor or human waves was often followed by days of calm as the Russians probed other sectors of the defense. Such stalemates created scenes reminiscent of World War I. From the Courland pocket, Jan Montyn wrote:

We saw a kilometer-wide strip of earth, churned up to the last blade of grass, riddled with craters, and covered with barbed wire entanglements. . . . Nothing moved. Everything that happened there, on either side of the dividing line . . . went on underground. It was hard to believe that under this ploughed-up strip of mud, curving away into the distant hills, there lived thousands of people. You could not see them, but you could smell them. There hung in the air a sickly, penetrating smell that became nauseatingly strong with the slightest breeze. It was the smell of the battlefield, the smell of corpses, or diarrhea. . . .

Two hours on, four hours off. Day and night. Round the clock. Mud. Darkness. Mist. The smell of putrefaction and death. Sniping. Machine-gunning. Barrage. Two hours on, four hours off. Waiting. It grows dark. It grows light. *And otherwise, nothing.*

I found that there was not just one enemy lurking out there, but a whole host. The soul-destroying monotony of guard duty was one of them. For you had to remain on the alert all the time. If you failed to keep under cover for just one instant, it could be fatal. Snipers were watching for their chance. Hunger and lack of sleep were enemies. The cold. The fits of insanity from which no one was immune: trench madness. Sometimes you would see someone's gaze stiffening. Shell shock. Quickly give him a shaking. Slap his face with the flat of your hand, as hard as you can. He will become a danger to himself and others. He may start to scream and provoke fire. He may start firing haphazardly at everything that moves, including you. He may crawl out of the trench, cut and run, towards certain death. . . .

But Hugo, the Belgian in our outfit, had his own unique method of working off his tensions. He did it by seeking out danger. He would take on the most amazing wagers. For a few cigarettes he was prepared to show himself briefly and wave to the other side. And he did it, too. He said he would place a hand grenade on top of his helmet and remove the firing pin. That was possible, he claimed. . . . A helmet is round and can have the same effect as an umbrella. The fragments would fly in all directions, but not downwards. A helmet is round.

---

18. Sajer, *Forgotten Soldier*, 416, 417.

. . . When the sound of the explosion had died away and we came out of hiding he was still standing there, clinging to the wall of the trench. Without his face.[19]

When the sun suddenly appeared one day and the temperature rose to zero, Montyn and his wretched comrades considered it a "miracle."

> It was as if we suddenly saw each other for the first time: filthy, our eyes ringed with black; emaciated, mostly bearded figures wrapped in a peculiar hotchpotch of rags and bits of uniform. For one day we were able to bask in the sun—a sunshine that was not confined to our side of the front line: not one shot was fired that day. . . .
>
> Coats were taken off, and the felt boots and the foot wraps, stiff with dirt, pus and congealed blood. Bare, swollen feet emerged, gray with putrefaction. Lie back! Put them up! Let the sun get at them! At last we could let everything dry out, even if just for a short time.[20]

Hideous as trench warfare was, once defenders were pressed back into the towns, life became immeasurably worse. Recalls Guy Sajer of the struggle for Gotenhafen:

> There were ruins everywhere, and a strong smell of gas and burning filled the air. The wide street which led down to the docks no longer had any definition. The wreckage of the buildings which had once lined it was crumbled right across the roadbed, obstructing all passage. Along with thousands of others, we were put to work clearing away the rubble, so that trucks filled with civilians could get down to the harbor. Every five or ten minutes, planes came over, and we had to freeze where we were. The street was strafed and burned twenty or thirty times a day. . . . We were no longer counting our dead and wounded: almost no one was entirely unhurt. . . . Heavily laden horses . . . pulled a continuous train of sledges loaded with bodies wrapped in sacking or even paper. . . .
>
> House-to-house fighting had already begun in the outlying sections of the town, while thousands of civilians still waited down by the docks. From time to time, Russian shells reached as far as the embarkation area, and exploded there.
>
> We were trying to snatch a short rest in a cellar, where a doctor was delivering a child. The cellar was vaulted and lit by a few hastily rigged lanterns. If the birth of a child is usually a joyful event, this particular birth only seemed to add to the general tragedy. The mother's screams no longer had any meaning in a world made of screams. . . . Once again, there was streaming blood, like the

---

19. Montyn, *Lamb*, 90, 96.
20. Ibid., 101–102.

blood in the streets. . . . A short while later, after a last look at the newborn child, whose tiny cries sounded like a tinkle of delicate glass through the roar of war, we returned to the flaming street. For the child's sake, we hoped he would die.[21]

After years of fighting and dying in a losing war, enduring battles more bloody and savage than anything known to the modern world, the doomed German units in the Baltic pockets should have simply disintegrated. And yet, they did not. Surrender, of course, was not an option. "Russia inspired such terror and had demonstrated such cruelty that no one even considered the idea," admitted Guy Sajer. "We had to hold, no matter what it cost. . . . We had to hold, or die."[22]

To the bitter end, that iron backbone of the German Army, discipline, remained unbroken. Once again, Landser, Guy Sajer:

> The captain spoke to us, and through his firm, official voice we caught the intense emotion of the crushing load which weighed on all of us. . . . [T]his man still wore the vestiges of a military uniform, and was still trying to impose some semblance of order in a situation of cataclysm which had swept an entire nation into a devastating retreat. This man, who knew that everything was lost, was still trying to save the *moment*. . . . This discipline, which had so often annoyed us in the past, touched us now like a soothing balm.[23]

And so, against fate, the handful of men fought on, contesting every inch of every block of every flaming "cauldron." Following an unprecedented air and artillery barrage on the thin German line at Heiligenbeil, the Soviets swept in to crush what little remained. Wrote a witness to a scene that became common:

> The Russian armored wedges drove forward, with the troops coming up behind roaring their *Uras!* But not all life was extinct. Covered with earth, the hardened Landser emerged from their holes. They threw their machine guns over the parapets of the trenches, shot into the gray-brown masses with their assault rifles and machine pistols, and dashed forward with their Panzerfausts against the enemy tanks.[24]

---

21. Sajer, *Forgotten*, 448–449.
22. Ibid., 416.
23. Ibid., 440.
24. Duffy, *Red Storm*, 205.

No amount of courage or discipline could compensate for numbers or equipment, however. Gradually, the coastal pockets were pressed back until German territory was measured in a few kilometers, or in some cases, to several hundred yards of sandy seashore. A tank sergeant remembers the last stand at Hoff:

> I was standing on the coastal cliffs with General [Hans] von Tettau, whose vehicle had been abandoned. The Russian infantry came storming towards us with wild cries of *Ura!* but von Tettau called out with quiet confidence to one of his staff officers: "Now then, gentlemen, let's give them something to remember!" We all proceeded to shoot at the attacking troops as calmly as if we had been on a rifle range. I picked up a rifle from one of the casualties and joined in. . . .
>
> The Russians then opened fire with mortars, but the bombs passed over us and landed on the beach. I looked in that direction and my stomach churned. Behind and beneath us, in the lee of the cliffs, the refugees were fleeing to the west, and the Russian shells were bursting among them.[25]

Frantic to escape such carnage, desperate civilians fled across the ice of the Frisches Haff, a bay several miles wide separating the mainland from a barrier island, or Nehrung. Along this slender strip of sand that led west towards Danzig, all were hoping to reach safety. Unfortunately, the bitter cold changed to rain just when many treks set out. Recounted one survivor of the perilous journey:

> The ice was breaking and at some places we had to drag ourselves with pains through water [nearly a foot] deep. We continually tried the surface with sticks. Bomb-craters compelled us to make detours. We often slipped and thought we were already lost. With our clothes wet through and through movement was difficult. But deadly fear drove us on in spite of our shivering bodies. I saw women do superhuman things. As leaders of treks they instinctively found the safest way for their carts. House utensils were lying scattered all over the ice, wounded people crept up to us with imploring gestures, dragged themselves along on sticks and were pushed forward by friends on little sledges.[26]

"Private cars and other vehicles of every kind frequently disappeared into crevices covered over by thin films of ice," reported one horrified witness.[27]

---

25. Ibid., 197–198.
26. Schieder, *Expulsion of the German Population*, 134–135.
27. Sajer, 439.

Juergen Thorwald describes the long, nightmarish experience of another refugee:

> The journey over the ice began. She watched the lead wagon ahead, and the thaw-water splashing around its wheels. The ice groaned and creaked. To the right and the left lay the victims of other days: sunken wagons with all their load, the frozen carcasses of horses—and some men and women, dead, grotesquely twisted. The girl tried to look straight ahead. But she saw it all.
>
> Soft parts of the ice had been covered with planks. But that meant little. The girl passed wagons that had broken through not more than an hour ago. There were many stops—more vehicles broke through the ice, they were being unloaded and, if possible, pulled out again. The wagon ahead of her broke through after half an hour. One of the women who had walked alongside had fallen into a hole—now they were fishing for her with poles. The coachman had cut the harness of the horses, and the dripping animals were trying to work out of the water in deadly fright. But the wagon was lost. She and those who followed drove around it.
>
> At seven o'clock Russian planes swooped down on them. They attacked farther ahead. She saw them dive, and heard the clatter of the machine guns and the dull explosions of their small bombs. There was panic, horses tore loose, distance was not kept, and a whole row of wagons broke through the overburdened ice. Some horses drowned. The shrill voices of women called for help. Some women, silent with a despair beyond all words, circled around holes in the ice that had swallowed a child, a mother, a husband. Or they ran to the next wagon and, on their knees, begged: "Please don't leave us," they whimpered, "oh, please! Please help—please don't leave us. . . ."
>
> Toward eight o'clock the shore line of the Nehrung appeared under a gray haze. But the way was still far, and the wrecks of the past days showed what toll the last stretch would take. At one point there lay so many dead people and animals that it seemed as though the sight of land had made them lose their caution and had killed them.
>
> The girl shut her eyes and dragged the horses around a crack in the ice and across a dead man's body. The horses shied. . . . It had been an old man. He had walked on two canes. She ran over him and closed her eyes again and leaned on the back of the horse.
>
> Still no respite. The north wind sprang up. The sky grew darker, its yellow tinge threatening more snow. Just as she began to distinguish the low growth of trees on the Nehrung, the snow began to fall. It fell, and quickly hid the lead wagon from her view. She heard the crack of breaking ice. But she moved on. She drove the horses forward. Once she got on a shaky floe of ice. The rear wheels broke through, but the horses pulled them out. . . .

To the right through the drifting snow, she saw the shaft of a wagon sticking upright out of the ice. The girl veered to the left, and suddenly the horses pulled ahead. Their front hooves broke through—but they touched bottom. They had reached the bank of the Nehrung.[28]

Understandably hesitant to risk such a crossing, thousands of refugees tried running the gauntlet along the coastal highways. If anything, the carnage along the crowded roads was worse than that on the ice. Wrote Robert Poensgen, a military dispatch rider:

> For kilometers on end the road was totally jammed with vehicles drawn up three and four abreast—petrol tankers, ammunition trucks, teams of horses, ambulances. It was impossible to move forwards or back. Russian combat aircraft now arrived in wave after wave, and threw bombs into that unprotected, inextricable mass. This is what hell must be like. Ammunition exploded, and burning petrol sprayed over dead, wounded and living, over men and horses. . . . It was the worst thing I have ever seen in all my years of active service—and I tell you I had already seen a lot.[29]

"Twice we were attacked by Soviet planes, swooping low and scattering missiles . . . ," remembered Guy Sajer from another road. "Each impact tore long, bloody furrows in the dense mass, and for a moment the wind was tinged with the warm smell of disemboweled bodies."[30]

"Never had I seen so many bodies . . . ," a witness added as he moved west along the coast. "Between the corpses were strewn dead horses, the overturned carts of the refugees, bogged-down military transport, burnt-out cars, weapons and equipment. . . . It was depressing enough to see the soldiers, who had nothing to eat for days and were totally exhausted, but the faces of the women were indescribable."[31]

"Demented mothers threw their children into the sea," said another horror-struck trekker. "[P]eople hanged themselves. . . . Everyone thought only of himself; no one was able to help the sick and the weak."[32]

While the butchery on land was in progress, the slaughter at sea continued. On the morning of April 13, Soviet aircraft pounced upon the refugee-laden *Karlsruhe* when the little freighter fell behind its con-

---

28. Thorwald, *Flight*, 88–89.
29. Duffy, *Red Storm*, 229.
30. Sajer, *Forgotten*, 441.
31. Duffy, 198.
32. Schieder, *Expulsion*, 135.

voy. Struck by a bomb and air torpedoes, the ship broke apart and sank in a matter of minutes. Of the one thousand people aboard, fewer than two hundred were rescued.[33]

Three days later, near midnight, torpedoes fired by a Soviet submarine exploded against the side of the *Goya*, a large transport carrying 7,000 people. Like the *Karlsruhe*, the *Goya* quickly broke in two and plunged to the bottom in four minutes. Added to the horror of those struggling in the black sea was a huge, fiery bubble bursting to the surface as the boilers exploded. When rescue ships finally reached the scene, only 183 survivors were plucked from the icy waters.[34]

Meanwhile, as the Soviets closed for the kill, Konigsberg, Memel, Gotenhafen, Pillau, and other besieged ports began their death dance. "Around me all hell broke loose," said Landser, Robert Poensgen, on the last moments of Danzig. "This whole area of the town was being thrashed by round after round of heavy and superheavy caliber. Houses broke apart like bundles of kindling, roof timbers were hurled high into the air and masonry crashed into the street. In an instant everything was shrouded in a red-brick dust. Yellow and red flames flashed and flared repeatedly through the veil."[35]

Added a comrade from Konigsberg:

> The city fell into ruins and burned. The German positions were smashed, the trenches ploughed up, embrasures leveled with the ground, companies buried, the signals system torn apart, and ammunition stores destroyed. Clouds of smoke lay over the remnants of the houses of the inner city. On the streets were strewn fragments of masonry, shot-up vehicles and the bodies of horses and human beings.[36]

In a world where smoke and fire and bombs and bullets had become the only reality, it was often the surreal that struck most Landsers during the final hours. Recalled Guy Sajer of Hela:

33. Ibid., 145.
34. Dobson, *Cruelest Night*, 166–168; Toland, *Last 100 Days*, 405.
35. Duffy, *Red Storm*, 228–229.
36. Ibid., 212.

The last victim I was to see was a dirty white horse. A Russian plane had been hit, and was disintegrating above us. We all watched as the forward part of the plane, whose racing engine gave off a long howl, plunged toward the ground. The noise terrified the animal, which slipped its collar and galloped, whinnying, toward the spot where the roaring mass of metal would land. It must have taken about three steps before it was hit. Its flesh was scattered for over fifteen yards in all directions.[37]

And within the greater overall tragedy was occurring a myriad of smaller ones. As the remnant of Danzig's defenders began withdrawing through the streets during a lull in the bombardment, dispatch riders on motorcycles led the way.

Girls from Zoppot and Danzig were sitting in some of the sidecars. They had been with the troops for some days now, and nobody objected to that. We noted the dearly beloved of the dispatch rider from the Pioneers—she was a pretty railway conductress, and he was determined to marry her at the first opportunity.

There was something sinister about the way the narrow gables of the old houses soared into the sky. They were thin, and they seemed to sway in the wind. The thought was still in my mind when someone yelled a warning from in front: "Watch out! The wall's coming down!" I saw the motor cycles buzz into confused movement in a fraction of a second, and then the wall broke into several pieces in the air and crashed on the crowd. There was a roar, a crack, a violent gust of air—and then an impenetrable cloud of dust. I stood as if paralyzed on the running board.

We all hastened to the scene of the catastrophe, where the debris lay nearly one metre deep over the motor cycles. All the soldiers were safe—for years now their reactions had been honed to lightning speed, and they had been able to leap to one side. But the girls had not moved from the sidecars and they were all buried. Cold sweat ran down our backs as we began to dig like madmen. The little Pioneer dispatch rider seemed to be out of his mind. We helped him to lift his dead bride from the sidecar. With extreme care he proceeded to wash her face, which was covered with a thick layer of dust.[38]

As the end neared, small, scattered units attempted to break out. Remembered one officer:

Every company was furnished with guides who knew the ground. It later transpired that they were useless, for local knowledge ceased to be any help in

37. Sajer, 452–453,
38. Duffy, 229–230.

the inferno which had once been the inner city. . . . Ghostly lunar landscapes came into being in place of the great avenues which used to lead through the city. Paths could be reconnoitered, and just an hour later they were impassable. There was a continual crashing from the impact of bombs, shells, and heavy Katusha rockets, while the remaining facades of the buildings collapsed into the streets and the ground was torn up by mighty bomb craters.[39]

While some soldiers and civilians were rescued by small craft still daring the coastline, others quickly fashioned rafts of tires, boards and anything that would float. Many more, however, died fighting among the ruins or were slaughtered on the beaches. As the cities burned and as Russian troops moved in, Soviet loudspeakers—between soothing blasts of waltz music—called on Germans to surrender quietly, promising food, freedom and safety.[40] At the same time, millions of leaflets signed by Ilya Ehrenburg, fluttered down on the Russians: "SOLDIERS OF THE RED ARMY! KILL THE GERMANS! KILL ALL GERMANS! KILL! KILL! KILL!"[41]

Like everyone else, Anna Schwartz was huddled in her basement when Danzig finally fell.

> In the following calm we heard the Russian panzer rolling in, and the first cheers of the Russian soldiers. Shortly afterwards Russian soldiers were heard coming down the steps of the cellar. The first Russian soldiers stood in front of us, and the first word we heard from them was: "Urr!" "Urr!" There was a stink of alcohol, sweat and dirty uniforms. After they had robbed us of our watches, with machine-pistols in their hands, they hastily disappeared into the next cellar, and did the same there. After five minutes the next two came, and so it continued, until we had no more jewelry, and the contents of our trunks had been turned upside down.
>
> In the meantime we heard the shrieks of women, who were being raped by Mongols. Suddenly a Russian officer appeared and called upon us in broken German, to leave the cellar at once. As quickly as we could, we took hold of our trunks and rucksacks, which had been searched over and over again, and rushed

39. Ibid., 213–214.
40. Schieder, *Expulsion*, 178.
41. Duffy, 274.

into the yard, which was full of guns and soldiers. All around the houses were burning, shells were exploding, and . . . wounded people and horses were screaming.[42]

After the fall of Konigsberg, Hans Graf von Lehndorff courageously held to his post as hospital surgeon. When Red soldiers burst into the building, bedlam erupted as the frenzy for watches and jewelry began.

The arrival of the first officers destroyed my last hopes of coming to tolerable terms. Any attempt to talk to them failed. Even for them I am only a coat rack with pockets; they see me only from the shoulders downward. A few nurses who got in their way were seized and dragged off and then released again thoroughly disheveled before they realized what was happening. The older nurses were the first victims. They wandered aimlessly along the corridors, but there was no place to hide, and new tormentors kept pouncing upon them.[43]

As terrible as the situation seemed, it was trivial compared to what occurred when the Russians discovered a distillery near the hospital. Dr. von Lehndorff:

They burst in here from the factory in crowds—officers, soldiers, riflewomen, all drunk. And not a chance of hiding anybody from them, because the whole neighborhood was lit up as bright as day by the burning buildings. . . . Now something like a tide of rats flowed over us, worse than all the plagues of Egypt together. Not a moment went by but the barrel of an automatic was rammed against my back or my belly, and a grimacing mask yelled at me for sulfa. Apparently most of these devils have got venereal disease. . . . On all sides we heard the desperate screams of women: "Shoot me then! Shoot me!" But the tormentors preferred a wrestling match to any actual use of their guns.

Soon none of the women had any strength left to resist. In a few hours a change came over them: their spirit died, you heard hysterical laughter which made the Russians even more excited. . . . [A] major who seemed to be still relatively reasonable, sent for me. . . . Thirty to forty Russians were rampaging among the patients. I was to tell him who these people were. Sick people, of course, what else? But what sort of sick people, he wanted to know. Well, all sorts; scarlet fever, typhus, diphtheria. . . . He gave a yell and hurled himself like a tank among his men. But he was too late; when the tumult had subsided, four women were already dead.[44]

---

42. Schieder, 178.
43. Von Lehndorff, *Token of a Covenant*, 71.
44. Ibid., 78–79.

When the hospital caught fire, von Lehndorff and his staff began evacuation.

> Soon the whole hillside was occupied by patients, and the Russians were rushing wildly among them like a horde of baboons, carrying off indiscriminately nurses or patients, harassing them and demanding watches for the hundredth time. . . . I shouldered again a rather heavy man, and had just crossed the footbridge when I was stopped by a Russian. . . . I had to drop the man. The Russian ransacked him, then shot him in the belly as if by mistake, and went on. The man sat there, looking at me, an inquiry in his eyes. If only I could have given him the finishing shot! I gave him a dose of morphine and left him lying by the side of the road.[45]

At night, the horror increased tenfold as the drunken mob went on a rampage of murder and rape.

"Grandma is too old," Klara Seidler pleaded when a young soldier forced her into a telephone booth.

"Grandmother must!" said the rapist over and over.

Near the booth, a young mother was grabbed as she tried to slip her three children into a cellar. When the children began screaming, a huge soldier hurled them headfirst into a wall, one after the other. Despite her own torture, Klara Seidler would never forget the sound of little skulls being crushed.

When the rapists left, Klara and other women tried in vain to shield the hysterical mother as another gang appeared. The shrieking woman was thrown down and one after another the soldiers continued the attack.[46]

Soon after the fall of Danzig, hundreds of women and girls pleaded with an officer for protection. The Russian pointed to a Catholic cathedral. After the females were safely inside, the officer yelled to his men, motioned to the church, and with bells ringing and organ pipes roaring the horror continued all night. Some women inside were raped more than thirty times.

"They even violated eight-year-old girls and shot boys who tried to shield their mothers," groaned a priest.[47]

---

45. Ibid., 83, 85.
46. Toland, 302.
47. Keeling, *Gruesome Harvest*, 58.

The bloody nightmare which enveloped the Baltic coast was neither more nor less than that which transpired wherever the Soviets occupied German soil. In many places—Silesia, Prussia, Pomerania, the German communities of Czechoslovakia, Rumania, Hungary, Jugoslavia—the horror had been in progress for weeks. There, the ghastly atrocities had abated little, if any, with the passage of time and to some it seemed as though Red soldiers were in a race with one another to see who could destroy, murder and, above all, rape the most. Some women and children were assaulted ten, twenty, even thirty times a night and for a female to be ravished one hundred times a week was not uncommon.

"One could hardly any longer call it raping . . . ," a victim moaned. "[T]he women were passive instruments."[48]

Thousands, of course, died from hemorrhaging and many who survived looked, acted and felt "like zombies." There was no reprieve for anyone, living or dead. "Russian soldiers even went so far as to violate some of the female corpses that lay in the mortuary at the cemetery prior to burial," revealed one clergyman from Rosenberg.[49]

Desperate to save her little child from further assault, one frantic mother begged a commanding officer for mercy. "He asked to see the girl," wrote a witness, "and when she appeared, he, too, raped her, and then sent her home."[50]

"Our fellows were so sex-starved," a Russian major laughed, "that they often raped old women of sixty, or seventy or even eighty—much to these grandmothers' surprise, if not downright delight. But I admit it was a nasty business, and the record of the Kazakhs and other Asiatic troops was particularly bad."[51]

Of all things German, nothing—not even the Nazi Party—aroused greater hatred among hard-core communists than the Christian religion, particularly the Catholic Church. Relates a priest from Grottkau:

---

48. Schieder, *Expulsion*, 257.
49. Kaps, *Silesia*, 173.
50. Ibid., 184.
51. DeZayas, *Nemesis at Potsdam*, 69.

He was utterly godless and the sight of my priest's robe apparently infuriated him. He kept insisting that I deny the existence of God and, seizing hold of my breviary, threw it onto the floor. Finally, he dragged me out into the street and pushed me against a wall in order to shoot me. . . . He had just placed me against the wall when all the men, women and children, who had been sheltering in the house . . . appeared on the scene. They stood around us, pale and terrified. Thereupon he began to scatter the crowd by shooting at random in every direction. When he and I were finally alone once more he pointed his revolver at me, but it was empty. He started reloading it, but whilst he was doing so, two other officers, who had apparently heard the shots, came into sight. They rushed up to him and snatched the revolver from his grasp. . . . [then] dragged him away.[52]

"He stood at the altar like a lord and eyed us triumphantly," a priest from another church remembered.

Then he ordered our old vicar to go outside with him. After a quarter of an hour they returned. The expression on the vicar's face was dreadful. He collapsed in front of the altar, muttering, "Shoot me, but shoot me here, at the altar. I refuse to leave the altar!"—The nuns screamed, "Don't shoot! Don't shoot!" The Russian grinned, triumphant in his power and strength. With a lordly gesture he walked away from the vicar.[53]

Lucky in these cases, most clergymen were not so fortunate. Many died in the prescribed Marxist manner: Bullet to the neck and skull bashed to bits.[54] For some Soviets, nuns were an especial target of debasement. Reveals a priest from Klosterbrueck:

They had been tortured and raped by officers for several hours. Finally they returned, their faces swollen and beaten black and blue. . . . [At] the neighboring village. . . . the Russians made all the nuns assemble in one room. Some of the younger nuns had managed to hide in the nick of time, in the water-cistern up in the attic. The rest of them were treated in a dreadful manner. They tried to defend themselves, but it was of no avail. They were brutally raped by the Russians,—even the oldest nuns, who were eighty. For four hours the Russians ransacked the house, behaving like wild animals. In the morning they then boasted in the village that there were no longer any virgins at the convent.[55]

52. Kaps, 211–212.
53. Ibid., 182.
54. Ibid., 528.
55. Ibid., 184–185.

"The nuns were completely exhausted when they came back. . . . We all sat there huddled together in one small room and prayed . . . ," wrote a witness from another parish. "Again and again we heard heavy footsteps approaching, and Russians came and went. At about midnight a new lot of fiends entered the room. They kicked those who had lain down on the floor in order to get a little rest; they fired shots at the ceiling, and tore the nuns' hoods off their heads. I shall never forget the terrible screams of the women and children."[56]

Like their lay sisters, nuns were raped with such sadistic regularity that some simply stopped praying. But most did not.

> Suddenly he dealt the priest a savage blow on the head, making it bleed. Thereupon the Russian became even more enraged; he rushed up to some of the nuns, ripped their garments, and began beating them with his sword. Finally he dragged one of the young nuns into a corner in order to rape her. There was nothing we could do, but pray to the Lord that she would be spared. Suddenly the door near the altar opened and a tall, young officer appeared. He immediately realized what was happening, ran towards the back of the chapel, seized hold of the other officer, threw him to the floor like a sack of flour, put his foot on his chest, and tore the sword out of his clutches. Then he called to two soldiers, and they picked up the old officer and threw him out of the chapel as if he were a log of wood. He turned to us and told us that we need no longer fear lest the man returned, and said that he would post guards in front of the chapel.[57]

As the case above makes clear, it was the confusing contradictions displayed by the Russian Army that proved most horrifying to Germans. Like some large, wild animal, victims could never be certain of its reaction in any given situation. Indeed, even in their most dire distress many Germans took note of these perplexing paradoxes. Within the span of a day, an hour, or just a few minutes, a German family might encounter the extremes of the Russian Army—from the correct, considerate captain who never drank and played perfect Chopin on the parlor piano to the bellowing, drunken major who entered a short time later and destroyed not only the piano but the

---

56. Ibid., 439.
57. Ibid., 183.

parlor as well. And even among individual soldiers themselves was a seeming jumble of contradictions. Described by their countrymen, Tolstoy and Dostojevsky, as "grown-up children ... totally unreliable in their thinking and acting," the incredible mood swings of the average Russian soldier was indeed terrifying to behold.[58]

"They are all like that," a farmer's wife insisted, shaking her head in disbelief. "They change from friend to foe from one second to another and become different people."[59]

Indeed, the same soldier who could brutally beat, bite, and rape a pleading mother could the next moment gently stroke and cuddle her infant. While many rapists were not discomfited in the least by a crying, screaming child, most were.

"They were shoving Fraulein Behn before them into the bedroom," one woman wrote, "when suddenly, catching sight of the baby and the four-year-old ... asleep together in the cot, they stopped short. 'Leetle child?' said one of them in German, clearly taken by surprise. For fully a minute the two soldiers stared at the cot, then slowly, on tiptoe, withdrew from the apartment."[60]

It was also noted by many that a sick child was often all that stood between a mother and rape. Most Russians displayed genuine affection for German children, feeding them, playing with them and granting concessions that would have meant certain death for adults. When little boys in a village were threatened by Soviet officials with summary execution if caught pilfering any more coal from railway cars, the orders apparently never reached the guards.

"[W]hen they saw the boys arrive with their wagons," said a viewer, "they turned their backs on them and kicked the coal down with their feet for the boys to pick up."[61]

"She has discovered that her little blond cherub-daughter never fails to delight the soldiers," recorded Regina Shelton of a friend. "While keeping her close, she permits the child to be talked to and cuddled by the strange men. Whether a national trait, as some claim, or sim-

---

58. Schieder, *Expulsion*, 228.
59. Horstmann, *We Chose to Stay*, 139.
60. Anonymous, *A Woman in Berlin*, 170.
61. Chadwick, *The War According to Anna*, 124.

ply the longing of lonely men for their families, no Russian we meet or hear about hurts this or any other child."[62]

Sadly, this was not entirely true. As countless tiny corpses attested, innocence was no assurance of safety. "Mrs. K. has lost her little girl, Gretel, who was nine," a Silesian priest reported. "She was shot by the Russians because she tried to protect her mother from being raped."[63]

Next to their mania for wristwatches, the novelty most sought by Soviets was the bicycle. Despite the chaos and horror all around, some Germans stared in disbelief as Russians "discovered" this strange new device.

"[T]hey seized every bicycle in the village," said a spectator, "but didn't know how to ride, fell off, and tried again until one corporal in a fit of rage smashed his machine to junk. Suddenly the rest followed him in an orgy of wheel smashing, and they left a mountain of wrecked bicycles on the street."[64]

"It was quite amusing," another observer added, "to watch them get on a bicycle, fall off, pick themselves up off the ground, and then seize hold of the bicycle, throw it down in a rage, and kick it."[65]

Though frustrated and angry, simple soldiers returned again and again in their efforts to master the machine. Noted one viewer: "To ride them was as blissful for these men as a new mechanical toy is to a child. They shouted with delight when all went well, and yelled in distress when they fell off or rode at full speed into a wall. No bicycle was safe from their clutches, and as there were not enough to go around, they fought over them amongst themselves."[66]

From their first step into the Reich, Russians were awed by the abundance. As often noted, many German women initially escaped rape by hiding in attics. Knowing only the mud and stick huts of their primitive homeland, some Soviets were frightened by stairs. Prowling below, however, Red troops entered a world they had hardly conceived of.

62. Shelton, *To Lose a War*, 110.
63. Kaps, *Silesia*, 247.
64. March, *Darkness Over Europe*, 242.
65. Kaps, 283.
66. Horstmann, *We Chose to Stay*, 104.

"Why you war?" an incredulous Russian asked of a German. "In Germany is everything. Here more to be taken out of one house than in our country out of whole village!"[67]

"Every drawer was full of things!" added a stunned comrade.[68]

The great number of automobiles, tractors, motorcycles, washing machines, stoves, mixers, radios, and other common articles of the modern world were beyond the comprehension of many Soviets. Even electricity and plumbing were a source of wonder. Some soldiers pried spigots from German kitchens, innocently assuming that they simply had to pound them into walls at home to receive running water. Others delicately packed light bulbs, eager to carry the magic back to their villages. Many Russians refused to believe that a toilet bowl was used for anything other than washing potatoes.

"[A]ll of us, officers and men, saw the riches and prosperity of a capitalist country and couldn't believe our eyes. We had never believed there could be such an abundance of goods," admitted one soldier.[69]

Aware that such wealth would have a profound impact on their men—and stir suspicions—commissars explained that all the property had been stolen from other people in other lands.[70] Only the simplest Red soldier accepted such words. Remembered Lali Horstmann: "'In Russia only men at the top have everything, we nothing,' he said, violently striking the table. 'Many others think as I do; if you repeat this, I will be shot,' he continued in a lower voice, looking around. Though he knew no other system than Communism, he was a human being."[71]

It was this cold, cruel reality, perhaps—more than motives of revenge or propaganda—which explained the plague-like destruction that swept eastern Germany. Not enough to murder, rape and plunder, the angry Red Army seemed bent on effacing everything it touched in recompense for the treatment it had received at the hands of its own government.[72] Homes lucky enough to escape the torch were com-

---

67. Kaps, *Silesia*, 148.
68. Anonymous, *A Woman in Berlin*, 237.
69. Elliott, *Pawns of Yalta*, 165.
70. Schieder, *Expulsion*, 229.
71. Horstmann, 138.
72. Howard Johnstone manuscript (Maple Hill, Kansas).

monly destroyed or defiled in a most revolting manner. When Erika Hansen's mother and sisters returned to their house in Schoeneiche, they were greeted by "a devastating stench that took their breath away."

"Human excrement had been smeared all over the walls . . . ," Erika noted in disgust. "Furniture had been smashed and parts had been dumped out of the windows. . . . Trash and dirt covered every room as if a tornado had roared through."[73]

When one Silesian pastor decided to assess the damage done to a local convent and church, he discovered "complete havoc."

> I walked through the empty rooms; all the bedding had been slit to pieces and feathers lay strewn all over the floor. Books, damaged beyond use, had been scattered about the rooms, and the Russians had poured syrup and preserves over them and, as if to add the crowning touch to the civilization they had brought us, had even covered them with human excrements. Incidentally, this description could be applied to every house in the town.[74]

The devastation on the countryside was fully as great as that in the towns. Indeed, the wave that rolled over the landscape was a blight of Biblical proportions. Barns were burned, grain destroyed, even orchards and nurseries were chopped down or deliberately flattened by armored vehicles. Relates a Russian soldier: "A lieutenant unsheathed a knife, walked up to a cow, and struck her a death-blow at the base of the skull. The cow's legs folded under, and she fell, while the rest of the herd, bellowing madly, stampeded and ran away. The officer wiped the sharp edge on his boots and said: 'My father wrote to me that the Germans had taken a cow from us. Now we are even.'"[75]

Like a machine out of control, the Red Army transferred its rage and hatred to everything it touched. "I recognized a great number of East Prussian horses harnessed to wagons and with riders on their backs," recalled a German prisoner. "The horses had become quite spiritless, used to the abominable paces forced upon them—a high-stepping trot changing into a furious gallop. It was torture to hear them

---

73. Hansen, "A Woman's Odyssey," 162.
74. Kaps, 424.
75. Duffy, Red Storm, 274.

tearing past on the paved road, heads jerked backwards, mouths torn and bleeding."[76]

Nothing escaped the fury. Continues the same witness: "A stork, probably just coming back from the south, was fired at with automatics by the Russians leading our group. Astonished, the bird rose into the air and winged its way towards Gross Germau which lay before us on a small hill. Over the village a volley of a hundred shots brought it down like a stone."[77]

Even carp ponds were dynamited and the fish left to rot. "Nothing is guiltless," proclaimed Comrade Ehrenburg in leaflets showering down on the front. "Kill, Kill, Kill!"

Of all the methods used to express its anger, the Red Army said it best with rape. From eight to eighty, healthy or ill, indoors or out, in fields, on sidewalks, against walls, the spiritual massacre of German women continued unabated. When even violated corpses could no longer be of use, sticks, iron bars and telephone receivers were commonly rammed up their vaginas.[78]

"This sort of thing," wrote a witness, "soon occurred to such an extent that it made many of the Soviet officers shudder."[79]

"Shudder" though many Red officers undoubtedly did, most lacked either the moral, physical or political authority to stop it. With no rules or regulations, no laws or discipline, the most depraved of the depraved had a field day, transforming their sadistic fantasies into fact. When Soviet soldiers captured the city of Neustettin in February 1945, they discovered several large camps of the Women's Reich Labor Service, an organization composed mostly of girls who worked on various projects from nursing to street repair. A young citizen of Brazil, nineteen-year-old Leonora Cavoa, was a member of one group. Because her coun-

76. Von Lehndorff, *Token of a Covenant*, 108.
77. Ibid., 96.
78. Lutz, "Rape of Christian Europe," 15; McKee, *Dresden 1945*, 281.
79. Thorwald, *Flight in the Winter*, 55.

try was on good terms with the Allies, Leonora was accorded special treatment by the commissar in charge. When her camp of five hundred girls was transferred to an old iron foundry, Leonora led the way.

The Commissar was very polite to us and assigned us to the foreign workers' barracks of the factory. But the allocated space was too small for all of us, and so I went to speak to the Commissar about it. He said that it was, after all, only a temporary arrangement, and offered that I could come into the typists' office if it was too crowded for me—which I gladly accepted. He immediately warned me to avoid any further contact with the others, as these were members of an illegal army. My protests that this was not true were cut off with the remark that if I ever said anything like that ever again, I would be shot.

Suddenly I heard loud screams, and immediately two Red Army soldiers brought in five girls. The Commissar ordered them to undress. When they refused out of modesty, he ordered me to do it to them, and for all of us to follow him. We crossed the yard to the former works kitchen, which had been completely cleared out except for a few tables on the window side. It was terribly cold, and the poor girls shivered. In the large, tiled room some Russians were waiting for us, making remarks that must have been very obscene, judging from how everything they said drew gales of laughter. The Commissar told me to watch and learn how to turn the Master Race into whimpering bits of misery.

Now two Poles came in, dressed only in trousers, and the girls cried out at their sight. They quickly grabbed the first of the girls, and bent her backwards over the edge of the table until her joints cracked. I was close to passing out as one of them took his knife and, before the very eyes of the other girls, cut off her right breast. He paused for a moment, then cut off the other side. I have never heard anyone scream as desperately as that girl. After this operation he drove his knife into her abdomen several times, which again was accompanied by the cheers of the Russians.

The next girl cried for mercy, but in vain—it even seemed that the gruesome deed was done particularly slowly because she was especially pretty. The other three had collapsed, they cried for their mothers and begged for a quick death, but the same fate awaited them as well. The last of them was still almost a child, with barely developed breasts. They literally tore the flesh off her ribs until the white bones showed.

Another five girls were brought in. They had been carefully chosen this time, all of them were well-developed and pretty. When they saw the bodies of their predecessors they began to cry and scream. Weakly, they tried desperately to defend themselves, but it did them no good as the Poles grew ever more cruel. They sliced the body of one of them open lengthwise and poured in a can of machine oil, which they tried to light. A Russian shot one of the other girls in the genitals before they cut off her breasts.

Loud howls of approval began when someone brought a saw from a tool chest. This was used to tear up the breasts of the other girls, which soon caused the floor to be awash in blood. The Russians were in a blood frenzy. More girls were being brought in continually.

I saw these grisly proceedings as through a red haze. Over and over again I heard the terrible screams when the breasts were tortured, and the loud groans at the mutilation of the genitals. . . . [I]t was always the same, the begging for mercy, the high-pitched scream when the breasts were cut and the groans when the genitals were mutilated. The slaughter was interrupted several times to sweep the blood out of the room and clear away the bodies. . . . When my knees buckled I was forced onto a chair. The Commissar always made sure that I was watching, and when I had to throw up they even paused in their tortures. One girl had not undressed completely, she may also have been a little older than the others, who were around seventeen years of age. They soaked her bra with oil and set in on fire, and while she screamed, a thin iron rod was shoved into her vagina until it came out her navel.

In the yard entire groups of girls were clubbed to death after the prettiest of them had been selected for this torture. The air was filled with the death cries of many hundred girls.[80]

In addition to the five hundred victims at the iron works, an estimated 2,000 other girls in the camps of Neustettin suffered a similar fate.[81]

And yet, as beastly and depraved as many crimes were, the average Soviet soldier remained an enigma. For every act of savagery, the Russian seemed capable of bestowing a kindness. "It is necessary, in order to understand all this," explained one man, "to have experienced, how a Russian soldier shared his last bread with German children, or how a Russian driver loaded an old woman, without being requested to do so, on his truck, and brought her home with her half broken-up hand-cart. But it is also necessary to have experienced, how the same man lay in ambush in a cemetery, in order to attack women and girls, and to plunder and rape them. Such things happened daily."[82]

"Always the extremes," added another victim. "Either 'Woman, come!' and excrement in the living room, or refined manners and bowings."[83]

80. Testimony of Leonora Cavoa Geier, *Deutschland-Journal*, April 23, 1965, issue 17, p. 7 (copy in possession of the author).
81. Ibid.
82. Schieder, *Expulsion*, 228.
83. Anonymous, *A Woman in Berlin*, 237.

The fate of a priest at Ritterswalde was the fate experienced by thousands of Germans:

> [T]hey treated us quite kindly. Two Russian soldiers then came back again to the chapel, offered us cigarettes, and sat down near to the altar. I remained standing in front of the altar, and we tried to converse with each other in a mixture of Polish, Russian, and German. Suddenly, however, a third Russian appeared in the doorway, caught sight of me, and aimed his revolver at me. One bullet hit me in the lung and the other caught me in the thigh. I collapsed in front of the altar.[84]

Understandably, many Germans, like the man above, found "life" in such an unpredictable world unbearable. As a consequence, many exercised the only option left.

"Father, I can't go on living!" one woman muttered to her priest. "Thirty of them raped me last night."[85]

Many times, clergymen like the above could thwart suicides, which in some towns carried off a quarter of the population. In most cases, however, they could not.

"We screamed, we begged them to leave us in peace," said a rape victim in Striegau, "but they showed us no mercy. We resolved to end our lives."

> Everyone had a knife and a piece of rope. Frau P. was first. Young Frau K. hanged her daughter and then herself. Her dear mother did the same with her sister. Now only two of us remained. I asked her to fix my rope for I was too upset to do it. Then we embraced one more time and kicked the luggage away on which we had stood. I, however, could touch the floor with my toes . . . the rope was too long. I tried over and over—I wanted to die. I looked to the right and to the left, we hung in a row. They were well off, they were dead. As for me, I had no choice but to free myself from the rope.[86]

Though not by their own hand, other determined women surrendered to suicide just as surely.

> [A] big Russian came in. He did not utter a single word, but looked around the room and then went to the back where all the young girls and women were

---

84. Kaps, *Silesia*, 258.
85. Ibid., 438.
86. Sorge, *Other Price*, 129.

sitting. He beckoned once with his finger to my sister. As she did not stand up at once, he went close up to her and held his machine pistol against her chin. Everyone screamed aloud, but my sister sat mutely there and was incapable of moving. Then a shot resounded. Her head fell to the side and the blood streamed out. She was dead instantly, without uttering a single sound. The bullet had gone from her chin to her brain and her skull was completely shattered. The Russian looked at us all, and went away again.[87]

Meanwhile, in what remained of the Reich, most Germans still knew surprisingly little of the savage fate befalling their countrymen. Doubters yet attributed the hair-raising reports of genocide to Dr. Goebbels's propaganda machine. By bits and pieces, however, the truth did emerge. When a small German counterattack temporarily recaptured Neustettin, young soldiers, unaware of the Russian rampage occurring behind the lines, began herding up their prisoners. "Then something unexpected happened," remembered an astonished Landser.

Several German women ran towards the Russians and stabbed at them with cutlery forks and knives. . . . [I]t was not until I fired a submachine gun into the air that the women drew back, and cursed us for presuming to protect these animals. They urged us to go into the houses and take a look at what they had done there. We did so, a few of us at a time, and we were totally devastated. We had never seen anything like it—utterly, unbelievably monstrous!

Naked, dead women lay in many of the rooms. Swastikas had been cut into their abdomens, in some the intestines bulged out, breasts were cut up, faces beaten to a pulp and swollen puffy. Others had been tied to the furniture by their hands and feet, and massacred. A broomstick protruded from the vagina of one, a besom from that of another. . . .

The mothers had had to witness how their ten and twelve-year-old daughters were raped by some 20 men; the daughters in turn saw their mothers being raped, even their grandmothers. Women who tried to resist were brutally tortured to death. There was no mercy. . . .

The women we liberated were in a state almost impossible to describe. . . . [T]heir faces had a confused, vacant look. Some were beyond speaking to, ran up and down and moaned the same sentences over and over again. Having seen the consequences of these bestial atrocities, we were terribly agitated and determined to fight. We knew the war was past winning; but it was our obligation and sacred duty to fight to the last bullet.[88]

---

87. Schieder, Expulsion, 145–146.
88. Testimony of "H. K.", Bergisch-Gladbach, Germany (copy in possession of the author).

6

THE LAST BULLET

WHILE THE END OF Nazi Germany loomed in the east, the end also steadily advanced from the west. Unlike the howling savagery to the east, fraught with nightmarish ferocity, defeat in the west came methodically, inexorably and, judged by the standards of the east, almost silently.

Following its devastating defeat during the Ardennes offensive of December 1944, the Wehrmacht withdrew and regrouped behind the "west wall," a mostly imaginary line that roughly traced the Reich's western border. There, as elsewhere, the German Army was a dim shadow of its former self, vastly outnumbered in men and materiel, but above all, totally overwhelmed in the air.

"We felt powerless before the immeasurable material superiority of the Americans, without which the Russians and British would have capitulated long since . . . ," revealed one German officer.[1]

Nevertheless, the hard-pressed Landser was still more than a match for the American "GI" and the British "Tommy." Whenever the two sides met on anything approaching equal numbers, the results were always the same.[2] Defending its homeland reinvigorated the German Army, of course, but during the fighting in Italy and North Africa, the outcome was similar. Asked his opinion of American troops during the fighting in North Africa—a campaign where Germany's ally, the Italian Army, had scattered and surrendered like sheep—one cap-

---

1. Woltersdorf, *Gods of War*, 121.
2. Fussell, *Wartime*, 123; J. D. Morelock, *Generals of the Ardennes* (Washington, D.C. : National Defense University Press, 1994), 21–22.

tive Landser told his US interrogators bluntly: "The Americans are to us what the Italians are to you."[3]

Though American commanders were understandably outraged by such sentiment, the panic created among Allied ranks during the Ardennes offensive only reinforced this assessment within the German Army. One reason for the Landser's low opinion of his American adversary could simply be attributed to lack of experience. Sights and sounds that many German soldiers had long since become accustomed to were terrifying novelties to most GIs. Remembered a British sergeant:

> The Americans will bunch, whereas we go up two sides of a road. . . . They were shouting at each other and firing at nothing. . . . It appeared that the American infantrymen were not trained in "battle noises." They seemed to drop to the ground and fire, whenever shots were heard close by. When passing a burning farmhouse, there was a sound of what appeared to be a machine-gun; no one could have been in the house, because of the flames, and it was obviously ammunition burning; but it took some time to get the Americans up and on again. As we [proceeded] I saw a figure in a long German greatcoat rise to his feet from the center of a field, and walk towards us with his hands up. The man was Volkssturm, about 50 or 60 years of age, a long, thin chap. Before we could do anything about it, three Americans let fly with their carbines and the figure fell. God, we were angry.[4]

While small arms fire was frightening, green US troops found artillery barrages utterly horrifying.

"[S]hells would not only tear and rip the body," said one frantic American, "they tortured one's mind almost beyond the brink of sanity."[5]

"[T]he pure physical terror that savages you when loud and violent death is screaming down from the sky and pounding the earth around you, smashing and pulping everything in search for you" was, a comrade added, "emasculating."[6]

Recalled another American newcomer:

> I asked [the sergeant] if he was hit and he sort of smiled and said no, he had just pissed his pants. He always pissed them, he said, when things started and then

3.   Fussell, 123.
4.   Strawson, *Battle for Berlin*, 100.
5.   Fussell, 278.
6.   Ibid.

he was okay. He wasn't making any apologies either, and then I realized something wasn't quite right with me. . . . There was something warm down there and it seemed to be running down my leg. . . . I told the sarge. I said, "Sarge, I've pissed too," or something like that and he grinned and said, "Welcome to the war."[7]

Accustomed to the bloodless "clean" kills of Hollywood, sudden, hideous sights also worked to unman the average American novice. After taking direct hits, some saw their buddies vaporize in a spray of "red spots." Others viewed comrades laying along roads, nothing more than "half a body, just naked buttocks and the legs."[8] With the war obviously nearing its end, and with sights like the above vivid in their minds, few GIs "went looking for a Purple Heart." Also, and as was the case in 1917, many American soldiers suffered what some observers called "spiritual emptiness"; a seeming uncertainty as to what exactly they were fighting for . . . or against.

Despite years of anti-Nazi propaganda and attempts to demonize the German soldier, front-line troops, as always, were first to discard hate. From released or escaped prisoners, it soon became apparent that Allied POWs were treated well and accorded all the rights of the Geneva Convention. Additionally, details that were seemingly trivial matters to politicians, propagandists and rear-echelon troops were all-important concerns to the actual fighters.

"One thing I'll say for the Germans," a British Tommy admitted, "they were better than we were with enemy dead; buried them properly and neatly with their equipment . . . over the crosses."[9]

Not surprisingly, "understandings" among the adversaries were quickly reached to make the war more tolerable to both parties. "We maintained very friendly communications with the Germans . . . ," confessed an American major. "Before they shelled Homberg they would let us know in advance the exact time. Before we shelled Leverkusen we would let the Germans know in advance. So everybody took cover ahead and nobody got hurt."[10] On countless other occasions front-line troops met, mixed, traded trinkets, even socialized.

7. Ibid.
8. Ibid., 272.
9. Strawson, *Berlin*, 101.
10. Douglas Botting, *From the Ruins of the Reich* (New York: Crown, 1985), 6.

In more than one instance, drunken American, British and German soldiers found themselves rioting together in the same bars and brothels and even standing in the same lines to use the same restrooms.[11]

Such incidents as the above had a way of putting an all-too human face on the "evil Hun." The same factors which worked on Allied attitudes of the German worked on German attitudes of the Allies. Unlike the East Front, German soldiers were well aware that their foe in the west were signatories of the Geneva Convention. Under this agreement, Landsers were guaranteed by law the status of POW upon capture or surrender. And like their Allied counterparts, with the end of war in sight, many "Jerrys" along the West Wall were unwilling to play hero. "I am neither looking for an Iron Cross," a German soldier declared, "nor a wooden one." Also, it was no secret that Landsers, high and low, considered the Western Allies the lesser of two evils. With the Red Army roaring across Germany from the east, many Germans were secretly hoping the Americans might occupy what remained of the Reich before the communists did.

Nevertheless, and although the war in the west was not characterized by the same "do or die" determination as it was in the east, thousands of patriotic German officers and men were committed to defend their homeland to the "last ditch." As the Americans and British pressed the Wehrmacht back from the West Wall, then over the Rhine, a glimpse at the task faced is given by an English officer from the town of Rees:

> They had been chased out of France, Belgium and Holland, into Germany, back over the Rhine, and now street by street across Rees into a corner. Yet they were still fighting it out.... The situation now was that the enemy were confined to the last hundred yards, at the very tip of the east end, but they were in a strong position with deep trenches and concrete and any attempts to get at it were met by heavy fire. I was going to make a last effort with C Company, when in came four or five prisoners, including a captain, who said he was in command. ... He was marched in front of me as I sat at my table poring over the map, and he gave me a spectacular Hitler salute which I ignored.... He was a nasty piece of work, cocksure and good-looking in a flashy sort of way, but I had to admire the brave resistance which he had put up. The strain of battle was apparent in the dark black chasms under his eyes.[12]

---

11. Ibid., 7; Interview with Walter B. Delge, Sr., Lecompton, Kansas, July, 1975.
12. Strawson, 98–99.

THE LAST BULLET
165

In spite of such fierce resistance, the massive weight of the Allied advance slowly ground all opposition into the mud. "[I]t must be stated that the morale of our men [in the west] is slowly sinking . . . ," admitted propaganda minister Joseph Goebbels. "[T]hey have now been fighting uninterruptedly for weeks and months. Somewhere the physical strength to resist runs out."[13]

If morale among troops was "slowly sinking," that of many civilians in the west had long since sunk. After enduring years of air attacks and now invasion, some Germans were more than willing to accept defeat. Unlike the terrified trekkers to the east, relatively few Germans in the west abandoned their homes. Despite the best efforts of Nazi propaganda, the racial and cultural ties with the Western Allies, particularly the Americans, was simply too strong to arouse the same depth of fear as did the Soviets. Hardly was there a German family that did not have at least one close relative in America and most felt that there was an essential goodness in any people who could give to the world a Mickey Mouse, Shirley Temple or Laurel and Hardy. Far from fleeing the advancing Allies, many civilians actually ran to greet them. Remembered a young German:

> [O]ne very sunny morning we saw across the fields a convoy of vehicles coming, and as they came closer we saw they were Americans, with little white stars on the side. There was a jeep up front and then tanks and troops carriers, and the bloke in the jeep had both his hands up, and in one hand he had a loaf of bread and in the other a lump of cheese. They came on very slowly . . . and as they came the Home Guard threw down their weapons and rushed toward the Americans, and my mother leapt up and started racing over the fields, with me about two hundred yards behind her, straight toward the American column. The man in the jeep turned out to be a very fat American sergeant, and my mother threw her arms around his neck and kissed him and hugged him in absolute joy and relief. It was all over.[14]

"Wherever we drove through the Rhineland those first weeks in April the feelings of the German people were unmistakable," reported war correspondent, Leonard Mosley.

13. Hugh Trevor-Roper, ed., *Final Entries, 1945* (New York: G.P. Putnam's Sons, 1978), 67.
14. Botting, *Ruins of the Reich*, 18.

The war was not yet over but they knew it was lost, and they were engaged in an instinctive effort to save something from the wreck. The mass of the people were casting off National Socialism like an old coat, almost without grief or regret, determined to forget it and to work to recreate, in cooperation with their conquerors, the things that had now been destroyed. . . . The men and women we stopped on the streets to ask the way were polite and helpful; they gathered round in bunches when they heard us speaking German, and bombarded us with questions: "How far had we advanced? When would the war be over? Where were the Russians?"[15]

When reports from recaptured towns and villages stated that Americans had treated civilians well and had not even engaged in looting, the desire among other Germans to surrender became overwhelming. Home Guard units were disbanded, white flags sprouted from doors and windows and many communities refused to aid the German Army in any way.

"Twice," recalled a British POW, "I watched an SS corporal go to a house and ask for water and each time the housewife, having seen his uniform, slammed the door in his face. He meekly retreated."[16]

In a desperate bid to shore up crumbling resistance, Dr. Goebbels's propaganda office warned citizens that "these Americans were combat troops whose only function was to fight; but after them come the rear-guard service troops and especially the Jews, who have in all other cases acted ruthlessly against the population."[17] Unfortunately, the truth in these words became apparent once the front-line troops pushed on.

Unlike the wild and almost unmanageable Red Army, US military commanders might have prevented much of the excesses committed by their men against helpless civilians had they but so willed it. In many cases, however, they did not. On the contrary, the words of some high-ranking officers seemed designed to encourage atrocities.

"We are engaged in a total war, and every individual member of the German people has turned it into such," US general Omar Bradley

15. Ibid., 6–7.
16. Crawley, *Spoils of War*, 12.
17. Steinert, *Hitler's War*, 305.

announced. "If it had not been Hitler leading the Germans, then it would have been someone else with the same ideas. The German people enjoy war and are determined to wage war until they rule the world and impose their way of life on us."[18]

"[T]he German is a beast," echoed Supreme Allied Commander, Dwight David Eisenhower, a man whose hatred of all things German was well known. In much the same vein as Stalin and Roosevelt, Eisenhower advocated the outright massacre of German army officers, Nazi Party members and others. In all, according to the American general, at least 100,000 Germans should be "exterminated."[19]

"In heart, body, and spirit . . . every German is Hitler!" faithfully trumpeted the US Army newspaper, *Stars and Stripes*. "Hitler is the single man who stands for the beliefs of Germans. Don't make friends with Hitler. Don't fraternize. If in a German town you bow to a pretty girl or pat a blond child . . . you bow to Hitler and his reign of blood."[20]

Not surprisingly, such sentiment from above quickly worked its way down. Soon after combat soldiers moved out of a community and rear echelon troops moved in, the reality of occupation became clear. Wrote one shocked reporter, William Stoneman of the *Chicago Daily News*:

> Frontline troops are rough and ready about enemy property. They naturally take what they find if it looks interesting, and, because they are in the front lines, nobody says anything. . . . But what front-line troops take is nothing compared to the damage caused by wanton vandalism of some of the following troops. They seem to ruin everything, including the simplest personal belongings of the people in whose homes they are billeted. Today, we have had two more examples of this business, which would bring tears to the eyes of anybody who has appreciation of material values.[21]

"We were crazy with happiness when the Americans came . . . ," one woman said, "[but] what [they] did here was quite a disappointment that hit our family pretty hard."

> They broke everything and threw it all outside. Later, we found only piles of rubbish. . . . Those who came in the first few days were fighting troops and they

18. Ibid., 305.
19. James Bacque, *Other Losses* (Toronto: Stoddart Pub. Co., 1989), 23.
20. Davidson, *Death and Life of Germany*, 54.
21. Keeling, *Gruesome Harvest*, 42–43.

had seen something of the war. But those who came later . . . hadn't seen anything at all. And many of these very young soldiers wanted to experience something, like repeat a little of the war. . . . We had original watercolors and so
forth on the walls, which weren't framed, and they wrote all over them. In the
cellar we had bottles of apple juice. When we wanted to get some later, after
the Americans had left, they'd drunk it all up and filled the bottles with urine.
Or, in our cooking pots was toilet paper, used toilet paper.[22]

In many towns, the invaders unlocked jails, prisons and concentration camps and invited the inmates to join the revelry. "They just opened
up the camps and let them go," noted Amy Schrott, a young German
raised in New Jersey. "The Russians and Poles were looting the houses
and killing the shopkeepers. Then they began raping the girls."[23]

When a prison camp at Salzwedel was thrown open, a mob of various nationalities literally tore the town to pieces. Locating the mayor,
a gang of Russians dragged the man, his wife and daughter to the cemetery. After lashing the mayor to a tombstone, a line of laughing men
began taking turns with his naked wife as she screamed on her hands
and knees. When a Mongolian started to rape his daughter, the father,
in a final fit of rage, tore the tombstone from the ground, then fell over
dead.[24]

A glimpse at the anarchy unleashed is given by Christabel Bielenberg of Furtwangen as she pedaled a bicycle near the town:

> It was like a drunken circus along the road. There were hordes of liberated
> Russian forced laborers, all dressed in clothes they had looted from all the ran-
> sacked shops, roaring with laughter and falling all over the road. And there
> were soldiers in huge army trucks tearing past all over the road in a crazy kind
> of way—it was a fantastic scene. . . .
>
> When we got to Furtwangen it was in pandemonium. All the radios had been
> requisitioned from their German owners and put in the windows facing out-
> ward toward the street—and each radio was playing a different program at full
> blast. All the freed Russians and Poles were waltzing down the street—it was just
> like a carnival going through the town. The Germans were walking round in a daze
> wearing white armbands as a sign of surrender. As for the French . . . [t]he troops
> were not French but Moroccan. . . . These were the men who occupied our area.

22. Owings, *Frauen*, 209.
23. Amy Schrott Krubel interview, Jan. 9, 1997, Topeka, Kansas.
24. Botting, *Ruins*, 19–20.

That was when the raping started. [They] raped up and down our valley in the first few days. Two people were shot trying to protect their wives. Then they moved out and another lot of French colonial troops moved in—Goums from the Sahara, tall, black, strange people in uniforms like gray dressing-gowns. They were terrifying. First they came into Rohrbach and stole all the chickens and my children's rabbits. A few days later they came at night and surrounded every house in the village and raped every female between 12 and 80. . . . What was so frightening about them was the silent way in which they moved. . . . [T]hey came up to the door and one of them asked: "Where's your husband?" I said that he was away and as I was talking to them I suddenly realized that one of them was standing right behind me—he had climbed in through a window and crept right up to me through that creaking wooden . . . house without making the slightest sound.[25]

While Moroccan and other French colonial troops had an especially bad reputation and raped on a massive scale in Germany and Italy, American and British soldiers were not above reproach. "Our own Army and the British Army . . . have done their share of looting and raping . . . ," a US sergeant admitted. "[W]e too are considered an army of rapists."[26]

"Many a sane American family would recoil in horror if they knew how 'Our Boys' conduct themselves . . . over here," added another GI.[27]

"We expected Russian lawlessness . . . ," said one German, "but we once believed the Americans were different."[28]

In part because of propaganda and the attitudes publicly espoused by western political and military leaders that "the only good German is a dead one," in part because of unfounded rumors of massacres and rapes committed at captured US field hospitals, in part because of genuine German atrocities, such as at Malmedy, wherein scores of American POWs were mowed down by SS troops during the Ardennes

25. Ibid., 22–23.
26. Kelling, 61; *Time Magazine*, Nov. 12, 1945; *Life Magazine*, Jan. 7, 1946.
27. *Time Magazine*, Nov. 12, 1945.
28. Freda Utley, *The High Cost of Vengeance* (Chicago: Henry Regnery Co., 1949), 248.
29. George Fowler, "Malmedy: The Case Against the Germans," *The Barnes Review* 2, no. 2 (Nov. 1996): 29.

campaign—because of these and other factors, large numbers of captured or surrendering Germans were simply slaughtered on the spot.[29] Among many American units, "take no prisoners" was the motto. For those members of the SS, Wehrmacht and Volkssturm lucky enough to survive capture, death often awaited behind the lines. In the transit from front to rear, hundreds of prisoners were allowed to suffocate, starve or freeze to death in railroad cars. Upon reaching the prison camps, thousands more perished. Wrote an eyewitness from Rheinberg in April:

> One inmate at Rheinberg was over 80 years old, another was aged nine. . . .
> Nagging hunger and agonizing thirst were their companions, and they died of
> dysentery. A cruel heaven pelted them week after week with streams of rain. . . .
> [A]mputees slithered like amphibians through the mud, soaking and freezing.
> Naked to the skies day after day and night after night, they lay desperate in the
> sand . . . or slept exhaustedly into eternity in their collapsing holes.[30]

With General Eisenhower turning a blind eye to the Geneva Convention, only the threat of retaliation against Allied POWs still held in Germany prevented a massacre of prodigious proportions.[31]

Despite the numerous atrocities committed on the western front, such savagery never became officially sanctioned. Considering the blood-thirsty propaganda they had been subjected to for almost a decade, as well as the active incitement of their political and military leaders, the average GI and Tommy comported himself amazingly well, and certainly far, far better than his Soviet counterpart. Efforts by writers in *Stars and Stripes* to draw favorable parallels between the American and Red Armies, in hopes of covering the crimes of the latter— "There is really not much difference between Joe and Ivan . . . both are fun-loving and happy-go-lucky"—were gross perversions of the truth.

Meanwhile, with the nation hopelessly locked in the grip of its enemies, the death struggle of the Reich began. For those armless, leg-

30. Bacque, *Other Losses*, 36.
31. Ibid., 23.

less, half-blind, and totally deaf German veterans who had imagined their war was over, they soon discovered otherwise. It was, noted an observer, "the last round-up of the old and the lame, the children and the dotards."[32] Recalled eighteen-year-old Landser, Guy Sajer:

> Some of these troops . . . must have been at least sixty or sixty-five, to judge by their curved spines, bowed legs, and abundant wrinkles. But the young boys were even more astonishing. . . . [W]e were looking literally at children, marching beside these feeble old men. The oldest boys were about sixteen, but there were others who could not have been more than thirteen. They had been hastily dressed in worn uniforms cut for men, and were carrying guns which were often as big as they were. They looked both comic and horrifying, and their eyes were filled with unease, like the eyes of children at the reopening of school. . . . Some of them were laughing and roughhousing. . . . [but] we noticed some heart-wringing details about these children, who were beginning the first act of their tragedy. Several of them were carrying school satchels their mothers had packed with extra food and clothes.[33]

Most children of the Volkssturm, as well as those in the "Hitler Youth," an organization similar to the American Boy Scouts, were armed with a motley array of old, discarded and almost worthless weapons, including .22 caliber rifles. For the most part, the "uniforms" of these new levies were a bizarre, rag-tag mix of civilian dress crossed with all branches of the service. Though there was no shortage of standard helmets, most were so large that they completely covered the eyes of the young wearer when a weapon was fired.[34]

"We looked like gypsies," remembered Siegfried Losch as he and his companions moved out to face the Red Army.[35] Surprisingly, the spirit of Losch and other youngsters was high.

"The morale among us young people was excellent," Losch continued. "We were ready to fight and die for [Hitler]. . . . Everybody felt that we were going to win the war and that he/she could be held responsible."[36]

Perhaps understandable among adolescents, few elders were so eager

32. Charman, *German Home Front*, 185.
33. Sajer, *Forgotten Soldier*, 395.
34. Siegfried Losch manuscript (copy in possession of the author), 6; Duffy, *Red Storm*, 164.
35. Losch manuscript, 6.
36. Ibid.

to fight for the Fuhrer at this late stage of the war. Nevertheless, most did. With unconditional surrender and prison camps staring them squarely in the face, with rape, torture, enslavement, and death looming for their families, most men saw fighting to the last as not only their duty, but their only option. For others, however, additional incentive was needed. Rumors that Roosevelt intended to hand over millions of German slaves to Stalin energized many laggards. "This news," wrote one official, "worked like a bombshell among some of the cowards."[37] There were even stronger incentives for wavering soldiers. Announced Commander-in-Chief of the Navy Admiral Karl Donitz, expressing the mood of all military branches:

I need not explain to you that in our situation capitulation is equivalent to suicide, is certain death, that capitulation implies the death, the annihilation sooner or later of millions of German people and that, compared with this, the toll of blood exacted by even the sternest battles is trifling. . . . Let us fly at anyone who, even in the smallest degree, falters in his loyalty to the National-Socialist state and to the Fuhrer. Such people can be swayed only by fear. . . . Anyone who, without an express order from the Fuhrer, leaves his area when under attack by the enemy or fails to fight to the last gasp . . . will be branded and treated as a deserter.[38]

Squads of ruthless army police, the Feldgendarmerie, roamed stealthily behind the fronts dispensing military justice on the spot. Any soldier unlucky enough to be stopped by these "chain dogs," and who could not provide a written order for his absence, was dead within minutes. No excuses were valid. Reveals tank commander, Hans von Luck:

I had sent one of my best sergeants, the highly decorated leader of an anti-tank platoon, to our workshop in the rear, with a couple of drivers, to bring forward some armored tractors that were being repaired. I had told him to put the screws on as we needed the vehicles urgently. He passed word to me through a messenger that he would be arriving with the vehicles the following morning. What happened then was told me the next day by one of the drivers. In tears, hardly able to control his voice, he said, "We were sitting together in the evening, after we had made sure that the last vehicles would be finished

37. Steinert, Hitler's War, 301.
38. Marlis G. Steinert, 23 Days (New York: Walker and Co., 1969), 19.

during the night, in a little inn, eating our day's ration and talking about the future, our homes and all the other things that soldiers talk about. Suddenly the door was pushed open and in rushed a staff officer with some military police-men. 'I am Chief Judge Advocate under the direct orders of Field Marshal [Felix] Schoerner. Why are you sitting about here while up at the front brave soldiers are risking their lives?"

My platoon leader replied: "I was ordered by my regimental commander, Colonel von Luck, to bring some armored vehicles that are being repaired here up to the front as quickly as possible. Work will be going on through the night. We'll be able to go back to the front tomorrow morning."

The judge advocate: "Where is your movement order?"

Answer: "I had it from the commander by word of mouth."

Advocate: "We know about that, that's what they all say when they want to dodge things. In the name of the Fuhrer and by the authority of the commander in chief Army Group Center, Field Marshal Schoerner, I sentence you to death by shooting on account of proven desertion."

"But you can't do that," shouted our platoon leader, "I've been at the front right through the war. Here, look at my medals."

Advocate: "But now, when it matters and everyone is needed up at the front, you soon decided you'd like to dodge things after all, didn't you? The sentence is to be carried out."

Then the military police took our platoon leader and shot him in the gar-den behind the inn.[39]

All too swiftly the work of these roving courts-martial became famil-iar sights on an already nightmarish landscape. As one civilian recalled:

As I walked along the winding . . . road I saw on a tree growing along the road-side a man hanging. His face was sunk forward on his chest and he was just dan-gling there. . . . He had a hand-written notice round his neck. It read "I was a coward." The sight of that terrible hanging thing frightened me and although I did not want to look at it, it kept drawing my gaze. It was a horrible sight. The man's face was blue-black in color, although his hands were natural color. I walked on quickly, trembling. Then I saw another body hanging, and then another. The rest of that frightening journey . . . was horrible. I had to pass so many of those dead men and I was alone on the road. Even in broad daylight and on a warm day I was shivering.[40]

39. Hans von Luck, *Panzer Commander* (New York: Praeger, 1989), 199.
40. Lucas, *Last Days of the Third Reich*, 101.
41. Fritz, *Frontsoldaten*, 94.

I DID NOT OBEY MY TRANSPORT COMMANDER, read the placards.
I WAS A DESERTER . . . I WAS TOO YELLOW TO FIGHT . . . THIS IS
WHAT BECOMES OF A COWARD.

"There was no mercy," muttered one horrified army officer.[41]

With death in front, death above, and now, cruelly, death behind, some frantic soldiers sought other means of escape. Self-mutilation was one method, noted Jan Montyn.

> Some boys were so desperate that they shot themselves in the foot or the arm, sometimes even in the shoulder or chest. There was a contradiction in this, because it required courage to do. But it was almost invariably found out, if not as a result of the victim's own behavior, then from the nature of the injury. Such cases were also handed over to the Feldgendarmerie. There was no need for the wound to heal. . . . Finally, there was the possibility of crossing the lines. To this end the Russians put out propaganda, for nights at a time. Metallic voices from loudspeakers, alternating with music. Usually in German, of course, but sometimes also in Dutch. They seemed to know exactly who were in the opposite trenches, probably because of information given to them by boys who had crossed the lines earlier. Sometimes one of us would even be addressed by name and nick-name.
>
> ". . . Lay down your arms. The Allied Forces are on the banks of the Rhine and the Oder. It is pointless to go on fighting. Come and join us. You will be treated correctly, in strict accordance with the provisions of the Geneva Convention. You will get good food, you will have a bed, a decent roof over your head. . . ." Sometimes sweet girls' voices came out of the loudspeaker, voices that not only sounded promising, but actually made promises, in quite specific terms.[42]

Desperate as many German soldiers were to escape the front, little did they realize that there was virtually no sanctuary anywhere in the Reich. Ran a secret memo of the Internal Intelligence Service:

> [E]very member of the community knows that we are facing the greatest national catastrophe and that it will have the most serious repercussions on every family and every individual. The population is suffering severely from the bombing terror. Human ties are being largely severed. Tens of thousands of men at the front do not know whether their relatives, their wives and children, are still alive or where they are. . . . In recent years the German people has accepted

42. Montyn, *Lamb to Slaughter*, 103.
43. Steinert, *23 Days*, 3–4.

every sacrifice. Now for the first time it is becoming weary and exhausted. Everyone is still trying to avoid admitting that this is the end. . . .

For the first time in this war the food position is making a noticeable impact. The available rations leave people hungry. The potato and bread supply is no longer adequate.[43]

With almost nothing moving on the roads, rails or waterways by day, and little by night, the dark specter of starvation spread swiftly across the Reich. Transports of food that normally took hours, now took days, even weeks, and those shipments that did successfully run the gauntlet arrived with spoiled or rotting cargoes. "My center . . . is the stomach," a woman in Berlin moaned. "All my thinking, feeling, desires, and hopes begin with food."[44]

A glimpse at the almost impossible task of staying fed is given by Ilse McKee, who was forced to pedal into the countryside to beg food from farms.

On one of those trips a Russian aircraft spotted me, a big, ancient-looking kite, rather harmless, I thought, until the gunner started to let fly. Immediately I was off my bike and into the ditch at the side of the road. I saw the bullets hit the road dangerously near, raising little puffs of dust. Then it went away. When it did not return I went back to my bike, which I had left lying in the road, mounted and rode on. Ten minutes later the Russian was back, and we played our little scene all over again. Even though I was badly scared now, I was determined not to give in, for if you are really hungry a few machine-gun bullets don't matter all that much. Seven times the wretch got me off the bike. When I got home I was bruised and dusty all over, but in my bag I carried a large loaf of bread and four pounds of gray flour.[45]

While hunger held the Reich tightly in its grip, thirst was no problem. When all else was in short supply—food, fuel, medicine, clothing—one essential of German life not only survived, but actually flourished—beer. Of the seventeen breweries in Berlin—a place that more resem-

44. Anonymous, *Woman in Berlin*, 16.
45. McKee, *Tomorrow the World*, 123.
46. Charman, *Home Front*, 195.

bled a lunar landscape than a city—eleven factories somehow managed to keep running.[46] In other cities the situation was the same as German men and women momentarily escaped the war "by other means."

"Enjoy the war, for the peace will be terrible," drunken people laughed as parties erupted throughout the doomed nation.

"Around ten o'clock the siren broke up the festivities with its harsh warning," remembered one Berliner. "While the guests hesitated and time was wasted in deciding where to take shelter, [a] blast shook the house. As it was too late to leave, the orchestra played louder, all joined in the dancing and singing to drown out the sound of explosions, to drink and forget."[47]

Like victims on a sinking ship, many Germans were determined to live each and every moment to its fullest.

> Everybody had linked arms and they were rocking to the tune of the song. . . .
> I pushed my way through the crowd, using my elbows, stepping on people's toes.
> They were all too happy to notice. An old man grabbed me and gave me a smacking kiss on my cheek. People were laughing and embracing one another all round
> me. Even the Party official on the rostrum was in a glorious mood.
> 'Ladies and gentlemen,' he shouted, lifting up a bottle of red wine. 'And now
> a bottle of Italian wine. Italy, you understand, the Axis, our gallant allies, Mussolini, fat stomach—too much macaroni.'
> The mob roared and started to sing a rather nasty little song about the Duce.
> . . . Very few could still walk in a straight line. "Today we're happy, tomorrow
> we're dead!" they shouted.[48]

Like drinking and revelry, sex was another way to forget the future. Already noted for its lusty attitude toward matters carnal before the war, Germany experienced a veritable sexual revolution as the end approached.

> A mattress on the floor. And that was all. Marika sat down on the mattress, I
> on the chair. I accepted a cigarette, although I rarely smoked. Where did I come
> from? she wanted to know. From Holland. Did I have brothers and sisters? Six.
> She had one brother, but she did not know whether he was still alive. She had
> fled from Riga, her parents had been killed. She had been here for less than a

---

47. Horstmann, We Chose to Stay, 40.
48. McKee, Tomorrow, 137–138.
49. Montyn, Lamb, 79.

month. And a question—no, many questions—burned on the tip of my tongue. . . . But at once she gave a barely perceptible shrug of her shoulders, lay down on the mattress, her eyes open, and muttered: "Come."[49]

Like the above, sex among passing strangers became pandemic and as the end neared encounters on park benches, in doorways or in plain view amid the rubble was simply too common to note. Additionally, wild orgies erupted spontaneously as thousands of men and women cast aside all inhibitions. When Werner Adamczyk and eleven other exhausted comrades entered a hay barn for the night, the young Landser imagined he was in for "a good night's sleep."

> I . . . was just dozing off when the large sliding door opened and a crowd of figures stormed into the barn. I jumped up and grabbed my rifle next to me. "Ivan is not getting me without a shot out of my rifle," was my instinctive thought. Well, it was an attack, but not by Ivan. It was an attack by the females of that farm. They were falling over us, hugging and kissing every soldier in the barn until they were consumed in what nature calls for. One girl or woman, as fat as an elephant, fell over me. In the dim light of the few bulbs lighting the barn, I could see that she was very ugly. . . .
>
> [T]he natural drive for love had overcome them, especially under the conviction that their lives would be over as soon as the Russians arrived here.[50]

Jan Montyn:

> It was Anna who, shortly after midnight, when the party was at its height, enticed me away, outside, without anyone noticing. Between the carts and across the yard, her fingers on her lip. Into the barn. The door was bolted with a wooden cross bar and she led me into the darkness, her hand squeezing mine confidentially. Up a ladder, and then we crawled through the hay, further and further, to the very back of the barn. There was a hollow in the hay, and a hanging oil lamp, and lo and behold, Karin, too. And Hanna. And another girl, no more than thirteen years old, whom I had not noticed at the party.
>
> Not a word was spoken. Everything seemed to have been agreed in advance. Karin and Hanna held me pressed down on my back in the dusty hay, a hand on my mouth. Anna was the one who pulled my trousers down. Anna was the one who crouched on me. And then, Hanna. And then Karin. And then, Anna again. And so it went on, while I, lying helpless on my back, was unable to move. Three pairs of eyes above me, three mouths. Groping hands. Breasts above white

---

50. Werner Adamczyk, *Feuer!* (Wilmington, N.C.: Broadfoot Pub. Co., 1992), 366.

lace bodices. Girls' legs under tucked-up, multicolored skirts. Whose was what? Who was who? While the younger girl watched motionless, wide-eyed. This was *her* first lesson in love. It was my second.[51]

When a climax was reached or the liquor wore off, the gray dawn of reckoning was always there to be faced anew. No amount of sex, drinking or merry-making could deny the fact that the end was now one day closer. Continues the secret Internal Intelligence Service memo:

> Now no one believes that with our present resources and possibilities catastrophe can be avoided. The last spark of hope lies in some salvation from without, in some quite extraordinary development. . . . Even this spark of hope is dying. . . . Many are coming round to the idea of doing away with themselves. The demand for poison, for a pistol or some other method of putting an end to one's life, is high everywhere. Suicide in sheer despair at the certainty of approaching catastrophe is the order of the day.[52]

"Better a horrible end than horror without end," explained those intent on taking their own lives.[53]

The one person in Germany who could not give up, was also the one person in Germany who *would not* give up. Adolf Hitler:

> No game is lost until the final whistle. . . . Like the great Frederick we, too, are combating a coalition, and a coalition, remember, is not a stable entity. It exists only by the will of a handful of men. If Churchill were suddenly to disappear, everything could change in a flash! We can still snatch victory in the final sprint! May we be granted the time to do so. All we must do is to refuse to go down![54]

On April 12, that which Hitler so fervently sought seemed about to occur—a miracle.

"My Fuhrer, I congratulate you! Roosevelt is dead . . . ," announced Joseph Goebbels when he excitedly phoned Hitler with the news. "[T]his is the 'miracle' . . . we have been waiting for, an uncanny historical parallel. This is the turning point."[55]

51. Montyn, 55–56.
52. Steinert, *23 Days*, 4.
53. Steinert, *Hitler's War*, 308.
54. Toland, *Last 100 Days*, 73.
55. Strawson, *Berlin*, 114; James P. O'Donnell, *The Bunker* (Boston: Houghton Mifflin Co., 1978), 94–95.

Though himself hopeful that a new American president might dissolve the alliance, might view the Soviet thrust into western Europe as the greater of two evils, Hitler wisely held a wait and see attitude. Recalled one who overheard the chancellor's comments to Goebbels: "He said something to the effect that, with this remarkable turn of events, the US Army and the Red Army might soon be exchanging artillery salvos over the roof of the Reich Chancellery."[56]

The realization that there would be no modern miracle, that the Allied coalition was in tact despite Roosevelt's death, became abundantly clear later that night when a massive British air raid began blasting the Berlin rubble to dust. Nevertheless, Adolf Hitler refused to "go down."

Clearly, Berlin was a political and post-war prize which neither the communists or capitalists could afford to lose if either hoped to dominate Europe. As the two armies approached the capital, there was the very real possibility that a fight would break out over the spoils. Unlike their leader, many German generals were secretly hoping the Americans would, as one officer phrased it, "roll up our backs," not because they held out hope of miracles or victory but because the more of Germany occupied by the West, the less that would be enslaved by the communists.[57] As a consequence, by mid-April 1945, only token resistance—or none at all—was offered on the western front while at the same time Germans fought to the death in the east.

Unbeknownst to either Hitler or his generals, Supreme Allied Commander in the west, Dwight D. Eisenhower, had no intention of capturing Berlin. Additionally, by ordering a halt on the Elbe River, the American general was in effect presenting a gift to the Soviet Union of central Germany and much of Europe. Not only was Winston Churchill shocked and angered by the decision, but so too were many of Eisenhower's lieutenants.[58]

"We had better take Berlin, and quick, and on to the Oder," argued George Patton, a general whose hatred of communism was no secret.[59]

56. O'Donnell, *The Bunker*, 95.
57. Toland, *100 Days*, 407.
58. O'Donnell, *Bunker*, 92; Toland, 326; Nadeau, *Stalin, Churchill, and Roosevelt*, 153–154; Davidson, *Death and Life of Germany*, 57.
59. Toland, 371.

Despite only sixty miles of undefended autobahns between him and Berlin, however, Eisenhower was firm.

"No German force could have stopped us," spit one staff officer in disgust. "The only thing that stood between [us] and Berlin was Eisenhower."[60]

On April 16, the pre-dawn quiet along the Oder River was shattered by a massive Soviet artillery barrage that signaled the final offensive of the war. One sector of the broad attack was the German position along the Seelow Heights. Remembered Russian general, Vasily Chuikov:

> The whole valley of the Oder rocked: forty thousand guns had opened fire. Forty thousand! It was as light as day on the bridgehead. An avalanche of fire descended on the Seelow Heights. The earth reared up in what seemed an unbroken wall reaching up to the sky itself. . . . The artillery bombardment, using every gun and mortar, and reinforced by bombers and dive-bombers, lasted twenty-five minutes. In its wake, and under cover of a double moving barrage, the infantry and tanks moved forward. Hundreds of powerful searchlights lit up the ground in front of the advancing troops.[61]

When the barrage lifted, survivors rose up from their smoking holes. The horror was recounted by a young German.

> The din of motors and clank of tracks was tremendous. The earth trembled. . . . From behind came an abrupt, heavy-throated chorus as 88 mm shells screeched overhead and smashed into the first tanks. Flames shot up, parts of metal and shell fragments rained over the foxholes. At least six tanks were on fire, but others kept coming on and on. In the reddish glare they stood out with clarity and were helpless before the withering fire of big guns. Red Army infantrymen began erupting from the middle of this massive conflagration. . . . [T]hey scrambled up the hill shouting like madmen. . . . We fired rifles and machine guns, and hundreds of Russians toppled over. The rest came on, still yelling.[62]

"Here they come," thought Siegfried Losch, a quiet seventeen-year-old who had never heard a shot fired in anger.

---

60. Lucas, *Last Days*, 196.
61. Strawson, *Berlin*, 123–124.
62. Ibid., 122–123.

My emotions were fear, of course. A lot of people were running in our direction. . . . I sighted my rifle and squeezed the trigger at the first Russian I saw. I
don't think I was shaking. I aimed real carefully and he kept on walking, so he
was either too far away or his number wasn't up yet. . . .

When I tried to reload, the extraction claw broke off and my rifle became
worthless. . . . It just so happened that a buddy from our company had been
hit by an artillery round fragment. He gave me his Enfield rifle and about 7
rounds of ammo. I then used two or three of them with little success. . . . Then
the word came that our C[ommanding] O[fficer] had been killed. Next we were
told to move back. As I ran zick-zack, as I had been taught in my pre-military
training, I noted that to my right and left bullets were hitting the surface. This
made me run faster. . . . In all this mixup we lost contact with all our buddies
with the exception of a fellow from Potsdam. We decided to keep on walking
toward Berlin and report to some organization.[63]

In much the same manner as young Losch, other brave but raw
recruits fled the wall of fire pell-mell. Within two days the massive
Soviet Army was over the Oder, its path to Berlin barred only by
pathetic pockets of resistance.

"'We' consisted of three men . . . ," Dutchman Jan Montyn recalled
with a smile. "A Dane about twenty-three years old, also from the navy,
a boy from the Hitler Youth who looked no more than fifteen, and I.
Three men, one machine gun. There we stood, mortal terror in our
hearts, keeping watch."

For an hour and a half nothing happened. Then the Russians came. They looked
like an entire army as they advanced towards us in the twilight, along the edge
of the wood. There were hundreds and hundreds of them. But silent. Utterly
silent. No sound but the rustling of thousands of leaves, the swishing of branches,
the creaking of boots. We threw hand grenades at random, we fired hit or miss
with everything we had—our aim being to make as much noise as possible and
so give the impression that the defense of the village consisted of more than a
single light machine gun, two sailors and a schoolboy in short trousers. It seemed
almost impossible that they would be misled by it. All the same, they withdrew
among the trees and we saw them no more. From time to time there was some
mortar fire. First a few misses. Then a direct hit. I was flung to the ground, binoc-
ulars and all. Deafened I scrambled up. I was unhurt. The . . . [round] landed
exactly between my two companions. Of the machine gun nothing was left but

---

63. Interview with Fred Losch, Aug. 14, 1997, Kansas City, Missouri; Losch manuscript, 8.

twisted scrap-iron. I sat there in a daze. It was suddenly very quiet. And it was
getting dark.

At half past eight I could stand it no longer. I ran.[64]

Devastating as defeat on the Oder had been, there was no wild rout—
the "chain dogs" made sure of that. "[T]here was one restriction on
our flight," revealed Jan Montyn, as he joined the retreat. "[W]e could
run as much as we liked, but we mustn't run too fast. Anyone in too
much of a hurry ran the risk of bumping into a Feldgendarmerie patrol.
The fatal narrow borderline was still in force; anyone who overstepped
it was a deserter. What happened to you then could be guessed from
the bodies hanging from the trees. In front of us the Feldgendarmerie,
behind us the Russians."[65]

"I saw lots of people with war decorations, who were not asked, they
were just shot," added a horrified Siegfried Losch as he pressed toward
Berlin.[66]

News of the disaster fifty miles to the east caused barely a ripple in
Berlin. By now, disasters were nothing new. "No excitement, no groups
talking in the streets," a French physician reported. "[H]ousewives
queue in front of the shops, men go to work, the squares are full of
children at play."[67]

Nevertheless, as the weary, dispirited troops began trailing into the
capital, few Berliners could doubt that the much dreaded final hour
had at last arrived. Wrote a woman in her diary:

> Standing in the door of the house I watched a troop of soldiers march by,
> dragging their feet. Some of them were limping. Stubble-faced, sunken-eyed,
> weighed down by their packs, they trudged silently, out of step, toward the
> city. . . . All these creatures are so wretched, they are no longer men. One nei-
> ther hopes nor expects anything from them any more—one feels only pity for
> them. They already give the impression of being defeated and taken prisoner.
> They looked past us with expressionless faces. . . . I didn't want to look at them
> any more.[68]

---

64. Montyn, *Lamb to Slaughter*, 150.
65. Ibid., 151.
66. Losch interview.
67. LeTissier, *Battle of Berlin*, 65.
68. Anonymous, *Woman in Berlin*, 34.

What was obvious to this woman was obvious to everyone else in Berlin. And yet, with no recourse left to rape, torture and enslavement but death, thousands of old men and boys, women and girls, made ready to die "on their feet, like Germans."

> Soldiers of the German front in the east!
>
> The hordes of our Judeo-Bolshevist foe have rallied for the last assault. They want to destroy Germany and to extinguish our people. You, soldiers of the east, have seen with your own eyes what fate awaits German women and children: the aged, the men, the infants are murdered, the German women and girls defiled and made into barracks whores. The rest are marched to Siberia. . . . If during these next days and weeks every soldier in the east does his duty, Asia's final onslaught will come to naught—just as the invasion of our Western enemies will in the end fail. Berlin stays German. Vienna will be German again. And Europe will never be Russian!
>
> Rise up to defend your homes, your women, your children—rise up to defend your own future! At this hour, the eyes of the German nation are upon you, you, my fighters in the east, hoping that your steadfastness, your ardor, and your arms will smother the Bolshevist attack in a sea of blood!
>
> *Adolf Hitler* [69]

---

69. Thorwald, *Flight in the Winter*, 210–211.

7

A SEA OF BLOOD

On the afternoon of April 24, 1945, Helmuth Weidling, along with an aide, Major Siegfried Knappe, entered Berlin, his automobile escorted by a pair of roaring motorcycles. Due to the chaotic conditions caused by the Russian advance, Weidling's corp had lost touch with other units and the general hoped to regain contact via the communications center below the Reich Chancellery. What the two officers saw on their short drive through the capital was sobering. Wrote Maj. Knappe:

The city was under fire from heavy artillery, which was probably mounted on a railroad car somewhere thirty or more kilometers away, and there was also some bombing by Russian aircraft. Fortunately, the artillery was not concentrated; it was scattered all over the city, with a heavy artillery shell landing somewhere in the city every few minutes.

Smoke and dust covered the city. Streetcars were standing disabled in the streets, their electric wires dangling. In the eastern suburbs, many buildings were burning and the civilian population was queuing up in bread lines and in line to get water from any source that was still working. Civilians were everywhere, scurrying from cover to cover because of the artillery shells and bombs. To avoid creating a possible panic, Goebbels had refused to issue orders for civilians to leave the city, even women and children, and now thousands more were fleeing into Berlin from the east. Defending Berlin was obviously going to be a very ugly business, and many civilians were going to die in the fighting.

Arriving at the Reich Chancellery at about 6:00 P.M., we left our car and driver to proceed on foot, taking the motorcycle runners with us. The area around the Reich Chancellery was pitted with deep craters. Fallen trees were scattered about like matchsticks, and the sidewalks were blocked by piles of rubble. The Reich Chancellery was badly damaged, with only shells of walls remaining in some places. The entrance hall . . . had been completely destroyed. The only part of the Reich Chancellery that was still usable was the underground bunker system. In the underground garage, we saw several Mercedes-Benzes we had seen Hitler use in parades and political rallies. There was an entrance to the passage to Fuhrer Headquarters in the underground bunker from the garage. SS guards at the entrance saluted Weidling, with his Knight's Cross and Swords. These first guards were SS unteroffiziers, but the deeper we went toward the bunker, the higher the rank of the guards became. . . .

Fuhrer Headquarters was about three levels down from the garage. We were stopped at many guard posts, even though Weidling was a general with many impressive military decorations, and we were searched by the guards before being admitted to the actual Fuhrer bunker. The SS guards were respectful, but here we were carefully investigated as to who we were, where we came from, and what our business was. We had to show proper identification and surrender our pistols.

Then we finally entered the antechamber to the offices of . . . General [Hans] Krebs, and . . . General [Wilhelm] Burgdorf. We were announced, and Burgdorf's adjutant . . . came to welcome us. He led us to the next room, where both Krebs and Burgdorf awaited us. . . . They had talked to us only briefly when Krebs said he would announce Weidling's presence to Hitler and see if Hitler wanted to talk to him. That was surprising, since Weidling had not come to see Hitler and knew of no reason Hitler would want to talk to him.

When Krebs and Burgdorf were out of the room, Weidling said quietly, "Something is wrong. They are behaving strangely." After about ten minutes, Burgdorf returned and told Weidling that Hitler wanted to see him. I stayed behind, of course. . . .

After about twenty more minutes, Weidling returned and told me that Hitler had ordered us to come into Berlin and take over the eastern and southern fronts of the city.[1]

This news, startling in itself, was soon transcended by what Weidling saw and heard in the bunker. Gone were the days of cool efficiency, the days when the German High Command was a well-oiled machine hitting on all cylinders. As Weidling discovered, shouting, arguments, and finger-pointing was now the order of the day.

"What a difference between the haphazard way things were being done now and the professional way things had been done in 1940 and 1941!" reflected Maj. Knappe.[2]

Weidling, Knappe and other visitors from "above" were also struck

1.   Siegfried Knappe and Ted Brusaw, *Soldat* (New York: Orion, 1992), 26–28.
2.   Ibid., 29.

by the ghastly atmosphere of the bunker. Sunless, cheerless, cool, and damp, the compound's pale and lethargic inhabitants haunted the hallways like beings from another world, or, as one inmate admitted, "like zombies."[3]

"Since 16 January, when Hitler had installed himself in his concrete shelter, we had to spend our time inside the bunker," revealed one of the chancellor's personal secretaries, Traudl Junge. "[I]t was our ninety-sixth day spent fifty feet underground, beneath sixteen-feet-thick slabs of cement resting on walls some six feet wide at their base."[4]

More recently, Hitler's mistress, Eva Braun, had moved in along with Joseph Goebbels and his large family. Adding to the cramped conditions, the Fuhrer's top adviser, Martin Bormann, was also ensconced below.

Perhaps most shocking of all to Weidling and other newcomers to the bunker was the appearance of Adolf Hitler himself. As one officer recalled:

> [T]hose of us who had known him in the earlier years before the war, when he was a human dynamo often bursting with restless energy, now noted, from about nineteen forty-two on, that he seemed to be aging at least five full years for every calendar year. Near the very end, on the day he celebrated his last birthday, he seemed closer to seventy than to fifty-six. He looked what I would call *physically* senile.[5]

During that birthday gathering on April 20, scores of officials and Party members from across Germany had arrived "to greet the Fuhrer, to shake his hand and swear their loyalty."[6] According to Traudl Junge, many of the visitors urged their leader to leave Berlin:

> "*Mein Fuhrer*, the city will soon be surrounded and you will be cut off from the south. There is still time to withdraw to Berchtesgaden from where you can command the southern armies."
>
> Hitler shook his head, bluntly turning down their suggestions. . . .
>
> "No, I can't," he answered. "If I did, I would feel like a lama turning an empty prayer wheel. I *must* bring about the resolution here in Berlin—or else go under."[7]

3. Galante, *Voices From the Bunker*, 12.
4. Ibid., 1.
5. O'Donnell, *The Bunker*, 36.
6. Galante, *Voices*, 141.
7. Ibid.

Emboldened by their leader's decision to go down fighting, others swore allegiance. "We shall never leave him in the lurch, whatever the danger . . . ," Dr. Goebbels vowed. "If history tells of this country that its people never abandoned their leader and that their leader never abandoned his people, that will be victory."[8]

And now, with his elevation to commander of the capital defenses, Gen. Weidling was being called upon to do the impossible—to keep not only Adolf Hitler and Berlin from "going under," but to prevent Germany from going down as well. With roughly 15,000 mostly ragged and battle-drained troops to work with, and with perhaps twice that number of poorly armed, poorly trained Volkssturm and Hitler Youth, Weidling was being asked to not only hold off half a million Soviet soldiers, and an equal number of reserves, but defeat and destroy them. Although Hitler had ordered the armies of Generals Walter Wenck and Theodor Busse to break the ring and relieve Berlin, Weidling well knew that this was a phantasm. Far from rescuing the capital, these units would be hard-pressed to prevent their own encirclement and destruction.

As the general and Major Knappe drove through the capital that night to their new headquarters at Templehof Airport, both understood well the hopeless nature of their task. While the inevitable defeat might be postponed for a few days, or weeks at most, nothing could save Berlin from becoming "one huge urban killing ground."[9]

"[I]t was on this night that the apocalyptic battle for the city of Berlin began in earnest," Maj. Knappe wrote. "The next day, Russian assault troops fought their way into the suburbs of the city."[10]

"Berliners!" cried Joseph Goebbels over the radio, "I call on you to fight for your city. Fight with everything you have got, for the sake of your wives and your children, your mothers and parents. . . . The battle for Berlin must become the signal for the whole nation to rise up in battle."[11]

8. Semmler, *Goebbels*, 198.
9. Knappe, *Soldat*, 30.
10. Ibid.
11. Charman, *Home Front*, 205.

Stirred by the summons of Joesph Goebbels, aware that Hitler himself was sharing their fate, thousands of men, women and children responded to the clarion, some riding street cars to the front lines in the suburbs. The speed of the Soviet onslaught and the haphazard nature of the defense created a logistical nightmare. Explained one Volkssturm commander:

> I had four hundred men in my battalion, and we were ordered to go into the line in our civilian clothes. I told the local Party leader that I could not accept the responsibility of leading men into battle without uniforms. Just before commitment we were given 180 Danish rifles, but no ammunition. We also had four machine-guns and a hundred Panzerfausts. None of the men had received any training in firing a machine-gun, and they were all afraid of handling the anti-tank weapons. Although my men were quite ready to help their country, they refused to go into battle without uniforms and without training. What can a Volkssturm man do with a rifle without ammunition? The men went home; that was the only thing we could do.[12]

Although many defenders were lost for similar reasons, others were determined to help in any way they could. Some women and children built barricades in the streets or dug anti-tank ditches. Old men and boys acted as couriers. Clerks, school teachers, government employees, even artists and musicians, hovered near the front in hopes of picking up weapons and uniforms from the battlefield. While Soviet forces converged upon the city, some of the first hammer-blows were delivered in the southern suburbs along the Teltow Canal. Remembered Russian general, Ivan Konev:

> I reached Teltow when the artillery preparation was almost over. Our troops had taken up assault positions and were poised to enter the city; there were tanks, motorized infantry and the artillery that was finishing its work. . . . The advance detachments began to cross the canal before the end of the artillery preparation. Everything was shaking. The entire locality was wrapped in smoke. Heavy artillery was demolishing the houses on the other side of the canal. Stones, slabs of concrete, fragments of wood and dust were flying into the air. We had over 600 guns per kilometer on a narrow frontage, and they were all pounding the northern bank. . . . The bombers—one flight after another—were also delivering their blows. . . .
>
> I remember how vast the city appeared to me. I noted the massive old build-

---

12. LeTissier, *Battle of Berlin*, 29.

ings, in which the district that lay before us abounded, and the density of these
buildings; I took note of everything that might complicate our task of capturing
Berlin. I also noticed the canals, rivers and streams that crossed Berlin in different directions. . . . Such a multiplicity of water obstacles promised additional
difficulties. Before us lay a front-line city, besieged and prepared for defense. . . .
As I gazed upon Berlin I reflected that its end would spell the end of the war
and that the sooner we took the city the sooner the war would be over.[13]

Once in the suburbs, it was not long before Konev and other Russians realized that the war was far from over. Near Oranienburg, a
member of the Hitler Youth wrote:

Our leader and the police fetched us from our homes and we had to assemble
in the SS barracks. . . . Then [we] were divided up by our companies and attached
to the SS and Volkssturm. We first saw action to the northeast of the town.
Most of us were killed by infantry fire, because we had to attack across open fields.
Then the fighting in the town; two days of it. In two days and two nights Oranienburg changed hands four times. That finished another part of us. Then the Russians started bombarding the town with Stalin-Organs [i.e., multi-tubed rocket
launchers], and when we wanted to finish and go home, we were stopped and
made to join the escape across the canal. My platoon leader, who refused, was
strung up on the nearest tree . . . but then he was already fifteen years old.[14]

Although resistance on the approaches to Berlin was generally light,
the further the Soviets advanced, the stiffer the defense became.
Increasingly, the Russians resorted to formula tactics. Said one German defender:

[A]ircraft flew over the buildings where resistance was suspected and where they
had spotted snipers posted on the roofs, dropping small-caliber bombs, or
possibly clusters of hand grenades. Simultaneously the tanks advanced, slowly
opening a passage with their fire. Behind the tanks came the infantry, usually
about thirty to forty men armed with submachine-guns. Behind the assault
troops came other shock troops, who searched the houses to left and right. As
soon as a cellar or building had been visited, the assault troops passed on, leaving one or two sentries. . . . The Russians did their mopping up very cautiously
and burnt with petrol all the houses from which they had been fired upon.[15]

As the Soviets pressed forward, they captured several prison camps.

13. Konev, *Year of Victory*, 153–154.
14. LeTissier, 96.
15. Ibid., 136.

While POWs of other nationalities were set free, Russian inmates were merely handed a rifle and pointed to the front.[16]

On a street in the suburbs, Werner Adamczyk and other nervous artillerymen waited while spotters located targets. As the young German gunner recalled:

> I could see a long line of women in front of a grocery store, waiting to be served out of the meager supply of food. Suddenly, we got a firing command. We were to fire three salvos directed less than a kilometer ahead. As our guns went off, the women in line ducked down to the floor. . . . After the salvos went off, we loaded the last shell and waited. . . .
>
> Then the moment of final destiny arrived. A Russian tank swerved around the corner of one of the streets ahead of us. Its turret was swinging from one side to the other, firing its shells at random. My breathing stopped when I saw one of its shells detonating in the middle of the row of women waiting in line at the grocery store. Several of them fell to the ground; screams of horrible panic and pain filled the air. . . . Some unknown men, maybe from the rest of our infantry, emerged in front of us and fired a "Panzerschreck" at that tank. It was a direct hit. The tank blew up in an inferno of fire. But fragments of it killed some more of the nearby women.
>
> Moments later, our gun barrels down for direct shooting, another tank appeared. Every gun fired its last round. At least two of our shells hit the tank and blew it to pieces.[17]

Young Siegfried Losch found himself sniping from windows with a group of paratroopers convalescing from the Italian front. After escaping the Oder, the seventeen-year-old had briefly considered shedding his uniform and blending with civilians. Loyalty to the Fatherland caused him to pause, however, and the ubiquitous Field Police gave him even more reasons to reconsider. Soon, Losch and his comrades found cover near the Olympic Stadium.

> There was no real organization. Every little group fought as good as it could. Confusion existed. For instance, there were members of the Volkssturm dressed in brown overcoats and Czechoslovakian helmets. I almost shot one man. He was rather old. I told him to change his uniform, if he wanted to survive. Then there were members of the Adolf Hitler school, a Nazi elite high school. These boys were armed like cowboys. Each one had several pistols. They picked the weapons up from dead soldiers. They were highly motivated. I remember,

16. Ibid., 101, 167.
17. Adamczyk, *Feuer!*, 370.

there was a T-34 tank about 60 yards from our position, firing ever so often along
the houses. Suddenly I heard a big bang from the T-34. One of those students
had knocked out the tank. He had crawled on the balcony across from us and
hiding behind some petunias he shot a bazooka [i.e., Panzerfaust] at the tank.
. . . He was maybe 14.[18]

As the incidents above illustrate, and as the Soviets soon discovered,
Berlin was a graveyard for tanks. The Panzerfaust, and its more lethal
cousin, the Panzershreck, was a simple, yet extremely effective tank-
killing device that could be fired with little or no training. Wagons,
carts and wheel-barrows loaded with the weapons were constantly
resupplying the fronts and doled out like loaves of bread. Additionally, the narrow streets of Berlin, lined with multi-storied stone and
brick ruins made perfect canyons for ambush.

General Wilhelm Mohnke describes a tank attack upon one of his
positions:

> They came on at dawn with tanks and infantry. Their tanks were highly unma-
> neuverable, blocked by rubble, and were sitting ducks in this classic street-fight-
> ing situation. Even young boys and old men, or women, for that matter, armed
> with bazookas and heroic despair, could get at them from point-blank range,
> usually under fifty yards, often from a cellar. . . . The Russians had brilliant
> tank commanders who had learned their business against us out on the steppes
> and in the open country. Even in city fighting, for example, in Stalingrad or War-
> saw, they had never come up against hostile, armed civilians. They realized their
> mistake only belatedly, after they had lost hundreds of tanks. . . .
>
> After that first frontal assault, they got smarter. They simply pulled back
> and plastered us with artillery, of which they had a plenitude. They never tried
> to storm our positions again.[19]

In other sectors as well, Soviet commanders screened their tanks with
sheets of iron or bags of cement and held them back until strong points
had been obliterated by artillery. A French POW watched a typical
operation outside the Schultheiss Brewery:

> The roadblock's defenders were bombarded by heavy mortars set up in some
> ruined houses nearby. Then the Russians set up a 75 or 105mm gun several
> hundred metres from the barricade. The Russian gunners were completely

---

18. Losch manuscript, 9; Losch interview, Aug. 14, 1997.
19. O'Donnell, *The Bunker*, 170–171.

exposed and, at the cost of several casualties, succeeded in getting some shots on the target, destroying the barricade and killing a number of Germans.

Then the Soviet infantry, about a hundred strong, charged in screaming, quickly swamped the remaining defenders, opened the barrier and regrouped on the street corner opposite the brewery. German losses were increased by the bitterness of the Soviet soldiers, who seemed to be drugged, and rarely took prisoners. We found numerous German corpses, civilians and soldiers, when we were able to get out of the brewery.[20]

With Berlin surrounded, the Soviets sought to sever the city's last link with the world by overrunning Templehof Airport. One of those defending the far approaches to the airfield scribbled in his diary:

> Russian artillery is firing without let-up. . . . We need infantry reinforcements, and we get motley emergency units. Behind the lines, civilians are still trying to get away right under the Russian artillery fire, dragging along some miserable bundle holding all they have left in the world. On and off, some of the wounded try to move to the rear. Most of them stay, though, because they are afraid of being picked up and hanged by flying courts-martial. The Russians burn their way into the houses with flame throwers. The screams of the women and children are terrible. . . .
>
> Afternoon. Our artillery retreats to new positions. They have very little ammunition. The howling and explosions of the Stalin organs, the screaming of the wounded, the roaring of motors, and the rattle of machine guns. Clouds of smoke, and the stench of chlorine and fire. Dead women in the street, killed while trying to get water. But also, here and there, women with bazookas, Silesian girls thirsting for revenge. . . .
>
> 8 P.M.: Russian tanks carrying infantry are driving on the airport. Heavy fighting.
>
> April 25: 5:30 A.M. New, massive tank attacks. We are forced to retreat. . . . Russian drive on the airport becomes irresistible. . . . Heavy street fighting—many civilian casualties. Dying animals. Women are fleeing from cellar to cellar. We are pushed northwest. . . . [H]eavy Russian air attacks. Inscriptions on the house walls: "The hour before sunrise is the darkest," and "We retreat but we are winning." Deserters, hanged or shot. What we see on this march is unforgettable.[21]

As the ferocious fighting approached the airport's perimeter, General Weidling realized he could not hold the vital link long. Major Knappe:

---

20. Le Tissier, *Berlin*, 129.
21. Thorwald, *Flight in the Winter*, 229–231.

During the evening, I entered a room where Weidling was meeting with [two generals]. They were discussing whether to defend Berlin dutifully or whether it would be appropriate to stay here and let the Russians pass by on both sides of us and then break through the Grunewald (woods to the west of the city), escape to the west, and surrender to the Western Allies. If we stayed to defend Berlin it would be necessary to move our headquarters to the center of the city, because within two days at the latest the Russians would be occupying this building. Weidling then made his decision to stay and defend Berlin. . . .

[We] . . . decided to move corps headquarters to a big antiaircraft bunker near the Berlin zoo. . . . The zoo bunker, a heavily fortified place with heavy antiaircraft guns on the roof, would be safe against bombing and artillery. . . .

When we left our headquarters, we had to be careful, because the railroad embankment behind our building was under fire and we had to cross it to get to our kubelwagen [i.e. Jeep] and motorcycle. We crossed it by dashing from cover to cover, finally arriving safely at our vehicles. As we drove through the city, the earth trembled with each exploding artillery shell, and a huge geyser of earth and debris erupted from the ground with each explosion. The noise was deafening, and the heaving of the earth was unsettling. A sliver of shrapnel from an exploding artillery shell finally punctured one of the tires on my kubelwagen.

While my driver was changing the tire, a woman watching from a house nearby offered me a cup of tea. She was about forty-five years old and matronly, with worn clothes, bedraggled hair, and a kind face. . . . Her apartment was in shambles from the artillery blasts. Small knickknacks, little pieces of her life, lay shattered on the floor about her.

"When will the Russians arrive, Herr Major?" she asked.

"In a matter of hours," I told her honestly. "A day at most. You will be safest if you stay in your basement." [22]

Like this helpless woman, females could do little else but sit in their cellars and wait. Unlike bombing raids, which had a certain rhyme and rhythm, death from artillery could come at any moment. Hence, life was now passed almost entirely underground talking . . . and thinking.

"The word 'Russians' is no longer mentioned. The lips won't pronounce it," confided one thirty-year-old female. While rape was on everyone's mind, she added, "not a single woman talked about 'it.'"

A nervous gaiety breaks out. All kinds of stories are making the rounds. Frau W. screeches: "Rather a Russki on the belly than an Ami on the head!"—a joke not quite fitting her mourning crepe. Fraulein Behn shouts through the cellar:

22. Knappe, *Soldat*, 34–36.

"Now let's be frank—I'll bet there's not a virgin among us!" No one answers. I find myself wondering. . . . Probably the janitor's younger daughter, who is only sixteen and who, ever since her sister's *faux-pas*, has been strictly watched. And certainly, if I know anything about the faces of young girls, the eighteen-year-old . . . who is sleeping peacefully in the corner.[23]

When those in hiding were finally forced by hunger and thirst to surface, the sights they saw were staggering. Continues the woman above:

> Walking south one is aware of approaching the front. The city railroad tunnel is already blocked. People standing in front of it said that at the other end a soldier in underpants is hanging, a sign saying "Traitor" dangling from his neck. They said he is hanging so low that one can twist his legs. This was reported by someone who saw it himself and had chased away some boys who were amusing themselves twisting the dead man's legs.
>
> The Berliner Strasse looks fantastic, half torn up and blocked by barricades. Queues in front of the shops, flak roaring overhead. Trucks moving citywards. Filthy mud-covered figures with vacant faces covered in blood-smeared bandages trudging along between them. In the rear hay carts driven by gray-heads. The barricades guarded by Volksturm men in patched uniforms. Soft-faced children under huge steel helmets, horrifying to hear their high voices. So tiny and thin in their far-too-loose uniforms, they can't be more than fifteen.[24]

"There are no more streets. Just torn-up ditches filled with rubble between rows of ruins . . . ," said another hungry scavenger, Ruth Andreas-Friedrich. "We climb across mountains of ruins, rummage through rubble and broken glass, crawl through unknown cellars, tear out other people's boxes and bags. Shellfire above us. We don't pay attention. We hardly bother to take cover. A fever has gotten hold of us."[25]

Rita Kuhn was also searching for food. As the little girl approached her neighborhood bakery, she soon became lost.

> I thought I was in another city. Everything looked very, very unfamiliar. The trees had lost all their leaves. And buildings on both sides were . . . little holes, big holes, and just the whole area is devastated. . . . I walked on, and I looked at the trees, and I saw pieces of clothing on the trees. Pretty soon, as I got closer to the bakery there were pieces of human flesh. They were all over, everywhere. On the trees, on the balconies, pieces of clothing, pieces of human flesh. . . . I

---

23. Anonymous, *A Woman in Berlin*, 14, 32, 35.
24. Ibid., 38.
25. Ruth Andreas-Friedrich, *Battleground Berlin* (New York: Paragon House, 1990), 6.

almost fell over a woman, lying there in the street, dead, with her legs blown off. . . . I came to where I thought the bakery was, and there was just a big hole. Sure enough, that's where it had hit, and people hadn't had time to take cover.[26]

Like this unfortunate group, once a source of food or water had been found, little or nothing could drive the desperate people away.

"Whole families take turns standing in line, each member doing a shift of several hours . . . ," wrote a witness. "With a few beefsteaks and loins of pork in sight, even the shakiest old grandma will hold her ground. There they stand like walls, those who not so long ago dashed into bunkers the moment three fighter planes were announced over Central Germany."[27]

"Just as we were about to drive past such a line," noted Major Knappe, "an artillery shell exploded beside the line of women. As the smoke began to clear, I could see that many of the women had been hit. Those women who were unhurt carried the dead, the dying, and the wounded into the entrances of nearby buildings and cared for them—and then again formed their queues so they would not lose their places in line!"[28]

When another direct hit on a food line killed and wounded over a dozen, one viewer was stunned to see victims merely wipe the blood from their ration cards and reform the line.[29] As the sounds of street fighting neared, however, few any longer risked the food and water sorties. Confined to their dark cellars, alone with their thoughts, it was now that dreadful anticipation came crushing down.

We sheltered in the air raid cellar of our house when the fighting came very close. . . . [W]e heard a series of thundering crashes which came nearer and nearer. One young boy in our cellar was brave enough to look out. He told us that two Russian tanks and a lot of soldiers on foot were coming and that the tanks were firing into the houses as they moved up the street. One tank was firing at the houses on the left. The boy suddenly jumped down from the slit through which he had been looking and almost immediately our house was struck by a shell. . . .

The noise moved past us. The sound of the firing grew less and less loud. We all sat quite still. . . . Each of us had our own thoughts. Mine were of my

26. Owings, *Frauen*, 464.
27. Anonymous, *Woman*, 43.
28. Knappe, *Soldat*, 32.
29. Anonymous, *Woman*, 43.

husband who was a sailor somewhere. . . . We all sat silent waiting, wondering and fearful. Very soon the Red Army would be here. Suddenly the door was pushed open and in the doorway was the silhouette of a man. Then another and another. Two pocket torches were switched on and their beam passed from one face to another in the cellar. "Alles Kaput," shouted one of the silhouettes, "Komm," and we made our painful way up the shelter stairs and into daylight. There they stood, the soldiers who had come into our cellar, laughing and shouting. "Alles Kaput." They looked about sixteen years old. The Ivans had arrived.[30]

As their frightened countrymen to the east had earlier discovered, Berliners also soon found that tough and hard as Russian shock troops might be, they were a far cry from the blood-thirsty monsters propaganda and imaginations had sketched them as. "The first troops were friendly and gave us food," said a teenager. "They had officers with them who spoke German very well and told us to be calm, that everything would be all right."[31] But also like their eastern brethren, Berliners soon learned that there was a world of difference between the first wave of Soviet soldiers and the second.

"These are good, disciplined and decent soldiers," one Russian officer explained to a Mother Superior at a maternity hospital. "But I must tell you—the ones coming up behind are pigs."[32]

With such warnings, some terrified women tried to follow the front, dodging from cellar to cellar, dying from bombs and bullets as they did, but staying just ahead of the horror behind. For most, however, it was too late.

> I step out into the dark corridor. Then they got me. Both men had been standing there waiting. I scream, scream. . . . One man seizes me by the wrists and drags me along the corridor. Now the other one also pulls, at the same time gripping my throat with one hand so that I can no longer scream. . . . I'm already on the ground, my head lying on the lowest cellar stair. I can feel the coldness of the tiles against my back. Something falls from my coat with a tinkling sound. Must be my house keys. . . .

---

30. Lucas, *Last Days of the Third Reich*, 49–50.
31. Pechel, *Voices From the Third Reich*, 430.
32. Botting, *From the Ruins of the Reich*, 68.

One man stands guard at the door upstairs while the other claws at my underwear, tears my garter belt to shreds and violently, ruthlessly has his way. . . .

When it's all over and, reeling, I try to get up, the other man hurls himself
upon me and with fists and knees forces me back on the floor. Now the first man
is standing guard, whispering: "Hurry, hurry. . . ."

Suddenly I hear loud Russian voices. Someone has opened the door at the top
of the staircase, letting in light. Three Russians come in, the third one a woman
in uniform. They look at me and laugh. My second attacker, interrupted, has
leaped to his feet. They both go off with the others, leaving me lying on the floor.
I pull myself up by the banister, gather my things together, and stagger along the
wall toward the door of the cellar. . . . My stockings are hanging over my shoes,
my hair has fallen wildly over my face, in my hand are the remains of the garter
belt.[33]

"What followed was worse than anything we had ever imagined,"
recalled nineteen-year-old Juliane Hartman.

One Russian went into the garage and the other headed for the house. Not
having the slightest idea of what would happen, I followed the man into the
house. First, he locked all of the doors behind him and put the keys in his pocket.
I began to feel a bit funny when we got to one of the bedrooms. I wanted to go
out on the balcony, but he pointed his gun at me and said, "*Frau komm!*" We had
already heard about a few of the horrible things going on, so I knew one thing
for certain and that was "Don't try to defend yourself." An upper-middle-class
child, I had never been told about the facts of life.[34]

A short time later, Juliane learned much more about the "facts of
life" when "an entire horde of Mongolians" stood facing her.[35]
Recounts Ruth Andreas-Friedrich, a German communist:

In the middle of the night I wake up. A flashlight is shining into my face.

"Come, woman," I hear a voice. The smell of cheap liquor assails me. . . . A
hand covers my mouth.

"Good woman . . . come," the voice repeats. A heavy body falls upon me.

"No, no," I gargle, half choked, trying to slip deeper into the pillows. The smell
of cheap liquor. Close to my ear panting breath. "O God! . . . Dear God!"[36]

Following her own ordeal, Andreas-Friedrich tried to console a young
Marxist friend:

---

33. Anonymous, *Woman*, 73–74.
34. Pechel, *Voices*, 454.
35. Ibid.
36. Andreas-Friedrich, *Battleground*, 10.

She sits huddled on her couch. "One ought to kill oneself," she moans. "This is no way to live." She covers her face with her hands and starts to cry. It is terrible to see her swollen eyes, terrible to look at her disfigured features.

"Was it really that bad?" I ask.

She looks at me pitifully. "Seven," she says. "Seven in a row. Like animals. . . ."

She is eighteen years old and didn't know anything about love. Now she knows everything. Over and over again, sixty times.

"How can you defend yourself?" she says impassively, almost indifferently. "When they pound at the door and fire their guns senselessly. Each night new ones, each night others. The first time when they took me and forced my father to watch, I thought I would die. . . ."

I shudder. For four years Goebbels told us that the Russians would rape us. That they would rape and plunder, murder and pillage.

"Atrocity propaganda!" we said as we waited for the Allied liberators.[37]

A German attorney and his Jewish wife were two more Berliners who had eagerly anticipated the arrival of Soviet troops. According to a witness:

> For months the couple had been looking forward to the liberation of Berlin, had spent nights by the radio, listening to foreign broadcasts. Then, when the first Russians forced their way into the cellar and yelled for women, there had been a free-for-all and shooting. A bullet had ricocheted off the wall and hit the lawyer in the hip. His wife had thrown herself on the Russians, imploring their help in German. Whereupon they had dragged her into the passage. There three men had fallen upon her while she kept yelling: "Listen! I'm a Jewess! I'm a Jewess!" By the time the Russians had finished with her, the husband had bled to death.[38]

Because of the close-quarter street fighting, German troops were often unwilling spectators to the horror taking place just beyond. "The nights, when the women in the occupied side streets were raped by Russian soldiers, were awful," a sixteen-year-old Hitler Youth reminisced. "[T]he screams were horrible. There were terrible scenes."[39] Added another Landser: "[I]t is just not a pretty sight to see a terrified, naked woman running along a roof top, pursued by a half-dozen soldiers brandishing bayonets, then leaping five or six stories to certain death."[40]

37. Ibid., 16.
38. Anonymous, *Woman*, 246–247.
39. Pechel, *Voices*, 470.
40. O'Donnell, *Bunker*, 282.

After witnessing such scenes as the above, resistance—already fierce—
soon turned fanatical. Ferocious as the fight became, little or nothing could stave off the inevitable. Nowhere was this fact more painfully
clear than in the bunker far below the Reich Chancellery. Traudl Junge:

> [A]n acute sense of anxiety had spread throughout the bunker. Outside, it was
> like the depths of hell. During the daytime the rumble of gunfire never stopped,
> and explosions that rocked the ground continued all night long. . . . Impris-
> oned in the bunker, we tried to get hold of some news about the outcome of
> the battle. It should have been at its height. Was that the noise of our guns and
> tanks? Nobody knew. . . .
>
> Hitler went out to the officers who were waiting in the corridor. "Gentlemen,"
> he said, "the end is approaching. I shall stay in Berlin and I shall kill myself when
> the moment comes. Any of you who wish to leave may do so. You are all free
> to go."[41]

When those present begged him to fly south to the Alps, while there
was still time, Hitler merely waved the words aside: "In this city I
have had the right to give orders; now I must obey the orders of Fate.
Even if I could save myself, I would not do it. The captain goes down
with his ship. How can I call on the troops to undertake the decisive
battle for Berlin if at the same moment I myself withdraw to safety?"[42]

While some in the bunker still held hope, pinning their last prayer
on General Wenck breaking the Russian ring and relieving the capital, Wenck himself suffered no such delusion.

"The idea of fighting through to Berlin . . . was completely absurd,"
the general later wrote. "The Army would have taken weeks to recover
and gain battle strength. From hour to hour our own position was
growing weaker. The Russians now attacked in overwhelming numbers."[43] Continues Traudl Junge:

> By 26 April, we were cut off from the outside world apart from a radio link.
> . . . It began to be obvious that we no longer had an army capable of saving us.
> . . . The sound of guns was coming closer and closer, but the atmosphere in
> the bunker remained the same. Hitler was haggard and absent-minded. . . .

41. Galante, *Voices*, 1, 3.
42. Strawson, *Battle for Berlin*, 142.
43. Ibid., 146–148.

[H]e was hollow-eyed and paler than ever. He seemed completely to have given up his role as leader. There were no briefing sessions, no more fixed schedules, no maps spread out on the table. Doors stood wide open. Nobody bothered with anything any more. Our single obsession was that the moment of Hitler's suicide was approaching.

Goebbels . . . arrived to discuss with Hitler their plans for a final radio broadcast. The population were to be told that the Fuhrer was staying in the besieged capital and that he would personally take part in the city's defense. It was a futile hope that this message would give the German people the courage and energy to achieve the impossible: the sad truth was that there were few able-bodied men left, and a large number of youngsters would sacrifice their lives in vain at a time when their Fuhrer had already given up.[44]

Despite the fast-approaching end, details of state continued. After destroying a Soviet tank single-handedly, a stunned and sleepless child was led down to the bunker and introduced to the Fuhrer.

"With a great show of emotion," noted a bystander, "Hitler pinned an Iron Cross on the puny chest of this little chap, on a mud-spattered coat several sizes too big for him. Then he ran his hand slowly over the boy's head and sent him back out into the hopeless battle in the streets of Berlin."[45]

As the circle closed on central Berlin, the combat became increasingly savage. "One of the worst things . . . was that the Russians always had fresh reserves to put into the fighting, so they could rest their troops . . . ," wrote Maj. Knappe. "[O]ur people had to just keep fighting, hour after hour and day after day, until they were killed or seriously wounded."[46]

"Gradually we lost all human appearance," a German soldier recounted. "Our eyes burned and our faces were lined and stained with the dust that surrounded us."[47]

"The dust from the rubble hung in the air like a thick fog . . . ," added General Weidling as he ducked and dodged from door to door to inspect his defenses. "Shells burst all round us. We were covered with bits of broken stones."[48]

---

44. Galante, *Voices*, 6–7.
45. David Fisher and Anthony Read, *The Fall of Berlin* (New York: W.W. Norton, 1992), 424.
46. Knappe, *Soldat*, 39.
47. LeTissier, *Berlin*, 119.
48. Strawson, *Battle for Berlin*, 150.

Another weary Landser took time to faithfully record the daily agony:

Continuous attacks throughout the night. The Russians are trying to break
through. . . . Increasing signs of disintegration and despair. . . . Hardly any
communications among the combat groups, in as much as none of the active
battalions have radio communications any more. Telephone cables are shot
through in no time at all. Physical conditions are indescribable. No relief or
respite, no regular food and hardly any bread. Nervous breakdowns from the
continuous artillery fire. Water has to be obtained from the tunnels and the Spree
[River] and then filtered. The not too seriously wounded are hardly taken in
anywhere, the civilians being afraid to accept wounded soldiers and officers into
their cellars when so many are being hanged as real or presumed deserters and
the occupants of the cellars concerned being ruthlessly turfed out as accomplices
by the members of the flying courts martial. . . .

Potsdamer Platz is a ruined waste. Masses of wrecked vehicles and shot-up
ambulances with the wounded still inside them. Dead everywhere, many of them
frightfully mangled by tanks and trucks. . . .

Violent shelling of the city center at dusk with simultaneous attacks on our positions. . . . Russians heading for Potsdamer Platz pass us in the parallel tunnel.[49]

As this diarist made note, while one battle raged above, another raged
below. Not only was Berlin one of the largest cities in the world, it
was also one of the most modern and beneath its surface stretched a
maze of subway tunnels, pedestrian passageways and huge drainage
pipes. With maps in hand, German commanders were quick to seize
the initiative . . . with devastating results. Admitted a Russian general:

Our troops would capture some center of resistance and think they had finished
with it, but the enemy, making use of underground passages, would send reconnaissance groups, as well as individual saboteurs and snipers into our rear. Such
groups of submachine-gunners, snipers, grenade throwers and men armed with
panzerfausts emerging from the underground communications fired on motor
vehicles, tanks and gun crews moving along already captured streets, severed
our lines of communication and created tense situations behind our firing lines.[50]

Though terrified by the black labyrinth, Soviet soldiers were compelled to enter them. Alexander Zhamkov and a squad of scouts crept
through one subway until they spotted a distant light.

49. LeTissier, Berlin, 186–187.
50. Konev, Victory, 176.

We decided to crawl the rest of the way. There was a niche in the wall . . . and a small electric bulb burning. Close by we heard Germans talking, and there was a smell of tobacco smoke and heat-up tinned meat. One of them flashed a torch and pointed it towards us, while the Germans remained in the shadows. We pressed ourselves to the ground and peered ahead. In front, the tunnel was sealed with a brick wall with steel shields set in the middle. We crawled forward another few metres. All of a sudden, bullets began to sing. We hid in the niches. After a while, we attacked, throwing hand grenades and firing Panzer-fausts, and broke through. Another 200 metres and another wall.[51]

"[T]hat is the worst possible sort of combat," said an underground fighter. "You see only flashes of fire coming at you: flame throwers and tracer ammunition."[52]

Nightmarish in its own right, frightened civilians crowding the subway platforms added immeasurably to the horror, as one soldier reveals:

> Platforms and waiting rooms resemble an army camp. . . . Exploding shells shake the tunnel roofs. Chunks of concrete collapse. Smell of powder and clouds of smoke in the tunnels. Hospital trains of the underground municipal railway roll along slowly. Suddenly a surprise. Water pours into our combat headquarters. Screams, weeping, cursing, people fight for the ladders which lead to the surface through the ventilation shafts. The masses pour over the railway sleepers leaving children and wounded behind. . . . The water rises over a meter before it slowly recedes. The terrible fear and panic lasts for more than an hour. Many drowned. The cause: on somebody's orders engineers had demolished the sides of the Landwehr Canal . . . in order to flood the tunnels to block underground enemy advances. . . .
>
> Late afternoon, we move to Potsdam Platz [station]. . . . Shells penetrate the roof. Heavy losses above, civilians and wounded. Smoke pours through the shell holes. . . . After one heavy shell explosion . . . by the station entrance next to the Pschorr brewery, there is a horrible sight: men, women and children are literally plastered to the walls.[53]

And, the soldier continues, as if the horror were not already great enough, "Flying courts-martial appear among us."

> Most are very young SS. . . . Hardly any decorations. They are blind and fanatical. Hopes of relief and the simultaneous fear of the courts-martial revitalize

---

51. Fisher and Read, *Fall of Berlin*, 422.
52. Pechel, *Voices*, 486.
53. Joachim Schultz-Naumann, *The Last Thirty Days* (Lanham, Maryland: Madison Books, 1991), 176.

the men again. General [Hans] Mummert bans the reappearance of any flying courts-martial in this defense sector. A division with the most bearers of the Knight's Cross and the oak leaf cluster does not deserve to be persecuted by such young fellows. Mummert is determined personally to shoot one such court-martial that interfered in his sector.[54]

As noted above, the chain dogs were omnipresent, insuring that few would "snap" and run to the rear. "[A]nywhere you went, you saw military police," a Hitler Youth member stated. "Even when the Russians were already in sight, you could see police a hundred yards farther on, still trying to check people. Whoever didn't have the right papers or the correct pass was strung up as a deserter."[55]

Of the one hundred and forty men originally in Lothar Ruhl's company, only a dozen or so were left. Nevertheless, said the brave seventeen-year-old, "An SS patrol stopped me and asked me what I was doing. Was I a deserter?"

They told me to go along with them and said that all cowards and traitors would be shot. On the way, I saw an officer, stripped of his insignia, hanging from a streetcar underpass. A large sign hung around his neck read, "I am hanging here because I was too much of a coward to face the enemy." The SS man said, "Do you see that? There's a deserter hanging already." I told him that I was no deserter; I was a messenger. He said, "That's what they all say." I wound up at an SS assembly point. One of our platoon leaders sat there. He saw me and yelled, "Hey, what are you doing with one of our men?" The answer was, "We picked him up." The platoon leader asked, "What do you mean 'picked him up?' This man is our messenger and I know him very well. Let him go so he can get back to his duties." They finally let me go.[56]

After one of many small counterattacks, German troops briefly reoccupied a battered neighborhood. Wrote a witness:

People who lived there had put out white flags of surrender. There was this one apartment house with white bed sheets waving from the windows. And the SS came—I'll never forget this—went into the house, and dragged all of the men out. I don't know whether these were soldiers dressed in civilian clothing, old men, or what. Anyway, they took them into the middle of the street and shot them.[57]

54. Ibid., 177.
55. Pechel, *Voices*, 471.
56. Ibid., 433–434.
57. Ibid., 471.

Two groups largely untroubled by flying courts-martial were the Hitler Youth and Volkssturm. Often living only blocks from where they fought, no military police were necessary to remind these men of the fate awaiting their mothers, wives, sisters, and daughters should they fail. Explained a Russian general:

> [T]he mood prevailing in the Volkssturm during the decisive fighting for Berlin may be described as one of hysterical self-sacrifice. Those defenders of the Third Reich, including mere boys, believed themselves to be the personification of the last hope of a miracle. . . . It is noteworthy that those men armed with panzerfausts usually fought to the end and during that last stage displayed much more fortitude than the German soldiers who had been through the mill and were demoralized by defeat and many years of strain.[58]

Far from passively defending a sector, the old men and boys launched furious, though forlorn, counterattacks. As a consequence, they died by the thousands. When one Hitler Youth unit joined the battle, it was five thousand strong. Five days later only five hundred were left.[59]

As the struggle for Berlin intensified and the carnage increased, doctors and nurses were taxed beyond their limits. Remembered one physician:

> [A]mputations were carried out on an old wooden table covered with a mattress. The surgeons operated without gloves, practically without antiseptics, and with instruments hardly boiled. Everything was defective or exhausted. It was impossible to change one's overalls and even washing one's hands became a problem. The oil lamps were dead and the last candles consumed. Fortunately we had found two bicycles equipped with electric lights, and the pedals turned by hand provided sufficient illumination for the operating tables.[60]

Moving in dark, smoky rooms, wading over floors awash in blood and body parts, exhausted medical personnel also endured a non-

58. Konev, *Victory*, 177.
59. LeTissier, *Berlin*, 198.
60. Ibid., 151.

stop barrage of curses, screamed at them in German, Russian, French, Spanish, and Dutch.

"All of us were now living a waking nightmare. We had lost any sense of clock or calendar time . . . ," said Ernst-Guenther Schenck, an intern compelled to perform surgery though his field was nutrition.[61]

> Minor casualties, the walking wounded, soldiers shot in the hand or the foot, were not even allowed to leave their assigned combat posts. Those dragged to us, or trundled in on stretchers, were usually unconscious. . . . Many a wounded soldier died, in horrible anguish, on the blood-smeared table as I operated. These were bewildered young men dragooned from half of Europe. I was up to my elbows in entrails, arteries, [and] gore.[62]

Assisting Dr. Schenck was a Catholic nun, who stuffed arms, legs, bones, and intestines into trash cans.[63]

Surprisingly, amid the smoking, flaming hell that was Berlin, another world existed, a world of strange and surreal contrasts. While men and women fought and died on one street, drunken revelers, bent on a final fling, yelled and laughed on an adjacent street. During brief lulls in the almost constant din of battle, shocked Landsers heard jazz and polka music blaring behind them in the German zone, and the screams of rape victims to their front in the Russian zone.[64] Len Carpenter, an English POW who had simply walked away from his prison, found himself wandering through this bizarre landscape, as if in a "coma."

> I remember going out and queuing up for some salt pork in the middle of the fighting and the queue being strafed by a Russian plane, and I remember joining in when the Germans started looting the shops and getting a big tin of jam and a typewriter, of all useless things. I remember the Hitler Youth boys singing as they marched past after driving the Russians out of Herrenstrasse railway station, and I remember the first Russians to arrive—they were Russians who had been fighting on the German side and when they took shelter in the

---

61. O'Donnell, *Bunker*, 147.
62. Ibid., 148.
63. Ibid., 161.
64. O'Donnell, *Bunker*, 239.

cellar with us I thought, "Just my luck to be caught by the Red Army with this lot in tow."[65]

When the Red Army did in fact arrive, Carpenter's "coma," if anything, worsened.

> [W]hen all the guns and shouting had died down I emerged into the streets. From quite a distance away I could hear the shrieks of young girls. A local cobbler who was a Communist went forward to meet the Russians and show them his Party card but all they did was pinch the leather jacket off his back. . . . I had a chit printed in four languages which said I was a British subject, but they weren't interested, they couldn't read, they just dropped it on the ground. I went with them on a plundering foray. We broke into a shoe shop with a lovely stock of shoes in it, and we broke into the wine and spirit shops, all sorts of places.[66]

By the last days of April 1945, all of Berlin save the city center was under Russian control. Consequently, almost everything that the capital had to give had fallen to the victors.

> I sense a strange, intangible something in the air, evil and menacing. Some of these fellows look past me in a strange way, exchanging glances with each other. One of them, short and yellow and smelling of alcohol, involves me in a conversation, tries to lure me sideways into a courtyard, points at two watches strapped to his hairy wrist, promising to give me one if I. . . .
>
> I retreat into the cellar corridor, sneak across the inner courtyard, think I've given him the slip when suddenly there he is, standing beside me, and following me into the cellar.[67]

"[H]e suddenly throws me onto the bed. Shut your eyes, clench your teeth, don't utter a sound. Only when the underwear is ripped apart with a tearing sound, the teeth grind involuntarily. The last underwear."[68]

> I feel fingers at my mouth, smell the reek of horses and tobacco. I open my eyes. Adroitly the fingers force my jaws apart. Eye looks into eye. Then the man above me slowly lets his spittle dribble into my mouth. . . .
>
> Paralysis. Not disgust, just utter coldness. The spine seems to be frozen, icy

65. Botting, *Ruins of the Reich*, 67.
66. Ibid., 67–68.
67. Anonymous, *Woman*, 67–68.
68. Ibid., 86.

dizziness encircles the back of the head. I find myself gliding and sinking deep down through the pillows, through the floor. . . .

Once more eye looks into eye. The lips above me open. I see yellow teeth, one front tooth half-broken. Slowly the corners of the mouth rise, tiny wrinkles form round the slit eyes. The man is smiling. . . .

When I got up I felt dizzy and wanted to vomit. My ruined underclothes fell round my feet. I staggered along the passage . . . to the bathroom. There I vomited. In the mirror I saw my green face, in the basin what I had vomited. I didn't dare rinse it as I kept on retching and we had so little water left in the bucket.[69]

After the horror stories from the east, most women in Berlin expected to be raped once or twice . . . but not dozens of times.

I felt wretched and sore and crept around like a lame duck. The widow, realizing immediately the reason why, got down her medicine chest from the loft where she had been hiding it. Without a word she handed me a jar containing vaseline, but her eyes were brimming. I too felt weak and was aware of something rising in my throat.

It occurred to me how fortunate I have been until now, how in the past lovemaking for me has never been a burden, but always a pleasure. I have never been forced, never had to force myself. Whatever it was like, it was good. What makes me so wretched at this moment is not the too-much, it's the abused body taken against its will, which reacts with pain. . . . Frigid is what I have remained during all these copulations. It cannot, it must not be different, for I wish to remain dead and unfeeling so long as I have to be prey. As a result I'm glad I feel so sore and sick. And yet there I stood blubbering, with the jar of vaseline in my hand, in front of the equally blubbering widow.[70]

Throughout ravaged Berlin, the victors ruthlessly laid claim to the "spoils of war."

"They queued up," whispers his wife, while Elvira just sits there speechless. "They waited for one another to finish. . . . She thinks there were at least twenty, but of this she isn't quite sure. She had to take almost all of it herself. The other one was unwell, they let her alone after four times. . . ."

I stare at Elvira. Her swollen mouth hangs from her deathly pale face like a blue plum. "Just let them see," says the distiller's wife. And without a word Elvira unbuttons her blouse, opens her chemise, and reveals her breasts covered with bruises and the marks of teeth. . . . [S]he herself started talking. We could hardly understand a word, her lips are so swollen. "I prayed all the time," she

69. Ibid., 86–87.
70. Ibid., 120, 121.

muttered. "I prayed: Dear God, I thank You for making me drunk. . . ." For even before queuing up, as well as after, the Ivans had forced liquor down the woman's throat.[71]

Nothing, it seemed, was a defense against the assaults. "Most of us tried to make ourselves look a lot older than we really were," said Hedwig Sass, who was in her early forties. "But then the Russians always said, 'You not old. You young.' They laughed at us because of the old clothes and eye-glasses we were wearing."[72] Added another woman: "The younger one, so the mother whispered to me, knowing that the Ivans didn't like menstruating women, had stuffed herself with cotton. But it didn't do her any good. Amidst howls and laughter the two rowdies had thrown the cotton all over the kitchen and laid the sixteen-year-old girl on the chaise lounge in the kitchen."[73]

The same woman continues:

> We sit around the kitchen table, everyone hollow-eyed, greenish-white from lack of sleep. We all whisper and breathe uneasily. . . . In turn we all stare at the bolted, barricaded back door, praying it will hold out. . . . All of a sudden the sound of steps on the back stairs, and the alien voices which seem so coarse and bestial to our ears. Silence and paralysis settle over the table. We stop chewing and hold our breath. Hands tremble, eyes open wide in horror. Then it's quiet again beyond the door; the sound of steps has died away. Someone whispers: "If it's going on like this. . . ."
>
> No one answers. Suddenly the refugee girl from Konigsberg throws herself screaming across the table: "I can't stand it any longer, I'm going to end it all. . . ." She had to submit to it several times last night, under the roof where she had fled, followed by a gang of pursuers. Her hair hangs over her face; she refuses to eat or drink.
>
> We sit, wait, listen. We can hear firing from a distance. Shots whip down our street.[74]

Like the frantic girl above, many females did indeed choose the ultimate escape. "There is no other talk in the city. No other thought either," revealed Ruth Andreas-Friedrich. "Suicide is in the air. . . . They are killing themselves by the hundreds.[75]

---

71. Ibid., 175–176.
72. Pechel, *Voices*, 457.
73. Anonymous, *Woman*, 165.
74. Ibid., 81–82.
75. Andreas-Friedrich, *Battleground*, 16, 17.

Those women who did not commit suicide sought out officers, commissars and other powerful men, offering their bodies in hopes of ending the brutal, random assaults.

Compelled by hunger and thirst to leave their holes, Germans were stunned by what they saw in the streets. To many, it was if Berlin had returned to the Dark Ages. Primitive, Asiatic carts, piled high with plunder, stood side by side with American-made tanks and jeeps. Over open fires Kulaks and Tartars roasted whole hogs and oxen on spits. Horses, cattle and sheep, many trailed by their young, filled the streets with a bedlam of sounds.

"The smell of cow-pat and horse dung was everywhere," one German recalled.

Not all foul odors were so rustic. Ruth Andreas-Friedrich:

> We hurry upstairs. An unbearable stench assails us.... Something slimy makes me slip. "They can't have been sober." Repulsed, I hold my nose. Andrik stands at the bathroom door. Aghast, he stares at the cause of the stench.
>
> "Buffaloes must have done this," he stammers, totally overwhelmed, and tries to flush the toilet. There is no water. Nor is there gas, electricity or telephone. Only chaos. Total and impenetrable chaos.
>
> Dagmar comes back from the cellar. "It's even worse down there," she reports and distractedly runs her hands through her hair. "It's a deluge, I tell you, a real deluge!"[76]

"Shoveling shit" soon became a new preoccupation for many a once-tidy hausfrau. Gagging and retching, the women tried mightily to remove piles of excrement left in living rooms, hallways and kitchens.[77]

"They certainly haven't much restraint, these conquerors," one disgusted woman wrote. "[T]hey relieve themselves against the walls; puddles of urine lie on the landings and trickle down the staircase. I'm told they behave just the same in the empty apartments placed at their disposal. . . . In a corner of the back staircase one of them is lying in a puddle of his own making."[78]

---

76. Ibid., 13.
77. Anonymous, *Woman*, 196.
78. Ibid., 113.

In their dazed, feral condition, many Germans themselves were in no frame of mind to maintain the veneer of civilization. "While looking for a rear entrance," said a witness, "we run into a woman who, with raised skirt, is quite unashamedly relieving nature in a corner of the yard. Another sight I've not seen before in Berlin."[79]

Like snarling, ravenous wolfpacks, many Berliners swiftly reverted to the law of the jungle. Ruth Andreas-Friedrich:

> In front of us a white ox comes trotting around the corner. With gentle eyes and heavy horns. . . . Frank and Jo look at each other. . . . In a moment we have surrounded the animal. . . .
>
> Five minutes later it is done. Five minutes later we all act as if we have gone mad. Brandishing kitchen knives, their sleeves rolled up, Frank and Jo are crouching around the dead animal. Blood drips from their hands, blood runs down their arms and trickles in thin lines across the trodden lawn. And suddenly, as if the underworld had spit them out, a noisy crowd gathers around the dead ox. They come creeping out of a hundred cellar holes. Women, men, children. Was it the smell of blood that attracted them? They come running with buckets. With tubs and vats. Screaming and gesticulating they tear pieces of meat from each other's hands.
>
> "The liver belongs to me," someone growls.
>
> "The tongue is mine . . . the tongue . . . the tongue!" Five blood-covered fists angrily pull the tongue out of the ox's throat. . . .
>
> "Ah," a woman screams, and rushing away from the crowd, she spins around twice and then hastens away. Above her head she waves the ox's tail.[80]

Records another viewer:

> [S]omeone had come rushing into the cellar with the glad tidings that a horse had collapsed outside. In no time the whole cellar tribe was in the street. The animal was still twitching and rolling its eyes when the first bread knives plunged into it—all this of course under fire. Everyone slashed and ripped just where he happened to be. When the philologist's wife reached out toward some yellowish fat, someone had rapped her over the fingers with the handle of a knife. "You there—you stay where you are!" She had managed nevertheless to cut out a piece of meat weighing six pounds. . . . [W]e no longer have any sense of shame.[81]

---

79. Ibid., 206.
80. Andreas-Friedrich, 9.
81. Anonymous, *Woman*, 207–208.

Meanwhile, in the rapidly shrinking pocket that was German Berlin, the death struggle continued. For fear of hitting comrades closing from all sides, Soviet artillerymen now lowered their guns to point-blank range. Nowhere was the fight more intense than in the streets surrounding the heavily fortified flak towers. Recounts a civilian near the Zoo tower:

> The barricades ... were defended by the remnants of Volkssturm units and some youngsters. The Russians had mounted some light guns outside our building to fire at these obstacles. The Russians pushed any men and women that appeared capable of work out of the cellars at gun-point and made them clear the streets of the rubble, scrap metal and steel plates used as anti-tank obstacles, and that without any tools. Many were killed by the fire of German soldiers still holding out.[82]

"[T]he smell of death now permeated everything," Major Knappe wrote from inside the Zoo bunker. "In addition to human corpses, many of the animals from the zoo had escaped and been killed. . . . The acrid smell of smoke mingled with the stench of decomposing corpses. Dust from pulverized bricks and plaster rose over the city like a heavy fog. The streets, littered with rubble and pockmarked with huge craters, were deserted."[83]

Atop the tower itself, anti-aircraft guns were lowered and fired non-stop into the surrounding streets.[84] Even so, admitted a soldier inside the bunker, "Russian pressure . . . cannot be contained much longer. We will have to withdraw again."[85]

"We experienced the violent shaking when all eight 125mm anti-aircraft guns fired a salvo at the Russians . . . ," remembered one Landser inside the Humboldthain flak-tower. "Their artillery fire was particularly fierce against the walls of the bunker since their infantry could not get in. The brave gunners were being killed mercilessly at their posts, and they were nearly all young Flak Auxiliaries, fourteen- to sixteen-year-olds. These brave youngsters continued to serve their guns fearlessly, and several were felled before our eyes."[86]

---

82. LeTissier, *Berlin*, 201.
83. Knappe, *Soldat*, 36, 38.
84. LeTissier, 211.
85. Ibid., 212.
86. Ibid., 133–134.

Among the thousands of civilians huddled behind the massive walls, one described the atmosphere:

> Of the actual fighting I saw nothing but we all heard a lot because the walls were not so thick that they kept out the sounds of shells and bombs bursting against the Flak tower walls. The tower soon became an emergency hospital and we were all expected to help. . . . More and more wounded were brought in and a lot died. Burial parties took the bodies outside and because there were not enough men to dig proper graves the bodies were just put into shell holes and covered with a sprinkling of earth. . . .
>
> There were suicides in the tower, as well. It was a ghastly time and when the shelling began to come really close it was clear that the Russians would soon be at the doors. We all knew what that meant and some of the girls decided not to wait until the Ivans came but to end their lives there and then.[87]

To keep Hitler abreast of the battle, General Weidling and Major Knappe were compelled to spend much of their time moving between headquarters and the Chancellery. Reveals Knappe:

> The whole area was in ruins. . . . Artillery shells exploded continuously, with thundering detonations. When I went outside now, the smoke from the burning city sliced through my nostrils and lungs like a jagged blade edge. The streets were full of both debris and bodies, although the bodies were hardly recognizable as such. The corpses of both soldiers and civilians who had been killed in the shelling and bombing were under debris, and everything was covered with a gray-and-red powder from the destruction of the buildings. The stink of death was suffocating. . . . [I]nfantry fighting was now everywhere. . . .
>
> When I made the trip to Fuhrer Headquarters now (approximately one kilometer), I had to dart from cover to cover, watching not only for incoming artillery rounds but for rifle and machine-gun fire as well. . . . Some of the SS troops defending the Chancellery were dug in before the building. . . . [These] one thousand SS troops defending Fuhrer Headquarters—were red-eyed and sleepless, living in a world of fire, smoke, death, and horror.[88]

In the bunker beneath the building itself, Ernst-Guenther Schenck was now in his seventh straight day at the operating table. "Casualties were now tumbling in from the fierce street fighting just three blocks away . . . and from the larger battle now raging for the Reichstag . . . ," said Dr. Schenck. "From time to time, soldiers who were

87. Lucas, *Last Days*, 63.
88. Knappe, *Soldat*, 41, 43.

still conscious and could talk, told me of their hopeless battle. The younger ones, many under sixteen, were terrified, bawling."[89]
Returning to Major Knappe:

> To the people at Fuhrer Headquarters, we represented the outside world. Nobody there had left the bunker for several days. They were safe in the bunker, with its many feet of concrete under many feet of earth, but they did not know what was going on outside—that the fighting was only a kilometer away or that the "rescuing" armies had been halted. Hitler and the high command were juggling divisions that no longer existed or were just skeletons of themselves.
>
> Every time I came into the bunker, Martin Bormann especially was eager to know what was happening. He was *always* there, in the big antechamber in front of Hitler's office and living quarters. Every time I came in he would insist that I sit down on one of the green leather chairs and have some of his goodies and tell him about the situation on the outside.[90]

The "situation" was always grim, of course, but Bormann, Goebbels, Hitler, and the other bunker dwellers needed accurate information on Russian proximity so that each might prepare for the end in his own fashion. Joining Major Knappe on what proved to be his final trip to the bunker was Gen. Weidling. Knappe continues:

> The bunker smelled damp, and the sound of the small engine that ran the exhaust system provided a constant background noise. . . . I saluted, and Hitler walked toward me. As he neared, I was shocked by his appearance. He was stooped, and his left arm was bent and shaking. Half of his face drooped, as if he'd had a stroke, and his facial muscles on that side no longer worked. Both of his hands shook, and one eye was swollen. He looked like a very old man, at least twenty years older than his fifty-six years.
>
> Weidling presented me to Hitler: "Major Knappe, my operations officer."
>
> Hitler shook my hand and said, "Weidling has told me what you are going through. You have been having a bad time of it."
>
> Being accustomed to saying "*Jawohl,* Herr General," I automatically said "*Jawohl,* Herr . . ." and then, realizing that this was wrong, I quickly corrected to "*Jawohl, mein Fuhrer.*" Hitler smiled faintly, and Goebbels smiled broadly— but Weidling frowned because his subordinate had made a social error.
>
> Hitler said goodbye, shook my hand again, and disappeared in the general direction of Goebbels's quarters. Although his behavior had not been lethar-

89. O'Donnell, *Bunker,* 143.
90. Knappe, 42.

gic, his appearance had been pitiful. Hitler was now hardly more than a physical caricature of what he had been. I wondered how it was possible that in only six years, this idol of my whole generation of young people could have become such a human wreck. It occurred to me then that Hitler was *still* the living symbol of Germany—but Germany as it was now. In the same six years, the flourishing, aspiring country had become a flaming pile of debris and ruin.[91]

One reason Weidling had come in person was to inform Hitler that his men could no longer hold out; permission for a breakout of the garrison was requested. The other reason the general had come was to urge his leader to escape while there was still time. To the first request, permission was granted; to the second, Hitler was firm. Others, including the Fuhrer's private pilot, Hans Baur, begged Hitler to leave.

"I had at my disposal a prototype six-engine Junkers with a range of over 6000 miles," Baur reminisced. "We could have gone to any Middle Eastern country well disposed towards the Fuhrer."[92]

To all the entreaties, however, Hitler's response was the same: "One must have the courage to face the consequences. Fate wanted it this way."[93]

Continues the chancellor's secretary, Traudl Junge:

> The bunker shook with the thundering of the Russian artillery bombardment and the air attack. Grenades and bombs exploded without interruption, and that alone was enough to warn us that the enemy would be at the door in a matter of hours. But inside the bunker there was no unusual activity. Most of the country's leaders were assembled, doing nothing but waiting for the Fuhrer's ultimate decision. Even Bormann, always energetic in the extreme, and the methodical Goebbels were sitting about without the smallest task to occupy them. . . . Hopes of victory had been upheld throughout recent days, but nobody held such illusions any longer. . . . It seemed amazing to me that, despite everything, we still ate and drank, slept and found the energy to speak.[94]

Despite the gloom and despair, many underground—and many above—did much more than eat and sleep. Some, said a witness, "went up the palm tree." Remembers Dr. Schenck:

91. Ibid., 44–45.
92. Galante, *Voices*, 18.
93. Ibid., 19.
94. Ibid., 12.

[M]any took to drink. Drink in turn relaxed inhibitions, releasing primitive animal instincts. . . . From time to time I had to leave a patient on the table while I took a five-minute break in the fresh air—to calm my nerves and to steady my scalpel hand. . . . Many of the same wild, red-eyed women who had fled their Berlin apartments in terror of rape by Red Army soldiers, now threw themselves into the arms, and bed rolls, of the nearest German soldiers they could find. And the soldiers were not unwilling. Still it came as a bit of a shock to me to see a German general chasing some half-naked Blitzmaedel [signalwoman] between and over the cots. The more discreet retired to Dr. Kunz's dentist chair upstairs in the Chancellery. That chair seemed to have had a special erotic attraction. The wilder women enjoyed being strapped in and made love to in a variety of novel positions. . . . Another diversion was group sex, but that was usually off in the dark corners.[95]

Returning to Traudl Junge:

As the hours went by, we became completely indifferent to everything. We weren't even waiting for anything to happen any more. We sat about, exchanging an occasional word and smoking. There was a great sense of fatigue, and I felt a huge emptiness inside me. I found a camp bed in a corner somewhere, lay down on it and slept for an hour. It must have been the middle of the night when I woke up. In the corridors and in the Fuhrer's apartments there was a great deal of coming and going by busy-looking valets and orderlies. I washed my face in cold water, thinking that it must be the moment for the Fuhrer's nighttime tea. When I went into his office, he held out his hand to me and asked: "Have you had some rest, my dear?"

Slightly surprised by the question, I replied, "Yes, *mein Fuhrer.*"

"Good. It won't be long before I have some dictation for you."[96]

Later, as Traudl wrote, Hitler spoke:

It is not true that I or anyone else in Germany wanted war back in 1939. It was desired and provoked solely by those international politicians who either come from Jewish stock or are agents of Jewish interests. After all my many offers of disarmament, posterity simply cannot pin any blame for this war on me. . . .

After a struggle of six long years, which in spite of many setbacks will one day be recorded in our history books as the most glorious and valiant manifestation of the nation's will to live, I cannot abandon this city which is the German capital. Since we no longer have sufficient military forces to withstand enemy attacks on this city . . . it is my desire to share the same fate that millions of other Germans have accepted. . . .

---

95. O'Donnell, *Bunker*, 155–156.
96. Galante, *Voices*, 13.

The people and the Armed Forces have given their all in this long and hard struggle. The sacrifice has been enormous. But my trust has been misused by many people. . . . It was therefore not granted to me to lead the people to victory. . . . The efforts and sacrifices of the German people in this war have been so great that I cannot believe that they have been in vain.[97]

At approximately 3:15 P.M., April 30, Adolf Hitler retired to his room, placed a pistol to his head, then squeezed the trigger.[98] Beside him, his newly-wed wife, Eva, also lay dead.

After administering poison to their children, Joseph and Magda Goebbels bid farewell to those remaining in the compound. Wrote one witness who watched as the couple prepared to leave the bunker for their final act in the courtyard above:

Going over to the coatrack in the small room that had served as his study, he donned his hat, his scarf, his long uniform overcoat. Slowly, he drew on his kid gloves, making each finger snug. Then, like a cavalier, he offered his right arm to his wife. They were wordless now. So were we three spectators. Slowly but steadily, leaning a bit toward each other, they headed up the stairs to the courtyard.[99]

Learning of Hitler's death, many in Berlin now resolved to escape the noose.

"I'll never forget sitting in a bunker and hearing of Hitler's end. It was like a whole world collapsing . . . ," explained a sixteen-year-old Hitler Youth. "Adolf Hitler's death left me with a feeling of emptiness."

Nonetheless, I remember thinking that my oath was no longer valid, because it had been made to Hitler. . . . So the oath was null and void. Now the trick was to get out of Berlin and avoid falling into the hands of the Russians. . . . Berlin burned: oceans of flames, horrible clouds of smoke. An entire pilgrimage of people began marching out of Berlin. I spotted an SS Tiger tank unit with room in one of the tanks, so they took me along.[100]

97. O'Donnell, 254; Strawson, *Battle for Berlin*, 143.
98. LeTissier, *Berlin*, 204.
99. O'Donnell, 263.
100. Pechel, *Voices*, 471–472.

"Even to a hardened soldier, [Berlin] was most unreal, phantas-magoric," said another of those fleeing. "Most of the great city was pitch dark; the moon was hiding; but flares, shell bursts, the burning downtown buildings, all these reflected on a low-lying, blackish-yellow cloud of sulphurlike smoke. . . . We made most excellent moving targets, like dummies in a shooting gallery."[101]

Young Siegfried Losch, whose war had begun seemingly a lifetime ago on the Oder, also joined the breakout:

> The bridge we had to cross was under fire. . . . I noted that a German tank was crossing the bridge and I took advantage of it by running on the opposite side from where the fire was coming. On the other side of the bridge we all gathered and found that no one was lost. As we walked along . . . more soldiers joined our group. . . . from all ranks and organizations, i.e. army, SS, air force and uniformed civilians. There was even a two star panzer general among us.[102]

Increasingly, as the Soviets realized what was taking place, the breakout became a massacre.

> Underfoot are the bodies of those who had not made it as far as the bridge. Sad their luck; let's hope ours is better for in a minute or two it will be our turn to race across. Every man on our lorry is firing his weapon; machine-gun, machine pistol or rifle. We roll onto the bridge roadway. The lorry picks up speed and races across the open space. It is not a straight drive but a sort of obstacle race, swerving to avoid the trucks, tanks and cars which are lying wrecked and burning on the bridge roadway. There is a sickening feeling as we bump over bodies lying stretched out, hundreds of them all along the length.[103]

Although most such groups quickly came to grief, a surprising number, by bluff, courage and sheer determination, did succeed in breaking through the ring. Once clear of the flaming capital, the ragged, bleeding columns struck west, hoping to reach the British and Americans.

Meanwhile, despite the death of their leaders and the collapse of organized resistance, the hopeless fight for Berlin continued, especially

---

101. O'Donnell, 280, 281.
102. Losch manuscript, 10.
103. Lucas, *Last Days*, 61.

among the elite SS. "Bolshevism meant the end of life ...," one young
German said simply. "[T]hat's the reason for the terribly bitter fight in
Berlin, which wasn't only street to street, but house to house, room
to room, and floor to floor.... [E]very single brick was bitterly fought
over."[104]

Rather than surrender and be murdered, most SS were determined
to die fighting. Of the three hundred members in one French battal-
ion who began the Battle of Berlin, only thirty were still standing. As
much might be said for the Balts, Letts, Danes, Dutch, Spanish, Swiss,
and other SS units.

"[They are] still fighting like tigers," reported a Russian general to
his commander, Marshal Georgi Zhukov, who was hoping to present
the German capital as a May Day prize to Stalin.[105]

"We all wanted to finish it off by the May 1 holiday to give our people something extra to celebrate," explained an exasperated Zhukov,
"but the enemy, in his agony, continued to cling to every building,
every cellar, floor and roof. The Soviet forces inched forward, block by
block, building by building."[106]

Finally, on the afternoon of May 2, General Weidling formally surrendered the city. While most obeyed their commander and laid down
their arms, many refused to submit. Remembered Lothar Ruhl:

> Now and again, we heard shots ... so I asked who was doing the shooting. I
> was told, "Come around to the back, the SS are shooting themselves." I said, "I
> don't want to see it." But I was told, "You have to watch." People were actually
> standing around shooting themselves. Mostly, they were not German SS men;
> they were foreigners, some West Europeans and some East Europeans. The group
> included a number of French and Walloons.[107]

"When the Russians [finally] rounded us up," Ruhl continues, "we
were divided into different march columns.... The Russians didn't
select anyone in particular; they just said, 'You go here, you go there,
and these men go sit in the square'.... No one was allowed to stand

104. Pechel, *Voices*, 470.
105. O'Donnell, *Bunker*, 218.
106. Georgi K. Zhukov, *Marshal Zhukov's Greatest Battles* (New York: Harper and Row, 1969), 287.
107. Pechel, 434.

up. If anyone tried, the Russians immediately fired live ammunition at head level."[108]

"We prisoners," said another weary Landser, "waiting as soldiers always have to wait, sat in the exhausted daze that the end of a battle brings. There was such a depression that we hardly talked, but dozed off into light sleep or smoked, waiting to know what was our fate."[109]

That "fate," as rumors had already hinted, was in fact contained in one chilling word—Siberia. Even so, many surviving soldiers quietly counted their blessings. Johannes Hentschel:

> I had begun to console myself. I was alive. Now, as we were herded out of the Reich Chancellery . . . where a truck was waiting to haul us away, destination unknown but suspected, we looked up and saw a very grim sight. Dangling bodies of some six or seven German soldiers were suspended from lampposts. They had been hanged. Each had a crude German placard pinned or tied to his limp body—TRAITOR, DESERTER, COWARD, ENEMY OF HIS PEOPLE.
>
> They were all so young. The oldest may have been twenty, the others in their mid-teens. Half of them wore Volkssturm armbands or Hitler-jungend uniforms. As we were shoved aboard our truck, prodded in the buttocks by bayonets, I saw that I could almost reach out and touch one of those lifeless boys. He looked sixteen perhaps. His wild, bulging, porcelain blue eyeballs stared down at me blankly, blinkless. I shuddered, looked away.[110]

Another soldier leaving Berlin for slavery was Wilhelm Mohnke. As the general and thousands of other dispirited captives marched east on the roads, they were stunned by what they saw.

> There was very little traffic moving in the same direction we were. But coming toward us now, column after column, endlessly, the Red Army support units. I say columns, but they resembled more a horde, a cavalcade scene from a Russian film. Asia on this day was moving into the middle of Europe, a strange and exotic panorama. There were now countless *panya* wagons, drawn by horse or pony, with singing soldiery perched high on bales of straw. Many of them had clothed themselves in all kinds of unusual civilian dress, including costumes that must have come from ransacked theater and opera wardrobes. . . . Those who noticed that we were Germans shook their brown fists and fired angry volleys

---

108. Ibid., 434.
109. Lucas, *Last Days*, 61.
110. O'Donnell, 360.

into the air. . . . Then came whole units of women soldiers, much better disciplined, marching on foot. . . . Finally came the *Tross*, or quartermaster elements. These resembled units right out of the Thirty Years' War.[111]

Behind the east-bound German prisoners, roughly 20,000 dead comrades lay buried beneath the rubble of a place that no longer resembled anything of this world. "The capital of the Third Reich is a heap
of gaunt, burned-out, flame-seared buildings," reported one of the first
American correspondents to reach Berlin. "It is a desert of a hundred thousand dunes made up of brick and powdered masonry. Over
this hangs the pungent stench of death. . . . It is impossible to exag-
gerate in describing the destruction. . . . Downtown Berlin looks like
nothing man could have contrived. Riding down the famous Frank-
furter Allee, I did not see a single building where you could have set
up a business of even selling apples."[112]

Added a German visitor later:

> The first impression in Berlin, which overpowers you and makes your heart beat
> faster, is that anything human among these indescribable ruins must exist in
> an unknown form. There remains nothing human about it. The water is pol-
> luted, it smells of corpses, you see the most extraordinary shapes of ruins and
> more ruins and still more ruins; houses, streets, districts in ruins. All people in
> civilian clothes among these mountains of ruins appear merely to deepen the
> nightmare. Seeing them you almost *hope* that they are not human.[113]

But, and almost miraculously, there *were* humans yet living in Berlin.
When the guns finally fell silent, these dazed survivors spilled from
their cracks and caves, trying to flee a nightmare, they knew not where.

"Crowds of people were laboriously trying to make their way through
the rubble," Traudl Junge noted. "Old and young, women and children, and a few men carrying small packs, pushing rusty carts or prams
full of assorted belongings. The Russian soldiers did not seem to be
paying much attention to these desperate human beings."[114]

Ruth Andreas-Friedrich:

---

111. Ibid., 333.
112. Keeling, *Gruesome Harvest*, 3.
113. Barnouw, *Germany 1945*, 138.
114. Galante, *Voices*, 151.

We clamber over bomb craters. We squeeze through tangled barbed wire and hastily constructed barricades of furniture. It was with sofas that our army tried to block the Russian advance! With oil cloth sofas, wing chairs and broken armoires. One could laugh if it didn't rather make one feel like crying.

Tanks riddled with holes block the way. A pitiful sight, pointing their muzzles toward the sky. A fatality comes from them. Sweet, heavy, oppressive. . . . Burned-out buildings left and right. God be with us, if it goes on this way. Silently we keep walking. The weight of our luggage is crushing us. . . .

Behind a projection in a wall sits an old man. A pipe in his right hand, a lighter in his left. He is sitting in the sun, completely motionless. Why is he sitting so still? Why doesn't he move at all? A fly is crawling across his face. Green, fat, shiny. Now it crawls into his eyes. The eyes . . . Oh God have mercy! Something slimy is dripping onto his cheeks. . . .

At last the water tower looms up in the distance. We are at the cemetery. The gate to the mortuary is wide open. Again that sweet, oppressive smell. . . . Bodies, nothing but bodies. Laid out on the floor. Row after row, body after body. Children are among them, adults and some very old people. Brought here from who knows where. That draws the final line under five years of war. Children filling mortuaries and old men decomposing behind walls.[115]

While stunned survivors drifted among the ruins like ghosts in a graveyard—or stood for hours in the interminable water lines—the conquerors celebrated in an orgy of drink, rape, music, and song.

"A rosy-cheeked Russian is walking up and down our line, playing an accordion," said one broken woman who had been raped dozens of times. "'Gitler kaputt, Goebbels kaputt, Stalin goot!' he shouts at us. Then he laughs, yells a curse, bangs a comrade on the shoulder and, pointing at him, shouts in Russian . . . 'Look at this one! This is a Russian soldier, who has marched all the way from Moscow to Berlin!' They are bursting out of their pants with the pride of conquerors. It is evidently a surprise to themselves that they have gotten this far."[116]

Although he had failed to present the German capital to Stalin as a May Day gift, and although the cost of taking Berlin had been enormous—well over 300,000 casualties—Marshal Zhukov was exuberant as well.[117]

115. Andreas-Friedrich, *Battleground*, 11–12.
116. Anonymous, *Woman*, 142.
117. Zhukov, *Greatest Battles*, n. 288.

What a stream of thoughts raced through my mind at that joyous moment! I relived the crucial Battle for Moscow, where our troops had stood fast unto death, envisioned Stalingrad in ruins but unconquered, the glorious city of Leningrad holding out through its long blockade of hunger, the thousands of devastated villages and towns, the sacrifices of millions of Soviet people who had survived all those years, the celebration of the victory of the Kursk salient—and now, finally, the goal for which our nation had endured its great sufferings: the complete crushing of Nazi Germany, the smashing of Fascism, the triumph of our just cause.[118]

No one was more quietly elated or deeply relieved, however, than Josef Stalin. And none more clearly perceived the great political and post-war prize that had been gained than the communist dictator.

"Stalin said," remembered Gen. Nikita Khrushchev, "that if it hadn't been for Eisenhower, we wouldn't have succeeded in capturing Berlin."[119]

118. Ibid., 287.
119. Nadeau, *Stalin, Churchill, and Roosevelt*, 163.

8

UNSPEAKABLE

German Wehrmacht! My comrades!

The Fuhrer has fallen. True to his great concept of protecting the people of Europe from Bolshevism, he put his life on the line and died a hero's death. With him one of the greatest heroes of German history is gone. . . .

The Fuhrer has appointed me to be his successor. . . . I assume command of all services of the German Wehrmacht with the desire to continue the fight against the Bolsheviks until the fighting troops and the hundreds of thousands of families of the eastern German region have been saved from enslavement or destruction. I must continue the fight against the British and the Americans for as long as they try to impede my struggle against the Bolsheviks. . . . Anyone who evades his duty now, and thus condemns German women and children to death or enslavement, is a coward and a traitor. . . .

German soldiers, do your duty. The life of our nation depends upon it!

Karl Donitz, Grand Admiral[1]

ALTHOUGH HITLER WAS DEAD and Berlin captured, and although the nation had been halved and further resistance was not only futile but nearly impossible, Germany's long death continued. As Donitz made clear, while there was no longer any question of the Reich's utter defeat and impending surrender, the shattered remnants of the German Army had to fight one last battle to gain

---

1.   Schultz-Naumann, *Last Thirty Days*, 51.

for the millions of fleeing refugees time to reach the Elbe River where the Americans and British had halted. Sadly, cruelly, Allied leaders were determined to halt the pathetic flight at all hazards. Swooping low over the roads, swarms of US and RAF fighters strafed and bombed the columns, slaughtering thousands. As the terrified trekkers scattered to the nearby woods and farms bombers appeared and blasted the hiding places to splinters.[2]

When survivors reached the broad Elbe, American forces under Eisenhower prevented a crossing. Although German soldiers were allowed to pass over and surrender, the general refused civilians the same right. When Soviet aircraft soon appeared, the Americans were forced back to avoid the bombing. Hence, three hundred thousand panic-stricken refugees risked the river and ultimately reached the west bank. Those thousands left standing on the opposite shore were abandoned to their fate.[3]

Unlike the Americans, British forces under Bernard Montgomery allowed all Germans, soldiers and civilians alike, to find haven within its lines. Horrified by what he had seen and heard, the field marshal's manly act saved thousands of women and children from rape, torture and death.

"[T]he Russians," Montgomery later wrote, "though a fine fighting race, were in fact barbarous Asiatics."[4]

When refugees did not come to the British, the British came to them. In the first days of May, Montgomery's men swept upward to occupy northern Germany. Although the English encountered fanatical opposition from small SS units at Bremen, the people of that port were overjoyed; not only would the bombs stop falling but they were saved from the Soviets.

"Their relief that no battle was to be fought over their heads was such that soon we were being hailed as liberators," remembered one Tommy.[5]

---

2.   Thorwald, *Flight in the Winter*, 265.
3.   LeTissier, *Battle of Berlin*, 212.
4.   DeZayas, *Nemesis at Potsdam*, 71.
5.   Strawson, *Battle for Berlin*, 157.

Expecting a bloodbath similar to Berlin, when Montgomery's troops reached Germany's second largest city, they were mystified. Noted a nervous Richard Brett-Smith as he rumbled in an armored car through the streets of Hamburg:

> There was something unnatural about the silence, something a little uncanny. As we drove up to that last great bridge across the Elbe, the final obstacle that could have held us up so long, it seemed impossible that we had taken Hamburg so easily. Looking down at the cold gray waters of the Elbe swirling far below, we sensed again that queer feeling that came whenever we crossed an enemy bridge, and it would have been no great surprise if the whole structure had suddenly collapsed. . . . But no, it did not blow up . . . we were across the last obstacle, and there were no more rivers to cross. . . . There was a lot of clicking of heels and saluting, and in a few moments Hamburg, the greatest port of Germany had been surrendered. . . .
>
> We had long guessed how disorganized the enemy was, and that his administration had broken down, but even so, the sight we now saw was stranger than we had ever expected. Thousands of infantry, Luftwaffe men, SS men, anti-tank gunners, Kriegsmarinen, Hungarians, Rumanians, ambulance men, Labour Corps men, Hitler Jugend boys, soldiers of every conceivable age and unit, jostled one another in complete disorder . . . down every road the Wehrmacht struggled to give itself up, its pride broken, its endurance at an end.[6]

Other German soldiers, a Canadian officer recalled, "[h]ungry and frightened, [were] lying in grain fields within fifty feet of us, awaiting the appropriate time to jump up with their hands in the air."[7]

For those Landsers who had fought for years in the savage, no-quarter nightmare that was the East Front, the first act of surrender, even to the Western Allies, was the most difficult and unnatural step in the world to take. Guy Sajer:

> Two of our men stood up, with their hands raised. . . . We wondered what would happen next. Would English machine guns cut them down? Would our leader shoot them himself, for giving up like that? But nothing happened. The old man, who was still beside me, took me by the arm, and whispered: "Come on. Let's go."
>
> We stood up together. Others quickly followed us. . . . We walked towards the victors with pounding hearts and dry mouths. . . .

---

6. Ibid., 115–116.
7. James Bacque, "The Last Dirty Secret of World War Two," *Saturday Night* 104, no. 9 (Sept. 1989): 31.

> We were roughly jostled together, and shoved into place by English soldiers
> with vindictive faces. However, we had seen worse in our own army, particularly
> in training. . . . The roughness with which the English handled us seemed com-
> paratively insignificant, and even marked by a certain kindness.[8]

"[I]n a time of total chaos," said an appreciative German, "only the British will still act like gentlemen."[9]

Though right on most counts, a number of ugly incidents did occur, illustrating that the Englishman was not immune to the years of vicious anti-German propaganda.

On May 3, RAF fighter-bombers attacked and sank the German refugee ship *Cap Arkona* as it neared Lubeck Bay. Among the thousands of drowning victims were large numbers of concentration camp inmates from Poland. When the British captured Lubeck a short time later and saw hundreds of corpses washing up on shore or bobbing in the bay, it seemed a clear case of the Nazi brutality the world had heard so much about. As Field Marshal Ernst Milch, in full military attire, stepped forward to formally surrender the garrison, an outraged English commando jerked the general's heavy baton from his hand and beat him savagely over the head.[10]

While the British were mopping up huge areas to the north, Americans were doing the same further south. For the most part, US forces were also greeted with white flags, cheers and tears of relief from a war-weary populace. When the Americans did meet determined defenders, it was often small pockets of old men and little boys. Reflected a GI: "I could not understand it, this resistance, this pointless resistance to our advance. The war was all over—our columns were spreading across the whole of Germany and Austria. We were irresistible. We could conquer the world; that was our glowing conviction. And the enemy had nothing. Yet he resisted and in some places with an implacable fanaticism."[11]

8.   Sajer, *Forgotten Soldier*, 456.
9.   O'Donnell, *The Bunker*, 293.
10. Dobson, *The Cruelest Night*, 149.
11. Lucas, *Last Days of the Third Reich*, 205.

Those defenders who survived to surrender were often mowed down where they stood. Gustav Schutz remembered stumbling upon one massacre site where a Labor Service unit had knocked out several American tanks.

"[M]ore than a hundred dead Labor Service men were lying in long rows—all with bloated stomachs and bluish faces," said Schutz. "We had to throw up. Even though we hadn't eaten for days, we vomited."[12]

Already murderous after the Malmedy Massacre and the years of anti-German propaganda, when US forces entered the various concentration camps and discovered huge piles of naked and emaciated corpses, their rage became uncontrollable. As Gen. Eisenhower, along with his lieutenants, Patton and Bradley, toured the prison camp at Ohrdruf Nord, they were sickened by what they saw. In shallow graves or lying haphazardly in the streets were thousands of skeleton-like remains of German and Jewish prisoners, as well as gypsies, communists, and convicts.

"I want every American unit not actually in the front lines to see this place," ordered Eisenhower. "We are told that the American soldier does not know what he is fighting for. Now, at least, he will know what he is fighting *against*."[13]

"In one camp we paraded the townspeople through, to let them have a look," a staff officer with Patton said. "The mayor and his wife went home and slashed their wrists."

"Well, that's the most encouraging thing I've heard," growled Eisenhower, who immediately wired Washington and London, urging government and media representatives to come quickly and witness the horror for themselves.[14]

Given the circumstances, the fate of those Germans living near this and other concentration camps was as tragic as it was perhaps predictable. After compelling the people to view the bodies, American and British officers forced men, women and children to dig up with their hands the rotting remains and haul them to burial pits. Wrote a witness at one camp:

12. Pechel, *Voices from the Third Reich*, 498.
13. Toland, *Last 100 Days*, 371.
14. Ibid.

[A]ll day long, always running, men and women alike, from the death pile to the death pit, with the stringy remains of their victims over their shoulders. When one of them dropped to the ground with exhaustion, he was beaten with a rifle butt. When another stopped for a break, she was kicked until she ran again, or prodded with a bayonet, to the accompaniment of lewd shouts and laughs. When one tried to escape or disobeyed an order, he was shot.[15]

For those forced to handle the rotting corpses, death by disease often followed soon after.

Few victors, from Eisenhower down, seemed to notice, and fewer seemed to care, that conditions similar to the camps existed throughout much of Germany. Because of the almost total paralysis of the Reich's roads and rails caused by around-the-clock air attacks, supplies of food, fuel, clothes, and medicine had thinned to a trickle in German towns and cities and dried up almost entirely at the concentration camps. As a consequence, thousands of camp inmates swiftly succumbed in the final weeks of the war to typhus, dysentery, tuberculosis, starvation, and neglect.[16] When pressed by a friend if there had indeed been a deliberate policy of starvation, one of the few guards lucky enough to escape another camp protested:

> "It wasn't like that, believe me; it wasn't like that! I'm maybe the only survivor who can witness to how it really was, but who would believe me!"
> "Is it all a lie?"
> "Yes and no," he said. "I can only say what I know about our camp. The final weeks were horrible. No more rations came, no more medical supplies. The people got ill, they lost weight, and it kept getting more and more difficult to keep order. Even our own people lost their nerve in this extreme situation. But do you think we would have held out until the end to hand the camp over in an orderly fashion if we had been these murderers?"[17]

As American forces swept through Bavaria toward Munich in late April, most German guards at the concentration camp near Dachau fled. To maintain order and arrange an orderly transfer of the 32,000 prisoners to the Allies, and despite signs at the gate warning, "NO ENTRANCE—TYPHUS EPIDEMIC," several hundred German sol-

---

15. Barnouw, *Germany 1945*, 68.
16. Ibid.; Howard A. Buechner, *Dachau* (Metairie, Louisiana: Thunderbird, 1986), 32.
17. Woltersdorf, *Gods of War*, 124–125.

diers were ordered to the prison.[18] When American units under Lt. Col. Felix Sparks liberated the camp the following day, the GIs were horrified by what they saw. Outside the prison were rail cars brim full with diseased and starved corpses. Inside the camp, Sparks found "a room piled high with naked and emaciated corpses. As I turned to look over the prison yard with unbelieving eyes, I saw a large number of dead inmates lying where they had fallen in the last few hours or days before our arrival. Since all the many bodies were in various stages of decomposition, the stench of death was overpowering."[19]

Unhinged by the nightmare surrounding him, Sparks turned his equally enraged troops loose on the hapless German soldiers. While one group of over three hundred were led away to an enclosure, other disarmed Landsers were murdered in the guard towers, the barracks, or chased through the streets. US Army chaplain, Captain Leland Loy:

[A] German guard came running toward us. We grabbed him and were standing there talking to him when . . . [a GI] came up with a tommy-gun. He grabbed the prisoner, whirled him around and said, "There you are you son-of-a-bitch!!" The man was only about three feet from us, but the soldier cut him down with his sub-machine gun. I shouted at him, "what did you do that for, he was a prisoner?" He looked at me and screamed "Gotta kill em, gotta kill em." When I saw the look in his eyes and the machine gun waving in the air, I said to my men, "Let him go." [20]

"[T]he men were deliberately wounding guards," recalled one US soldier. "A lot of guards were shot in the legs so they couldn't move. They were then turned over to the inmates. One was beheaded with a bayonet. Others were ripped apart limb by limb."[21]

While the tortures were in progress, Lt. Jack Bushyhead forced nearly 350 prisoners up against a wall, planted two machine-guns, then ordered his men to open fire. Those still alive when the fusillade ended were forced to stand amid the carnage while the machine-gunners reloaded. A short time later, army surgeon Howard Buechner happened on the scene:

18. Buechner, *Dachau*, 8.
19. Ibid., 64.
20. Ibid., 75–76.
21. Ibid., 104.

Lt. Bushyhead was standing on the flat roof of a low building. . . . Beside him one or more soldiers manned a .30 caliber machine gun. Opposite this building was a long, high cement and brick wall. At the base of the wall lay row on row of German soldiers, some dead, some dying, some possibly feigning death. Three or four inmates of the camp, dressed in striped clothing, each with a .45 caliber pistol in hand, were walking along the line. . . . As they passed down the line, they systematically fired a round into the head of each one.[22]

"At the far end of the line of dead or dying soldiers," Buechner continued, "a small miracle was taking place."

The inmates who were delivering the coup de grace had not yet reached this point and a few guards who were still alive were being placed on litters by German medics. Under the direction of a German doctor, the litter bearers were carrying these few soldiers into a nearby hospital for treatment.

I approached this officer and attempted to offer my help. Perhaps he did not realize that I was a doctor since I did not wear red cross insignia. He obviously could not understand my words and probably thought that I wanted him to give up his patients for execution. In any event, he waved me away with his hand and said "Nein," "Nein," "Nein."[23]

Despite his heroics and the placing of his own life in mortal danger, the doctor's efforts were for naught. The wounded men were soon seized and murdered, as was every other German in the camp.

"We shot everything that moved," one GI bragged.

"We got all the bastards," gloated another.

In all, over five hundred helpless German soldiers were slaughtered in cold blood. As a final touch, Lt. Col. Sparks forced the citizens of Dachau to bury the thousands of corpses in the camp, thereby assuring the death of many from disease.[24]

Though perhaps the worst, the incident at Dachau was merely one of many massacres committed by US troops. Unaware of the deep hatred the Allies harbored for them, when proud SS units surrendered they naively assumed that they would be respected as the unsurpassed fighters that they undoubtedly were. Lt. Hans Woltersdorf was recovering in a German military hospital when US forces arrived.

22. Ibid., 86.
23. Ibid., 87.
24. Ibid., 64, 98.

Those who were able stood at the window, and told those of us who were lying down what was going on. A motorcycle with sidecar, carrying an officer and two men from the Waffen-SS, had arrived. They surrendered their weapons and the vehicle. The two men were allowed to continue on foot, but the officer was led away by the Americans. They accompanied him part of the way, just fifty meters on. Then a salvo from submachine guns was heard. The three Americans returned, alone.

"Did you see that? They shot the lieutenant! Did you see that? They're shooting all the Waffen-SS officers!"

That had to be a mistake! Why? Why?!

Our comrades from the Wehrmacht didn't stand around thinking for long. They went down to the hospital's administrative quarters, destroyed all files that showed that we belonged to the Waffen-SS, started new medical sheets for us with Wehrmacht ranks, got us Wehrmacht uniforms, and assigned us to new Wehrmacht units.[25]

Such stratagems seldom succeeded, however, since SS soldiers had their blood-type tattooed under the left arm.

"Again and again," continues Woltersdorf, "Americans invaded the place and gathered up groups of people who had to strip to the waist and raise their left arm. Then we saw some of them being shoved on to trucks with rifle butts."[26]

When French forces under Jacques-Philippe Leclerc captured a dozen French SS near Karlstein, the general sarcastically asked one of the prisoners why he was wearing a German uniform.

"You look very smart in your *American* uniform, General," replied the boy.

In a rage, Leclerc ordered the twelve captives shot.

"All refused to have their eyes bandaged," a priest on the scene noted, "and all bravely fell crying "Vive la France!"[27]

Although SS troops were routinely slaughtered upon surrender, anyone wearing a German uniform was considered lucky if they were merely slapped, kicked, then marched to the rear. "Before they could be properly put in jail," wrote a witness when a group of little boys

25. Woltersdorf, 121–122.
26. Ibid., 123.
27. Landwehr, *Charlemagne's Legionnaires*, 174–177.

were marched past, "American GIs . . . fell on them and beat them bloody, just because they had German uniforms."[28]

After relatively benign treatment by the British, Guy Sajer and other Landsers were transferred to the Americans. They were, said Sajer, "tall men with plump, rosy cheeks, who behaved like hooligans."

> Their bearing was casual. . . . Their uniforms were made of soft cloth, like golf-ing clothes, and they moved their jaws continuously, like ruminating animals. They seemed neither happy nor unhappy, but indifferent to their victory, like men who are performing their duties in a state of partial consent, without any real enthusiasm for them. From our filthy, mangy ranks, we watched them with curiosity. . . . They seemed rich in everything but joy. . . .
>
> The Americans also humiliated us as much as they could. . . . They put us in a camp with only a few large tents, which could shelter barely a tenth of us. . . . In the center of the camp, the Americans ripped open several large cases filled with canned food. They spread the cans onto the ground with a few kicks, and walked away. . . . The food was so delicious that we forgot about the driving rain, which had turned the ground into a sponge. . . .
>
> From their shelters, the Americans watched us and talked about us. They prob-ably despised us for flinging ourselves so readily into such elementary con-cerns, and thought us cowards for accepting the circumstances of captivity. . . . We were not in the least like the German troops in the documentaries our charm-ing captors had probably been shown before leaving their homeland. We pro-vided them with no reasons for anger; we were not the arrogant, irascible Boches, but simply underfed men standing in the rain, ready to eat unseasoned canned food; living dead, with anxiety stamped on our faces, leaning against any sup-port, half asleep on our feet; sick and wounded, who didn't ask for treatment, but seemed content simply to sleep for long hours, undisturbed. It was clearly depressing for these crusading missionaries to find so much humility among the vanquished.[29]

Ironically, it was those very same soldiers who had fought with such ruthless savagery during the war and whose government had not even been a signatory to the Geneva Convention that now often exhib-ited most kindness and compassion to the fallen foe. Undoubtedly, these battle-hardened Soviet shock troops had seen far too much blood and death during the past four years to thirst for more. Panzer com-mander, Col. Hans von Luck:

---

28. Barnouw, *Germany 1945*, 67–68.
29. Sajer, *Forgotten Soldier*, 456–457.

So there we stood with our hands up; from all sides the Russians came at us with their tommy guns at the ready. I saw to my dismay that they were Mongolians, whose slit eyes revealed hatred, curiosity, and greed. As they tried to snatch away my watch and Knight's Cross, a young officer suddenly intervened.

"Stop, don't touch him. He's a *geroi* (hero), a man to respect."

I looked at him and just said, "*Spasivo* (thank you). . . .

This correct young Russian officer took us at once to the nearest regimental command post, where he handed us over to a colonel of the tank corps. . . . It turned out before long that it had been his tank regiment on which we had inflicted such heavy losses at Lauban. This burly man, who made such a brutal first impression, slapped his thigh and laughed.

"You see," he cried, "that's poetic justice: you shot up my tanks and forced us to retreat; now in recompense I have you as my prisoner."

He fetched two glasses and in Russian style filled them to the brim with vodka, so that together we would drain them with one swallow.[30]

In numerous other instances surprised Landsers in the east were treated correctly, given food, clothing, cigarettes, and accorded prisoner of war status. Left to the Russian soldiers themselves, there would have been no gulags, no slavery, and no Siberia for their defeated enemy—it was enough for the average Ivan to have simply survived.

Finally, after fighting for as much time as he dared, Admiral Donitz signed the articles of unconditional German surrender on May 7 and the Third Reich ceased to exist.

"With this signature," Field Marshal Alfred Jodl announced to the Allies, "the German people and the German armed forces are for better or worse delivered into the victor's hands. . . . In this hour I can only express the hope that the victors will treat them with generosity."[31]

For those resolved to fight to the death as long as their nation fought on, formal capitulation was the signal that they now could lay down their arms with honor in tact. Many, like famous flying ace Hans-Ulrich Rudel, were determined to face the ignominy of defeat with all the dignity they could muster. When the one-legged pilot landed his plane

30. Von Luck, *Panzer Commander*, 212–213.
31. Strawson, *Berlin*, 158.

to surrender at an American-occupied airfield, a GI rushed up, poked a pistol into his face, then grabbed for the colonel's decorations. Rudel promptly slammed the canopy shut. A short time later, as the hobbling ace was escorted to the officers' mess, other prisoners sprang to their feet and gave the Nazi salute. At this, the indignant US commander demanded silence, then asked Rudel if he spoke English. "Even if I can speak English, we are in Germany and here I speak only German. As far as the salute is concerned, we are ordered to salute that way, and being soldiers, we carry out our orders. Besides, we don't care whether you object to it or not. The German soldier has not been beaten on his merits but has simply been crushed by overwhelming masses of materiel."[32]

For surrendering SS units lucky enough to escape savage beatings or execution, there were sometimes humiliations worse than death. When one group of survivors, after six bloody years of war, pinned on their medals in a final act of pride, they were mobbed by US souvenir-seekers who plucked from them the last vestige of their valor.[33]

Meanwhile, behind the Russian front, the final pockets of German resistance surrendered. At the Courland enclave on the Baltic, 190,000 soldiers and 14,000 Lettish volunteers laid down their arms.[34] After seventy days of desperate, heroic struggle, the besieged garrison of Breslau also lowered its flag. Soon after surrender, the already haggard females of Breslau began pondering "whether life had not been sweeter during the worst days of the siege."[35] Remembered one girl:

> Rape began almost immediately and there was a viciousness in the acts as if we women were being punished for Breslau having resisted for so long. . . . Let me say that I was young, pretty, plump and fairly inexperienced. A succession of Ivans gave me over the next week or two a lifetime of experience. Luckily very few of their rapes lasted more than a minute. With many it was just a matter

32. Toland, *100 Days*, 583.
33. Lucas, *Last Days*, 91.
34. Duffy, *Red Storm*, 152.
35. Thorwald, *Flight*, 279.

of seconds before they collapsed gasping. What kept me sane was that almost from the very first one I felt only a contempt for these bullying and smelly peasants who could not act gently towards a woman, and who had about as much sexual technique as a rabbit.[36]

At devastated Dresden, Chemnitz and other cities that now for the first time experienced Soviet occupation, the situation was the same.

"On the morning of May 9th, the Russian troops swarmed into town," wrote a priest from Goerlitz.

> By noon, the Russians, flushed with victory, were looting all the houses and raping the womenfolk. Most of the soldiers were under the influence of drink, and as a result the number of atrocities began to increase at an alarming rate.
> . . .
> As soon as it grew dark the streets re-echoed with the screams of women and girls who had fallen into the hands of the Russians. Every ten minutes or so, parties of soldiers raided the house. As I was attired in the dress of my order, I tried to protect the occupants of the house by pointing to the cross I was wearing. . . . All went well until about three o'clock in the morning. Just as we were beginning to hope that the dreadful night was over, four drunken Russians appeared and started searching the house for two girls who had hidden in a room on the fourth floor. After ransacking our apartment, they went upstairs. . . . They found the two girls and locked the three of us in the room. I went down on my knees and begged them not to molest us. Thereupon they forced me onto a chair; one of them stood in front of me, pointing his loaded revolver at me, and made me look on whilst the others raped the poor girls. It was dreadful.[37]

"There were no limits to the bestiality and licentiousness of these troops . . . ," echoed a pastor from Milzig. "Girls and women were routed out of their hiding-places, out of the ditches and thickets where they had sought shelter from the Russian soldiers, and were beaten and raped. Older women who refused to tell the Russians where the younger ones had hidden were likewise beaten and raped."[38]

"Fear is always present," young Regina Shelton added. "It flares into panic at tales of atrocities—mutilated nude bodies tossed by the wayside—a woman nailed spread-eagle to a cart and gang-raped while

36. Lucas, *Last Days*, 69.
37. Kaps, *Tragedy of Silesia*, 464–465.
38. Ibid., 430.

bleeding to death from her wounds—horrible diseases spread to their victims by sex-drunken Mongolians."[39]

"Is this the peace we yearned for so long?" cried Elsbeth Losch from a town near Dresden. "When will all this have an end?"[40]

While the rape of Germany was in progress, a horror unimaginable was transpiring in Czechoslovakia. On May 5, when rumors swept through Prague that US forces were only seven miles away, the citizens of the Czech capital rose up against the Nazi occupation. Before the day was out most of the German garrison had been isolated and surrounded.[41] Meanwhile, the roundup of prisoners, including many refugees, began. Years of pent hatred for the German minority in their midst now had a free hand among the population. Wrote Juergen Thorwald:

> Crowds of Czechs awaited the transports of German prisoners in the streets to pelt them with stones, spit into their faces, and beat them with any object that came to hand. German women, children, and men ran the gauntlet, with arms over their heads, to reach the prison gates under a hail of blows and kicks. Women of every age were dragged from the groups, their heads were shaved, their faces smeared with paint, and swastikas were drawn on their bared backs and breasts. Many were violated, others forced to open their mouth to the spittle of their torturers.[42]

On May 9, with the fighting ended, the mob turned its attention to the thousands of Germans locked in prisons. "Several trucks loaded with German wounded and medical personnel drove into the [prison] court," Thorwald continues. "The wounded, the nurses, the doctors had just climbed from their vehicles when suddenly a band of insurgents appeared from the street and pounced upon them. They tore away their crutches, canes, and bandages, knocked them to the ground, and with clubs, poles, and hammers hit them until the Germans lay still."[43]

39. Shelton, *To Lose a War*, 110.
40. Letter of Elsbeth Losch, Lehnmuhle, Germany, to "Dear Heta," May 14, 1945 (copy in possession of the author).
41. Nadeau, *Stalin, Churchill, and Roosevelt*, 178–179.
42. Thorwald, *Flight*, 287.
43. Ibid., 302.

"So began a day as evil as any known to history," muttered Thorwald.

In the street, crowds were waiting for those who were marched out of their prisons. . . . [T]hey had come equipped with everything their aroused passions might desire, from hot pitch to garden shears. . . . They . . . grabbed Germans—and not only SS men—drenched them with gasoline, strung them up with their feet uppermost, set them on fire, and watched their agony, prolonged by the fact that in their position the rising heat and smoke did not suffocate them. They . . . tied German men and women together with barbed wire, shot into the bundles, and rolled them down into the Moldau River. . . . They beat every German until he lay still on the ground, forced naked women to remove the barricades, cut the tendons of their heels, and laughed at their writhing. Others they kicked to death.[44]

"At the corner opening onto Wasser Street," said Czech, Ludek Pachmann, "hung three naked corpses, mutilated beyond recognition, their teeth entirely knocked out, their mouths nothing but bloody holes. Others had to drag their dead fellow-Germans into Stefans Street. . . . 'Those are your brothers, kiss them!' And so the still-living Germans, lips pressed tightly together, had to kiss their dead."[45]

As he tried to escape the city, Gert Rainer, a German soldier disguised as a priest, saw sights that seemed straight from hell:

[A] sobbing young woman was kneeling, showering kisses on a child in her arms. . . . The child's eyes had been gouged out, and a knife still protruded from his abdomen. The woman's torn clothing and disheveled hair indicated that she had fought like a fury. Lost in her sorrow, she had not noticed the approaching stranger. He bent down to her and put her in mind that she had better not stay here. She was in danger of being shot herself.

"But that's what I want!" she suddenly cried. "I don't want to go on living without my little Peter!"

In their sadistic ecstasy, people turned public mass murder into a folk festival. . . . Five young women had been tied to an advertising pillar, the rope wrapped about them several times. Their seven children had been packed into a gutter of sorts at their feet. . . . [A] Czech woman, perhaps 50 years of age, was pouring gasoline over the tied-up mothers. Others were spitting in their faces, slapping them and tearing whole fistfuls of hair. Then the oldest of them, laughing frenetically, lit a newspaper and ran around the pillar holding the burning paper to the gasoline-soaked victims. Like a flash, the pillar and the five others disappeared in flames

---

44. Ibid., 302–303.
45. Herta Ruthard Collections (Lisle, Ontario, Canada), "The Furies of Hell—Here They Were Unleashed" (copy in possession of the author).

several meters high. . . . The spectators had not noticed that one of the burning Germans had torn through the charring rope and thrown herself into the flames that licked up through the grating. With strength borne of a courage beyond death, she lifted out the grating and, lying on her stomach, tried to reach down into the tangle of blazing children. Lifeless, she lay in the flames.

In the meantime, the other four women, on fire from their feet to their hair, had slumped down as the common support of the rope was gone. That was the cue for their murderers to begin dancing around the pillar, cheering and rejoicing. The howling of the butchers grew even louder.

On Wenzels Square there was not one lamp-post without a German soldier strung up from it. The majority of them had been war-injured. . . . A crowd literally jumping for joy surrounded an arena-like clearing, in the center of which two men held a stark-naked young German woman. Each of her breasts had been pierced with a large safety-pin, from which Iron Crosses were hung. A rod bearing a swastika flag at one end had been stabbed through her navel. . . . A naked German lay motionless beside her trampled child. She had been beaten to death. A gaping head wound revealed her brain, oozing out.

Several men had been dragged down from a Wehrmacht truck. Their hands were tied, the other end of the rope fastened to the hitch beneath the back end of the truck. . . . A young Czech climbed into the driver's seat. When the truck started, the spectators fell into a frenzy of hatred. . . . The five captives were pulled along by ropes some 60 feet long. As yet they could keep up with the truck. But the more the driver picked up speed, the more it became impossible for them to keep on their feet. One after the other fell, jerked forward, and was dragged along at ever-increasing speed. After but a few rounds, the Germans were mangled beyond recognition. One single lump of blood, flesh and dirt comprised the pitiful haul of this chariot of bestiality.[46]

At the huge sports stadium, thousands of Germans were herded onto the field to provide amusement for a laughing, howling audience. "Before our very eyes . . . [they] were tortured to death in every conceivable way," remembered Josefine Waimann. "Most deeply branded on my memory is the pregnant woman whose belly . . . uniformed Czechs slashed open, ripped out the fetus and then, howling with glee, stuffed a dachshund into the torn womb of the woman, who was screaming dreadfully. . . . The slaughter happening in the arena before our very eyes was like that in ancient Rome."[47]

The horror born at Prague soon spread to the rest of Czechoslova-

---

46. Ingomar Pust, "Screams From Hell," *Kronenzeitung* (March 29, 1994), 24.
47. Ruthard Collections, article from "Friedlaender Heimatbriefe" (in possession of the author).

kia, particularly the Sudentland, where Germans had lived for over seven centuries.

"Take everything from the Germans," demanded Czech president, Edvard Benes, "leave them only a handkerchief to sob into!"[48]

"You may kill Germans, it's no sin," cried a priest to a village mob.[49]

At Bilna, wrote a chronicler,

> men and women were rounded up in the market square, had to strip naked and were made to walk single-file while being beaten by the population with whips and canes. Then ... the men had to crawl on all fours, like dogs, one behind the other, during which they were beaten until they lost control of their bowels; each had to lick the excrement off the one in front of him. This torture continued until many of them had been beaten to death. . . . What was done to the women there simply cannot be described, the sadistic monstrousness of it is simply too great for words.[50]

"When I passed through Czechoslovakia after the collapse," one German soldier recalled, "I saw severed human heads lining window sills, and in one butcher's shop naked corpses were hanging from the meat hooks."[51]

When the fury had finally spent itself in Czechoslovakia, over 200,000 people had been butchered. Similar purges of German minorities occurred in Rumania, Hungary and Yugoslavia where men, women and children, by the hundreds of thousands, were massacred in cold blood. The slaughter throughout Europe was not confined to ethnic Germans alone. Following the Allied occupation of France, over 100,000 French citizens were murdered by their countrymen because of collaboration with the Germans or anti-communist activities. Similar, though smaller, reckonings took place in Belgium, Holland, Denmark, and Norway.

While the bloody pogroms were in progress across Europe, US and British forces were quietly carrying out a secret sweep of their own.

48. Ibid., "Paradise Lost," 1.
49. Ibid.
50. Ibid., "40 Years Ago: Sudeten German History Book", 4.
51. Ibid., "The Furies of Hell," 2.

When the Western Allies overran Germany and Austria, millions of Soviet citizens fell into their hands. Among the many points discussed at Yalta was one especially dear to Stalin—the repatriation of all Soviet citizens, including large numbers of POWs and slave laborers.[52] Among all Soviet nationals, however, Stalin was particularly anxious to lay hands on Andrei Vlasov, the fiercely anti-communist general who had hoped to lead his million-man army in the liberation of Russia. Eager as always to please "Uncle Joe," Roosevelt and Churchill happily agreed to send back all Soviets encountered, irregardless of laws, treaties or the dictates of common humanity. Although several repatriations of Russian prisoners had occurred shortly after Yalta, fear of German reprisals against Allied POWs prevented more.[53] Now, with the war over and the threat of German riposte removed, the return of Russians began in earnest.

Since Soviet soldiers captured or surrendering in German uniform were guaranteed protection under the Geneva Convention, most Russian prisoners felt certain they were beyond Stalin's grasp; that the Western democracies, founded on freedom, liberty and law, would honor the treaty and protect them.[54] Although many British and American soldiers initially despised their Russian captives, both for being an enemy, as well as "traitors" to their country, attitudes among many began to soften upon closer examination.

"When the screening began, I had little sympathy for these Russians in their battered German uniforms . . . ," wrote William Sloane Coffin, Jr., who acted as translator for several colonels who interrogated the prisoners. "But as the colonels, eager to establish their cover and satisfy their curiosity, encouraged the Russians to tell their personal histories, I began to understand the dilemma the men had faced."[55]

They spoke not only of the cruelties of collectivization in the thirties but of arrests, shootings and wholesale deportations of families. Many of the men them-

---

52. Nikolai Tolstoy, *The Secret Betrayal, 1944–1947* (New York: Charles Scribner's Sons, 1977), 254.
53. Ibid., 142, 325.
54. Elliott, *Pawns of Yalta*, 248–249
55. Ibid., 94.

selves had spent time in Soviet jails. . . . Soon my own interest was so aroused that I began to spend evenings in the camp hearing more and more tales of arrest and torture. . . . Hearing . . . the personal histories of those who had joined Vlasov's army made me increasingly uncomfortable with the words "traitor" and "deserter," as applied to these men. Maybe Stalin's regime was worthy of desertion and betrayal?[56]

Added a Russian prisoner, one of thousands captured by the Germans who joined Vlasov rather than starve in a POW camp:

You think, Captain, that we sold ourselves to the Germans for a piece of bread? Tell me, why did the Soviet Government forsake us? Why did it forsake millions of prisoners? We saw prisoners of all nationalities, and they were taken care of. Through the Red Cross they received parcels and letters from home; only the Russians received nothing. In Kassel I saw American Negro prisoners, and they shared their cakes and chocolates with us. Then why didn't the Soviet Government, which we considered our own, send us at least some plain hard tack? . . . Hadn't we fought? Hadn't we defended the Government? Hadn't we fought for our country? If Stalin refused to have anything to do with us, we didn't want to have anything to do with Stalin![57]

"I lost, so I remain a traitor . . . ," conceded Vlasov himself, who, though he might easily have saved himself, chose instead to share the fate of his men. As the Russian general reminded his captors, however, if he was a traitor for seeking foreign aid to liberate his country, then so in their own day were George Washington and Benjamin Franklin.[58]

Despite the Geneva Convention, despite the strong likelihood that returnees would be massacred, Gen. Eisenhower and other top leaders were determined that Russian repatriation would be carried out to the letter. Terrible portents of what lay ahead had come even before the war was over.

When the British government prepared to return from England thousands of Soviets in the winter of 1944/45, many prisoners attempted suicide or tried to escape. Once the wretched cargo was finally forced onto ships, heavy guards were posted to prevent the pris-

56. Ibid.
57. Tolstoy, *Secret Betrayal*, 41.
58. Ibid, 292.

oners from leaping overboard. Upon reaching Russian ports, few British seamen could doubt the fate of their charges once they were marched out of sight by the NKVD, or secret police. At Odessa on the Black Sea, noisy bombers soon appeared and circled tightly over the docks while loud sawmills joined the chorus to drown the sounds of screams and gunfire echoing from the warehouses. Within half an hour, the airplanes flew away, the sawmills shut down, and all was quiet again.[59] A similar scenario was played out when four thousand Soviets were forcibly repatriated from the United States.[60]

To prevent Russian riots in Europe when the war was over, Allied authorities kept the operations top secret, with only a minimum of officers privy to the moves. Additionally, rumors and counter-rumors were planted, stating that the prisoners would be transferred to cleaner camps soon or even set free.[61] Not all Americans had the stomach for it. As a translator, William Sloane Coffin, Jr. had not only grown to like and respect the men, but empathize with their plight. On the night before the surprise repatriation from the camp at Plattling, the Russians staged a theatrical performance in honor of several US interrogators. Sickened by their own treachery, the officers spent the night drinking and ordered Coffin to fill in for them instead.[62]

> For a while I thought I was going to be physically ill. Several times I turned to the [Russian] commandant sitting next to me. It would have been easy to tip him off. There was still time. The camp was minimally guarded. Once outside the men could tear up their identity cards, get other clothes. . . . Yet I couldn't bring myself to do it. It was not that I was afraid of being court-martialed. . . . But I too had my orders. . . . The closest I came was at the door when the commandant said good night. . . . I almost blurted out . . . "Get out and quick." But I didn't. Instead I drove off cursing the commandant for being so trusting.[63]

In the pre-dawn darkness the following day, as tanks and searchlights surrounded the camp, hundreds of US soldiers moved in. Surprised though they were, some Russians acted swiftly.

59. Ibid., 128–130.
60. Elliott, *Yalta*, 90.
61. Ibid., 91.
62. Ibid., 94.
63. Ibid., 95.

"Despite the fact that there were three GIs to every Russian," Coffin noted, "I saw several men commit suicide. Two rammed their heads through windows sawing their necks on the broken glass until they cut their jugular veins. Another took his leather boot-straps, tied a loop to the top of his triple-decker bunk, put his head through the noose and did a back flip over the edge which broke his neck."[64]

With clubs swinging, troops ruthlessly drove the startled survivors into waiting trucks which were soon speeding toward the Soviet lines.[65]

"[W]e stood over them with guns and our orders were to shoot to kill if they tried to escape from our convoy," said an American officer in one group. "Needless to say many of them did risk death to effect their escape."[66]

Much like the British and American sailors who had delivered a living cargo to its executioner, Allied soldiers knew very well the journey was a one-way trip. "We . . . understood they were going to their deaths. Of this, there was never any doubt whatsoever," a British Tommy admitted. "It was that night and the following day that we started to count the small-arms fire coming from the Russian sector to the accompaniment of the finest male voice choir I have ever heard. The voices echoed round and round the countryside. Then the gunfire would be followed by a huge cheer."[67]

In much the same way as above were the rest of Vlasov's Russian Liberation Army forced from the camps in Germany and Austria and handed to Stalin. Many, maybe most, were dead within days of delivery.

"When we captured them, we shot them as soon as the first intelligible Russian word came from their mouths," said Captain Alexander Solzhenitsyn.[68]

Another group of "traitors" Stalin was eager to have repatriated were the Cossacks. Long known for its courage and fierce independence, the colorful nation fled Russia and years of communist persecution

64. Ibid., 1–2.
65. Tolstoy, *Betrayal*, 357.
66. Ibid., 323.
67. Ibid., 186.
68. Elliott, *Yalta*, 195.

when the German Army began its withdrawal west.[69] Recorded an Allied soldier:

> As an army they presented an amazing sight. Their basic uniform was German, but with their fur Cossack caps, their mournful dundreary whiskers, their knee-high riding boots, and their roughly-made horse-drawn carts bearing all their worldly goods and chattels, including wife and family, there could be no mistaking them for anything but Russians. They were a tableau from the Russia of 1812. Cossacks are famed as horsemen and these lived up to their reputation.[70]

Like the Americans who returned Vlasov's army, the British were eager to appease Stalin by handing back the hapless Cossacks. Unlike the Americans though, the British realized that by separating the thirty thousand followers from their leaders would make the transfers simpler. When the elders were requested to attend a "conference" on their relocation elsewhere in Europe, they complied. Honest and unsophisticated—many having served in the old Imperial Army—the Cossack officers were easily deceived.[71]

"On the honor of a British officer . . . ," assured the English when the people asked about their leaders. "They'll all be back this evening. The officers are only going to a conference."[72]

With the beheading of the Cossack Nation, the job of repatriating the rest was made easier, but not easy. When the men, women and children at the various Cossack camps refused to enter the trucks and go willingly to their slaughter, Tommies, armed with rifles, bayonets and pick handles, marched in. "WE PREFER DEATH than to be returned to the Soviet Union . . . ," read signs printed in crude English. "We, husbands, mothers, brothers, sisters, and children PRAY FOR OUR SALVATION!!!"[73]

Wrote one British officer from the Cossack camp at Lienz, Austria:

> As soon as the platoon approached to commence loading, the people formed themselves into a solid mass, kneeling and crouching with their arms locked around each others' bodies. As individuals on the outskirts of the group were

---

69. Tolstoy, 152.
70. Ibid., 160.
71. Ibid., 178.
72. Ibid., 172.
73. Ibid., 202.

pulled away, the remainder compressed themselves into a still tighter body, and as panic gripped them [they] started clambering over each other in frantic efforts to get away from the soldiers. The result was a pyramid of hysterical, screaming human beings, under which a number of people were trapped. The soldiers made frantic efforts to split this mass in order to try to save the lives of these persons pinned underneath, and pick helves and rifle butts were used on arms and legs to force individuals to loosen their hold. When we eventually cleared this group, we discovered that one man and one woman [had] suffocated. Every person of this group had to be forcibly carried onto the trucks.[74]

When one huddled mob was beaten into submission, the troops waded into another. Recalled a Cossack mother as the Tommies cut and clubbed their way forward:

There was a great crush; I found myself standing on someone's body, and could only struggle not to tread on his face. The soldiers grabbed people one by one and hurried them to the lorries, which now set off half-full. From all sides in the crowd could be heard cries: "Avaunt thee, Satan! Christ is risen! Lord have mercy upon us!"

Those that they caught struggled desperately and were battered. I saw how an English soldier snatched a child from its mother and wanted to throw him into the lorry. The mother caught hold of the child's leg, and they each pulled in opposite directions. Afterwards I saw that the mother was no longer holding the child and that the child had been dashed against the side of the lorry.[75]

As in the case above, soldiers tried first to wrench children from their mothers' arms for once a child had been hurled into a truck the parents were sure to follow. In the tumult, some victims managed to break free and run. Most were mowed down by machine-guns. Those not hit drowned themselves in the nearby river or cut the throats of their entire family. In the Lienz operation alone, as many as seven hundred men, women and children committed suicide or were cut down by bullets and bayonets.[76]

Eventually, the entire Cossack nation had been delivered to the Soviets. Within days, most were either dead or bolted into cattle cars for the one-way ride to Siberia.[77]

---

74. Ibid., 208.
75. Ibid., 208–209.
76. Ibid., 212.
77. Ibid., 221.

Certainly, not every British or American officer had a heart for the repatriations, known broadly—and aptly—as "Operation Keelhaul." Some actually placed their careers on the line. When Alex Wilkinson was ordered to turn over Russians in his district to the Soviets, the British colonel replied: *"Only if they are willing to go."*

> It was then suggested to me that they should be collected and put into the trains whether they liked it or not. I then asked how they were to be put into the trains? And I was told that a few machine-guns might make them change their minds. To which I replied "that will *not* happen while I am here.[78]

When Wilkinson agreed to obey orders "on the one condition that the trains go west NOT EAST," his commander was furious.

"Within a fortnight of that meeting," said the Colonel, "I was relieved of my command and sent back to England with a report that 'I lacked drive.'"[79]

Another British officer who "lacked drive" was Sir Harold Alexander. "To compel . . . repatriation," the field marshal wrote his government from Italy, "would certainly either involve the use of force or drive them into committing suicide. . . . Such treatment, coupled with the knowledge that these unfortunate individuals are being sent to an almost certain death, is quite out of keeping with the traditions of democracy and justice, as we know them."[80]

Unfortunately, such courageous acts had little impact on the removals. Alexander, like Wilkinson, was soon sent elsewhere and officers less inclined to cause trouble took their place. Nevertheless, word of what was occurring did trickle out, forcing top Allied officials to issue denials.

"[I]t is not and has not been the policy of the US and British Government [sic] involuntarily to repatriate any Russian . . . ," assured a spokesman for Supreme Allied Command.[81]

"[N]o instances of coercion have been brought to our attention . . . ," echoed US Secretary of State George C. Marshall. "[I]t is against Amer-

---

78. Ibid., 354.
79. Ibid.
80. Elliott, *Yalta*, 114–115.
81. Ibid., 120.

ican tradition for us to compel these persons, who are now under our authority, to return against their will."[82]

With what little public concern there was allayed by such announcements, the Allies worked feverishly to fulfill their pact with Stalin. "We ought to get rid of them *all* as soon as possible," wrote an impatient Winston Churchill.[83]

Another category of Russians the Allies repatriated were the POWs in German hands. Because of Stalin's well known equation of capture or surrender on the battlefield with treason, few of these starved, diseased and ragged Red Army veterans were eager to return where, at best, a slow, agonizing death in Siberia awaited. And even for those stalwart patriots who steadfastly refused to collaborate with the Germans and remained in their prison camps, where they ate tree bark, grass, and their dead comrades, a "tenner"—or ten years in Siberia— was almost mandatory.[84] When a curious Russian guard queried one such repatriate what he had done to deserve a twenty-five year sentence, the hapless prisoner replied, "Nothing at all."

"You're lying," the guard laughed, "the sentence for 'nothing at all' is ten years."[85]

Yet another group on the seemingly endless list Stalin wanted returned were Soviet slave laborers. Again, the Allies made haste to comply.

"We had to go round the farms to collect the Russians who had been working as laborers on the farms," one British lieutenant remembered. "[They were] mostly old men and women, and [we] were amazed and somewhat perplexed to have people who had literally been slaves on German farms, falling on their knees in front of you and begging to be allowed to stay, and crying bitterly—not with joy—when they were told they were being sent back to Russia."[86]

"It very quickly became apparent," added another English officer, "that 99% of these people did not wish to return to the Motherland,

82. Ibid., 121.
83. Tolstoy, *Betrayal*, 276.
84. Elliott, 205.
85. Ibid., 206.
86. Ibid., 123.

because (a) they feared the Communist Party and the life they had lived in Soviet Russia and (b) life as slave-laborers in Nazi Germany had been better than *life* in Russia."[87]

Because of their exposure to the West with its freedoms and high standard of living, Stalin rightly feared the "contaminating" influence these slaves might have on communism at home and abroad if allowed to remain.

Another body of Russians Stalin demanded the return of were the emigres, or those "whites" who had fought the Bolsheviks in 1917 and fled to the West upon defeat. Included in the number were individuals who had been mere children at the time of the revolution. Indeed, so willing were the Allies to comply with Stalin's every demand, that Soviet authorities were themselves surprised at how easily this latter group of "traitors" were delivered to the executioner.[88]

The roundups and repatriations continued across Europe until eventually over five million Soviet citizens had been delivered to death, torture and slavery.[89] However, if the Allies expected to enamor Stalin by their actions, they were mistaken. In fact, quite the opposite occurred. Rightly regarding the repatriations as a Western betrayal of its natural allies, the Red dictator and other Soviet leaders viewed the entire program as proof of American and British moral decay and a blatant, "groveling" attempt at appeasement.[90]

Curiously, it was Liechtenstein, one of the tiniest nations in Europe, that Stalin had most respect for, for it was Liechtenstein—a country with no army and a police force of only eleven men—that had the moral integrity to do what others did not dare. When the communists angrily demanded the return of all Soviet citizens within the little nation's boundaries for "crimes against the Motherland," Prince Franz Joseph II politely but firmly requested proof. When none was forthcoming, the Soviets quietly dropped the matter. Remembered an interviewer: "I asked the Prince if he had not had misgivings or fears as to the suc-

87. Tolstoy, *Betrayal*, 314–315.
88. Ibid., 250; Elliott, *Yalta*, 86, 104.
89. Elliott, 96; Juergen Thorwald, *The Illusion—Soviet Soldiers in Hitler's Armies* (New York: Harcourt, Brace, Jovanovich, 1974), 314.
90. Tolstoy, *Betrayal*, 193, 250, 368.

cess of this policy at the time. He seemed quite surprised at my question. 'Oh no,' he explained, 'if you talk toughly with the Soviets they are quite happy. That, after all, is the language they understand.'"[91]

When the camps were finally cleared and the dark deed was done, many soldiers who had participated wanted nothing more than to forget the entire episode. Most found, however, that they could not.

"My part in the . . . operation left me a burden of guilt I am sure to carry the rest of my life," confessed William Sloane Coffin, Jr.[92]

"The cries of these men, their attempts to escape, even to kill themselves rather than be returned to the Soviet Union . . . still plague my memory," echoed Brigadier General Frank L. Howley.[93]

"It just wasn't human," an American GI said simply.[94]

Well aware that some grim details from Operation Keelhaul were bound to surface, Allied leaders were quick to squash rumors and reassure the public. "[T]he United States Government has taken a firm stand against any forced repatriation and will continue to maintain this position . . . ," said a spokesman for the War Department long after most of the Russian returnees were either dead or enslaved. "There is no intention that any refugee be returned home against his will."[95] To do otherwise, General Eisenhower later chimed, "would . . . violate the fundamental humanitarian principles we espoused."[96]

Even as he was soothing public concern over Russian repatriation, Eisenhower's "humanitarian principles" were at work in the numerous American concentration camps.

"God, I hate the Germans," Eisenhower had written his wife in 1944.[97] As Mrs. Eisenhower and anyone else close to the general knew, Dwight

91. Ibid., 394.
92. Elliott, 104.
93. Ibid.
94. Ibid., 93.
95. Ibid., 120.
96. Ibid., 102.
97. Bacque, "The Last Dirty Secret," 34.

David Eisenhower's loathing of all things German was nothing short of pathological.

With the final capitulation on May 8, the supreme allied commander found himself in control of over five million ragged, weary, but living, enemy soldiers.[98] "It is a pity we could not have killed more," muttered the general, dissatisfied with the body-count of the greatest blood-bath in world history.[99] And so, the Allied commander settled for next best: If he could not kill armed Germans in war, he would kill disarmed Germans in peace. Because the Geneva Convention guaranteed POWs of signer nations the same food, shelter and medical attention as their captors, and because these laws were to be enforced by the International Red Cross, Eisenhower simply circumvented the treaty by creating his own category for prisoners. Under the general's reclassification, German soldiers were no longer considered POWs, but DEFs—Disarmed Enemy Forces. With this sleight-of-hand, and in direct violation of the Geneva Convention, Eisenhower could now deal in secret with those in his power, free from the prying eyes of the outside world.[100]

Even before war's end, thousands of German POWs had died in American captivity from starvation, neglect and, in many cases, outright murder. Wrote a survivor from one camp in April 1945:

> Each group of ten was given the outdoor space of a medium-sized living room. We had to live like this for three months, no roof over our heads. Even the badly wounded only got a bundle of straw. And it rained on the Rhine. For days. And we were always in the open. People died like flies. Then we got our first rations. . . . [W]e got one slice of bread for ten men. Each man got a tiny strip of that one slice. . . . And this went on for three long months. I only weighed 90 pounds. The dead were carried out every day. Then a voice would come over the loudspeaker: "German soldiers, eat slowly. You haven't had anything to eat in a long time. When you get your rations today from the best fed army in the world, you'll die if you don't eat slowly."[101]

When two members of the US Army Medical Corp stumbled upon one of Eisenhower's camps, they were horrified by what they saw:

98. Ibid., 32.
99. Bacque, *Other Losses*, 160.
100. Bacque, "Last Dirty Secret," 34, 37, 38.
101. Pechel, *Voices From the Third Reich*, 505–506.

Huddled close together for warmth, behind the barbed wire was a most awesome sight—nearly 100,000 haggard, apathetic, dirty, gaunt, blank-staring men clad in dirty field gray uniforms, and standing ankle-deep in mud. . . . The German Division Commander reported that the men had not eaten for at least two days, and the provision of water was a major problem—yet only 200 yards away was the River Rhine running bankfull.[102]

With German surrender and the threat of retaliation against Allied POWs entirely erased, deaths in the American concentration camps accelerated dramatically. While tens of thousands died of starvation and thirst, hundreds of thousands more perished from overcrowding and disease. Said sixteen-year-old Hugo Stehkamper:

I only had a sweater to protect me from the pouring rain and the cold. There just wasn't any shelter to be had. You stood there, wet through and through, in fields that couldn't be called fields anymore—they were ruined. You had to make an effort when you walked to even pull your shoes out of the mud. . . .

[I]t's incomprehensible to me how we could stand for many, many days without sitting, without lying down, just standing there, totally soaked. During the day we marched around, huddled together to try to warm each other a bit. At night we stood because we couldn't walk and tried to keep awake by singing or humming songs. Again and again someone got so tired his knees got weak and he collapsed.[103]

Added a starving comrade from a camp near Remagen:

The latrines were just logs flung over ditches next to the barbed wire fences. To sleep, all we could do was to dig out a hole in the ground with our hands, then cling together in the hole. . . . Because of illness, the men had to defecate on the ground. Soon, many of us were too weak to take off our trousers first. So our clothing was infected, and so was the mud where we had to walk and sit and lie down. There was no water at all at first, except the rain. . . .

We had to walk along between the holes of the soft earth thrown up by the digging, so it was easy to fall into a hole, but hard to climb out. The rain was almost constant along that part of the Rhine that spring. More than half the days we had rain. More than half the days we had no food at all. On the rest, we got a little K ration. I could see from the package that they were giving us one tenth of the rations that they issued to their own men. . . . I complained to the American camp commander that he was breaking the Geneva Convention, but he just said, "Forget the Convention. You haven't any rights."

---

102. Bacque, "Secret," 36.
103. Pechel, *Voices*, 491.

Within a few days, some of the men who had gone healthy into the camps were dead. I saw our men dragging many dead bodies to the gate of the camp, where they were thrown loose on top of each other onto trucks, which took them away.[104]

"The Americans were really shitty to us," a survivor at another camp recalled. "All we had to eat was grass."[105] At Hans Woltersdorf's prison, the inmates survived on a daily soup made of birdseed. *Not fit for human consumption*, read the words on the sacks.[106] At another camp, a weeping seventeen-year-old stood day-in, day-out beside the barbed wire fence. In the distance, the youth could just view his own village. One morning, inmates awoke to find the boy dead, his body strung up by guards and left dangling on the wires. When outraged prisoners cried "Murderers! Murderers!" the camp commander withheld their meager rations for three days. "For us who were already starving and could hardly move because of weakness . . . it meant death," said one of the men.[107]

"Civilians from nearby villages and towns were prevented at gunpoint from passing food through the fence to prisoners," revealed another German from his camp near Ludwigshafen.[108]

There was no lack of food or shelter among the victorious Allies. Indeed, American supply depots were bursting at the seams. "More stocks than we can ever use," one general announced. "[They] stretch as far as [the] eye can see." Instead of allowing even a trickle of this bounty to reach the compounds, the starvation diet was further reduced. "Outside the camp the Americans were burning food which they could not eat themselves," said a starving Werner Laska from his prison.[109]

Horrified by the silent, secret massacre, the International Red Cross—which had over 100,000 tons of food stored in Switzerland—

---

104. Bacque, *Other Losses*, 38.

105. Ibid., 39.

106. Woltersdorf, *Gods of War*, 176.

107. Bacque, *Other Losses*, 38–39.

108. Letter from "Anonymous," March 14, 1998 (copy in possession of the author).

109. Bacque, "Secret," 34; Martin Brech, "In 'Eisenhower's Death Camps', Part I," *The Journal of Historical Review* 10, no. 2 (Summer 1990): 162; Werner Wilhelm Laska, "In a U.S. Death Camp—1945," *The Journal of Historical Review* 10, no. 2 (Summer 1990): 173.

tried to intercede. When two trains loaded with supplies reached the camps, however, they were turned back by American officers.[110]

"These Nazis are getting a dose of their own medicine," a prison commandant reported proudly to one of Eisenhower's political advisors.[111]

"German soldiers were not common law convicts," protested a Red Cross official, "they were drafted to fight in a national army on patriotic grounds and could not refuse military service any more than the Americans could."[112]

Like this individual, many others found no justification whatsoever in the massacre of helpless prisoners, especially since the German government had lived up to the Geneva Convention, as one American put it, "to a tee."

"I have come up against few instances where Germans have not treated prisoners according to the rules, and respected the Red Cross," wrote war correspondent Allan Wood of the *London Express*.[113]

"The Germans even in their greatest moments of despair obeyed the Convention in most respects," a US officer added. "True it is that there were front line atrocities—passions run high up there—but they were incidents, not practices; and maladministration of their American prison camps was very uncommon."[114]

Nevertheless, despite the Red Cross report that ninety-nine percent of American prisoners of war in Germany have survived and were on their way home, Eisenhower's murderous program continued apace.[115] One officer who refused to have a hand in the crime and who began releasing large numbers of prisoners soon after they were disarmed was George Patton.[116] Explained the general:

I emphasized [to the troops] the necessity for the proper treatment of prisoners of war, both as to their lives and property. My usual statement was . . . "Kill all the Germans you can but do not put them up against a wall and kill them. Do your killing while they are still fighting. After a man has surrendered, he

110. Bacque, *Other Losses*, 50; Bacque, "Secret," 34.
111. Bacque, *Other Losses*, 150.
112. Keeling, *Gruesome Harvest*, 28.
113. Ibid., 28–29.
114. Ibid., 29.
115. Ibid.
116. Bacque, *Other Losses*, 51.

should be treated exactly in accordance with the Rules of Land Warfare, and just as you would hope to be treated if you were foolish enough to surrender. Americans do not kick people in the teeth after they are down."[117]

Although other upright generals such as Omar Bradley and J. C. H. Lee issued orders to release POWs, Eisenhower quickly overruled them. Mercifully, for the two million Germans under British control, Bernard Montgomery refused to participate in the massacre. Indeed, soon after war's end, the field marshal released and sent most of his prisoners home.[118]

After being shuttled from one enclosure to the next, Corporal Helmut Liebich had seen for himself all the horrors the American death camps had to give. At one compound, amused guards formed lines and beat starving prisoners with clubs and sticks as they ran the gauntlet for their paltry rations. At another camp of 5,200 men, Liebich watched as ten to thirty bodies were hauled away every day. At yet another prison, there was "35 days of starvation and 15 days of no food at all," and what little the wretched inmates did receive was rotten. Finally, in June 1945, Liebich's camp at Rheinberg passed to British control. Immediately, survivors were given food and shelter and for those like Liebich—who now weighed 97 pounds and was dying of dysentery—swift medical attention was provided.[119]

"It was wonderful to be under a roof in a real bed," the corporal reminisced. "We were treated like human beings again. The Tommies treated us like comrades."[120]

Before the British could take complete control of the camp, however, Liebich noted that American bulldozers leveled one section of the compound where skeletal—but breathing—men still lay in their holes.[121]

117. Ibid., 149.
118. Bacque, "Last Dirty Secret," 31, 34, 36.
119. Bacque, *Other Losses*, 134–135; Laska, "In a U.S. Death Camp—1945," 169.
120. Bacque, *Other Losses*, 135.
121. Ibid.

If possible, Germans in French hands suffered even more than those held by Americans. When France requested slaves as part of its war booty, Eisenhower transferred over 600,000 Germans east.[122]

"Gee! I hope we don't ever lose a war," muttered one GI as he stared at the broken, starving wrecks being selected for slavery.[123]

"When we marched through Namur in a column seven abreast, there was also a Catholic procession going through the street," remembered one slave as he moved through Belgium. "When the people saw the POWs, the procession dissolved, and they threw rocks and horse shit at us. From Namur, we went by train in open railroad cars. At one point we went under a bridge, and railroad ties were thrown from it into the cars filled with POWs, causing several deaths. Later we went under another overpass, and women lifted their skirts and relieved themselves on us."[124]

Once in France, the assaults intensified. "[W]e were cursed, spat upon and even physically attacked by the French population, especially the women," Hans von der Heide wrote. "I bitterly recalled scenes from the spring of 1943, when we marched American POWs through the streets of Paris. They were threatened and insulted no differently by the French mob."[125]

Like the Americans, the French starved their prisoners. Unlike the Americans, the French drained the last ounce of labor from their victims before they dropped dead. "I have seen them beaten with rifle butts and kicked with feet in the streets of the town because they broke down of overwork," remarked a witness from Langres. "Two or three of them die of exhaustion every week."[126]

"In another camp," a horrified viewer added, "prisoners receive only one meal a day but are expected to continue working. Elsewhere so many have died recently that the cemetery space was exhausted and another had to be built."[127]

---

122. Bacque, "Secret," 38.
123. Keeling, *Gruesome Harvest*, 24.
124. Pechel, *Voices*, 491–492.
125. Hans von der Heide, "From the Allied Camps to the Revisionist Camp," *The Journal of Historical Review* 12, no. 2 (Summer 1992): 180.
126. Keeling, 23.
127. Ibid.

Revealed the French journal, *Figaro*: "In certain camps for German prisoners of war . . . living skeletons may be seen . . . and deaths from undernourishment are numerous. We learn that prisoners have been savagely and systematically beaten and that some have been employed in removing mines without protection equipment so that they have been condemned to die sooner or later."[128]

"Twenty-five percent of the men in [our] camp died in one month," echoed a slave from Buglose.[129]

The enslavement of German soldiers was not limited to France. Although fed and treated infinitely better, several hundred thousand POWs in Great Britain were transformed into virtual slaves. Wrote historian Ralph Franklin Keeling at the time:

> The British Government nets over $250,000,000 annually from its slaves. The Government, which frankly calls itself the "owner" of the prisoners, hires the men out to any employer needing men, charging the going rates of pay for such work—usually $15 to $20 per week. It pays the slaves from 10 cents to 20 cents a day . . . plus such "amenities" as slaves customarily received in the former days of slavery in the form of clothing, food, and shelter.[130]

When prisoners were put to work raising projects for Britain's grand "Victory in Europe" celebration, one English foreman felt compelled to quip: "I guess the Jerries are preparing to celebrate their own downfall. It does seem as though that is laying it on a bit thick."[131]

In vain did the International Red Cross protest:

> The United States, Britain, and France . . . are violating International Red Cross agreements they solemnly signed in 1929. Investigation at Geneva headquarters today disclosed that the transfer of German war prisoners captured by the American army to French and British authorities for forced labor is nowhere permitted in the statues of the International Red Cross, which is the highest authority on the subject in the world.[132]

---

128. Ibid., 22.
129. Bacque, "Secret," 44.
130. Keeling, *Gruesome Harvest*, 25.
131. Ibid.
132. Ibid., 27.

Meanwhile, those Germans not consigned to bondage continued to perish in American prisons. Landsers who did not succumb to hunger or disease often died of thirst, even though streams sometimes ran just a few feet from the camps. "[T]he lack of water was the worst thing of all," remembered George Weiss of his enclosure where the Rhine flowed just beyond the barbed wire. "For three and a half days we had no water at all. We would drink our own urine. It tasted terrible, but what could we do? Some men got down on the ground and licked the ground to get some moisture. I was so weak I was already on my knees."[133]

"[O]thers," observed American guard, Martin Brech, "tried to escape in a demented or suicidal fashion, running through open fields in broad daylight towards the Rhine to quench their thirst. They were mowed down."[134]

As if their plight were not already hideous enough, prisoners occasionally became the targets of drunken and sadistic guards who sprayed the camps with machine-gun fire for sport.[135] "I think . . ," Private Brech continued, "[that] soldiers not exposed to combat were trying to prove how tough they were by taking it out on the prisoners and civilians."

> I encountered a captain on a hill above the Rhine shooting down at a group of German civilian women with his .45 caliber pistol. When I asked, "Why?" he mumbled, "Target practice," and fired until his pistol was empty. . . . This is when I realized I was dealing with cold-blooded killers filled with moralistic hatred.[136]

While continuing to deny the Red Cross and other relief agencies access to the camps, Eisenhower stressed among his lieutenants the need for secrecy. "Ike made the sensational statement that . . . now that hostilities were over, the important thing was to stay in with world public opinion—apparently whether it was right or wrong . . . ," recorded George Patton. "After lunch [he] talked to us very confidentially on the necessity for solidarity in the event that any of us are called before a Congressional Committee."[137]

---

133. Bacque, *Other Losses*, 40.
134. Brech, "Eisenhower's Death Camps, Part 1," 162.
135. Letter from "Anonymous," March 14, 1998 (copy in possession of the author); Bacque, *Other Losses*, 92.
136. Brech, "Death Camps," 162.
137. Bacque, *Other Losses*, 148.

To prevent the gruesome details from reaching the outside world—and sidetrack those that did—counter-rumors were circulated stating that, far from mistreating and murdering prisoners, US camp commanders were actually turning back released Germans who tried to slip back in for food and shelter.[138]

Ultimately, at least 800,000 German prisoners died in the American and French death camps. "Quite probably," one expert later wrote, the figure of one million is closer to the mark. And thus, in "peace," did ten times the number of Landsers die than were killed on the whole Western Front during the whole of the war.[139]

Unlike their democratic counterparts, the Soviet Union made little effort to hide from the world the fate of German prisoners in its hands. Toiling by the hundreds of thousands in the forests and mines of Siberia, the captives were slaves pure and simple and no attempt was made to disguise the fact. For the enslaved Germans, male and female, the odds of surviving the Soviet gulags were even worse than escaping the American or French death camps and a trip to Siberia was tantamount to a death sentence. What little food the slaves received was intended merely to maintain their strength so that the last drop of energy could be drained from them.

And so, with the once mighty Wehrmacht now disarmed and enslaved, and with their leaders either dead or awaiting trial for war crimes, the old men, women and children who remained in the dismembered Reich found themselves utterly at the mercy of the victors. Unfortunately for these survivors, never in the history of the world was mercy in shorter supply.

---

138. Ibid., 149.
139. Bacque, "Secret," 38.

(*left*) Ilya Ehrenburg

(*below*) Hamburg

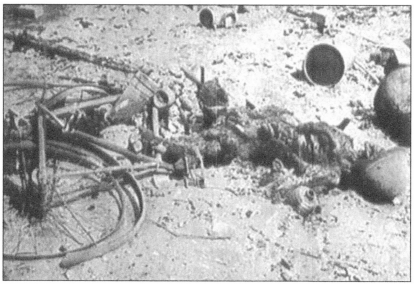

(*above*) After the Fire Storm

(*left*) Arthur Harris

BOTH PHOTOS COURTESY OF
NATIONAL ARCHIVES

The "Good War"

(*above*) The *Wilhelm Gustloff*

(*opposite, top*) Yalta: Winston Churchill, Franklin Roosevelt and Josef Stalin
COURTESY OF NATIONAL ARCHIVES

(*opposite, bottom*) Fire Bombs Over Germany
COURTESY OF NATIONAL ARCHIVES

264

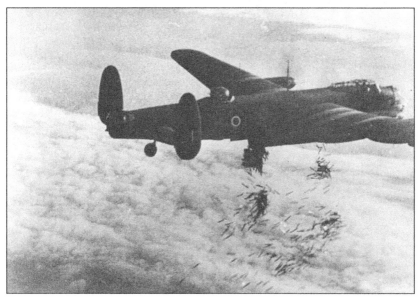

(*above*) Dresden
COURTESY OF GERMAN FEDERAL ARCHIVE

(*left*) Kurt Vonnegut
COURTESY OF NATIONAL ARCHIVES

(*opposite, top*) Berlin: The Battle Below
COURTESY OF RUSSIAN STATE ARCHIVES

(*opposite, bottom*) Adolf Hitler:
The Final Review
COURTESY OF NATIONAL ARCHIVES

The Fall of Berlin

Total War

(*above*) On the Road to Siberia

(*below*) The Dachau Massacre

(*above*) American Death Camp

(*below*) Germany in Ruins

BOTH PHOTOS COURTESY OF NATIONAL ARCHIVES

(*left*) Andrey Vlasov

(*below*) Henry Morgenthau

(*right*) Leni Riefenstahl

(*below*) Expulsion: Millions on the Move

(*above*) The Spoils of War

(*left*) Victor Gollancz

(*right*) Jan Montyn
COURTESY OF JAN MONTYN

(*below*) German POWs in Kiev
COURTESY OF TOM PETTYS

Public execution of Germans on Kreschatik. Kiev, 1946.
COURTESY OF TOM PETTYS

9

A WAR WITHOUT END

W HAT HAD TAKEN the German nation over two millennia to build, had taken its enemies a mere six years to destroy. When the fighting finally ended on May 8, 1945, the Great German Reich which had been one of the most modern industrial giants in the world lay totally, thoroughly and almost hopelessly demolished. Germany, mused an American newsman drifting through the rubble, resembled nothing so much as it resembled "the face of the moon."[1] Omar Bradley agreed. After viewing for himself the blackened, smoking wreck, the US general reassured his countrymen, "I can tell you that Germany has been destroyed utterly and completely."[2]

What Leonard Mosley found at Hanover epitomized the condition of all German cities at war's end. Hanover, wrote the British reporter, was the most "sullen and desolate city [that] I have ever seen."

> Even from there, five miles away, the devastation was appalling. . . . Hanover looked like a wound in the earth rather than a city. As we came nearer, I looked for the familiar signs that I used too know, but the transformation that had been made by bombardment seemed complete. I could not recognize anywhere; whole streets had disappeared, and squares and gardens and brooks with them, covered in piles of bricks and stone and mortar. . . . The city was a gigantic open sore.[3]

To the shock and surprise of not only Mosley and the victorious armies, but to the survivors as well, life actually existed among and

---

1. Crawley, *The Spoils of War*, 30.
2. Keeling, *Gruesome Harvest*, 1.
3. Barnouw, *Germany 1945*, 17–18.

under the seemingly sterile rock piles. Like cave-dwellers from the
Stone Age, men, women and children slept, ate, whispered, suffered,
cried, and died below the tons of jagged concrete, broken pipes and
twisted metal. As one victor who viewed Berlin recorded:

> A new race of troglodytes was born, one or other of whom periodically would
> bob up from nowhere at one's feet among rank weeds and rubble. . . . After a
> time those who had to live among the ruins became inured or deadened to them;
> this was very noticeable, especially among the children, many of whom them-
> selves were little veterans without an arm, an eye, or a leg, at the age of seven
> or ten or twelve. They took their disablement with amazing calm, but they
> grew up fast. They had to, to survive.[4]

Another horrifying feature of the razed cities was the nauseating
stench that hung over them like a pall. "[E]verywhere," remembered
a witness, "came the putrid smell of decaying flesh to remind the living that thousands of bodies still remained beneath the funeral pyres
of rubble."[5]

"I'd often seen it described as 'a sweetish smell'—but I find the word
'sweetish' imprecise and inadequate," a Berlin woman scratched in her
diary. "It strikes me not so much a smell as something solid, tangi-
ble, something too thick to be inhaled. It takes one's breath away and
repels, thrusts one back, as though with fists."[6]

In their own tally of bombing casualties, the British estimated they
had killed 300,000–600,000 German civilians. That some sources from
the Dresden raid set the toll there alone at 300,000–400,000 dead would
suggest that the British figures were absurdly—and perhaps deliberately—low.[7] Whatever the accurate figure, the facts are that few German families survived the war in tact. Those who did not lose a father,
a brother, a sister, a mother—or all the above—were by far the exception to the rule. In many towns and villages the dead quite literally
outnumbered the living. For some, the hours and days following the
final collapse was simply too much. Unwilling to live any longer in a

---

4.   Constantine FitzGibbon, *Denazification* (New York: W.W. Norton, 1969), 86.
5.   Crawley, *Spoils*, 30.
6.   Anonymous, *Woman in Berlin*, 308–309.
7.   Garrett, *Ethics and Airpower*, xi; Thomas Weyersberg Collections (copy in author's posses-
     sion); McKee, *Dresden 1945*, 182.

world of death, misery and alien chaos, thousands took the ultimate step. Wrote once-wealthy Lali Horstmann of a scenario that was replayed over and over throughout Germany:

> Wilhelm, our gardener and gamekeeper, had committed suicide by hanging himself from a tree in the woods, having first slashed the wrist arteries of his wife and three-year-old son, refusing to leave them behind him in a world of strife and disorder. They had been found in time to revive them, but he himself was stark and cold. Despite his stalwart looks, Wilhelm was a sensitive man. . . . Yesterday drunken soldiers had upset his treasured beehives, used his jars of preserves as shooting targets and driven the couple and child out of the house. He had not been able to stand the strain of these repeated scenes and now lay on the ground covered with a blanket.[8]

"Thousands of bodies are hanging in the trees in the woods around Berlin and nobody bothers to cut them down," a German pastor noted. "Thousands of corpses are carried into the sea by the Oder and Elbe Rivers—one doesn't notice it any longer."[9]

For Germany, May 8, 1945, became known as "The Hour Zero"—the end of a nightmare and the beginning of a dark, uncertain future. Most assumed, no doubt, that awful though the coming weeks and months would be, the worst was nevertheless behind them. But these people were wrong. The worst yet lay ahead. Though the shooting and bombing had indeed stopped, the war against Germany continued unabated. World War II was history's most catastrophic and terrifying war, but what still lay ahead would prove, as *Time* magazine later phrased it, "History's most terrifying peace."[10]

Although forced to the shadows by public opprobrium, the Morgenthau Plan for Germany was never actually abandoned by Franklin Roosevelt. Indeed, up until his death, the American president had secretly favored the "Carthaginian" approach to the conquered Reich. When Roosevelt's successor, Harry Truman, met at Potsdam with Stalin

8.   Horstmann, *We Chose to Stay*, 117.
9.   Keeling, *Gruesome Harvest*, 67.
10. Botting, *Ruins of the Reich*, 122; Keeling, xii.

and the new British prime minister, Clement Attlee, in July 1945, most of the teeth in Morgenthau's scheme remained on the table. With the signature of the Big Three, the plan went into effect.[11]

"It is not the intention of the Allies," stated the joint declaration, "to destroy or enslave the German people."[12]

Despite such solemn pronouncements meant to mollify a watching world, it soon became abundantly clear to the Germans themselves that the victors came not as peace-minded "liberators," as propagandists were wont to declare, but as conquerors fully as vengeful, ruthless and greedy as any who ever won a war.

The plundering of Germany by the Soviet Union first began when the Red Army penetrated Prussia in 1944. With war's end, Stalin's methodical looting in the Russian Occupation Zone became prodigious. Steel mills, grain mills, lumber mills, suger and oil refineries, chemical plants, optical works, shoe factories, and other heavy industries were taken apart down to the last nut and bolt and sent east to the Soviet Union where they were reassembled. Those factories allowed to remain in Germany were to operate solely for the benefit of Russia. Electric and steam locomotives, their rolling stock, and even the tracks they ran on were likewise sent east.[13] While the Soviet government pillaged on a massive scale, the common Red soldier was even more meticulous. Wrote one woman from Silesia:

> The Russians systematically cleared out everything, that was for them of value, such as all sewing machines, pianos, grand-pianos, baths, water taps, electric plants, beds, mattresses, carpets, etc. They destroyed what they could not take away with them. Trucks often stood for days in the rain, with the most valuable carpets and articles of furniture in them, until everything was completely spoiled and ruined. . . .
>
> If fuel was required, then whole woods were generally felled, or window-frames and doors were torn out of the empty houses, broken up on the spot, and immediately used for making fire. The Russians and Poles even used the staircases and banisters as fire-wood. In the course of time, even the roofs of houses were removed and used for heating. . . . Empty houses, open, without window-panes, overgrown with weeds and filthy, rats and mice in uncanny numbers,

11. Davidson, *Death and Life of Germany*, 6; Keeling, 83.
12. Keeling, xi.
13. Ibid., 51–52.

unharvested fields, land which had been fertile, now completely overgrown with weeds and lying fallow. Not in a single village did one see a cow, a horse or a pig. . . . The Russians had taken everything away to the east, or used it up.[14]

As this woman made clear, what was not looted was destroyed. Like millions of other refugees, Regina Shelton found her way home at the end of the war.

> We have been warned by others who have witnessed signs of Russian occupancy to expect bedlam and to abandon our hopeless mission altogether. Thus we expect the worst, but our idea of the worst has not prepared us sufficiently for reality. Shocked to the point of collapse, we survey a battlefield—heaps of refuse through which broken pieces of furniture rise like cliffs; stench gags us, almost driving us to retreat. Ragged remnants of clothes, crushed dishes, books, pictures torn from frames,—rubble in every room. . . . Above all, the nauseating stench that emanates from the largest and totally wrecked living room! Spoiled contents oozes from splintered canning jars, garbage of indefinable origin is mixed with unmistakable human excrement, and dried stain of urine discolors crumpled paper and rags. We wade into the dump with care and poke at some of all but unrecognizable belongings. . . . The wardrobes with doors torn from their hinges are empty, their contents looted or mixed in stinking heaps.[15]

Americans were not far behind their communist counterparts and what was not wantonly destroyed, was pilfered as "souvenirs."

"We 'liberated' German property," winked one GI. "The Russians simply stole it."

Unlike its primitive Soviet ally, the United States had no need for German plants and factories. Nevertheless, and as Ralph Franklin Keeling points out, the Americans were far and away the "most zealous" at destroying the Reich's ability to recover. Continues the historian:

> Although America went about the business of dismantling and dynamiting German plants with more fervor than was at first exhibited in any other zone, our motive was quite different from the motives of our allies. Russia is anxious to get as much loot as possible from Germany and yet to make it produce abundantly for Russia to help make her new five year plan successful, and ultimately to absorb the Reich into the Soviet Union. France is ravenous for loot, has been anxious to destroy Germany forever and to annex as much of her territory as possible. Britain has found uses for large amounts of German booty,

---

14. Schieder, *Expulsion of the German Population*, 242.
15. Shelton, *To Lose a War*, 138.

wants to get rid of Germany as a trade competitor, while retaining her market for British goods. The United States has no use for German plant and equipment as booty. . . . [but wants] to eliminate German competition in world trade. We are willing to permit the German people to subsist on their own little plot of land, if they can, but we are determined that they never again shall engage in foreign commerce on an important scale.[16]

While the US may have spurned German plants and factories, not so the Reich's hoard of treasure. Billions of dollars in gold, silver and currency, as well as priceless paintings, sculptures and other art works were plucked from their hiding places in caves, tunnels and salt mines and shipped across the Atlantic. Additionally, and of far greater damage to Germany's future, was the "mental dismantling" of the Reich. Tons of secret documents revealing Germany's tremendous organizational talent in business and industry were simply stolen, not only by the Americans, but by the French, English and British Commonwealth. Hundreds of the greatest scientists in the world were likewise "compelled" to immigrate by the victors. As one US Government agency quietly admitted, "Operation Paper-Clip" was the first time in history wherein conquerors had attempted to bleed dry the inventive power of an entire nation.[17]

"The real gain in reparations of this war," *Life* magazine added, was not in factories, gold or artworks, but "in the German brains and in the German research results."[18]

While the Soviet Union came up short on German scientists and technicians simply because most had wisely fled and surrendered to the West, Russia suffered no shortage of slave labor. Added to the millions of native dissidents, repatriated refugees, and Wehrmacht prisoners toiling in the gulags, were millions of German civilians snatched from the Reich. As was commonly the case, those who were to spend years in slavery were given mere minutes to make ready. In cities, towns

---

16. Keeling, *Gruesome Harvest*, 52, 53.
17. Walendy, *Methods of Reeducation*, 17.
18. Ibid.

and villages, posters suddenly appeared announcing that all able-bodied men and women were to assemble in their local square at a given time or face arrest and execution.

"The screaming, wailing and howling in the square will haunt me the rest of my life," remembered one horrified female.

> Mercilessly the women were herded together in rows of four. Mothers had to leave tiny children behind. I thanked God from the bottom of my heart that my boy had died in Berlin shortly after birth.... The ... wretched victims [were] then set in motion to the crack of Russian whips. It was foggy and damp, and a drizzling rain swept into our faces. The streets were icy and slippery; in many places we waded ankle-deep in ice water. Before long one of the women collapsed, and being unable to rise, remained lying there.
>
> So we marched along, mile after mile. I had never believed it possible to go so far on foot, but I was so indifferent that I scarcely could think. I just pushed one foot along mechanically after the other. ... Only rarely did we exchange words. Each of my suffering fellow-creatures had enough torment of her own and many had eyes swollen and sore from weeping.[19]

For those forced east on foot, the trek became little better than a death march. Thousands dropped dead in their tracks from hunger, thirst, disease, and abuse. "It took all of our remaining strength to stay in the middle of the extremely slow-moving herds being driven east," said Wolfgang Kasak. "We kept hearing the submachine guns whenever a straggler was shot. ... I will never forget ... the shooting of a 15-year-old boy right before my very eyes. He simply couldn't walk anymore, so a Russian soldier took potshots at him. The boy was still alive when some officer came over and fired his gun into the boy's ear."[20]

"One young girl jumped from a bridge into the water, the guards shot wildly at her, and I saw her sink," recalled Anna Schwartz. "A young man, who had heart-disease, jumped into the Vistula. He was also shot. The fourth day we could hardly move further. Thirst was such a torture, and we were so tired. Many had got open sores on their feet from walking."[21]

Those who traveled by rail to Siberia fared even worse. As one slave recorded:

19. Lutz, "Rape of Christian Europe," 14.
20. Pechel, et all, *Voices From the Third Reich*, 520.
21. Schieder, *Expulsion*, 180.

120 people were forced into each wagon, women and men separately. . . .
The wagons were filthy from top to bottom, and there was not a blade of straw.
When the last man had been driven in by blows with rifle-butts, we could only
stand packed together like sardines. . . . When we were being loaded, the Russians treated us like cattle, and many people became demented. A bucket of water
and crumbs of bread, served up to us on a filthy piece of tent canvas, were our
daily food. The worst part were the nights. Our legs got weak from continual
standing, and the one leant against the other. . . . [T]he journey lasted 28 days.
When the train stopped, mostly for the night, we were not left in peace. The
guards came to the wagons, and hammered on them from all sides. We could
not understand why this was done. But this happened almost every night. 10
to 15 men had already died during the first eight days. We others had to carry
out the corpses naked under guard, and they were piled up at the end of the train
like wood in empty wagons. Every day more and more died.

Our condition was made worse by the fact that in all the wagons there were
some Poles and Lithuanians. . . . They thought . . . that they had more rights than
we, and made room for themselves by lying on top of weak persons; they took
no notice when these screamed because of being stifled by the weight. When the
food came, they stormed it, and very little remained over for us Germans. We
slowly perished in the course of this death-journey.

Thirst was worse than hunger. The iron fittings of the wagons were damp
through the vapor and breath. Most of the people scratched this off with their
dirty fingers and sucked it; many of them got ill in this way. The mortality
increased from day to day, and the corpse wagons, behind the train, continually increased in number.[22]

When the trains finally reached their destinations, there was sub-
stantially more room in each car since a third to one half of all prisoners normally died in transit. Continues the above witness:

The rest of us poor wretches looked like a crowd of walking corpses. After
we had stumbled out of the train, we had to parade in front of it. . . . We were
covered from head to foot with a crust of dirt and filth, and looked terrible.
The Russians led us in this state stumbling or rather creeping through the
roads of the Ural [Mountains]. The Russian population stood on the edge of the
road with terror in their faces, and watched the procession of all these miserable
people. Those who could not walk any further, were driven on, step by step, by
being struck with rifle-butts.

We now stopped in front of a sauna-bath. This was fatal for most of us. For
everyone was thirsty and rushed to the basins, which were full of dirty water,

---

22. Ibid., 161.

and each drank until he was full. This immediately caused the awful dysentery illness. . . . When we finally came to camps, more than a half of what remained of us poor wretches already had typhoid.[23]

"[N]ow the dying really began . . . ," remembered Anna Schwartz.

[O]ur camp. . . [was a] large piece of land with a barbed wire fence, 2 metres high. Within this fence, at a distance of 2 metres, there was another small barbed wire fence, and we were not allowed to go near it. At every corner, outside the fence, was a sentry turret, which was occupied by guards day and night. There was a searchlight outside, which lit up the whole camp at night time. . . . The huts, in which we were quartered, were full of filth and vermin, swarms of bugs over-whelmed us, and we destroyed as much of this vermin as we could. We lay on bare boards so close together, that, if we wanted to turn round, we had to wake our neighbors to the right and left of us, in order that we all turned round at the same time. The sick people lay amongst us, groaning and in delirium. . . .

Typhoid and dysentery raged and very many died, but death meant rather release than terror to them. The dead were brought into a cellar, and when this was full up to the top, it was emptied. Meanwhile the rats had eaten from the corpses, and these very quickly decayed. . . . Also the wolves satisfied their hunger. . . .

After three weeks the [doctors] came to examine us medically. We went by huts to the outside hospital, and had to strip ourselves naked; we then went one by one into the so-called consulting room. When we opened the door, we saw that the whole room was full of officers; this also upset us and caused tears, but that did not help, we had to go in naked. . . . [They] laughed at our blushing, and also at our figures, which were distorted through our having got so thin. Some officers pinched our arms and legs, in order to test the firmness of the flesh. This occurred every three months.[24]

While Anna's camp worked on a railroad and was driven day-in, day-out "like a herd of draught animals," and while others toiled in fields, factories, peat bogs, and lumber camps, thousands more were relegated to the mines. Wrote Ilse Lau:

It is a strange feeling to be suddenly 120 metres beneath the earth. Around us everything was dark, there was only one electric bulb for lighting the lift. We lit our miners lamps, and then began working. . . . There was water everywhere on the ground of the mine gallery. If one stepped carelessly from the rails, on which the coal trucks were pushed along, one got wet up to the knees. . . . [W]e

---

23. Ibid., 161–162.
24. Ibid., 181, 182.

sometimes had to remain as much as 16 hours down in the pit. When we had finally finished our work by summoning up our last strength, we were not allowed to go up in the lift, but had to climb up the ladders (138 metres). We were often near to desperation. We were never able to sleep enough, and we were always hungry.[25]

"Every day . . . in the coal-pit camp even as many as 15 to 25 [died]," added fellow slave, Gertrude Schulz. "At midnight the corpses were brought naked on stretchers into the forest, and put into a mass grave. . . . On Sundays our working hours were a little shorter, and ended at 5 o'clock in the afternoon. Then catholics and protestants assembled . . . for divine service. Often a commissar came and shouted out: 'That won't help you.'"[26]

Just as faith in the Almighty was often the thin divide that separated those who lived from those who died, so too did simple acts of kindness offer strength and rays of hope in an otherwise crushing gloom. As Wolfgang Kasak and his comrades stood dying of thirst, a Russian woman appeared with buckets of water.

"The guards drove the woman away," Kasak said. "But she kept on bringing water, bucket after bucket, to the places where no Russians were standing guard. I know now the Russian soldiers closed one eye and took a long time in following their orders to keep the woman from giving us something to drink."[27]

Siegfried Losch, the youth who had become a recruit, soldier, veteran, deserter, prisoner, and slave before he had seen his eighteenth year, was at work one Sunday morning when an old grandmother approached.

Her clothing indicated that she was very poor. Judging from her walk . . . she suffered from osteosclerosis. Indeed, her figure was more like that of the witch in Hansel and Gretl. But her face was different. . . . [T]he face emanated . . . warmth as only a mother who has suffered much can give. Here was the true example of mother Russia: Having suffered under the Soviet regime, the war, having possible lost one or more of her loved ones. . . . She probably was walking toward her church. When she was near me, she stopped and gave me some small coins. . . . Then she made a cross over me with tears in her eyes and

25. Ibid., 170, 171.
26. Ibid., 175.
27. Pechel, *Voices*, 520.

walked on. I gave her a "spasibo" (thank you!) and continued my work. But for the rest of the day I was a different person, because somebody cared, somebody let her soul speak to me.[28]

Precious as such miracles might be, they were but cruel reminders of a world that was no more. "We were eternally hungry . . . ," recalled Erich Gerhardt.

> Treatment by the Russian guards was almost always very bad. We were simply walking skeletons. . . . From the first to the last day our life was a ceaseless suffering, a dying and lamentation. The Russian guards mercilessly pushed the very weakest people forward with their rifle-butts, when they could hardly move. When the guards used their rifle-butts, they made use of the words, "You lazy rascal." I was already so weak, that I wanted to be killed on the spot by the blows.[29]

"We were always hungry and cold, and covered with vermin . . . ," echoed a fellow slave. "I used to pray to God to let me at least die in my native country."[30]

Cruelly, had this man's prayers been answered and had he been allowed to return to Germany, the odds were good indeed that he would have died in his homeland . . . and sooner than he imagined. Unbeknownst to these wretched prisoners dreaming of home, the situation in the former Reich differed little, if any, from that of Siberia. Indeed, in many cases, "life" in the defeated nation was vastly worse.

Because German's entire infrastructure had been shattered by the war, it was already assured that thousands would starve to death before roads, rails, canals, and bridges could be restored. Even when much of the damage had been repaired, the deliberate withholding of food from Germany guaranteed that hundreds of thousands more were doomed to slow death. Continuing the policy of their predecessors, Harry Truman and Clement Attlee allowed the spirit of Yalta and Morgenthau to dictate their course regarding post-war Germany.

---

28. Losch Manuscript, 35–36.
29. Schieder, *Expulsion*, 159.
30. Kaps, *Tragedy of Silesia*, 167.

No measures were to be undertaken, wrote the US government to General Eisenhower, "looking toward the economic rehabilitation of Germany or designed to maintain or strengthen the German economy." Not only would food from the outside be denied entry, but troops were forbidden to "give, sell or trade" supplies to the starving. Additionally, Germany's already meager ability to feed itself would be sharply stymied by withholding seed crop, fertilizer, gas, oil, and parts for farm machinery. Because of the enforced famine, it was estimated that thirty million Germans would soon succumb.[31] Well down the road to starvation even before surrender, those Germans who survived war now struggled to survive peace.

"I trudged home on sore feet, limp with hunger ... ," a Berlin woman scribbled in her diary. "It struck me that everyone I passed on the way home stared at me out of sunken, starving eyes. Tomorrow I'll go in search of nettles again. I examine every bit of green with this in mind."[32]

"The search for food made all former worries irrelevant," added Lali Horstmann. "It was the present moment alone that counted."[33]

While city-dwellers ate weeds, those on the land had food taken from them and were forced to dig roots, pick berries and glean fields. "[O]ld men, women and children," a witness noted, "may be seen picking up one grain at a time from the ground to be carried home in a sack the size of a housewife's shopping bag."[34]

The deadly effects of malnutrition soon became evident. Wrote one horrified observer:

> They are emaciated to the bone. Their clothes hang loose on their bodies, the lower extremities are like the bones of a skeleton, their hands shake as though with palsy, the muscles of the arms are withered, the skin lies in folds, and is without elasticity, the joints spring out as though broken. The weight of the women of average height and build has fallen way below 110 pounds. Often women of child-bearing age weigh no more than 65 pounds.[35]

---

31. Freda Utley, *The High Cost of Vengeance* (Chicago: Henry Regnery Co., 1949), 16; Davidson, *Death and Life*, 86; Interview with Martha Dodgen, Topeka, Kansas, Dec. 12, 1996.
32. Anonymous, *Woman*, 303.
33. Horstmann, *We Chose to Stay*, 123.
34. Keeling, *Gruesome Harvest*, 68.
35. Ibid., 71–72.

"We were really starving now . . . ," said Ilse McKee. "Most of the time we were too weak to do anything. Even queuing up for what little food there was to be distributed sometimes proved too much."[36]

Orders to the contrary, many Allied soldiers secretly slipped choco-late to children or simply turned their backs while elders stole bread. Others were determined to follow orders implacably. "It was a com-mon sight," recalled one GI, "to see German women up to their elbows in our garbage cans looking for something edible—that is, if they weren't chased away."[37] To prevent starving Germans from grubbing American leftovers, army cooks laced their slop with soap. Tossing crumbs or used chewing gum to scrambling children was another pas-time some soldiers found amusing.[38]

For many victims, especially the old and young, even begging and stealing proved too taxing and thousands slipped slowly into the final, fatal apathy preceding death.

"Most children under 10 and people over 60 cannot survive the com-ing winter," one American admitted in October 1945.[39]

"The number of still-born children is approaching the number of those born alive, and an increasing proportion of these die in a few days," added another witness to the tragedy. "Even if they come into the world of normal weight, they start immediately to lose weight and die shortly. Very often mothers cannot stand the loss of blood in childbirth and perish. Infant mortality has reached the horrifying height of 90 per cent."[40]

"Millions of these children must die before there is enough food," echoed an American clergyman traveling in Germany. "In Frankfurt at a children's hospital there have been set aside 25 out of 100 children. These will be fed and kept alive. It is better to feed 25 enough to keep them alive and let 75 starve than to feed the 100 for a short while and let them all starve."[41]

---

36. McKee, *Tomorrow the World*, 150–151.
37. Brech, "Eisenhower's Death Camps," 165.
38. Interview with Amy Schrott Krubel, Topeka, Kansas, Jan. 9, 1997.
39. Keeling, 73.
40. Ibid., 72.
41. Ibid., 72–73.

From Wiesbaden, a correspondent of the *Chicago Daily News* reported:

> I sat with a mother, watching her eight-year-old daughter playing with a doll and carriage, her only playthings. . . . Her legs were tiny, joints protruding. Her arms had no flesh. Her skin drawn taut across the bones, the eyes dark, deep-set and tired.
>
> "She doesn't look well," I said.
>
> "Six years of war," the mother replied, in that quiet toneless manner so common here now. "She hasn't had a chance. None of the children have. Her teeth are not good. She catches illness so easily. She laughs and plays—yes; but soon she is tired. She never has known"—and the mother's eyes filled with tears—"what it is not to be hungry."
>
> "Was it that bad during the war?" I asked.
>
> "Not this bad," she replied, "but not good at all. And now I am told the bread ration is to be less. What are we to do; all of us? For six years we suffered. We love our country. My husband was killed—his second war. My oldest son is a prisoner somewhere in France. My other boy lost a leg. . . . And now. . . ."
>
> By this time she was weeping. I gave this little girl a Hershey bar and she wept—pure joy—as she held it. By this time I wasn't feeling too chipper myself.[42]

When a scattering of reports like the above began filtering out to the American and British publics, many were shocked, horrified and outraged at the secret slaughter being committed in their name. Already troubled that the US State Department had tried to keep an official report on conditions in Germany from public scrutiny, Senator James Eastland of Mississippi was forced to concede:

> There appears to be a conspiracy of silence to conceal from our people the true picture of conditions in Europe, to secrete from us the fact regarding conditions of the continent and information as to our policies toward the German people. . . . Are the real facts withheld because our policies are so cruel that the American people would not endorse them?
>
> What have we to hide, Mr. President? Why should these facts be withheld from the people of the United States? There cannot possibly be any valid reason for secrecy. Are we following a policy of vindictive hatred, a policy which would not be endorsed by the American people as a whole if they knew true conditions?[43]

"Yes," replied a chamber colleague, Senator Homer Capehart of Indiana:

---

42. Ibid., 72.
43. Ibid., 76.

The fact can no longer be suppressed, namely, the fact that it has been and continues to be, the deliberate policy of a confidential and conspirational clique within the policy-making circles of this government to draw and quarter a nation now reduced to abject misery. In this process this clique, like a pack of hyenas struggling over the bloody entrails of a corpse, and inspired by a sadistic and fanatical hatred, are determined to destroy the German nation and the German people, no matter what the consequences. . . .

[T]he cynical and savage repudiation of . . . not only . . . the Potsdam Declaration, but also of every law of God and men, has been deliberately engineered with such a malevolent cunning, and with such diabolical skill, that the American people themselves have been caught in an international death trap. . . . [T]his administration has been carrying on a deliberate policy of mass starvation without any distinction between the innocent and the helpless and the guilty alike.[44]

The murderous program was, wrote an equally outraged William Henry Chamberlain, "a positively sadistic desire to inflict maximum suffering on all Germans, irrespective of their responsibility for Nazi crimes."[45]

Surprisingly, one of the most strident voices raised against the silent massacre was that of influential Jewish journalist, Victor Gollancz. It was not a matter of whether one was "pro-German" or "anti-Soviet," argued the London publisher, but whether or not a person was "pro-humanity."[46]

The plain fact is . . . we are starving the German people. . . . Others, including ourselves, are to keep or be given comforts while the Germans lack the bare necessities of existence. If it is a choice between discomfort for another and suffering for the German, the German must suffer; if between suffering for another and death for the German, the German must die.[47]

Although Gollancz felt the famine was not engineered, but rather a result of incompetence and indifference, others disagreed.

"On the contrary," raged the *Chicago Daily Tribune*, "it is the product of foresight. It was deliberately planned at Yalta by Roosevelt, Stalin, and Churchill, and the program in all its brutality was later confirmed

44. Ibid., 75.
45. Ibid., 82.
46. Barnouw, *Germany 1945*, 151.
47. Keeling, 77.

by Truman, Attlee, and Stalin. . . . The intent to starve the German people to death is being carried out with a remorselessness unknown in the western world since the Mongol conquest."[48]

Because of these and other critics, Allied officials were forced to respond. Following a fact-finding tour of Germany, Eleanor Roosevelt, wife of the late president, professed to see no suffering beyond what was considered "tolerable." And General Eisenhower, pointing out that there were food shortages all throughout Europe, noted that Germany suffered no more nor less than its neighbors. "While I and my subordinates believe that stern justice should be meted out to war criminals . . . we would never condone inhuman or un-American practices upon the helpless," assured the general as Germans died by the thousands in his death camps.[49]

Although some nations were indeed suffering shortages, none save Germany was starving. Many countries were actually experiencing surpluses of food, including Denmark on Germany's north border, a nation only waiting Eisenhower's nod to send tons of excess beef south.[50]

"England is not starving . . . ," argued Robert Conway in the *New York News*. "France is better off than England, and Italy is better off than France."[51]

When Senator Albert Hawkes of New Jersey pleaded with President Truman to head off catastrophe and allow private relief packages to enter Germany, the American leader offered various excuses, then cut the senator short:

> While we have no desire to be unduly cruel to Germany, I cannot feel any great sympathy for those who caused the death of so many human beings by starvation, disease, and outright murder, in addition to all the destruction and death of war. . . . I think that . . . no one should be called upon to pay for Germany's misfortune except Germany itself. . . . Eventually the enemy countries will be given some attention.[52]

---

48. Ibid.
49. Ibid., 80, 81.
50. Ibid., 78.
51. Ibid.
52. Ibid., 80.

In time, Germany did receive "some attention." Late in 1945, the British allowed Red Cross shipments to enter their zone, followed by the French in theirs. Months later, even the United States grudgingly permitted supplies to cross into its sector.[53] For thousands upon thousands of Germans, however, the food came far too late.

Even as the starvation of Germany was in progress, the defilement of German womanhood continued without pause. Although violent, brutal and repeated rapes persisted against defenseless females, Russian, American, British, and French troops quickly discovered that hunger was a powerful incentive to sexual surrender.

"[R]ape represents no problem to the military police because," explained an American officer matter-of-factly, "a bit of food, a bar of chocolate, or a bar of soap seems to make rape unnecessary."[54]

"Young girls, unattached, wander about and freely offer themselves for food or bed . . . ," reported the *London Weekly Review*. "Very simply they have one thing left to sell, and they sell it."[55]

"Bacon, eggs, sleep at your home?" winked Russian soldiers over and over again, knowing full well the answer would usually be a five-minute tryst among the rubble. "I continually ran about with cooking utensils, and begged for food . . . ," admitted one girl. "If I heard in my neighborhood the expression 'pretty woman,' I reacted accordingly."[56]

Despite Eisenhower's edict against fraternization with the despised enemy, no amount of words could slow the US soldier's sex drive. "Neither army regulations nor the propaganda of hatred in the American press," noted newswoman, Freda Utley, "could prevent American soldiers from liking and associating with German women, who although they were driven by hunger to become prostitutes, preserved a certain innate decency."[57]

53. De Zayas, *Nemesis at Potsdam*, 133.
54. Keeling, *Gruesome Harvest*, 64.
55. Ibid., 64.
56. Schieder, *Expulsion*, 259.
57. Utley, *High Cost*, 17.

"I felt a bit sick at times about the power I had over that girl," one troubled British soldier said. "If I gave her a three-penny bar of chocolate she nearly went crazy. She was just like my slave. She darned my socks and mended things for me. There was no question of marriage. She knew that was not possible."[58]

As this young Tommy made clear, desperate German women, many with children to feed, were compelled by hunger to enter a bondage as binding as any in history. With time, some victims, particularly those consorting with officers, not only avoided starvation, but found themselves enjoying luxuries long forgotten.

"You should have seen all the things he brought me, just so I wouldn't lack for anything!" recalled one woman kept by an officer on Patton's staff. "Nylon stockings, and the newest records, perfume, and two refrigerators, and of course loads of cigarettes and alcohol and gas for the car. . . . It was a wild time—the champagne flowed in streams, and when we weren't totally drunk, we made love."[59]

Unlike the above, relatively few females found such havens. For most, food was used to bait or bribe them into a slavery as old and unforgiving as the Bible. Wrote Lali Horstmann from the Russian Zone:

> He announced that women were needed to peel potatoes in a soldiers' camp and asked for volunteers. Their work would be paid for with soup and potatoes. The girl next to me whispered: "My sister was taken away four days ago on the same pretext and has not returned yet. A friend of mine escaped and brought back stories of what happened to her and the others."
>
> When a frail, hungry-looking, white-haired woman lifted her arm to offer her services, the golden-toothed one did not even glance at her, but pointed his pistol at the young girl . . . of whom the others had been talking. As she did not move, he gave a rough command. Two soldiers came to stand beside him, four more walked right and left of the single file of women until they reached her and ordered her to get into the truck. She was in tears as she was brutally shoved forward, followed by others who were protesting helplessly.[60]

"[A] Pole discovered me, and began to sell me to Russians," another girl confessed.

---

58. Botting, *From the Ruins of the Reich*, 250.
59. Bernt Engelmann, *In Hitler's Germany* (New York: Pantheon, 1986), 334–335.
60. Horstmann, *We Chose to Stay*, 105.

He had fixed up a brothel in his cellar for Russian officers. I was fetched by him. . . . I had to go with him, and could not resist. I came into the cellar, in which there were the most depraved carryings on, drinking, smoking and shouting, and I had to participate. . . . I felt like shrieking.

Then a room was opened, and the door shut behind me. Then I saw how the Pole did a deal with a Russian, and received money. My value was fixed at 800 zlotys. The Russian then gave me 200 zlotys for myself, which he put in my pocket. I did not give him the money back, because I could buy food. . . .

My employer . . . was continually after me, and followed me even when I went into the cellar. I was chased about like a frightened deer, he even turned up in the wash-house if he thought I was there. We often had a struggle but how was I to escape him? I could not run away, or complain to anyone, but had to keep to my work, as I had my mother with me. I did as little as I could. It was, however, not possible to avoid everything.[61]

While many women endured such slavery—if only to eat—others risked their all to escape. Remembered an American journalist:

As our long line of British Army lorries . . . rolled through the main street of Brahlstorf, the last Russian occupied town, a pretty blond girl darted from the crowd of Germans watching us and made a dash for our truck. Clinging with both hands to the tailboard, she made a desperate effort to climb in. But we were driving too fast and the board was too high. After being dragged several hundred yards she had to let go and fell on the cobblestone street. That scene was a dramatic illustration of the state of terror in which women . . . were living.[62]

By the summer of 1945, Germany had become the world's greatest slave market where sex was the new medium of exchange. While the wolf of hunger might be kept from the door, grim disease was almost always waiting in the wings.

"As a way of dying it may be worse than starvation, but it will put off dying for months—or even years," commented an English journalist.[63]

In addition to all the venereal diseases known in the West, German

61. Schieder, *Expulsion*, 268.
62. Keeling, 59.
63. Ibid., 64.

women were infected by a host of new evils, including an insidious strain of Asiatic syphilis. "It is a virulent form of sickness, unknown in this part of the world," a doctor's wife explained. "[I]t would be difficult to cure even if we were lucky enough to have any penicillin."[64]

Another dreaded concern—not only for those who were selling themselves, but for the millions of rape victims—was unwanted pregnancy. Thousands who were if fact pregnant sought and found abortions. Thousands more lived in dreadful suspense. Jotted one Berlin woman in her diary:

> I calculated that I'm now just two weeks overdue. So I decided to consult a woman's doctor whose sign I had seen on a house round the corner. She turned out to be a blond woman of about my age, practicing in a semi-gutted room. She had replaced the missing windowpanes with X-ray negatives of human chests. She refused to talk and went straight to work. "No," she said, after the examination, "I can't find a thing. You're all right."
>
> "But I'm overdue. That's never happened to me before."
>
> "Don't be silly! It's happening to almost every woman nowadays. I'm overdue myself. It's lack of food. The body's saving its blood. Try and put some flesh on your ribs. Then things'll begin to work again."
>
> She charged me 10 Marks—which I gave her with a bad conscience. . . . Finally I risked asking her if women made pregnant by Russians come to her for help. "I'd rather not talk about that," she said dryly, and let me go.[65]

And for those infants who were carried and delivered, their struggle was usually brief.

"[T]he mortality among the small children and infants was very high," wrote one woman. "[T]hey simply had to starve to death. There was nothing for them. . . . Generally, they did not live to be more than 3 months old—a consolation for those mothers, who had got the child against their will from a Russian. . . . The mother worked all the time and was very seldom able to give the child the breast."[66]

As the above implied, simply because a mother sold her body to feed a child did not necessarily save her from back-breaking labor. Indeed, with the end of war, Germans old and young were dragooned by the

---

64. Horstmann, 106.
65. Anonymous, *Woman in Berlin*, 301–302.
66. Schieder, *Expulsion*, 276.

victors for the monumental clean-up and dismantling of the devastated Reich. Sometimes food was given to the workers—"a piece of bread or maybe a bowl of thin, watery soup"—and sometimes not. "We used to start work at six o'clock in the morning and get home again at six in the evening," said a Silesian woman. "We had to work on Sundays, too, and we were given neither payment nor food for what we did."[67]

From the blasted capital, another female recorded:

> Berlin is being cleaned up. . . . All round the hills of rubble, buckets were being passed from hand to hand; we have returned to the days of the Pyramids—except that instead of building we are carrying away. . . . On the embankment German prisoners were slaving away—gray-heads in miserable clothes, presumably ex-Volksturm. With grunts and groans, they were loading heavy wheels onto freight-cars. They gazed at us imploringly, tried to keep near us. At first I couldn't understand why. Others did, though, and secretly passed the men a few crusts of bread. This is strictly forbidden, but the Russian guard stared hard in the opposite direction. The men were unshaven, shrunken, with wretched doglike expressions. To me they didn't look German at all.[68]

"My mother, 72 years of age, had to work outside the town on refuse heaps," lamented a daughter in Posen. "There the old people were hunted about, and had to sort out bottles and iron, even when it was raining or snowing. The work was dirty, and it was impossible for them to change their clothes."[69]

Understandably, thousands of overworked, underfed victims soon succumbed under such conditions. No job was too low or degrading for the conquered Germans to perform. Well-bred ladies, who in former times were theater-going members of the upper-class, worked side by side with peasants at washtubs, cleaning socks and underclothes of Russian privates. Children and the aged were put to work scrubbing floors and shining boots in the American, British and French Zones. Some tasks were especially loathsome, as one woman makes clear: "[A]s a result of the war damage . . . the toilets were stopped up and filthy. This filth we had to clear away with our hands, without any utensils to do so. The excrement was brought into the yard, shoveled into carts,

67. Kaps, *Tragedy of Silesia*, 149.
68. Anonymous, *Woman in Berlin*, 268, 287.
69. Schieder, 257.

which we had to bring to refuse pits. The awful part was, that we got
dirtied by the excrement which spurted up, but we could not clean
ourselves."[70]

Added another female from the Soviet Zone:

> We had to build landing strips, and to break stones. In snow and rain, from six
> in the morning until nine at night, we were working along the roads. Any Russ-
> ian who felt like it took us aside. In the morning and at night we received cold
> water and a piece of bread, and at noon soup of crushed, unpeeled potatoes,
> without salt. At night we slept on the floors of farmhouses or stables, dead
> tired, huddled together. But we woke up every so often, when a moaning and
> whimpering in the pitch-black room announced the presence of one of the
> guards.[71]

As this woman and others make clear, although sex could be bought
for a bit of food, a cigarette or a bar of soap, some victors preferred
to take what they wanted, whenever and wherever they pleased. "If
they wanted a girl they just came in the field and got her," recalled
Ilse Breyer who worked at planting potatoes.[72]

"Hunger made German women more 'available,'" an American soldier revealed, "but despite this, rape was prevalent and often accompanied by additional violence. In particular I remember an eight-
een-year old woman who had the side of her face smashed with a
rifle butt and was then raped by two GIs. Even the French complained
that the rapes, looting and drunken destructiveness on the part of
our troops was excessive."[73]

Had rapes, starvation and slavery been the only trials Germans were
forced to endure, it would have been terrible enough. There were other
horrors ahead, however—some so sadistic and evil as to stagger the
senses. The nightmarish fate that befell thousands of victims locked
deep in Allied prisons was enough, moaned one observer, to cause even
the most devout to ask "if there really were such a thing as a God."

---

70. Ibid., 256.
71. Thorwald, *Flight in the Winter*, 181.
72. Interview with Ilse Breyer Broderson, Independence, Missouri, Sept. 12, 1997.
73. Brech, "Eisenhower's Death Camps," 165.

10

THE HALLS OF HELL

SOON AFTER the Allied victory in Europe, the purge of Nazi Party members from government, business, industry, science, education, and all other walks of German life commenced. While a surprising number of Nazis were allowed—even compelled—to man their posts temporarily to enable a smooth transition, all party members, high and low, were sooner or later excised from German daily life. In theory, "de-Nazification" was a simple transplanting of Nazi officials with those of democratic, socialist or communist underpinnings. In practice, the purge became little more than a cloak for an orgy of rape, torture and death.

Because their knowledge of the language and culture was superb, many of the intelligence officers accompanying US and British forces into the Reich were Jewish refugees who had fled Nazi persecution in the late 1930s. Although their American and English "aides" were hardly better, the fact that many of these "39ers" became interrogators, examiners and screeners, with old scores to settle, insured that Nazis—or any German, for that matter—would be shown no mercy.

One man opposed to the vengeance-minded program was George Patton. "Evidently the virus started by Morgenthau and [Bernard] Baruch of a Semitic revenge against all Germans is still working . . . ," wrote the general in private. "I am frankly opposed to this war-criminal stuff. It is not cricket and it is Semitic. . . . I can't see how Americans can sink so low."[1]

---

1. Martin Blumenson, *The Patton Papers—1940–1945* (New York: Houghton Mifflin Co., 1972), pages?

Soon after occupation, all adult Germans were compelled to register at the nearest Allied headquarters and complete a lengthy questionnaire on their past activities. While many nervous citizens were detained then and there, most returned home, convinced that at long last the terrible ordeal was over. For millions, however, the trial had but begun.

"Then it started," remembered Anna Fest, a woman who had registered with the Americans six weeks earlier.

> Such a feeling of helplessness, when three or four heavily armed military police stand in front of you. You just panic. I cried terribly. My mother was completely beside herself and said, "You can't do this. She registered just as she was supposed to." Then she said, "If only you'd gone somewhere else and had hidden." But I consider that *senseless*, because I did not feel guilty. . . . That was the way it went with everyone, with no reason given.[2]

Few German adults, Nazi or not, escaped the dreaded knock on the door. Far from being dangerous fascists, Freddy and Lali Horstmann were actually well-known anti-Nazis. Records Lali from the Russian Zone:

> "I am sorry to bother you," he began, "but I am simply carrying out my orders. Until when did you work for the Foreign Office?"
>
> "Till 1933," my husband answered.
>
> "Then you need fear nothing," Androff said. . . . "We accuse you of nothing, but we want you to accompany us to the headquarters of the NKVD, the secret police, so that we can take down what you said in a protocol, and ask you a few questions about the working of the Foreign Office. . . ."
>
> We were stunned for a moment; then I started forward, asking if I could come along with them. "Impossible," the interpreter smiled. My heart raced. Would Freddy answer satisfactorily? Could he stand the excitement? What sort of accommodation would they give him?
>
> "Don't worry, your husband has nothing to fear," Androff continued. "He will have a heated room. Give him a blanket for the night, but quickly, we must leave. . . ."
>
> There was a feeling of sharp tension, putting the soldier on his guard, as though he were expecting an attack from one of us. I took first the soldier, then the interpreter, by their hands and begged them to be kind to Freddy, repeating myself in the bustle and scraping of feet that drowned my words. There was a bang-

---

2. Owings, *Frauen*, 334.

ing of doors. A cold wind blew in. I felt Freddy kiss me. I never saw him again.[3]

"[W]e were wakened by the sound of tires screeching, engines stopping abruptly, orders yelled, general din, and a hammering on the window shutters. Then the intruders broke through the door, and we saw Americans with rifles who stood in front of our bed and shone lights at us. None of them spoke German, but their gestures said: 'Get dressed, come with us immediately.' This was my fourth arrest."[4]

Thus wrote Leni Riefenstahl, a talented young woman who was perhaps the world's greatest film-maker. Because her epic documentaries—*Triumph of the Will* and *Olympia*—seemed paeans to not only Germany, but Nazism, and because of her close relationship with an admiring Adolf Hitler, Leni was of more than passing interest to the Allies. Though false, rumors also hinted that the attractive, sometimes-actress was also a "mistress of the devil"—that she and Hitler were lovers.[5]

"Neither my husband nor my mother nor any of my three assistants had ever joined the Nazi Party, nor had any of us been politically active," said the confused young woman. "No charges had ever been filed against us, yet we were at the mercy of the [Allies] and had no legal protection of any kind."[6]

Soon after Leni's fourth arrest, came a fifth.

> The jeep raced along the autobahns until, a few hours later . . . I was brought to the Salzburg Prison; there an elderly prison matron rudely pushed me into the cell, kicking me so hard that I fell to the ground; then the door was locked. There were two other women in the dark, barren room, and one of them, on her knees, slid about the floor, jabbering confusedly; then she began to scream, her limbs writhing hysterically. She seemed to have lost her mind. The other woman crouched on her bunk, weeping to herself.[7]

As Leni and others quickly discovered, the "softening up" process began soon after arrival at an Allied prison. When Ernst von Salomon, his Jewish girl friend and fellow prisoners reached an American holding pen near Munich, the men were promptly led into a room and bru-

3. Horstmann, *We Chose to Stay*, 198–200.
4. Riefenstahl, *A Memoir*, 308.
5. Ibid., 327.
6. Ibid.
7. Ibid., 309.

tally beaten by military police. With his teeth knocked out and blood spurting from his mouth, von Salomon moaned to a gum-chewing officer, "You are no gentlemen." The remark brought only a roar of laughter from the attackers. "No, no, no!" the GIs grinned. "We are Mississippi boys!" In another room, military policemen raped the women at will while leering soldiers watched from windows.[8]

After such savage treatment, the feelings of despair only intensified once the captives were crammed into cells.

"The people had been standing there for three days, waiting to be interrogated," remembered a German physician ordered to treat prisoners in the Soviet Zone. "At the sight of us a pandemonium broke out which left me helpless. . . . As far as I could gather, the usual senseless questions were being reiterated: Why were they there, and for how long? They had no water and hardly anything to eat. They wanted to be let out more often than once a day. . . . A great many of them have dysentery so badly that they can no longer get up."[9]

"Young Poles made fun of us," said a woman from her cell in the same zone. "[They] threw bricks through the windows, paperbags with sand, and skins of hares filled with excrement. We did not dare to move or offer resistance, but huddled together in the farthest corner, in order not to be hit, which could not always be avoided. . . . [W]e were never free from torments."[10]

"For hours on end I rolled about on my bed, trying to forget my surroundings," recalled Leni Riefenstahl, "but it was impossible."

> The mentally disturbed woman kept screaming—all through the night; but even worse were the yells and shrieks of men from the courtyard, men who were being beaten, screaming like animals. I subsequently found out that a company of SS men was being interrogated.
>
> They came for me the next morning, and I was taken to a padded cell where I had to strip naked, and a woman examined every square inch of my body. Then I had to get dressed and go down to the courtyard, where many men were standing, apparently prisoners, and I was the only woman. We had to line up before an American guard who spoke German. The prisoners stood to attention, so I

8.   Botting, *From the Ruins of the Reich*, 263.
9.   Von Lehndorff, *Token of a Covenant*, 128–129.
10. Schieder, *Expulsion of the German Population*, 258.

tried to do the same, and then an American came who spoke fluent German. He pushed a few people together, then halted at the first in our line. "Were you in the Party?"

The prisoner hesitated for a moment, then said: "Yes."

He was slugged in the face and spat blood.

The American went on to the next in line.

"Were you in the Party?"

The man hesitated.

"Yes or no?"

"Yes." And he too got punched so hard in the face that the blood ran out of his mouth. However, like the first man, he didn't dare resist. They didn't even instinctively raise their hands to protect themselves. They did nothing. They put up with the blows like dogs.

The next man was asked: "Were you in the Party?"

Silence.

"Well?"

"No," he yelled, so no punch. From then on nobody admitted that he had been in the Party and I was not even asked.[11]

As the above case illustrated, there often was no rhyme or reason to the examinations; all seemed designed to force from the victim what the inquisitor wanted to hear, whether true or false. Additionally, many such "interrogations" were structured to inflict as much pain and suffering as possible. Explained one prisoner:

> The purpose of these interrogations is not to worm out of the people what they knew—which would be uninteresting anyway—but to extort from them special statements. The methods resorted to are extremely primitive; people are beaten up until they confess to having been members of the Nazi Party. . . . The authorities simply assume that, basically, everybody has belonged to the Party. Many people die during and after these interrogations, while others, who admit at once their party membership, are treated more leniently.[12]

"A young commissar, who was a great hater of the Germans, cross-examined me. . . ," said Gertrude Schulz. "When he put the question: "Frauenwerk [Women's Labor Service]?", I answered in the negative. Thereupon he became so enraged, that he beat me with a stick, until I was black and blue. I received about 15 blows . . . on my left upper

---

11.   Riefenstahl, *Memoir*, 310.

12.   Von Lehndorff, *Token*, 127.

arm, on my back and on my thigh. I collapsed and, as in the case of the first cross-examination, I had to sign the questionnaire."[13]

"Both officers who took our testimony were former German Jews," reminisced a member of the women's SS, Anna Fest. While vicious dogs snarled nearby, one of the officers screamed questions and accusations at Anna. If the answers were not those desired, "he kicked me in the back and the other hit me."

> They kept saying we must have been armed, have had pistols or so. But we had no weapons, none of us. . . . I had no pistol. I couldn't say, just so they'd leave me in peace, yes, we had pistols. The same thing would happen to the next person to testify. . . . [T]he terrible thing was, the German men had to watch. That was a horrible, horrible experience. . . . That must have been terrible for them. When I went outside, several of them stood there with tears running down their cheeks. What could they have done? They could do nothing.[14]

Not surprisingly, with beatings, rape, torture, and death facing them, few victims failed to "confess" and most gladly inked their name to any scrap of paper shown them. Some, like Anna, tried to resist. Such recalcitrance was almost always of short duration, however. Generally, after enduring blackened eyes, broken bones, electric shock to breasts—or, in the case of men, smashed testicles—only those who died during torture failed to sign confessions.

Alone, surrounded by sadistic hate, utterly bereft of law, many victims understandably escaped by taking their own lives. Like tiny islands in a vast sea of misery, however, miracles did occur. As he limped painfully back to his prison cell, one Wehrmacht officer reflected on the insults, beatings, and tortures he had endured and contemplated suicide.

> I could not see properly in the semi-darkness and missed my open cell door. A kick in the back and I was sprawling on the floor. As I raised myself I said to myself I could not, should not accept this humiliation. I sat on my bunk. I had hidden a razor blade that would serve to open my veins. Then I looked at the New Testament and found these words in the Gospel of St. John: "Without me ye can do nothing."
>
> Yes. You can mangle this poor body—I looked down at the running sores

13. Schieder, *Expulsion*, 173.
14. Owings, *Frauen*, 335, 336.

on my legs—but myself, my honor, God's image that is in me, you cannot touch. This body is only a shell, not my real self. Without Him, without the Lord, my Lord, ye can do nothing. New strength seemed to rise in me.

I was pondering over what seemed to me a miracle when the heavy lock turned in the cell door. A very young American soldier came in, put his finger to his lips to warn me not to speak. "I saw it," he said. "Here are baked potatoes." He pulled the potatoes out of his pocket and gave them to me, and then went out, locking the door behind him.[15]

Horrific as de-Nazification was in the British, French and, especially, the American Zones, it was nothing compared to what took place in Poland, behind Soviet lines. In hundreds of concentration camps sponsored by an apparatus called the "Office of State Security," thousands of Germans—male and female, old and young, high and low, Nazi and anti–Nazi, SS, Wehrmacht, Volkssturm, Hitler Youth, all—were rounded up and imprisoned. Staffed and run by Jews, with help from Poles, Czechs, Russians, and other concentration camp survivors, the prisons were little better than torture chambers where dying was a thing to be prolonged, not hastened. While those with blond hair, blue eyes and handsome features were first to go, anyone who spoke German would do.[16]

Moments after arrival, prisoners were made horrifyingly aware of their fate. John Sack, himself a Jew, reports on one camp run by twenty-six-year-old Shlomo Morel:

> "I was at Auschwitz," Shlomo proclaimed, lying to the Germans but, even more, to himself, psyching himself like a fighter the night of the championship, filling himself with hate for the Germans around him. "I was at Auschwitz for six long years, and I swore that if I got out, I'd pay all you Nazis back." His eyes sent spears, but the "Nazis" sent him a look of simple bewilderment. . . . "Now sing the Horst Wessel Song!" No one did, and Shlomo, who carried a hard rubber club, hit it against a bed like some judge's gavel. "Sing it, I say!"
>
> "*The flags held high . . .*," some Germans began.
>
> "Everyone!" Shlomo said.

15. Wilfried Strik-Strikfeldt, *Against Stalin and Hitler* (New York: John Day Co., 1973), 243.
16. Botting, *Ruins of the Reich*, 262; John Sack, *An Eye for an Eye* (New York: Basic Books, 1993), 87.

"The ranks closed tight. . . ."

"I said everyone!" . . .

"Blond!" Shlomo cried to the blondest, bluest-eyed person there. "I said sing!" He swung his rubber club at the man's golden head and hit it. The man staggered back.

"Our comrades, killed by the Reds and Reactionaries. . . ."

"Sonofabitch!" Shlomo cried, enraged that the man was defying him by not singing but staggering back. He hit him again, saying, "Sing!"

"Are marching in spirit with us. . . ."

"Louder!"

"Clear the street for the Brown Battalions. . . ."

"Still louder!" cried Shlomo, hitting another shouting man. . . .

"Millions of hopeful people. . . ."

"Nazi pigs!"

"Are looking to the swastika. . . ."

"Schweine!" Shlomo cried. He threw down his rubber club, grabbed a wooden stool, and, a leg in his fist, started beating a German's head. Without thinking, the man raised his arms, and Shlomo, enraged that the man would try to evade his just punishment, cried, "Sonofawhore!" and slammed the stool against the man's chest. The man dropped his arms, and Shlomo started hitting his now undefended head when *snap!* the leg of the stool split off, and, cursing the German birchwood, he grabbed another stool and hit the German with that. No one was singing now, but Shlomo, shouting, didn't notice. The other guards called out, "Blond!" "Black!" "Short!" "Tall!" and as each of these terrified people came up, they wielded their clubs upon him. The brawl went on till eleven o'clock, when the sweat-drenched invaders cried, "Pigs! We will fix you up!" and left the Germans alone.

Some were quite fixed. . . . Shlomo and his subordinates had killed them.[17]

The next night it was more of the same . . . and the next night and the next and the next. Those who survived the "welcoming committees" at this and other camps were flung back into their pens.

"I was put with 30 women into a cell, which was intended to accommodate one person," Gerlinde Winkler recalled. "The narrow space, into which we were rammed, was unbearable and our legs were all entangled together. . . . The women, ill with dysentery, were only allowed to go out once a day, in order to relieve themselves. A bucket without a cover was pushed into the cell with the remark: 'Here you

17. Sack, *Eye*, 102–103.

have one, you German sows.' The stink was insupportable, and we were not allowed to open the little window."[18]

"The air in the cells became dense, the smell of the excrement filled it, the heat was like in Calcutta, and the flies made the ceiling black," wrote John Sack. "*I'm choking*, the Germans thought, and one even took the community razor blade and, in despair, cut his throat open with it."[19]

When the wretched inmates were at last pried from their hellish tombs, it was only for interrogation. Sack continues:

> As many as eight interrogators, almost all Jews, stood around any one German saying, "Were you in the Nazi Party?" Sometimes a German said, "Yes," and the boys shouted, "*Du schwein*! You pig!" and beat him and broke his arm, perhaps, before sending him to his cell. . . . But usually a German said, "No," and the boys . . . told him, "You're lying. You were a Nazi."
>
> "No, I never was."
>
> "You're lying! We know about you!"
>
> "No, I really wasn't—"
>
> "*Du lugst*! You're lying!" they cried, hitting the obstinate man. "You better admit it! Or you'll get a longer sentence! Now! Were you in the Nazi Party?"
>
> "No!" the German often said, and the boys had to beat him and beat him until he was really crying, "I was a Nazi! Yes!"
>
> But sometimes a German wouldn't confess. One such hard case was a fifty-year-old. . . .
>
> "Were you in the Party?"
>
> "No, I wasn't in it."
>
> "How many people work for you?"
>
> "In the high season, thirty-five."
>
> "You must have been in the Party," the boy deduced. He asked for the German's wallet, where he found a fishing license with the stamp of the German Anglers Association. Studying it, he told the German, "It's stamped by the Party."
>
> "It's not," said the German. He'd lost his left arm in World War I and was using his right arm to gesture with, and, to the boy, he may have seemed to be Heiling Hitler. The boy became violent. He grabbed the man's collar, hit the man's head against the wall, hit it against it ten times more, threw the man's body onto the floor, and, in his boots, jumped on the man's cringing chest as though jumping rope. A half dozen other interrogators, almost all Jews, pushed the man onto a couch, pulled off his trousers, and hit him with hard rubber clubs and

---

18. Schieder, *Expulsion*, 163.
19. Sack, 74.

hard rubber hoses full of stones. The sweat started running down the Jews' arms, and the blood down the man's naked legs.

"*Warst du in der Partei?*"

"*Nein!*"

"*Warst du in der Partei?*"

"*Nein!*" the German screamed—*screamed*, till the boys had to go to Shlomo's kitchen for a wooden spoon and to use it to cram some rags in the German's mouth. Then they resumed beating him. . . . The more the man contradicted them, the more they hated him for it.[20]

After undergoing similar sessions on a regular basis, the victim was brought back for the eighth time.

By now, the man was half unconscious due to his many concussions, and he wasn't thinking clearly. The boys worked on him with rubber and oak-wood clubs and said, "Do you still say you weren't in the Party?"

"No! I didn't say I wasn't in the Party!"

"You didn't?"

"No!" said the punch drunk man. "I never said it!"

"You *were* in the Party?"

"Yes!"

The boys stopped beating him. They practically sighed, as if their ordeal were over now. They lit up cigarettes. . . .

"Scram," one said to the German. The man stood up, and he had his hand on the doorknob when one of the boys impulsively hit the back of his head, and he fell to the floor, unconscious. "*Aufstehen, du Deutsches schwein.* Stand up, you German pig," the boys said, kicking him till he stood up and collapsed again. Two boys carried him to his cell and dropped him in a corner. . . .

Of course, the boys would beat up the Germans for "Yes"es as well as "No"s. In Glatz, the Jewish commandant asked a German policeman, "Were you in the Party?"

"Of course! I was obliged to be!"

"Lie down," the commandant said, and six weeks later the boys were still whipping the German's feet.[21]

Some torture sessions lacked even the pretense of an examination. Remembered Eva Reimann:

My cell door opened. The guard, who, because of the foul smell, held a handkerchief to his nose, cried, "Reimann Eva! Come!" I was led to a first-floor room. . . .

20. Ibid., 74–75, 76.
21. Ibid., 77, 78.

He shouted at me, "Take off your shoes!" I took them off. "Lie down!" I lay down. He took a thick bamboo stick, and he beat the soles of my feet. I screamed, since the pain was very great. . . . The stick whistled down on me. A blow on my mouth tore my lower lip, and my teeth started bleeding violently. He beat my feet again. The pain was unbearable. . . .

The door opened suddenly, and, smiling obligingly, a cigarette in his mouth, in came the chief of the Office, named Sternnagel. In faultless German he asked me, "What's wrong here? Why do you let yourself be beaten? You just have to sign this document. Or should we jam your fingers in the door, until the bones are broad? . . .

A man picked me up by the ankles, raised me eight inches above the floor, and let me fall. My hands were tied, and my head hit hard. . . . I lay in a bloody puddle. Someone cried, "Stand up!" I tried to, and, with unspeakable pain, I succeeded. A man with a pistol came, held it to my left temple, and said, "Will you now confess?" I told him, "Please shoot me." Yes, I hoped to be freed from all his tortures. I begged him, "Please pull the trigger."[22]

After barely surviving his "interrogation," one fourteen-year-old was taken to the camp infirmary. "My body was green, but my legs were fire red," the boy said. "My wounds were bound with toilet paper, and I had to change the toilet paper every day. I was in the perfect place to watch what went on. . . . All the patients were beaten people, and they died everywhere: at their beds, in the washroom, on the toilet. At night, I had to step over the dead as if that were normal to do."[23]

When the supply of victims ran low, it was a simple matter to find more. John Sack:

One day, a German in pitch-black pants, the SS's color, showed up in Lola's prison. He'd been spotted near the city square by a Pole who'd said, "Fascist! You're wearing black!" At that, the German had bolted off, but the Pole chased him a mile to the Church of Saints Peter and Paul, tackled him by a gold mosaic, hit him, kicked him, and took him to Lola's prison. Some guards, all girls, then seized the incriminating evidence: the man's black pants, pulling them off so aggressively that one of the tendons tore. The man screamed, but the girls said, "Shut up!" and they didn't recognize that the pants were part of a boy scout uniform. The "man" was fourteen years old.

The girls decided to torture him [with]. . . . fire. They held down the German boy, put out their cigarettes on him, and, using gasoline, set his curly black hair afire.[24]

---

22. Ibid., 152–153.
23. Ibid., 172–173.
24. Ibid., 87–88.

At the larger prison camps, Germans died by the hundreds daily.

"You pigs!" the commandant then cried, and he beat the Germans with their stools, often killing them. At dawn many days, a Jewish guard cried, *"Eins! Zwei! Drei! Vier!"* and marched the Germans into the woods outside their camp. "Halt! Get your shovels! Dig!" the guard cried, and, when the Germans had dug a big grave, he put a picture of Hitler in. "Now cry!" the guard said. "And sing *All the Dogs Are Barking!*" and all the Germans moaned,

> *All the dogs are barking,*
> *All the dogs are barking,*
> *Just the little hot-dogs,*
> *Aren't barking at all.*

The guard then cried, "Get undressed!" and, when the Germans were naked, he beat them, poured liquid manure on them, or, catching a toad, shoved the fat thing down a German's throat, the German soon dying.[25]

Utterly unhinged by years of persecution, by the loss of homes and loved ones, for the camp operators, no torture, no sadism, no bestiality, seemed too monstrous to inflict on those now in their power. Some Germans were forced to crawl on all fours and eat their own excrement as well as that of others. Many were drowned in open latrines. Hundreds were herded into buildings and burned to death or sealed in caskets and buried alive.[26]

Near Lamsdorf, German women were forced to disinter bodies from a Polish burial site. According to John Sack:

The women did, and they started to suffer nausea as the bodies, black as the stuff in a gutter, appeared. The faces were rotten, the flesh was glue, but the guards— who had often seemed psychopathic, making a German woman drink urine, drink blood, and eat a man's excrement, inserting an oily five-mark bill in a woman's vagina, putting a match to it—shouted at the women . . . "Lie down with them!" The women did, and the guards shouted, "Hug them!" "Kiss them!" "Make love with them!" and, with their rifles, pushed on the backs of the women's heads until their eyes, noses and mouths were deep in the Polish faces' slime. The women who clamped their lips couldn't scream, and the women who screamed had to taste something vile. Spitting, retching, the women at last stood up, the wet tendrils still on their chins, fingers, clothes, the wet seeping into

---

25. Ibid., 110.
26. Ibid., 111; Botting, *Ruins of the Reich*, 185.

the fibers, the stink like a mist around them as they marched back to Lamsdorf. There were no showers there, and the corpses had all had typhus, apparently, and sixty-four women . . . died.[27]

Not surprisingly, the mortality rate at the concentration camps was staggering and relatively few survived. At one prison of eight thousand, a mere 1,500 lived to reach home.[28] And of those "lucky" individuals who did leave with their lives, few could any longer be called human.

When a smattering of accounts began to leak from Poland of the unspeakable crimes being committed, many in the West were stunned. "One would expect that after the horrors in Nazi concentration camps, nothing like that could ever happen again," muttered one US senator, who then reported on beatings, torture and "brains splashed on the ceiling."[29]

"Is this what our soldiers died for?" echoed a Briton in the House of Commons.[30]

Added Winston Churchill: "Enormous numbers [of Germans] are utterly unaccounted for. It is not impossible that tragedy on a prodigious scale is unfolding itself behind the Iron Curtain."[31]

While Churchill and others in the West were expressing shock and surprise over the sadistic slaughter taking place in the Soviet Zone, precious little was said about the "tragedy on a prodigious scale" that was transpiring in their own backyard.

Among the millions imprisoned by the Allies were thousands of Germans accused of having a direct or indirect hand in war crimes. Because the victorious powers demanded swift and severe punishment, Allied prosecutors were urged to get the most damning indictments in as little time as possible. Unfortunately for the accused, their captors seemed determined to inflict as much pain as possible in the process.

27. Sack, *Eye For an Eye*, 130–131.
28. Ibid., 131.
29. Ibid., 111.
30. Ibid.
31. Ibid.

"[W]e were thrown into small cells stark naked," Hans Schmidt later wrote. "The cells in which three or four persons were incarcerated were six and a half by ten feet in size and had no windows or ventilation."

When we went to the lavatory we had to run through a lane of Americans who struck us with straps, brooms, cudgels, buckets, belts, and pistol holders to make us fall down. Our head, eyes, body, belly, and genitals were violently injured. A man stood inside the lavatory to beat us and spit on us. We returned to our cells through the same ordeal. The temperature in the cells was 140 Fahrenheit or more. During the first three days we were given only one cup of water and a small slice of bread. During the first days we perspired all the time, then perspiration stopped. We were kept standing chained back to back for hours. We suffered terribly from thirst, blood stagnation and mortification of the hands. From time to time water was poured on the almost red-hot radiators, filling the cells with steam, so that we could hardly breathe. During all this time the cells were in darkness, except when the American soldiers entered and switched on electric bulbs . . . which forced us to close our eyes.

Our thirst became more and more cruel, so that our lips cracked, our tongues were stiff, and we eventually became apathetic, or raved, or collapsed.

After enduring this torture for several days, we were given a small blanket to cover our nakedness, and driven to the courtyard outside. The uneven soil was covered with pebbles and slag and we were again beaten and finally driven back on our smashed and bleeding feet. While out of breath, burning cigarettes were pushed into our mouths, and each of us was forced to eat three or four of them. Meanwhile the American soldiers continued to hit us on eyes, head, and ears. Back in our cells we were pushed against burning radiators, so that our skin was blistered.

For thirteen days and nights we received the same treatment, tortured by heat and thirst. When we begged for water, our guards mocked us. When we fainted we were revived by being drenched with cold water. There was dirt everywhere and we were never allowed to wash, our inflamed eyes gave us terrible pain, we fainted continuously.

Every twenty minutes or so our cell doors were opened and the soldiers insulted and hit us. Whenever the doors were opened we had to stand still with our backs to the door. Two plates of food, spiced with salt, pepper, and mustard to make us thirstier, were given us daily. We ate in the dark on the floor. The thirst was the most terrible of all our tortures and we could not sleep.

In this condition I was brought to trial.[32]

---

32. Utley, *High Cost of Vengeance*, 190–191.

During the Nazi war crimes trials and hearings, almost any method that would obtain a "confession" was employed. Eager to implicate high-ranking German officers in the Malmedy Massacre, American investigator Harry Thon ordered Wehrmacht sergeant Willi Schafer to write out an incriminating affidavit:

> Next morning Mr. Thon appeared in my cell, read my report, tore it up, swore at me and hit me. After threatening to have me killed unless I wrote what he wanted, he left. A few minutes later the door of my cell opened, a black hood encrusted with blood, was put over my head and face and I was led to another room. In view of Mr. Thon's threat the black cap had a crushing effect on my spirits. . . . Four men of my company . . . accused me, although later they admitted to having borne false testimony. Nevertheless I still refused to incriminate myself. Thereupon Mr. Thon said that if I continued to refuse this would be taken as proof of my Nazi opinions, and . . . my death was certain. He said I would have no chance against four witnesses, and advised me for my own good to make a statement after which I would be set free. . . . I still refused. I told Mr. Thon that although my memory was good, I was unable to recall any of the occurrences he wished me to write about and which to the best of my knowledge had never occurred.
>
> Mr. Thon left but returned in a little while with Lieutenant [William] Perl who abused me, and told Mr. Thon that, should I not write what was required within half an hour, I should be left to my fate. Lieutenant Perl made it clear to me that I had the alternative of writing and going free or not writing and dying. I decided for life.[33]

Another Landser unable to resist the pressure was Joachim Hoffman:

> [W]hen taken for a hearing a black hood was placed over my head. The guards who took me to my hearing often struck or kicked me. I was twice thrown down the stairs and was hurt so much that blood ran out of my mouth and nose. At the hearing, when I told the officers about the ill treatment I had suffered, they only laughed. I was beaten and the black cap pulled over my face whenever I could not answer the questions put to me, or gave answers not pleasing to the officers. . . . I was beaten and several times kicked in the genitals.[34]

Understandably, after several such sessions, even the strongest submitted and signed papers incriminating themselves and others. "If you confess you will go free," nineteen-year-old Siegfried Jaenckel was told.

---

33. Ibid., 192–193.
34. Ibid., 193.

"[Y]ou need only to say you had an order from your superiors. But if you won't speak you will be hung."[35] Despite the mental and physical abuse, young Jaenckel held out as long as he could: "I was beaten and I heard the cries of the men being tortured in adjoining cells, and whenever I was taken for a hearing I trembled with fear. . . . Subjected to such duress I eventually gave in, and signed the long statement dictated to me."[36]

Far from being isolated or extreme cases, such methods of extorting confessions were the rule rather than the exception. Wrote author Freda Utley, who learned of the horror after speaking with American jurist Edward van Roden:

> Beatings and brutal kickings; knocking-out of teeth and breaking of jaws; mock trials; solitary confinement; torture with burning splinters; the use of investigators pretending to be priests; starvation; and promises of acquittal. . . . Judge van Roden said: "All but two of the Germans in the 139 cases we investigated had been kicked in the testicles beyond repair. This was standard operating procedure with our American investigators." He told of one German who had had lighted matchsticks forced under his fingernails by the American investigators to extort a confession, and had appeared at his trial with his fingers still bandaged from the atrocity.[37]

In addition to testimony given under torture, those who might have spoken in defense of the accused were prevented. Moreover, hired "witnesses" were paid by the Americans to parrot the prosecution's charges.[38]

When criticism such as Utley's and van Roden's surfaced, and even as victims were being hung by the hundreds, those responsible defended their methods. "We couldn't have made those birds talk otherwise . . . ," explained Colonel A. H. Rosenfeld. "It was a trick, and it worked like a charm."[39]

---

35. Ibid., 194.
36. Ibid.
37. Ibid., 186.
38. Ibid., 197; Joseph Halow, *Innocent at Dachau* (Newport Beach, Cal.: Institute for Historical Review, 1992), 311.
39. Utley, *High Cost*, 197.

Meanwhile, as the judicial charade was in progress behind prison walls, tortures of another kind stalked the land. Indeed, during the first post-war years conquered Germany was little better than a vast concentration camp. Coinciding with the ruthless Allied program of denazification and "reeducation," was the American and British policy of non-fraternization. In theory, "nonfrat" was little more than a simple segregation of victors from vanquished to ensure that the occupation was both efficient and economical. In cold, hard fact, however, the program was a deliberate attempt to further degrade and demonize Germans and crush what little pride and respect remained. Ran one post-war pamphlet issued to US troops:

> [T]he shooting is over but there is a lot to be done. . . . Look out, the people are still a formidable enemy. . . . There are children who shuffle from one foot to another outside your mess hall; they'll be too polite or too scared to ask for food but you can see in their eyes how hungry they are. . . . Old men and women pulling carts, young girls in threadbare clothing . . . are still better off than thousands of the Greeks and Dutch and Poles they enslaved. . . . The ragged German trudging along the street with a load of firewood may not look vicious but he has a lot in common with a trapped rat.[40]

With centuries of colonial experience to draw upon, the British Government issued similar directives to its soldiers stationed in "darkest Germany":

> Do play your part as a representative of a conquering power and keep the Germans in their place. Give orders—don't beg the question. Display cold, correct, dignified curtness and aloofness. Don't try to be kind—it will be regarded as weakness. Drop heavily on any attempt to take charge or other forms of insolence. Don't be too ready to listen to stories from attractive women—they may be acting under orders. Don't show any aversion to another war if Germany does not learn her lesson this time.[41]

While non-fraternization became the official vehicle to dispossess Germans of their homes and property and deny them access to shops, stores and restaurants, unofficially the edicts acted as a license for the conquerors to abuse, insult and mistreat the conquered whenever the urge struck.[42]

---

40. Davidson, *Death and Life of Germany*, 81.
41. Botting, *Ruins of the Reich*, 206.
42. Crawley, *Spoils of War*, 53, 57.

"I HATE GERMANS," a sign over an American major's desk warned. Not surprisingly, many enlisted men took such hints to heart. Wrote one US soldier, Joseph Halow:

> I recall one Jewish-American translator who, when driving his Jeep . . . never missed a chance to hit a puddle at high speed, drenching as many German pedestrians as he could with cold, muddy water. I was along on one of these occasions. After swerving to splash a large crowd of Germans walking along a dirt road, he grinned at me and freely admitted that it was all deliberate, that he thought the Germans had it coming. Although I could understand his feelings, I deplored this habit, for by then I knew the painstaking care with which my own German acquaintances, very few of them able to buy new clothes, cleaned and mended their old clothes.[43]

Another sport Allied soldiers in jeeps enjoyed was hooking with a cane the ankles of women they passed and upending them. German men were bashed over the head.[44] Joseph Halow remembered another incident that became all too common:

> As I was standing in front of the Excelsior Hotel, about to board a bus . . . I noticed a crowd gathered at the corner. Hurrying over, I discovered the attraction. A US Army enlisted man was beating a German, who offered no resistance. He soon fell to the pavement, saying over and over: "Aber ich habe nichts getan!" ("But I've done nothing!") His pleas were useless to calm the frenzied GI. I asked a bystander what had happened, and learned that the German had insulted an American girl by calling her a "whore."
>
> As the German lay there the enlisted man began kicking him furiously, in the side, in the chest, all over his writhing body. Two American lieutenants stood among the onlookers. I asked if there was nobody who could stop the attack. One of the officers showed obvious distaste, but continued to watch in silence. When I asked him directly if he couldn't order the man to stop, he merely shrugged his shoulders wordlessly.[45]

Nor was such random brutality lost on the Germans themselves. Wrote American, Freda Utley:

> I remember one young German, who had been in occupied France, saying to me, "When I was a soldier in France, I never had a chance to enjoy life and kick other people around as you do. We were strictly disciplined and told to

---

43. Halow, *Innocent*, 41.
44. Crawley, *Spoils*, 57.
45. Halow, 89–90.

be polite and considerate to the French; we lived with them in their houses, and did not throw them into the gutter as you do us. We have learned our lesson though; if there is ever a next time you have taught us Germans what is permitted to a conqueror.[46]

Although some soldiers wholeheartedly embraced the non-fraternization edict with a vindictiveness to satisfy even Eisenhower, most GIs and Tommies remained true to their better nature. Peter Fabian, a young artillery officer in a British division, recalled one day when a "very distraught" German farmwife rushed up to him.

> She had run all the eight miles from the farm. She said she had scalded her baby and begged us to help save it. So I went to our Medical Officer, who was a woman, and asked her if she could do anything. She said she thought she could but she didn't have any transport. So I nicked some transport. I took a jeep without proper authority—and drove the MO and the [mother] over to the farm. We found the baby almost dead. It was scalded all over. The mother had covered the burns in flour, which was the last thing you should do. So the MO had to spend two or three hours getting the flour off. . . .
>
> [T]he next day, Monday morning, I was on the carpet sharpish in front of the Colonel, my Commanding Officer, who was a Christian and hated Germans. He said: "How dare you speak to the Germans! You've absolutely no right. Don't you know there's a law about that sort of thing! Next time you'll be in serious trouble." This made me very, very angry, so I retorted: "Well, now I know how you *Christians* feel about these things, but I'm afraid we have other standards." He didn't answer to that. He just went red in the face and said: "Alright, go." I never heard anymore.[47]

Such islands of humanity—tiny havens that they were—could not materially ease the dreadful conditions existing throughout Germany, nor could they ameliorate the vast sea of human suffering. One year after war's end, the former Reich was still a land of "troglodytes" with urban-dwellers clinging precariously to their caves and cracks. After viewing for himself conditions in Hamburg, Victor Gollancz was horrified. Penned the Jewish publisher to his wife in England:

> In one room were living a soldier, his wife (who is expecting a baby in a fortnight) and his seventy-two-year-old mother. They live, eat, cook, work,

46. Utley, *High Cost*, 236.
47. Botting, *Ruins of the Reich*, 206–207.

and sleep in the one room. There is one bed; a table; two chairs; a very small side-table; and a little cooking stove. . . . The old mother sleeps in the bed; *on the floor*, on a filthy rug but no mattress, sleep the husband and wife. The wife's clothes were wretched, and she was barefoot. She has no baby clothes or cradle—nothing. People like this have literally *nothing*. Their chief concern is to get a basket or something to put the baby in. I asked the old mother whether she had enough to eat, and she replied with a smile, "*Nein, nein, ich bin immer hungrig*"—as if that were the fault of her appetite.

This was all pretty shaking, but it was heaven—I really mean this—in comparison with the next place. . . . The place was a cellar under rubble in one of the huge devastated areas. For light and air there was one tiny window. On a table was a sort of open lamp with a naked flame. . . . The air was so thick that I could hardly keep my glasses free enough from steam to see. . . . There was one bed in which the husband and wife were sleeping; on a sort of couch was the son, crippled in the war; and on the floor, on an indescribably filthy "mattress" which was all broken open with the sawdust spilling out, was the daughter. She looked fifty but I suspect she was about twenty-five. This was an extraordinary creature, with a huge nose, a bony, emaciated face, and several front teeth missing. She also appeared to be pretty crippled, and her hand was shaking terribly, I suppose from hunger. There was no free space in the cellar at all and again they lived, ate and slept here. Nobody could work—the young man could not because he was crippled, and the father because he was too weak. . . . The woman cried when the Salvation Army people gave her some money.[48]

As Gollancz made note, one of the few relief organizations that dared face and fight the incredible suffering, irregardless of Allied political pressure, was the Salvation Army. With characteristic warmth and compassion that seemed all the more startling amid the crushing climate of hate and revenge, the charity dispensed food, clothing and shelter. But even the heroic efforts of the Salvation Army and its well-funded, well-organized staff could hardly make a dent in the growing catastrophe.

In Berlin alone, an estimated 50,000 orphans struggled to survive. "[S]ome of them," wrote a witness, were "one-eyed or one-legged

48. Ibid., 126–127.

veterans of seven or so, many so deranged by the bombing and the Russian attack that they screamed at the sight of any uniform, even a Salvation Army one."[49]

Given the feral conditions and the scarcity of resources, competition among the swarms of orphans was keen, especially in winter. "Every time a lorry drove out of a coal depot," one British officer recalled, "hundreds of little kids would run out after it to pick up any pieces of coal that fell off as it swept past, and many of them were run over in the melee."[50]

While occupation troops dined on five-course meals complete with fried sole, Dutch steak and ice cream, thousands of starving children felt fortunate if a potato peel or crust of moldy bread was unearthed.[51] Christopher Leefe remembered an incident that occurred during dinner at a British mess:

> [W]e were about halfway through when there was a terrific commotion in the hall outside and the mess waiter burst in dragging a small boy behind him. The boy had been caught robbing our rooms. He had climbed up a drainpipe and got in through a window four stories up. He had nicked a few cigarette lighters and a watch and was just about to make his getaway when he got caught. So there he stood, this little German ragamuffin, in front of us grand British officers. He was only about 10, thin as a bean pole, clothes hanging on him like sacks—when kids are starving their clothes always look too big for them. He was stood in front of the senior officer present . . . and the major asked him, "Why did you do it?. . ."
>
> The boy just stood there and said nothing. He was blonde and Aryan and defiant, and suddenly the major leaned forward and whacked him across the face with his hand. "YOU FUCKING LITTLE KRAUT!" he yelled. "Come on, where have you put it all?" Bash, bash! The boy just stood there with the tears streaming down his face and the German mess waiter behind him snarling at him in German. His eyes were so blue and his hair was so blonde and he stood there so arrogant and defiant that I've always asked myself right to this day: "God, I wonder how many of our boys would be as tough as that?"
>
> The point is that none of us could have cared a bit for that little boy. He was probably an orphan, his father dead on the Eastern Front, his mother rotting

49. Garrett, *Ethics and Airpower*, 141.
50. Botting, *Ruins*, 251.
51. Ibid., 214.

under the rubble of the bombed-out ruins, and here he was—starving and risking his life climbing up drainpipes in the middle of a British tank regiment. So what? We didn't feel any compassion for him or any of the Germans.[52]

Children who could not live by their wits, died. Those who didn't starve or freeze, were crushed by the walls of their caves or torn to shreds by unexploded bombs which lay scattered across Germany by the ton.

"I saw a friend playing with a hand grenade," said nine-year-old Martha Suentzenich. "It exploded and blew off his head. He jumped around like a chicken with blood going everywhere."[53]

On their own, orphans aged fast, and little girls aged fastest of all. Like their older sisters, the children soon discovered that selling themselves could stave off starvation.

"Germany's youth is on the road . . . because there was not enough to eat at home," the *New York Times* reported. "Homeless, without papers or ration cards . . . these groups rob Germans and displaced persons. They are . . . wandering aimlessly, disillusioned, dissolute, diseased, and without guidance."[54]

Just as pangs of conscience were creeping over many Allied soldiers—as well as New York reporters—so too were others beginning to recoil at the ruthless reign of terror transpiring in Germany. Over the next months and years, voices, heretofore muted or silent, at last were raised. George Kennan, a high-ranking US State Department official, was outraged by what he saw in Germany:

> Each time I had come away with a sense of sheer horror at the spectacle of this horde of my compatriots and their dependents camping in luxury amid the ruins of a shattered national community, ignorant of the past, oblivious to the abundant evidences of present tragedy all around them, inhabiting the same sequestered villas that the Gestapo and SS had just abandoned, and enjoying the

---

52. Ibid., 207–208.
53. Interview with Martha Suentzenich Dodgen, Topeka, Kansas, Dec. 12, 1996.
54. Keeling, *Gruesome Harvest*, 67.

same privileges, flaunting their silly supermarket luxuries in the face of a veritable ocean of deprivation, hunger and wretchedness, setting an example of empty materialism and cultural poverty before a people desperately in need of spiritual and intellectual guidance.[55]

Added fellow American and historian, Ralph Franklin Keeling:

While the Germans around them starve, wear rags, and live in hovels, the American aristocrats live in often unaccustomed ease and luxury. . . . [T]hey live in the finest homes from which they drove the Germans; they swagger about in fine liveries and gorge themselves on diets three times as great as they allow the Germans. . . . When we tell the Germans their low rations are necessary because food is so short, they naturally either think we are lying to them or regard us as inhuman for taking the lion's share of the short supplies while they and their children starve.[56]

One of the underlying concerns that many critics of Allied policy had was that the atrocious example being set by the democracies would soon drive all Germans into Soviet hands; that the victims, despite their deep-seated aversion, would soon view communism as the lesser of two evils.

"What we are doing is to utterly destroy the only semi-modern state in Europe so that Russia can swallow the whole," warned George Patton prophetically, shortly before he was sacked by Eisenhower.[57]

As the general had earlier made clear, and in spite of the worldwide sympathy expressed for Jews persecuted by the Nazis before and during the war, a rising tide of voices were equally horrified by Jewish treatment of Germans after the war. Certainly no anti-Semite herself, as fervently anti-Nazi as she was anti-communist, journalist Freda Utley gave substance to the growing mood of many in her book, *The High Cost of Vengeance*:

Unfortunately for the future, the revengeful attitude of some Military Government officials who were Jews, the fact that Morgenthau gave his name to the policy of genocide underwritten by President Roosevelt, and the abuse by many non-German Jews of their privileged position as D[isplaced] P[ersons]

55. Botting, 215.
56. Keeling, 101.
57. Bacque, *Other Losses*, 149.

have converted more Germans to anti-Semitism than Hitler's racial laws and propaganda. Under the Nazis many, if not most, Germans sympathized with the Jews and were ashamed of the atrocities committed by the Nazis. But according to what I was told by German Jews, since the defeat of Germany and the Allied occupation more and more Germans formerly free of anti-Semitic prejudice are saying that after all Hitler was right; the Jews are the cause of German misery and the unjust treatment Germans receive at the hands of the victorious democracies. . . .

Jeanette Wolff, the intrepid Jewish Social-Democratic leader . . . told me that it was tragic for the German Jews that the behavior of many American Jews and DP's was giving legitimate grounds for anti-Semitism in Germany. . . . Jeanette Wolff's views were not exceptional. Whereas hatred of the German people too often drives out all pity and sense of justice among those Jews who escaped from Germany in the thirties or never lived in Germany, the German Jew who stayed at home and suffered under Hitler's terror, whose relatives and friends were murdered, and who themselves endured the horrors of the concentration camps, are for the most part without hatred of the German *people*, and still feel themselves to be Germans. It is the American Jews (often of Polish or Russian origin) and the returned exiles who seem determined to avenge the agony of the Jewish people in Hitler's Reich by punishing the whole German people.

I suppose the explanation lies in the fact that the Jews who stayed in Germany know from experience that the German people as a whole were not responsible for Nazi crimes. Many of them owe their survival to the risks taken by plain ordinary Germans to save them by hiding them or feeding them. And the Jews who emerged alive from the concentration camps know that many Germans suffered the same hunger and torture as the Jews because they opposed the tyranny of the Nazis and spoke out against the persecution of Jews.[58]

While politics and fear of further anti-Semitism motivated many critics, nothing more than genuine compassion for innocent victims compelled others to speak out. In his Christmas Eve 1945 message, Pope Pius XII appealed to the world to end the "ill-conceived cruelty" that was secretly destroying the German people.[59] As powerful as the Pope's plea undoubtedly was, a report later filed by Herbert Hoover was perhaps more shocking and had greater implications. After visiting Germany, the former US president told of homeless children freez-

---

58. Utley, *High Cost*, 243–245.
59. Austin J. App, "Mass Expulsions: 'Tragedy on a Prodigious Scale,' " *The Barnes Review* 2, no. 10 (October 1996): 22.

ing to death by the hundreds, of men and women fainting at their work stations from hunger, of motorists taking special care not to run down diseased and emaciated pedestrians as they crossed the streets.[60] Also sifting to the surface were horrific tales of Allied torture chambers.

"AMERICANS TORTURE GERMANS TO EXTORT CONFESSIONS,'" ran British headlines. "[A]n ugly story of barbarous tortures inflicted in the name of allied justice. . . . strong men were reduced to broken wrecks ready to mumble any admission demanded by their prosecutors."[61]

Embarrassed and aghast, many Americans were horror-struck. Viewing Allied atrocities against Germany as a whole, it was, said Henrick Shipstead on the floor of the US Senate, "America's eternal monument of shame, the Morgenthau Plan for the destruction of the German-speaking people."[62] Although Henry Morgenthau was gone—ousted by President Truman—and although some of the more savage aspects of the plan had been shelved, the agreement signed by the victorious Allies at Postdam was in many respects even more draconian than the original.

Even as the chorus of critics over the sadistic treatment of Germany grew, a nightmare of almost unbelievable proportions was developing behind the Iron Curtain. Here, in the centuries-old provinces of Prussia, Pomerania, but especially Silesia, the seeds sown at Yalta and Postdam bore a rich and terrible fruit. What transpired in this former German region was, announced an American historian at the time, "the most staggering atrocity in all history. It is deliberate, it is brutal, it is enormous—and it is an Allied crime. It is an American, British, Russian, Morgenthau, Postdam crime."[63]

It was, an American bishop said simply, "the greatest crime of the age."[64]

---

60. Crawley, *Spoils of War*, 61.
61. Grenfell, *Unconditional Hatred*, 191.
62. De Zayas, *Nemesis at Potsdam*, 134.
63. App, "Mass Expulsions," 24.
64. Ibid., 21.

11

CRIME OF THE AGE

A S WAS THE CASE throughout eastern Germany during the
spring of 1945, while millions had fled in terror from the Red
Army or found themselves snared by the swift Soviet advance,
millions more had held to their homes, determined to somehow
weather the storm. With defeat following soon after, thousands of starving, bedraggled refugees returned east, trusting that it was better to
suffer and die at home, surrounded by all that was familiar, than suffer and die on the roads as homeless vagabonds. Unbeknownst to
this multitude of wretched humanity, they were living on borrowed
time—they no longer had a home.

Under agreements articulated at Yalta and codified at Potsdam, Russia would receive vast stretches of German and Polish territory in
the east and, in recompense, Poland would absorb large tracts of the
former Reich in the west, including much of Prussia, Pomerania and
the extremely rich, industrialized province of Silesia. What such an
action implied was chillingly revealed by Winston Churchill. When a
Polish official expressed doubt that such a massive uprooting of people could be carried out, the British prime minister waved all concerns
aside: "Don't mind the five or more million Germans. Stalin will see
to them. You will not have trouble with them: they will cease to exist."[1]

Even as the Red Army was overrunning eastern Germany in 1945,
armed Polish militiamen were hard on their heels, eager to lay claim
to what would soon be theirs. For survivors who thought they had seen
and suffered everything under the passing Soviets, they soon discovered that they had not.

---

1.   Keeling, *Gruesome Harvest*, 13.

"The weeks during which the Russians had occupied the village seemed peaceful in comparison," wrote an incredulous woman from Silesia.[2]

"There is something strange and frightening about this Polish militia," another viewer added. "It consists, not of soldiers and policemen, but of rabble—youths, dirty and unkempt, cruel and cunning."[3]

As these witnesses and many more made note, the malice of the Polish invaders was more extreme than even that of the Red Army. Unlike the typical Russian, who harbored no great, personal ill-will for the average German, the centuries of conflict between neighboring Poland and Germany had nurtured a deep and abiding hatred.[4]

"[T]he Russians . . . are spiteful in a manner that is different from that of the Poles," observed one clergyman. "The maliciousness of the Polish militia . . . is cold and venomous, whereas Russian maliciousness is somehow warm-blooded."[5]

"They were constantly drunk and gave vent to their rage upon the Germans," records Silesian, Maria Goretti.

> Four drunken Poles, led by a Polish worker, who had formerly been employed in my house, had forced their way into the vicarage and were beating my sister-in-law and my housekeeper. When I appeared on the scene they immediately made for me, swearing at me obscenely. One of them held my hands so that I could not move and the others hit me in the face and on the head with their fists. Then someone dealt me such a blow on the chin that I fell to the ground. They kicked me and dragged me towards the door. I managed to struggle to my feet and ran out into the yard, but they pursued me and soon caught up with me. Then they tripped me up and I fell on a stone and cut my face. They continued to belabor me as I lay there, until I thought my last hour had come. . . . That was the thanks I got from the Poles for having protected them during the Hitler regime.[6]

"[T]here was hardly a German in the whole village who was not beaten on some occasion or other . . . ," another pummeled victim

---

2.   Kaps, *Tragedy of Silesia*, 194.
3.   Ibid., 135.
4.   Schieder, *Expulsion of the German Population*, 235.
5.   Kaps, *Silesia*, 189.
6.   Ibid., 195.

revealed. "To mention but three examples of Polish methods of tormenting the Germans: they pushed one German under the weir; they
made another villager lie on the ground and eat grass; on another occasion they made one of the villagers lie on the floor and then they
climbed onto the table and jumped down onto his stomach."[7]

Because many militiamen came with wives, sweethearts and sometimes children, massive rapes did not occur.[8] For the victims of beatings, torture and around-the-clock terror, however, this was cold comfort. All residents were fair and easy game.

"Since all Germans are required to wear white arm bands, they are
marked prey for these willful adolescents and can be easily identified
and herded off for any type of labor or humiliation," noted Regina
Shelton. "The few German men in town, most of them well beyond
their prime and found physically unfit for military service during
the war, bear the brunt of degradation and terrorism. Sooner or later,
each is arrested on whatever pretext comes to a Polish mind."[9]

Arrests were random, sudden and usually based on rumors or
hearsay. Remembered one man from the city of Neisse:

> I had just stepped outside, after finishing my soup, when a civilian and a Russ-
> ian, wearing the uniform of the Young Communists Movement, came up to me.
> . . . He informed me that I was suspected of having mishandled Poles. I denied
> this accusation. The young Russian, who was about twenty-six, thereupon hit
> me in the face and shouted, "You fat German pig, never worked, only eat and
> drink, hit workers, and go with women." I objected to this accusation most
> strongly, whereupon he hit me in the face a second time. Then they marched me
> off, allegedly to interrogate me. They took me to the cellar in the boys' school,
> where four Russians promptly seized hold of me and began beating me. Blood
> streamed out my nose, mouth, and ears, and finally I collapsed.[10]

From the village of Falkenhain, another man adds:

> [A] Polish militiaman appeared at the house and said to me, "German man
> says you got wireless." I replied, "German man telling lies." The Pole thereupon
> kicked me in the stomach, arrested me, and took me to . . . the headquarters of

---

7.   Ibid., 478–479.
8.   Ibid., 186.
9.   Shelton, *To Lose a War*, 149.
10. Kaps, *Silesia*, 535–536.

the so-called Polish commandant. I was interrogated for hours and they kept asking me whether I had hidden any valuables anywhere. They hit me in the face and mouth and kicked me in the stomach. Then they locked me up in a cell, which was so small that there was only enough room to stand or sit, but not to lie down.[11]

"We were crowded together like a lot of animals . . . ," said a prisoner at Trebnitz. "Swarms of lice ran about on the rags on which we slept. At night they plagued us to such an extent that we hardly got a wink of sleep, but it was hopeless to try and catch them as it was so dark in the cell. There was an old bucket in each cell which we had to use when we needed to relieve nature. Needless to say, the stench from the bucket was horrible. The militia guards . . . took a special delight in tormenting the poor prisoners every day, either by beating or kicking them or by setting the dogs at them. They were highly amused whenever one or other of the prisoners got bitten."[12]

When the prison "interrogations" began, many of the torture sessions were simply an attempt to discover where Germans had buried imaginary gold, silver and jewels. Almost any method was used to inflict pain, including crushed genitals, sharpened slivers tapped under toenails, red hot pokers, and of course, vicious beatings.[13] To drown the hideous shrieks echoing through the streets, radios were often turned to full volume.[14] Those who managed to survive these sadistic torture sessions could only pray that their agony was ended. Almost always, it was not. Time and again, hundreds of thousands of victims were forced to endure the horror over and over.[15]

"At ten o'clock they . . . started interrogating me again," recalled one beaten and bruised man.

> They made me get undressed and lie down on a chair, and then they dealt me about seventy strokes with their whips. Every time I tried to get up they hit me in the face and kicked me in the stomach. . . . When they had finished flogging me, they said, "Now will you tell us where you've hidden your valuables?" I replied, "I haven't hidden anything." They then made me lie on the floor, on

---

11.   Ibid., 479.
12.   Ibid., 537–538.
13.   Ibid., 203.
14.   Ibid., 322.
15.   Ibid.

my stomach with the soles of my feet upwards, and one of the brutes started hitting my toes with a hammer until the bones splintered.[16]

When one form of savagery failed to work, the sadists laughingly moved on to the next.[17] With knives and bayonets the young torturers cut swastikas into the bellies and backs of screaming victims. For those who fainted, a splash of water revived them so that the torture could continue.[18]

No one escaped the horror. Returning Landsers, those who thought they had faced all the terrors six years of war could offer, soon discovered that indeed, they had not. Records one of those young soldiers on his own personal journey through hell:

> My father and I were locked up in a cell together. . . . Soon afterwards they came and took my father away. I heard someone shout, "Trousers down! Lie down, you swine!" Then I heard the sound of blows descending on naked flesh, followed by screams, moans, and groans, and at the same time derisive laughter, jeers, oaths, and more blows. I trembled with rage and indignation at the thought that the Poles had flogged my father, an old man of sixty-eight. Then I heard a faint moaning sound, and after that all was quiet. . . . [T]hen the door was opened, and I heard a Polish voice shout, "Out you get, you swine, you son of a bitch. Trousers down! Get a move on! Quick!" Before I had time to realize what they were about to do to me, four of them, an ugly grin on their faces, seized hold of me. They pulled my trousers down, and pushed me over a stool . . . and then they started flogging my bare thighs and posterior with a whip. I bit my lips to prevent myself from screaming, for I was determined not to let these devils see how much they were hurting me. But I was unable to control the twitching of my body, and I wriggled about like a worm. . . . Then I fainted.[19]

Days and nights on end, the sadism continued. When the radios were turned up or accordions started to play, the horror commenced. "As soon as we heard them," one quaking victim recalled, "we knew that the torture was due to begin."[20]

---

16. Ibid., 479.
17. Ibid., 203.
18. Ibid., 231.
19. Ibid., 539–542.
20. Ibid., 532.

Not all crimes were committed in secret behind prison walls. Those individuals fortunate enough to escape the hell of Polish prisons found themselves slaves in all but name. Thousands were thrown into labor camps and toiled in the fields, forests and factories until they dropped. "One day they were in the bloom of health, and in 14 days corpses," noted a German at Grottkau. "The Poles laughed when they saw the great number of corpses."[21]

While hundreds perished daily in the work camps, millions more who held to their homes were subject to slave labor on a moment's notice.

"Any half-grown Polish militiaman . . . had the right to stop the Germans on the street, even when they were going to church, and take them off to work somewhere," disclosed one observer.[22]

"We were brought to the town in long columns like criminals under guard," remembered Josef Buhl, a photographer from Klodebach. "It reminded one of the slave trade of the middle ages, when we were drawn up on the town's square. We were examined like goods for sale."[23]

As the weeks and months passed more and more Poles—men, women and children—migrated into eastern Germany crowding the residents and expropriating their property. "Every house received one or several families," Josef Buhl goes on. "They lived in the best rooms and not only did they take the best furniture for themselves, but also the cattle and our clothes."[24]

Homes not stolen outright were subject to plunder raids at any moment.

"The Germans," a woman in Liegnitz wrote, "were forced to open cupboards, chests of drawers and such-like furniture, and then the Poles took what they wanted with the words: 'All mine.' If he took a fancy to the beds, the mattresses and other furniture, a day later a truck stopped before the house, and everything was put into it."[25]

Continues Josef Buhl:

21. Schieder, *Expulsion*, 249.
22. Kaps, *Silesia*, 303.
23. Schieder, 320.
24. Ibid., 317–318.
25. Ibid., 240.

All German signs had to disappear. The German names of places were changed into tongue-twisting Polish ones. The sign-posts received new inscriptions in the Polish language. One could not find one's way about in one's own home. . . . Our school had become Polish, and German children were not allowed to go into the street. The Polish riffraff was allowed to molest and beat German women and children with sticks on their way to and from their work. The Germans had no right of complaint. We were utterly defenseless and at the mercy of the mob.[26]

On the countryside, land-hungry Poles fanned out and greedily seized the rich, productive farms. Recounts a witness:

Three militiamen would appear at the farm and say to the farmer, "In five minutes you must be out of here. The house and the land and everything now belongs to a Polish farmer!" Then they would stand there with a watch in their hands, counting the minutes. If the farmer and his family failed to get out of the house by the time the five minutes were up, the Polish militiamen attacked them with cudgels and drove them out of the farmyard. The Polish farmer then moved in and took possession of everything.[27]

Many Poles, more prudent, stole farms but wisely retained the owners as slaves. "I now farmer, you Hitler, *work*," snapped one usurper to a hapless German who suddenly found himself enslaved on his own farm.[28] Soon, concludes Josef Buhl, "everything belonged to them. . . . Work was the only thing they did not take from us."[29]

"[The] Poles ventured to commit more and more excesses against Germans," said a Pomeranian farmer. "They drove us out of our beds at night, beat us, and took us away for days at a time, and locked us up. . . . [W]hen the Germans were sleeping, there would suddenly come into the room a horde of Poles, for the most part drunk; the German families had to move, just as they were. . . . Thus our conditions of life steadily got worse."[30]

"Generally," concluded a woman in Silesia, "no other course remained open to the Germans than to leave their property, in order not to die of starvation."[31]

26. Ibid., 318, 321.
27. Kaps, 215.
28. Ibid., 239.
29. Schieder, 318.
30. Ibid., 219.
31. Ibid., 245.

And thus, by tens and twenties, by hundreds and thousands, many Germans "voluntarily" abandoned their ancestral homes and began drifting west with no clear goal in mind. Surprisingly, despite the daily terror and torture they faced, many eastern Germans displayed a dogged determination to ride out the storm, naively assuming that since life could obviously get no worse, it must only get better. Nevertheless, the fate of all Germans in the east had been sealed at Potsdam.[32]

Although the timing varied greatly from region to region, when the fateful day arrived there was no mistaking the matter. Commonly, the shattering of glass and doors were the first sounds a victim heard, soon followed by angry shouts to clear the home within thirty, ten, or even five minutes.

"Cold-bloodedly and sarcastically, they informed us that we must leave the house at once . . . ," one German remembered. "[S]ome of them were already ransacking the rooms. They told us we could each of us take a blanket, so we hurriedly stuffed two pillows inside the blanket. But when the Polish officer, who, incidentally, was rushing up and down in the room like a maniac, striking his whip against his riding-boots, saw the pillows, he said, 'Leave those here. We Poles want something as well!'"[33]

"I was dumbfounded," admitted Heinrich Kauf:

> My wife had been confined the evening before with a little girl. I was still standing at her bedside, and did not know what to do. First I went to the mayor. . . . He said quite abruptly: "Leave your wife at home. You must go away with the children". . . . [W]hen I came back home again, the Polish militia was already there and shouted out: "Get out at once!" Then I called my neighbor Mrs. Dumel, and got the horses and carts ready. I put my wife and child with the bedding into the cart, and in my great haste forgot to take the necessary things for the other children.[34]

While militiamen stood with watches in hand, frantic residents rushed in a mad attempt to scoop up what little remained to them.

32. De Zayas, *Nemesis at Potsdam*, 108.
33. Kaps, *Silesia*, 160–161.
34. Schieder, *Expulsion*, 315.

"I was only allowed 10 minutes," recalled an elderly woman, "and was just able to drag my grandchild, who was 1 year old, down the stairs. . . . When I wanted to fetch my cloak out of my house, the Poles did not let me in again remarking, that the 10 minutes were passed."[35]

"You have seven minutes. Six minutes. Five minutes. Four," the impatient men yelled.[36]

For those who tarried beyond the time limit, whips, sticks and clubs were used freely. Once in the streets, the victims were strip-searched.[37] Recalled Isabella von Eck:

> As I was 75 years of age, I was put onto a farm-cart with 2 dying women and 2 girls of 10 and 12 years of age, who had venereal diseases, all of whom could not walk. Just in front of the yard a Polish officer beat me with a heavy riding whip, until I took my fur off. Then a soldier sprang onto the cart, and tore open my clothes as far as my chemise; he found my purse with jewelry, and took it for himself. The German paper money he threw at my feet. Very many men and women were thrashed in the course of the search, until they bled; their faces were covered with stripes, and their eyes full of blood.[38]

"A Polish girl took my shoes from my feet, which I had kept on when sleeping for weeks . . . ," another grandmother sobbed. "My hair was hanging down and disheveled, as the Russians had taken all my hair-clips and combs. . . . I was 6 times searched in my vagina for jewelry."[39]

"Polish militiamen on horseback drove the poor people through the streets, lashing them with whips," wrote one witness from a town near Breslau. "The entire population of Zobten lined up on the square in front of the town hall. They were all clutching small bundles containing their belongings. Women and children were weeping and screaming. The men folk wore an expression of utter despair on their faces. Every now and again the Poles cracked their whips and brutally lashed the poor people standing on the square."[40]

"We stand numb before the bankruptcy, our own and that of generations before us," muttered Regina Shelton to herself. "They had

---

35. Ibid., 299.
36. Sack, *An Eye for an Eye*, 138.
37. Schieder, 310.
38. Ibid., 297.
39. Ibid., 299.
40. Kaps, 397.

made this land ours by their sweat and blood. How can a whole people be uprooted, disowned, tossed aside like useless flotsam—how?
With the stroke of a pen, with a new line drawn on a map, we are
sentenced to homelessness."[41]

"As they left town in an endless procession," a viewer from Gruen-
berg reminisced, "Polish soldiers fell upon them, beating and flog-
ging them in a blind rage. . . . Robbed of all they possessed and literally stripped of the last of their belongings, . . . these poor creatures
trudged along in the wind and the rain, with no roof or shelter over
their heads, not knowing where they would find a new abode."[42]

And thus, from throughout eastern Germany, from farms, villages,
towns, and cities, began the greatest death march in history. Crippled and starved, diseased and enfeebled, with virtually nothing to
their name, set adrift in a hostile, hate-filled land already bled to the
bone, it was preordained that millions would never survive the trek.
Except for those able-bodied individuals held as slaves and young girls
retained for sex, roughly eleven million Germans took to the roads.

"The Poles had by their conduct made the departure from our home
easy," confessed Josef Buhl. "It almost caused us joy."[43]

"Almost," but not quite. As the long lines of misery began wending
their way west, many, like Anna Kientopf, well knew that they would
never see their ancestral homes again. "I remained further behind, and
went slowly. I often looked back, the farm was in the evening sun; it
was an old farm, where I had been born. My parents had lived and
worked there before us, and had been buried in the cemetery. . . .
The sheep and cows were peacefully grazing. Who would milk them
this evening and the following days?"[44]

"Wherever we looked on the road," Isabella von Eck took note, "the

---

41. Shelton, *To Lose a War*, 184.
42. Kaps, 428.
43. Schieder, 324.
44. Ibid., 287.

same wretched columns were to be seen, wheel-barrows were pushed by women, loaded with luggage and small children, aged and sick people sat in cases with wheels."[45]

While millions set out afoot, thousands more were expelled by rail. Recalled Regina Shelton:

> The train stands ready, sliding doors gaping to receive us into the dark space of the freight cars. It seems to stretch for miles beyond the platform, and many of the cars are already occupied. The revulsion of having to clamber up and into the inhospitable black holes is given short shrift by the militia swarming among the evacuees and counting heads to fill each car to capacity. Straw is pushed to the walls around the cavernous rectangle. When the quota in our car is filled, we are told to spread out the straw. Baggage stacked against the walls, each family builds a lair of sorts, and the lucky ones garner a corner as far away from the door and the cold as possible.
>
> Then the platform is empty, except for the militiamen on guard. At a signal the sliding doors clang shut and are latched from the outside. . . . When the train jerks into motion, we still do not know where it will carry us. . . . The small window draws me like a magnet. Stepping over bags and around huddled or sprawling bodies, I make my way to it to stand by it as long as the train keeps rolling to see the familiar scenes glide by for the last time.[46]

In addition to those traveling overland, thousands of freezing Germans were crammed like cordwood onto barges and boats and floated down rivers.

Almost immediately, the ragged refugees were set upon and robbed by gangs of Russians, Jews, Gypsies, and other DPs moving in the opposite direction. Poles who already occupied the villages and towns through which the people passed were also laying in wait. "Polish civilians lined both sides of the road and the refugees were systematically robbed and beaten as they walked by," said one victim.[47]

If anything, those trapped in cattle cars were even more vulnerable. As Maria Popp recorded:

> Whole bands of fellows attacked every wagon, and when 2 left it 3 got in. The train kept stopping to help the plundering, and no-one was left in peace. There

---

45. Ibid., 297.
46. Shelton, 191.
47. De Zayas, *Nemesis*, 114.

were about 70–80 persons in each wagon, and each one was separately searched for valuables or money. Anyone, who was wearing good clothes, had to take them off, even shoes if the plunderers liked them. If anyone refused, he was beaten until he yielded. . . . Very few of us were able to think clearly, and no-one dared to help the cripples and the dying. . . . The crutches were snatched out of their hands, and one of them was literally kicked to death. I shall never forget his screams.[48]

"Throughout the whole journey," recounts another of those fleeing, "the Poles continued to rob the expellees on the train, both during the day and by night. I saw one Pole hit the Mother Superior . . . in the face because she refused to give him the only suitcase she had."[49]

And while some were robbing, others were raping. Many females were violated thirty or more times during the trek. "Women who resisted were shot dead," a horrified viewer divulged, "and on one occasion . . . a Polish guard [took] an infant by the legs and crush[ed] its skull against a post because the child cried while the guard was raping its mother."[50] When the weary travelers halted for the night they were compelled to bed down in barns, deserted homes or nearby woods. "'[B]ut even there the Poles did not leave us in peace," moaned a victim.[51] Moving among the wretched refugees, the attackers robbed and raped at will.

"Our cart was plundered the same night by the Poles, who stole everything that they liked," revealed Heinrich Kauf, whose wife had given birth the day before. "The next morning we continued our journey, and I took my wife out of the village in a hand-cart. We had scarcely got out of it, when a Polish woman came, and took the bedding away from my sick wife."[52]

Like Kauf, many others lost to thieves not only their possessions but their sole means of transport.

"One cart I saw," wrote a wanderer, "was being drawn by six children, instead of by a horse, and there was a pregnant woman pushing it.

48. Schieder, *Expulsion*, 307.
49. Kaps, *Silesia*, 253.
50. De Zayas, 114.
51. Schieder, 299.
52. Ibid., 315.

Old women of seventy were laboriously pulling handcarts, and I saw some Sisters of Mercy with ropes tied round their chests engaged in the same task. Venerable Catholic priests were toiling along the roads with the members of their parish, pulling and pushing carts."[53]

Slow and agonizing as every mile was, the columns nevertheless continued to creep ahead for only death and misfortune awaited those who dallied. The old and sick were first to go and their withered remains littered the roadside by the thousands. Little children and newborns were next.

"Nursing infants suffer the most . . . ," one observer remarked of a refugee train. "[T]heir mothers are unable to feed them, and frequently go insane as they watch their offspring slowly die before their eyes. Today four screaming, violently insane mothers were bound with rope to prevent them from clawing other passengers."[54]

"[A] young married couple . . . ," added a diarist, "were pushing a perambulator, containing a cardboard box. They said, 'Our baby is in that box. We are going to bury it. We buried our other little one a week ago. They died of starvation. . . . There is no food, no doctor, and no medicine to be had!"[55]

As the refugees approached the Niesse and Oder Rivers, there was renewed hope. Once over these streams which marked the new boundary between Germany and Poland, many felt their great trial would be, for the most part, over. Unfortunately, when the trekkers reached the rivers, the worst leg of the odyssey began. To the Polish soldiers and civilians along the frontier, it was one final chance to wreak vengeance on the hated Germans. Many made the most of it. One last time, what little remained to the refugees was tossed, stolen or destroyed. One last time, women were publicly strip-searched and their vaginas meticulously probed for hidden valuables. One last time,

53. Kaps, *Silesia*, 127.
54. Keeling, *Gruesome Harvest*, 15.
55. Kaps, 187.

victims were forced to crawl on all fours and eat grass, dirt . . . or worse. Those who balked were beaten or killed.[56]

The horror and chaos of the moment is vividly captured by Anna Kientopf:

> We had to pass through a lane of Polish soldiers, and people were taken out of the column. These had to drop out, and go to the farms on the highway with their carts, and all that they had with them. No one knew what this meant, but everyone expected something bad. The people refused to obey. Often it was single individuals, particularly young girls, who were kept back. The mothers clung to the girls and wept. Then the soldiers tried to drag them away by force and, as this did not succeed, they began to strike the poor terrified people with rifle-butts and riding whips. One could hear the screams of those who were whipped, far away. . . .
>
> Polish soldiers also came to us with riding whips in their hands. With flushed faces, they ordered us to get out of the column, and to go to the farms. Else and Hilde Mittag began to weep. I said: "Come, it is no use resisting. They will beat us to death. We will try to escape afterwards." Russians were standing there looking on cynically. In our desperation we begged them for help. They shrugged their shoulders and indicated to us, that the Poles were the masters. Just as everything already seemed to be hopeless, I saw a senior Polish officer. I pointed to my 3 children, and asked what I could do. . . . [H]e answered: "Go to the highway."
>
> We got hold of our cart and got away, as quickly as we could. The trek carts were getting congested. . . . From the other direction came large trucks driven by Russians. They ruthlessly forced their way through us. We tried to go forward. . . . Then we were again stopped. . . . Four Polish soldiers tried to separate a young girl from her parents, who clung in desperation to her. The Poles struck the parents with their rifle-butts, particularly the man. He staggered, and they pulled him across the road down the embankment. He fell down, and one of the Poles took his machine pistol, and fired a series of shots. For a moment there was a deathly silence, and then the screams of the 2 women pierced the air. They rushed to the dying man, and the four Poles disappeared in the forest. When we finally went on, the desperate weeping of the 2 women echoed behind us, mingled with the screams of the people, who were being beaten. . . .
>
> [T]here was only one thing for us to do, and that was to go forward, to cross the Oder at any price. We saw more dead people at the side of the road. . . . We kept pushing forward, as hard as we could. . . . At last we reached the bridge over the Oder. . . . We were ready to give everything, which we still possessed,

56. Ibid., 130, 256.

if we could only pass over the Oder. . . . Our one object was to get away from these robbers and murderers. . . . When there were still only 6–8 carts in front of us, the barrier was closed, and that was the end for that day.

What was now to happen? Our disappointment was boundless, for we were just before our goal, and were not allowed to pass through.[57]

After spending "a terrible night" in a drenching downpour, Anna and her family again moved toward the river the following day. In addition to robbery and rape, Poles also used this last opportunity to dragoon the able-bodied for slavery. Anna:

Families were ruthlessly torn asunder there, and the individuals among them, who were capable of work, were taken away. Father Liefke said: "My God, my God, this is a bitter life. I am more than 70 years old. When mother died, I thought: that is hard. Then Hermann and Arthur were killed in the war, and I thought: that is still harder. Then the Russians came, and robbed us of everything, and then I thought: that is the hardest blow of all; but what we are now suffering, is the hardest, and I shall not survive it for long. If it were not for Anni and the 2 little children, I should kill myself.[58]

Many, rather than endure further torture, did in fact end their suffering then and there on the Oder/Neisse line. "The only thing they let me keep was this rope, and I'm going to hang myself with it before the day's over," vowed a man who could stand no more.[59]

When demented refugees attempted to escape the horror on the bridge above by crossing over the river below, Polish guards systematically shot them dead. "Why don't you drive us into a big enclosure like a herd of cattle, surround us with machine-guns, and shoot us on the spot!" one crazed woman cried.[60]

For those survivors who finally entered the bridge, there was one last gauntlet to run.

"They robbed us and flogged us as we crossed the bridge," remembered a victim. "Children screamed, grown-ups collapsed, and some of them died and were left lying there on the ground at the end of the bridge. Others fell into the icy waters of the Neisse, but the Poles

---

57. Schieder, 292–293.
58. Ibid., 294–295.
59. Kaps, 130.
60. Ibid., 130, 131.

were indifferent to their fate. They drove us on unmercifully across the bridge."[61]

Anna Kientopf:

> Now we thought, that the worst was past, but at the other end of the bridge, there were Russian soldiers with their green caps, and also girls in uniform. We were again controlled, all our sacks were opened, and turned upside down. Many lost the few valuables, which they still possessed. From me they took my wedding ring, which I foolishly had [put back] on my finger. Then we had to collect the sacks together, and were forced with blows to leave the Oder bridge as quickly as possible. They drove us without mercy down the steep embankment.[62]

For the miserable refugees, the first hint that there would be no happy ending to the story came when those reaching the west bank of the Neisse/Oder line found thousands of Germans desperately trying to reach the east bank. With what little shelter that remained in the war-ravaged Reich already jammed to overflowing, with starvation stalking the land, with murder, rape and slavery the order of the day, many earlier refugees from Prussia, Pomerania and Silesia were frantic to return to homes that were no longer theirs. As one viewer recorded:

> [C]rowds kept calling to the Silesians who were trekking eastwards, "Turn back! There's no sense in going on. You can't get across the Neisse! The Poles will take all your belongings from you. They'll rob you like they did us and throw you out of Silesia. Go back where you've come from!" On hearing this, those who were aiming to get back to Silesia grew confused. Many of them refused to believe what they were told and pushed on; others, however, decided to turn back.[63]

For those weary, starving trekkers moving west, signs greeted them at every turn in every town and every village: "Refugees not permitted to stay. They must move on." "Move on! Move on!" "There is a famine in Goerlitz. . . . There are not enough food supplies. . . . If you disregard this warning you will probably die of starvation."[64]

61. Ibid., 256.
62. Schieder, 295.
63. Kaps, 128.
64. Ibid.

Threats such as these were not idle words, as one witness makes clear:

The inhabitants of Goerlitz resemble living corpses—deathly pale, sunken-cheeked, and haggard. . . . Many of the refugees are unable to move on, for their strength is at an end and they are slowly wasting away. Dray-carts come to collect the bodies of those who have died of starvation. I counted sixteen coffins on one dray-cart, coffins of grown-ups and children. . . . I actually saw people collapse on the street, weak with hunger.[65]

With waning hope and fading strength, the expellees trudged deeper into Germany. Unable to walk any further, thousands simply dropped dead by the wayside.[66] Increasingly, and with building momentum, Berlin became the star of hope for many. If there was any succor yet left in the world, here, most felt, was where it would be found. What the people discovered upon reaching the former capital, however, were endless ruins, rotting corpses, "living skeletons" boiling grass for food, and still more signs: "Attention, refugees! Newcomers banned from settling in Berlin. Use detours. Avoid entering the city limits. Continue westward."[67]

Few heeded such words . . . few could. A British officer was on hand at one Berlin rail station when a transport arrived from the east:

The train was a mixture of cattle and goods trucks, all of which were so packed that people lay on the tops, clung to the sides or hung on the bumpers. Children were tied by ropes to ventilation cocks, heating pipes, and iron fittings.

The train stopped and a great long groan rose from the length and breadth of it. For a full minute no one moved a limb. Eyes that were full of anguish examined the people on the platform. Then people began to move, but everyone seemed crippled with cold and cramp. Children seemed dead, purplish blue in the face; those who had clung to doors and fittings could not use their hands or arms, but went about, arms raised or outstretched, hands clenched. They hobbled, legs numbed, to fall on the platform.

The people who had arrived days before pressed back to make room, and looked on in silence. Soon the platform was filled with cries of disillusionment as the newcomers learned how they had been deceived. Their hair was matted. They were filthy, covered with soot and grime. Children had running sores, and scratched themselves continually. Old men, unshaven, red-eyed, looked like

65. Ibid., 129.
66. App, "Mass Expulsions," 22.
67. Barnouw, *Germany 1945*, 187.

drug addicts, who neither felt, nor heard, nor saw. Everyone seemed to be a unit of personal misery, complete unto himself.[68]

"Filthy, emaciated, and carrying their few remaining possessions wrapped in bits of cloth," noted a reporter for the *New York Daily News*, "they shrank away crouching when one approached them in the railway terminal, expecting to be beaten or robbed or worse."[69]

Each train that unloaded held horrors that soon seemed common:

> Red Army soldiers lifted 91 corpses from the train, while relatives shrieked and sobbed as their bodies were piled in American lend-lease trucks and driven off for internment in a pit near a concentration camp.... "Many women try to carry off their dead babies with them," a Russian railway official said. "We search the bundles whenever we discover a weeping woman, to make sure she is not carrying an infant corpse with her."[70]

Barges and small craft also docked in Berlin. One boat, a Red Cross worker revealed, "contained a tragic cargo of nearly 300 children, half dead from hunger, who had come from a 'home' . . . in Pomerania. Children from two to fourteen years old lay in the bottom of the boat, motionless, their faces drawn with hunger, suffering from the itch and eaten up by vermin."[71]

Those expellees who did not wander off into the wilderness of rubble that was Berlin, to root, grub and die like moles, remained camped in the railroad stations for weeks, even months, where they died from disease and starvation by the thousands.[72] At one depot alone, "an average of ten have been dying daily from exhaustion, malnutrition and illness . . . ," protested an American official, Robert Murphy, to the US State Department. "Here is retribution on a large scale, but practiced not on the [Nazis], but on women and children, the poor, the infirm."[73]

"It was a pathetic sight . . . ," echoed British Foreign Secretary, Ernest Bevin, after a trip to Berlin. "The most awful sight one could see."[74]

---

68. Botting, *Ruins of the Reich*, 187.
69. De Zayas, *Nemesis*, 114.
70. Keeling, *Gruesome Harvest*, 15.
71. De Zayas, 107.
72. Pechel, *Voices From the Third Reich*, 447; Botting, *Ruins*, 187.
73. De Zayas, 115.
74. Botting, 190.

When horrifying accounts such as the above began circulating in the US and Britain, readers were shocked and sickened. Vengeful and bloody-minded as many in the West had been during war, with peace most no longer had a stomach for the cold and calculated slaughter of a fallen foe.

"[A]n apparently deliberate attempt is being made to exterminate many millions of Germans . . . by depriving them of their homes and of food, leaving them to die by slow and agonizing starvation," influential British philosopher, Bertrand Russell, warned in the *London Times*. "This is not done as an act of war, but as part of a deliberate policy of 'peace.'"[75]

"The scale of this resettlement and the conditions in which it takes place are without precedent in history," added Anne O'Hare McCormick in the *New York Times*. "No one seeing its horrors first-hand can doubt that it is a crime against humanity."[76]

Wrote an equally outraged American academic, Austin J. App:

> Cannot each of us write a letter to President Truman and another to each of our senators begging them not to make the United States a partner to the greatest mass atrocity so far recorded in history? Calling it the greatest mass atrocity so far recorded in history is not rhetoric. It is not ignorance of history. It is sober truth.
>
> To slice three or four ancient provinces from a country, then loot and plunder nine million people of their houses, farms, cattle, furniture, and even clothes, and then . . . expel them "from the land they have inhabited for 700 years" with no distinction "between the innocent and the guilty" . . . to drive them like unwanted beasts on foot to far-off provinces, unprotected, shelterless, and starving is an atrocity so vast that history records none vaster.[77]

Fortunately, these voices of protest and the pressure they exerted on Western leaders were welcome signs that the physical torment of Germany was nearing an end. Unfortunately, by the time the horror became common knowledge, the deed was all but done. Of the roughly eleven million expellees hurled from their homes in Prussia, Pomerania and Silesia, an estimated two million, mostly women and children,

---

75. De Zayas, 108.
76. Ibid., 123.
77. App, "Mass Expulsions," 24.

perished. Equally as horrifying, though less well known, were the nearly one million Germans who died during similar expulsions in Czechoslovakia, Hungary, Rumania, Bulgaria, and Yugoslavia. Additionally, an estimated four million more ethnic Germans were sent east to Russia and elsewhere where their odds of surviving as slaves were worse than as refugees.[78]

While Western leaders such as Winston Churchill expressed astonishment at the tragedy they had wrought in eastern Germany, little was said about the deliberate starvation of the rest of the Reich, and utter silence prevailed concerning the Allied torture chambers in Germany and Poland, the on-the-spot massacre of Nazi Party members and SS troops, or the death camps run by Eisenhower. Indeed, taken as a whole, it is not improbable that far more Germans died during the first two years of "peace" than died during the previous six years of war.[79] It was truly, as *Time* magazine had earlier termed it, "history's most terrifying peace." But, and as the American journal failed to add, before there had been history's most terrifying peace, there had been history's most terrifying war.

Like Winston Churchill, other prominent figures who had lent a guiding hand to Allied atrocities began distancing themselves from the deeds when some of the first damning details became known. When particulars of Dresden and the terror-bombing campaign began to surface, RAF commander Arthur Harris insisted matter-of-factly that he was only following orders; "orders," said Harris, from "higher up." And even Ilya Ehrenburg, that most virulent of propagandists and a man whose words to the advancing Red Army did more perhaps than all causes combined to insure the rape and slaughter of millions, even Ehrenburg had the temerity to plead innocence years after the war.

> I had feared that after the crimes the invaders had perpetrated in our country, our Red Army men might try to settle accounts. In dozens of articles I kept on

78. De Zayas, 184; Botting, 191; Keeling, 13.
79. Crawley, *Spoils of War*, 45.

saying that we should not and, indeed, could not exact vengeance, for we were Soviet people, not Fascists. . . . There were, of course, cases of violence, of looting: in every army there are criminals, hooligans and drunkards, but our officers took measures against excesses. . . . Patrols protected the population. . . . [I]solated cases of excesses committed in East Prussian towns . . . aroused our general indignation. . . . pity welled up in my heart. . . . [T]he feeling of revenge was alien to me.[80]

Despite such protests and similar ungainly attempts to put as much time and space between themselves and their dark deeds as possible, Ehrenburg and other Allied leaders actually had very little to fear. They had, after all, won the war. With a more-than-willing army of apologists, polemicists, journalists, film-makers, and "historians" to cover their tracks, none of the major, or minor, Allied war criminals ran any risk of being called to account for their acts. Far from it. At the lower levels, those who actually committed the atrocities at Dachau, Nemmersdorf and a thousand other points on the map, were quietly forgiven while at the upper end, US generals became American presidents and English prime ministers became British knights.

Meanwhile, as the voices of conscience were drowned in a flood of Allied adulation and celebration, much of the world's attention was riveted on Nuremberg. There, the victors sat in judgment over the vanquished. There, the accused German leaders were tried, there they were convicted, and there they were dutifully hung, *for planning aggressive war . . . for waging criminal war . . . for crimes against peace and humanity . . . for crimes planned . . . for crimes committed . . . for crimes against.* . . . And all this, it may be presumed, spoken slowly, solemnly, and with a straight face.

From afar, Austin J. App watched the ongoing charade in Nuremberg with mounting indignation. Like a good many others, the American academic had followed closely the course of the war and he, for one, was appalled and outraged by the utter hypocrisy displayed.

Germans still have much to feel guilty of before God. But they have nothing to feel guilty of before the Big Three. Any German who still feels guilty before the Allies is a fool. Any American who thinks he should is a scoundrel.[81]

---

80. Ehrenburg, *The War*, 163, 169, 173, 175.
81. App, "Mass Expulsions," 24.

Epilogue

OF VICTORS AND VICTIMS

SLOWLY, SLOWLY, Germany came home. Like a planet blown to atoms by some vast cosmic explosion, the scattered debris began drifting back to its center of gravity. One, two, three, even ten years after the war, German prisoners and slaves took their first steps back on the long road home. Unlike the river of misery and fear that had flowed outward in 1945, only a trickle of broken and starved humanity seeped back. Millions had perished in captivity—some in British and French slave colonies, some in Eisenhower's death camps, but more in the vast Soviet gulag system. Of the nearly one hundred thousand Landsers marched off after the fall of Stalingrad alone, barely 5,000 lived to see their homeland again. Some camps in Siberia had death rates of seventy, eighty and ninety percent. Though the survival rate was better in the west, the physical and mental abuse was perhaps even more extreme. Thus, when inmates, east and west, heard of their impending reprieve from what seemed a death sentence, most were stunned.

"I stood there as if rooted to the spot and said absolutely nothing at all," Anna Fest recounted when she learned of her impending release from an American prison in 1947. "I have no idea how I got back to the barracks. I only know once I was inside, I threw myself on the bed and wept horribly."[1]

Wrote a fellow German from Russia:

July 12th, 1949, is a date I shall never forget. Our hopes had been dashed to the ground so often, but this time it really was true and we were going to be set free

---

1. Owings, *Frauen*, 338.

and return to Germany. . . . Naturally we were all so happy and excited at the prospect of one thousand persons being released, that we found it impossible to go to sleep. And yet at heart we were inclined to be skeptical for we had been disappointed so often. Those of us who were at the hospital were taken to the railway-station by lorry, but the rest of the men who were being released had to go there on foot and were escorted by armed guards. In fact, they were driven to the station like a herd of cattle and pushed and beaten by the guards with the butt-end of their rifles. The good mood that everyone had been in quickly vanished, and most of the men were convinced that their last hour had come. Forty-five men were crowded into each of the trucks of the goods train which was to take us homewards. Each man was given a piece of bread and marmalade as his ration for three days, and then the trucks were locked and barred from the outside.[2]

Tragically, and in a scenario similar to that of the eastern expellees, the last leg home was often the most deadly. Diseased, emaciated, underfed, the physical strain proved simply too great for many.

"[D]uring the 3 weeks' journey 53 men died, and were thrown out of the train . . . ," one amputee recalled. "Almost all the occupants were sick with diarrhea."[3]

"[M]y best pal, who came from my native town, died of heat-stroke," added another returnee. "It is tragic to think that, after having survived so much suffering and hardship, he should die on the way home."[4]

Incongruously, the death trains were often decorated with green boughs, pictures of Stalin and colorful banners: GREAT STALIN, WE THANK YOU FOR OUR RETURN.[5] When the Russian zone of Germany was reached the wagons unloaded their cargoes of agony. Remembered a Berlin nurse who greeted one transport:

> Almost all of the 800 or 900 in the train were sick or crippled. You might say they were all invalids. With 40 to 50 packed in each of those little boxcars, the sick had to sleep beside the dead on their homeward journey. I did not count them but I am sure we removed more than 25 corpses. Others had to be taken to hospitals. I asked several of the men whether the Russian guards or doctors had done anything on the trip to care for the sick. They said "No." I met only one alert, healthy man in the lot and. . . . [h]e was just a kid of 17.[6]

---

2.   Kaps, *Tragedy of Silesia*, 171.
3.   Schieder, *Expulsion of the German Population*, 168.
4.   Kaps, *Silesia*, 171.
5.   Schieder, *Expulsion*, 189.
6.   Keeling, *Gruesome Harvest*, 21.

Understandably, few who survived years of communist captivity were willing to linger long in the Soviet sector. Thus, most opted to continue their journey to the American, British or French zones. Young Siegfried Losch was one:

> The train took us to about two miles from the British zone border. From there we had to walk. As sick as we were I could not help noting that the speed of our march increased as we were coming close to the border. After all we had seen, we knew, that one Russian officer could have at his pleasure sent all of us back. . . .
>
> On the border, Russian soldiers made another head count. Then they raised the barrier and we were in West Germany. What a relief that was. We shook each others hands and many cried with joy. . . .
>
> We had never seen or heard anything about the Salvation Army. There they were standing right on the border with a truck and much food. We had to form a single file and walk by the truck. I was surprised how quickly the mob let itself be organized. Then everybody received a hot cup of chocolate milk. . . . Next, everybody got a sandwich. A real white bread sandwich! with sliced sausage inside. . . . [S]ausage was something we only dreamed about. . . .
>
> [W]ith tears in our eyes we were asked to "please" board some apparently brand new Mercedes buses. It was *warm* inside. . . . [N]ow in the heated vehicles the warm air made the warm welcome by our hosts complete. We felt good all over. . . . WE WERE HOME!!!!! We were in Germany![7]

"They even brought us to the railroad and furthermore not in the big trucks, but in a perfectly normal *car*," reminisced Anna Fest after she and a friend were finally released. "And they bought us tickets and we were seated in the train and nobody was there to guard us and nobody locked us in. We essentially could do and let happen whatever we wanted, but we were *afraid*. We didn't even know how to move around freely on the train and maybe walk down the aisle. We didn't dare do that. We sat there just so, a couple bawling miserably."[8]

As might be imagined, such homecomings were almost always otherworld experiences. Everyone—mothers, wives, children, all—had long since given up. Thus, with the sudden and unexpected appearance of surviving men and women, it was as if ghosts had returned from the grave. Having himself experienced all the horrors that war and prison

---

7.   Losch manuscript, 44–45.
8.   Owings, *Frauen*, 339.

had to give, young Guy Sajer found the chasm separating his past from his present almost unbridgeable.

I was still five miles from my house and from the end of my journey, and the place where it had all begun. It was a beautiful day, and I should have been impelled by joy to run the whole way, toward the incredible fact that drew closer with each step. However, my throat was knotted with anguish, and I could scarcely breathe. . . . A cold sweat suddenly began to pour down my emaciated body. The despair which had settled over me in the East was suddenly violated by a reality I had almost forgotten, which was about to impose itself on me once more, as if nothing had happened. The transition was too great, too brutal. . . . My head was spinning like a boat with a broken rudder, as I walked slowly toward the encounter which I had so much longed for, and which I suddenly feared.

A plane flew over very low across the sunny countryside. Unable to stop myself, I plunged into the ditch on the other side of the road. The plane throbbed overhead for a moment, and then vanished, as suddenly as it had come. I pulled myself up by the trunk of an apple tree, without understanding what had just happened. I felt stunned. My blurred eyes watched the grass, which had been crushed by my weight, slowly straightening up again. . . . This grass was not so tall, but otherwise reminded me of the grass on the steppe. It seemed familiar, and I let myself fall down again. The brilliance of the day rose over the points of the blades, forcing me to shut my eyes. . . . I managed to calm down, and fell asleep. . . .

When I woke, I set out again, to complete my journey. My sleep must have lasted for several hours; the sun was setting behind the hill, and I arrived at twilight—which was preferable to the glare of full day. I felt anxious enough about meeting my own family; I didn't want to meet anyone I used to know. . . . So I arrived at the end of the day I had longed for so much, and started down the street as if I had just left it the day before. I tried to walk slowly, but each step seemed to resound like a parade step. . . . As I turned the corner . . . I saw my house. My heart was pounding so hard that my chest ached.

Someone appeared at the corner: a small old woman, whose shoulders were covered by a worn cloak. Even the cloak was familiar to me. My mother was carrying a small milk can. She was walking toward a neighboring farm, which I knew well. She was also walking toward me. I thought I was going to fall. She was coming down the middle of the road. . . . My heart contracted so hard I thought I would faint. My mother walked past me.

I leaned against a wall to keep my balance. A bitter taste filled my mouth, as if it had filled with blood. I knew that within a few minutes she would come back the same way. I felt like running, but at the same time, couldn't move, and stood paralyzed, letting the minutes trickle by.

After a few moments ... she reappeared, going the other way, grayer and more shadowy in the deepening darkness. She came closer and closer. I was afraid to move, afraid of frightening her. And then it was unbearable. I summoned up my courage and spoke. . . .

She stopped. I took several steps toward her, and then I saw that she was about to faint. The milk can fell to the ground, and I caught her in my trembling arms.[9]

"This whole experience had the quality of a dream rather than reality," said Siegfried Knappe as he approached the home of his wife, Lilo, nearly five years after the war.

When she opened the door and saw me, her expression was as unbelieving as my mother's had been. I was so excited that I thought my heart would surely stop! I stepped inside the door and we fell into each other's arms. Having her in my embrace was breathtaking, and I felt almost light-headed. We just clung to each other, both of us racked with sobs.

Then I saw Klaus and Alexander standing behind her. I knelt before Klaus and said, "Hello, Klaus," and he caught on to who I was and shyly let me hug him. Lilo knelt by Alexander, who was four, and said, "It is Daddy." I said, "Hello, Alexander," and he looked at Lilo and said, "He still knows me!" Lilo and I looked at each other and began to laugh, but the laughter abruptly turned to tears and we clung to each other as if we could never part again.[10]

Unfortunately, most homecomings had no such happy endings. Some soldiers limped back to find only rubble where houses had stood and only the graves of those they had loved. There were other cruel surprises.

"I had my own little house," one returning Landser recalled. "How happy I was that it was still standing! [But] when I rang the bell, Americans came to the door—my wife's new friends. They asked me what the hell I wanted."[11]

After years of waiting without a word, many women, like the above, simply gave up. Thousands turned to prostitution or concubinage to avoid starvation and make ends meet. When returning husbands stood face to face with the post-war reality, often heavily rouged and smeared

---

9.   Sajer, *Forgotten Soldier*, 462–464.
10. Knappe, *Soldat*, 362.
11. Pechel, *Voices From the Third Reich*, 506.

with lipstick, some murdered their mates on the spot, then took their own lives.[12]

"You've turned into shameless bitches—every one of you . . . ," a returned soldier shouted at his Berlin wife. "You've lost all your standards, the whole lot of you!"[13]

Like the man above, thousands of ex-Landsers were unprepared and ill-equipped to deal with the unpleasant truths of defeat and occupation. For the year 1946, there were 25,000 divorces in Berlin alone.[14]

Despite the epidemic of dissolving families, many were determined, come what may, to reunite and remain together. Some women, not content to sit and passively await their men, set off in search of them instead. Renate Hofmann was one. After a terrifying odyssey across half of Germany, the woman finally tracked her husband to a hospital in Munich.

> There was no doctor in sight, and no one told me anything about my husband's burns and what to expect. So, looking straight ahead, I walked through the door and saw a bed in front of me in which someone was sitting. It had to be my husband. Unfortunately, he noticed my hesitation, as brief as it was. A doctor should have made me aware of the severity of the burns so that my husband wouldn't notice that I didn't recognize him.
>
> We fell into one another's arms. We talked and I immediately realized it was the same voice, nothing had changed. My husband got out of bed and put on his robe—the same motions, the same movements, the same figure. But it had still been a shock, because the face was no longer there—it was gone.[15]

Bittersweet as the anticipated reunion was, Renate at last knew peace. "We were reunited as a family once again," sighed the grateful wife.[16]

Sadly, many women who found loved ones alive realized too late it would have been far, far better had they discovered them dead. Refusing to believe the worst, Regina Shelton rushed into a village tavern one day in "breathless expectation" of finding her father.

12. Anonymous, *Woman in Berlin*, 245–246.
13. Ibid., 316.
14. Hermann Glaser, *The Rubble Years* (New York: Paragon House, 1986), 49.
15. Pechel, *Voices*, 449.
16. Ibid.

I see a lonely figure in something vaguely resembling a Russian uniform. He sits at the table by the tile stove where the regulars used to have their friendly card games and mugs of beer. He sits without moving, and I am struck motionless by the sight. Now and then, the breeze from the open window touches him and makes him shiver as if from an icy wind. The only other sign of life is a steady rivulet out of the corner of one eye, tracing a shiny line along the parchment nose and joining the saliva that drools from the slack, half-open mouth. The hairless skull hangs low on his chest, arms dangle between his wide-spread legs, and a drop from his chin falls at regular intervals between them on the floor. Except for the drip and the chill that trembles through him occasionally, he resembles a broken statue, with rags tossed over its ragged edges. . . . Sunken eyes glisten feverishly in their hollows, glazed, vacant, dead. Like a scarecrow bleached by sun, wind, and rain, the figure is of an indefinable color, skin and rags blending to an ashen gray.

The greeting has frozen on my lips. What is there to say to a man who seems no longer human? whose instincts, surely, more than any conscious decision have carried the remains of his body to the place where he used to be a man? who lights like a homing pigeon on the very spot that was his point of departure into regions beyond nightmare? . . . In an irrational reversal of my earlier thoughts, I tiptoe by him, no longer wishing the man to be Father. . . .

In the kitchen, the others are huddled in a helpless hush, not knowing how to approach this intruder from the nether-world who has given them no sign of being aware of where he is or who they are. Mia . . . is almost out of her mind and without a clue how to cope with the repulsive creature who is her husband. . . . His obvious state of near-starvation at last gets Mia's practical mind working. She carries a bowl of steaming soup to him. When she comes back, she whispers, horror-stricken: "He can't even eat any more. You should have seen him sinking his whole face into the soup and slurping it, not even using a spoon. And he kept trying to drink it while it was coming back up. It's terrible!"[17]

"Oh great God! How miserable can it get?" asked Ruth Andreas-Friedrich from Berlin.

Sometimes, when walking through the streets, one can barely stand to look at all the misery. Among the smart American uniforms, the well-fed figures in the occupying forces, the first German soldiers appear ragged and haggard, sheepishly looking around like caught offenders. Prisoners of war from who knows where. They drag themselves through the streets. Seeing them one wants to look away because one feels so ashamed of their shame, of their wretched pitiful looks.

17. Shelton, *To Lose a War*, 154–155.

... They shamble around like walking ruins. Limbless, invalid, ill, deserted and lost. A gray-bearded man in a tattered uniform leans against a wall. With his arms around his head he is quietly weeping. People pass by, stop and shyly form a circle around him. He does not see them.[18]

Given the despair and horror of their homeland, millions were understandably desperate to escape. Thousands of nubile German women opted for marriages of convenience and fled the Fatherland forever with American or British husbands. Likewise, thousands of German men joined the French Foreign Legion or immigrated legally or illegally to Canada, South America and the US. While countless numbers were leaving their war-ravaged homeland, wretched POWs continued to trickle back.

"Everywhere," remembered one staring returnee, "there were just women and boys working in patched old uniforms, examining bricks, searching through the ruins for anything that could be used. Then the train journey [continued] with its unending procession of shattered towns, villages, factories. . . . The sight made us draw in our breaths . . . , it made us fear for the future. . . . We had been committed to Germany, but now we had to find new meaning in our lives. Each one of us would have to struggle alone for himself and his family, without being able to stand shoulder to shoulder with other soldiers, without the comradeship . . . to support us."[19]

It was just such sentiment as this, springing from the hearts of desperate, but determined, souls, that enabled the German nation to begin the long climb back, one brick at a time. Fortunately for all concerned, by the late 1940s, with the inevitable rift between East and West in full rupture, Great Britain and the United States were more intent on erecting a bulwark against Soviet expansion than in flailing a fallen enemy even further. Although the once proud German nation would remain little more than a degraded vassal of the victors, the sudden shift in Allied attitude at least granted to Germans the tools needed to rescue themselves and their children from utter extinction. This proved all the incentive needed.

---

18. Barnouw, *Germany 1945*, 172.
19. Fritz, *Frontsoldaten*, 222, 226–227.

With a will and energy never before witnessed in the modern world, Germans set to work at a furious pace, as if in some mad race to place as much brick and mortar as possible between themselves and the nightmare. While old men, cripples and children worked as frenetically as any, it was upon females that much of the burden fell.

"Did you ever see anything like it! Aren't those German women wonderful?" marveled one American who viewed the phenomenon.[20]

"I used to think that it was only in China you could see women working like that," a comrade added. "I never imagined white people could do it. I admire their guts."[21]

While rubble magically disappeared in the cities and buildings rose from the ruins, food was also rising on the countryside. "The Germans are making every effort to help themselves . . . ," noted one astonished visitor. "It is not unusual to see a milch cow hitched to a plow, a woman leading the cow and a small boy guiding the plow."[22]

As they were being transported through Germany, Hans Woltersdorf and other POWs also beheld the spectacle:

> The people waved to us, furtively, to be sure, but with their will to live obviously unbroken. Stress with its inevitable diseases, to which they ought to have been subject in these exhausting times, passed them by without a trace. They were still sound in mind and body; they did not crave health cures and hospitals. Despite the superhuman achievements that the war had demanded of them, they were throwing themselves into hard work not to rest until once again they achieved a miracle, an economic miracle. . . .
>
> Just yesterday these people were prepared to defy an enemy who broke all written and unwritten rules of war to wage a war of annihilation against their homes, their kitchens, chairs and beds; who drove them into cellars night after night, where they were buried alive, burned, smothered, and killed, and first lived through all the tortures of hell and met fates that would forever remain unknown, because the victims had taken their testimonies with them to the grave. Now they were there again, like ants, ready to help, to work, to worry, to obey, to hope, and once more to adapt themselves to the view that the victims were really the guilty.[23]

20. Utley, *High Cost of Vengeance*, 37.
21. Ibid.
22. Keeling, *Gruesome Harvest*, 68.
23. Woltersdorf, *Gods of War*, 170.

As Hans Woltersdorf observed, and as Allied occupation troops would later attest, the one element almost totally lacking in the German heart during the post-war years was, surprisingly, the spirit of hatred and revenge.[24] In their heedless, headlong struggle to survive, there simply was no time or energy left in Germans to dwell on what was or what might have been.

"Forget the past," read the new national motto, "only the future counts."[25]

Paradoxically, while the defeated had neither the time nor inclination to look back, the victors did. Continuing the process begun before the war, the Western propaganda offensive against Germany proceeded with renewed vigor following the war. In thousands of books, articles, and movies, the world was reminded over and over again that the Nazi Party in particular, and all Germans in general, were solely responsible for the war; that they and they alone had committed beastly atrocities; that only the German people and their leaders were war criminals; that German guilt was somehow something "unique." Curiously, many who argued this thesis and were often its most violent proponents were also those who had been furthest removed from the actual fighting itself. Additionally, almost all who promoted the notion of singular guilt were those with a personal, political, or financial stake in perpetuating the fiction of the "Good War," the "war to end evil" and the "Crusade in Europe."

Among those closest to the fight, however, post-war propaganda had negligible results. Indeed, far from being filled with hatred as they were expected to be, many maturing Allied soldiers and airmen—those who actually fought on the ground or bombed from the air—were some of the least vindictive and some of the most forgiving. After boarding with Germans, dining with Germans, drinking with Germans, and sometimes, after courting and falling in love with Germans, many

---

24. Engelmann, *In Hitler's Germany*, 331.
25. Ibid., 333.

Allied troops ultimately began to understand and identify with Germans. Too late, most came to the shocking realization that in no appreciable way was their former enemy different from themselves. Ashamed by the sadistic, blood-thirsty propaganda they had swallowed so eagerly and obeyed so blindly, many young men—Americans, British, French, and even Russians—knew all too well from experience that neither Nazis or Germans had a corner on crime and that there was nothing "unique" about guilt or evil.

One of the most outspoken opponents of singular war guilt was the intrepid American journalist, Freda Utley. "[A]n atrocity ceases to be one when committed in a 'good cause,' that is, *our own*," wrote the hard-hitting author in her 1949 book, *The High Cost of Vengeance.*

> I thought it was high time we stopped talking about German guilt, since there was no crime the Nazis had committed, which we or our allies had not also committed. I had referred to our obliteration bombing, the mass expropriation and expulsion from their homes of twelve million Germans on account of their race; the starving of the Germans during the first years of the occupation; the use of prisoners as slave laborers; the Russian concentration camps, and the looting perpetrated by Americans as well as Russians. . . . Compared with the rape and murder and looting engaged in by the Russian armies at the war's end, the terror and slavery and hunger and robbery in the Eastern zone today, and the genocide practiced by the Poles and Czechs, the war crimes and crimes against humanity committed by the Germans condemned at Nuremberg to death or lifelong imprisonment appeared as minor in extent if not in degree.[26]

J. F. C. Fuller agreed. "For fifty or a hundred years, and possibly more," announced the British major general, "the ruined cities of Germany will stand as monuments to the barbarism of their conquerors."[27]

Another backward-looking Briton, an RAF crewman, expressed in simple, yet profound, terms a thought that thousands of other Allied soldiers and airmen no doubt pondered for the rest of their lives: "Had the Germans won the war, should we or ought we to have been tried as war criminals? . . . [T]he thoughts live with me to this day."

For the most part though, such reflections were kept strictly pri-

---

26. Utley, *High Cost*, 182, 183–184.
27. Ibid., 183.

vate and even the public utterances of Freda Utley, General Fuller
and a few courageous others were all but lost in a storm of voices
that had a personal, as well as psychological, stake in whitewashing
history. Hotly argued the still-maddened majority:

> "They got exactly what they deserved."
> "We felt we were fighting an inhuman philosophy. . . ."
> "We became a force of retribution. . . ."
> "I always said that the only good German was a dead one and I still say that!"

Hopefully, for the sake of these speakers and the millions more
who could utter such words, hopefully they had never witnessed a
screaming child running like a living torch through a flaming street,
never watched as a man drank his own urine to stay alive while a
river ran just beyond his prison fence, never heard the animal shrieks
of the tortured as their genitals were mutilated or the groans of a bleeding woman begging for a bullet while the line awaiting its turn grew
longer—hopefully they had never seen such things, for only then can
one understand how they might parrot over and over and over again
the standard refrain, "they got exactly what they deserved" . . . and
never lose a moment's sleep.

But even an avalanche of such savage hatred and mindless moral-
izing could not erase the memories of those who *had* seen and heard
such things. And worse, nothing could clear the consciences or still the
nightmares of those who had not only seen and heard such things, but
who had actually *committed* them. Whether it was revealed in the
jarring, inward-searching prose of the American, Kurt Vonnegut, or
whether it was the brooding, haunting verse of the Russian, Alexander Solzhenitsyn, for the future of mankind, thank God, these men
and other brave souls faced up to their past and in the end, each was
finally able to know pity, compassion and ultimately, remorse.

> This strange state of mind which fell upon us for a little while after the guns
> had been silenced was a vague obscenity. It was the faint, lingering aftertaste
> of having achieved something monstrous. We had unleashed powers beyond
> our comprehension. Entire countries lay in waste beneath our hands—and, in
> the doing of it, our hands were forever stained. It was of no avail to tell ourselves

that what we had done was what we had had to do, the only thing we could have done. It was enough to know that we had done it. We had turned the evil of our enemies back upon them a hundredfold, and, in so doing, something of our own integrity had been shattered, had been irrevocably lost.

We who had fought this war could feel no pride. Victors and vanquished, all were one. We were one with the crowds moving silently along . . . the old women hunting through the still ruins . . . the bodies piled like yellow cordwood . . . the dreadful vacant eyes of the beaten German soldiers . . . the white graves and the black crosses and the haunting melancholy of our hearts. All, all, were one, all were the ghastly horror of what we had known, of what we had helped to do. . . . Face it when you close this book.

We did.[28]

---

28. McKee, *Devil's Tinderbox*, 308–309.

BIBLIOGRAPHY

Adamczyk, Werner. *Feuer! An Artilleryman's Life on the Eastern Front.* Wilmington, N.C.: Broadfoot Publishing Co., 1992.

Andreas-Friedrich, Ruth. *Battleground Berlin—Diaries, 1945–1948.* New York: Paragon House, 1990.

Anonymous. *A Woman in Berlin.* New York: Harcourt, Brace, 1954.

Anonymous. Letter (March 14, 1998). Subject: American POW camps.

App, Austin J. "Mass Expulsions: 'Tragedy on a Prodigious Scale.'" *The Barnes Review* 2, no. 10 (Oct. 1996): 21–24.

Bacque, James. *Other Losses—An Investigation into the Mass deaths of German Prisoners at the Hands of the French and Americans after World War II.* Toronto: Stoddart Publishing Co., 1989.

Bacque, James. "The Last Dirty Secret of World War Two." *Saturday Night* 104, no. 9 (Sept. 1989): 31–38.

Baird, Jay W. *To Die for Germany—Heroes in the Nazi Pantheon.* Bloomington: Indiana University Press, 1990.

Baker, Mignon Fries. Letter.

Barker, Ralph. *The RAF at War.* Alexandria, Virginia: Time-Life Books, 1981.

Barnes, Harry Elmer. "Sunrise at Campobello: Sundown at Yalta." *The Barnes Review* 3, no. 9 (Sept. 1997): 3–7.

Barnouw, Dagmar. *Germany 1945—Views of War and Violence.* Bloomington: Indiana University Press, 1996.

Bielenberg, Christabel. *The Past is Myself.* Dublin: Ward River Press, 1982.

Blumenson, Martin, ed. *The Patton Papers.* Boston: Houghton-Mifflin, 1974

Botting, Douglas. *From the Ruins of the Reich—Germany, 1945–1949.* New York: Crown, 1985.

Brech, Martin. "In 'Eisenhower's Death Camps': Part I—A U.S. Prison Guard's Story." *The Journal of Historical Review* 10, no.2 (Summer 1990): 161–166.

Broderson, Ilse. Interview (Sept. 12, 1997), Independence, Missouri.

Bruner, Olga Held. Manuscript.

Buechner, Howard A. *Dachau—The Hour of the Avenger*. Metairie, Louisiana: Thunderbird Press, 1986.

Buhite, Russell D. *Decisions at Yalta—An Appraisal of Summit Diplomacy*. Wilmington, Delaware: Scholarly Resources, Inc., 1986.

Cavoa, Leonora Geier. "In Their Terror All Were Alike—East German Suffering: 'War Crimes.'" *Der Freiwillige* (June 1995): 10–11.

Charman, Terry. *The German Homefront, 1939–1945*. New York: Philosophical Library, 1989.

Chadwick, Kamilla C. *The War According to Anna—A Paean to My Mother*. Woodside, Calif.: Seven Stones Press, 1986.

Clemens, Diane Shaver. *Yalta*. New York: Oxford University Press, 1970.

Connors, Michael F. *Dealing in Hate—The Development of Anti-German Propaganda*. Torrance, Calif.: Institute for Historical Review, 1970.

Crawley, Aidan. *The Spoils of War—The Rise of Western Germany Since 1945*. Indianapolis: Bobbs-Merrill, 1964.

Davidson, Eugene. *The Death and Life of Germany—An Account of American Occupation*. New York: Alfred Knopf, 1959.

Delge, Walter B., Sr. Interview.

De Zayas, Alfred M. *Nemesis at Potsdam:The Anglo-Americans and the Expulsions of the Germans—Background, Execution, Consequences*. London: Routledge & Kegan Paul, 1977.

———. *The Wehrmacht War Crimes Bureau, 1939–1945*. Lincoln: University of Nebraska Press, 1989.

Dobson, Christopher, and John Miller and Ronald Payne. *The Cruelest Night*. Boston: Little, Brown, 1979.

Donitz, Karl. *Memoirs—Ten Years and Twenty Days*. Annapolis, Maryland: Naval Institute Press, 1959.

Douglas, Gregory. *Gestapo Chief—The 1948 Interrogations of Heinrich Muller*. 3 vols. San Jose: R. James Bender Publishing, 1995–1998.

Duffy, Christopher. *Red Storm on the Reich—The Soviet March on Germany, 1945*. New York: Atheneum, 1991.

Einsiedel, Heinrich von. *I Joined the Russians—A Captured German Flier's Diary of the Communist Temptation*. New Haven, Conn.: Yale University Press, 1953.

Elliott, Mark R. *Pawns of Yalta—Soviet Refugees and America's Role in their Repatriation*. Urbana: University of Illinois Press, 1982.

Engelmann, Bernt. *In Hitler's Germany: Daily Life in the Third Reich*. New York: Pantheon, 1986.

Ehrenburg, Ilya. *The War: 1941–1945*. Cleveland: World Publishing Co., 1964.

FitzGibbon, Constantine. *Denazification*. New York: W.W. Norton, 1969.

Fowler, George. "Malmedy: The Case Against the Germans." *The Barnes Review* 2, no. 2 (Nov. 1996): 25–30.

Fritz, Stephen G. *Frontsoldaten—The German Soldier in World War II.* Lexington: University Press of Kentucky, 1995.

Fussell, Paul. *Wartime—Understanding and Behavior in the Second World War.* New York: Oxford University Press, 1989.

Gaede, Carl W. Letter (April 12, 1998). Springs, Pa.

Garrett, Stephen A. *Ethics and Airpower in World War II—The British Bombing of German Cities.* New York: St. Martin's Press, 1993.

Glaser, Hermann. *The Rubble Years—The Cultural Roots of Postwar Germany, 1945–1948.* New York: Paragon House, 1986.

Grenfell, Russell. *Unconditional Hatred.* New York: Devin-Adair, 1953.

Halow, Joseph. *Innocent at Dachau.* Newport Beach, Calif.: Institute for Historical Review, 1992.

Hansen, Erika M. Manuscript.

Harris, Arthur. *Bomber Offensive.* London: Greenhill Books, 1990.

Hastings, Max. *Bomber Command—The Myths and Reality of the Strategic Bombing Offensive, 1939–1945.* New York: Dial Press/James Wade, 1979.

"H.K." Testimonial. Bergisch-Gladback, Germany.

Horstmann, Lali. *We Chose to Stay.* Boston: Houghton Mifflin, 1954.

Irving, David. *The Destruction of Dresden.* London: William Kimber & Co., LTD.

Johnstone, Howard. Manuscript.

Kaps, Johannes, ed. *The Tragedy of Silesia, 1945–46—A Documentary Account with a Special Survey of the Archdiocese of Breslau.* Munich: Christ Unterwegs, 1952/53.

Kaufman, Theodore N. *Germany Must Perish!* Newark, N.J.: Argyle Press, 1941.

Keeling, Ralph Franklin. *Gruesome Harvest—The Allies' Postwar War Against the German People.* 1947. Reprint. Torrance, Calif.: Institute for Historical Review, 1992.

Knappe, Siegfried and Ted Brusaw. *Soldat—Reflections of a German Soldier, 1936–1949.* New York: Orion Books, 1992.

Koehn, Ilse. *Mischling, Second Degree—My Childhood in Nazi Germany.* New York: Greenwillow, 1977.

Konev, Ivan. *Year of Victory.* Moscow: Progress Publishers, 1969.

Krubel, Amy Schrott. Interview (Jan. 9, 1997), Topeka, Kansas.

Landwehr, Richard. *Charlemagne's Legionnaires—French Volunteers of the Waffen-SS, 1943–1945.* Silver Spring, Maryland: Bibliophile Legion Books, Inc., 1989.

Laska, Werner Wilhelm. "In a U.S. Death Camp—1945." *The Journal of Historical Review* 10, no. 2 (Summer 1990): 166–175.

LeTissier, Tony. *The Battle of Berlin, 1945.* New York: St. Martin's, 1988.

Losch, Elsbeth. Letter, May 14, 1945.

Losch, Siegfried. Manuscript.

Losch, Siegfried. Letter (Oct. 10, 1997).

Lucas, James. *Last Days of the Third Reich—The Collapse of Nazi Germany, May 1945.* New York: William Morrow and Company, Inc., 1986.

Lucas, James. *War on the Eastern Front, 1941–1945.* London: Jane's Publishing Co., 1979.

Lutz, Elizabeth. "Rape of Christian Europe—The Red Army's Rampage in 1945." *The Barnes Review* 3, no. 4 (Apr. 1997): 9–16.

McKee, Alexander. *Dresden 1945—The Devil's Tinderbox.* New York: E.P. Dutton, 1982.

McKee, Ilse. *Tomorrow the World.* London: J.M. Dents and Sons, 1960.

March, Tony, ed. *Darkness Over Europe—First Person Accounts of Life in Europe During the War Years, 1939–1945.* New York: Rand McNally, 1969.

Middlebrook, Martin. *The Battle of Hamburg—Allied Bomber Forces Against a German City in 1943.* New York: Charles Scribner's Sons, 1981.

Montyn, Jan and Dirk Ayelt Kooiman. *A Lamb to Slaughter.* New York: Viking, 1985.

Morelock, J. D. *Generals of the Ardennes.* Washington, D.C.: National Defense University Press, 1994.

Nadeau, Remi. *Stalin, Churchill, and Roosevelt Divide Europe.* New York: Praeger, 1990.

Neumann, Manfred. Letter, January 14, 1998.

Nugent, John H. and George Fowler. "The Geneva & Hague Conventions—and the 'Holocaust'." *The Barnes Review* 2, no. 2 (Nov. 1996): 11–17.

O'Donnell, James P. *The Bunker—The History of the Reich Chancellery Group.* Boston: Houghton Mifflin Co., 1978.

Owings, Alison. *Frauen—German Women recall the Third Reich.* New Brunswick, N.J.: Rutgers University Press, 1994.

Pechel, Peter, Dennis Showalter and Johannes Steinhoff. *Voices From the Third Reich—An Oral History.* Washington, D.C.: Regnery Gateway, 1989.

Pust, Ingomar. "The Expulsion—A Forgotten Tragedy." *Kronenzeitung* (March 9, 1994); and "Screams From Hell" (March 29, 1994).

Rauss, Erhard, et al. *Fighting in Hell—The German Ordeal on the Eastern Front.* Mechanicsburg, Penn.: Stackpole Books, 1995.

Read, Anthony and David Fisher. *The Fall of Berlin.* New York: W.W. Norton, 1992.

Riefenstahl, Leni. *A Memoir.* New York: St. Martin's Press, 1993.

Ruthard, Herta. Papers. Lisle, Ont., Canada.

Sack, John. *An Eye for an Eye.* New York: Basic Books, 1993.

Sajer, Guy. *The Forgotten Soldier.* New York: Harper and Row, 1967.

Schieder, Theodor, ed. *The Expulsion of the German Population from the Territories East of the Oder-Neisse Line—Documents on the Expulsion of the Germans from Eastern-Central-Europe, vol. I.* Bonn: Federal Ministry for Expellees, Refugees and War Victims.

Schultz-Naumann, Joachim. *The Last Thirty Days—The War Diary of the German Armed Forces High Command from April to May 1945.* Lanham, Maryland: Madison Books, 1991.

Semmler, Rudolf. *Goebbels—The Man Next to Hitler.* London: Westhouse, 1947.

Shelton, Regina Maria. *To Lose a War—Memories of a German Girl.* Carbondale: Southern Illinois University Press, 1982.

Solzhenitsyn, Alexander. *Prussian Nights—A Poem*. New York: Farrar, Straus and Giroux, 1977.

Sorge, Martin K. *The Other Price of Hitler's War—German Military and Civilian Losses Resulting from World War II*. Westport, Conn.: Greenwood Press, 1986.

Stahlberg, Alexander. *Bounden Duty—The Memoirs of a German Officer, 1932–45*. London: Brassey's, 1990.

Steinert, Marlis G. *Hitler's War and the Germans—Public Mood and Attitude During the Second World War*. Athens: Ohio University Press, 1977.

Steinert, Marlis G. *23 Days—The Final Collapse of Nazi Germany*. New York: Walker and Co., 1969.

Strawson, John. *The Battle for Berlin*. New York: Charles Scribner's Sons, 1974.

Strik-Strikfeldt, Wilfried. *Against Stalin and Hitler—Memoir of the Russian Liberation Movement, 1941–1945*. New York: John Day Co., 1973.

Suentzenich, Martha Dodgen. Interview (Dec. 12, 1996), Topeka, Kansas.

Thorwald, Juergen. *Flight in the Winter: Russia Conquers—January to May, 1945*. New York: Pantheon, 1951.

Thorwald, Jurgen. *The Illusion—Soviet Soldiers in Hitler's Armies*. New YorK: Harcourt, Brace, Jovanovich, 1974.

Toland, John. *The Last 100 Days*. New York: Random House, 1965.

Tolstoy, Nikolai. *The Secret Betrayal, 1944–1947*. New York: Charles Scribner's Sons, 1977.

Trevor-Roper, Hugh, ed. *Final Entries, 1945—The Diaries of Joseph Goebbels*. New York: G.P. Putnam's Sons, 1978.

Utley, Freda. *The High Cost of Vengeance*. Chicago: Henry Regnery Co., 1949.

Vassiltchikov, Marie. *Berlin Diaries, 1940–1945*. New York: Alfred Knopf, 1987.

Veale, F.J.P. *Advance to Barbarism—The Development of Total Warfare from Serajevo to Hiroshima*. New York: Devon-Adair Co., 1968.

Von Der Heide, Hans. "From the Allied Camps to the Revisionist Camp." *The Journal of Historical Review* 10, no. 2 (Summer 1990): 177–185.

Von Einsiedel, Heinrich. *I Joined the Russians—A Captured German Flier's Diary of the Communist Temptation*. New Haven, Conn.: Yale University Press, 1953.

Von Kardorff, Ursula. *Diary of a Nightmare—Berlin, 1942–1945*. New York: John Day, 1966.

Von Lehndorff, Hans Graf. *Token of a Covenant—Diary of an East Prussian Surgeon, 1945–47*. Chicago: Henry Regnery Co., 1964.

Von Luck, Hans. *Panzer Commander—The Memoirs of Colonel Hans von Luck*. New York: Praeger, 1989.

Vonnegut, Kurt, Jr. *Slaughterhouse-Five, or the Children's Crusade—A Duty-Dance with Death*. New York: Delacorte, 1969.

Walendy, Udo. *The Methods of Reeducation*. Vlotho/Weser, Germany: Verlag fur Volkstum und Zeitgeschichtsforschung, 1979.

Weber, Mark. "Churchill Wanted to 'Drench' Germany with Poison Gas." *The Journal of Historical Review* 6, no. 4 (Winter 1985–86): 501–503.

Weyersberg, Thomas A. Letters.

Woltersdorf, Hans Werner. *Gods of War—A Memoir of a German Soldier.* Novato, Calif.: Presidio Press, 1990.

Wulff, Renate Rich. Interview (Dec. 18, 1996), Topeka, Kansas.

Zhukov, Georgi K. *Marshal Zhukov's Greatest Battles.* New York: Harper and Row, 1969.

Ziemke, Earl F. *The Soviet Juggernaut.* Alexandria, Virginia: Time-Life Books, 1980.

INDEX

References to illustrations appear in italics.

Forrestal, James V., 100–101
Franz Joseph II, 250–51
fraternization. *See* non-fraternization policy
Frederick the Great, and Hitler influence, 48, 178
French Army, 233; colonial troops, 168–69; POWs, abuses, 257–58, 260
French POWs, 5, 70, 93
French SS, 219, 233
Freyer, Margret, 107, 108, 110, 112, 113–15, 116–17, 120, 122
Fries, Mignon, 80
Fuller, J. F. C., 357, 358
Furtwangen, Germany, 168–69

General Stueben (ship), 133–34
Geneva Convention: Allied breaks, 170, 231–34, 252–60; Allied stance, 164, 243; German stance, 126–27, 163, 164, 255; Soviet protection, 242; Soviet refusals, 49, 234, 249. *See also* prisoners of war
geographical changes, post-war. *See* postwar geography
Gerhardt, Erich, 287
German air forces (Luftwaffe), 14, 43, 46
German army. *See* Wehrmacht
German High Command, 186–87, 200–201, 213–15, 216–17
German history, 48, 326
Germany Must Perish (Kaufman), 7
Gliewe, Hans, 131–32, 133
Goebbels, Joseph: anti-American propaganda, 166; in Berlin, 44–45, 187, 188–89, 201, 214, 215, 217; on Dresden bombing, 123; on Geneva Convention, 126; on morale, 44–45, 165; on Roosevelt's death, 178; on Russian Army, 92, 199; suicide, 217
Goerlitz, Germany, 237, 340–41
Gollancz, Victor, *274*, 291, 317–18
Goretti, Maria, 326
Goring, Hermann, 46
Gotenhafen, Germany, 88, 91, 138, 143
Goya (ship), 143
Great Britain: area bombing denial, 36–37, 43, 124, 344; area bombing policy, 15–16, 36–39, 96, 101–102, 123–25; Dresden bombing reports, 123–24; German bombing on, 15, 38, 46; Soviet alliance realities, 97–98. *See also* Churchill, Winston; Royal Air Force (RAF)
Gros, Martha, 30, 31, 33–34

Guderian, Heinz, 69–70
guerrilla agents, 58, 59
gulags. *See* slavery

Haag, Friedrich, 58
Hague Treaty, 49
Halow, Joseph, 316
Hamburg, Germany: bombing, 1943, 13–15, *261*; bombing, civilian accounts, 30–31, 32–33; postwar life, 317–18; surrender, 227
hangings, 59, 173, 182, 193, 195, 204, 220, *276*, 279. *See also* Feldgendarmerie; suicide
Hanke, Karl, 129
Hanover, Germany, 277
Hansen, Erika, 154
Harris, Arthur, 15, 16, 39, 101, 124, *262*, 344
Hartman, Juliane, 198
Hawkes, Albert, 292–93
Hecht, Ben, 7, 9
Heiligenbeil pocket, 139
Held, Olga, 19, 23, 28, 125–26
Henry, Harald, 58
Hentschel, Johannes, 220
The High Cost of Vengeance (Utley), 321–22, 357
Hitler, Adolf, *267*; American portrayals, 167; deterioration, 187, 200–201, 214–15; Geneva Convention, 126, 127; and German High Command, 186–87, 214–15, 216–17; Germans' faith in, 42; rise to power, 6; suicide, 200, 201, 215, 216–17; surrender refusal, 45, 47–48, 96, 127–28, 129, 178, 179, 183, 187–88; war planning and execution, 45–49, 179, 187–88; writings, 6, 183, 216–17
Hitler Youth, 171, 188, 190, 205, 217
Hoff, Germany, 140
Hoffman, Joachim, 313
Hoffmeister, Kate, 32
Hofmann, Renate, 75, 86, 352
Homberg, Germany, 163
homecomings, 44, 281, 325, 347–55
home confiscation, 75, 330, 331, 332–33, 334
home destruction: American Army, 167–68; bombing accounts, 40–42, 108, 109, *269*; Soviet Army, 76, 77–78, 153–54, 210, 280–81
Hoover, Herbert, 322–23
horses: battle damages, 58, 144, 154–55; as food, 211; ice travel, 140–41
Horstmann, Lali, 44, 75, 79, 83, 153, 279, 288, 294, 300
"hospital city" status, 103, 106, 125

Made in the USA
Coppell, TX
21 April 2024

31541661R00229